# Boarding School Juliet

To LOVE, or not to LOVE

vol. 15

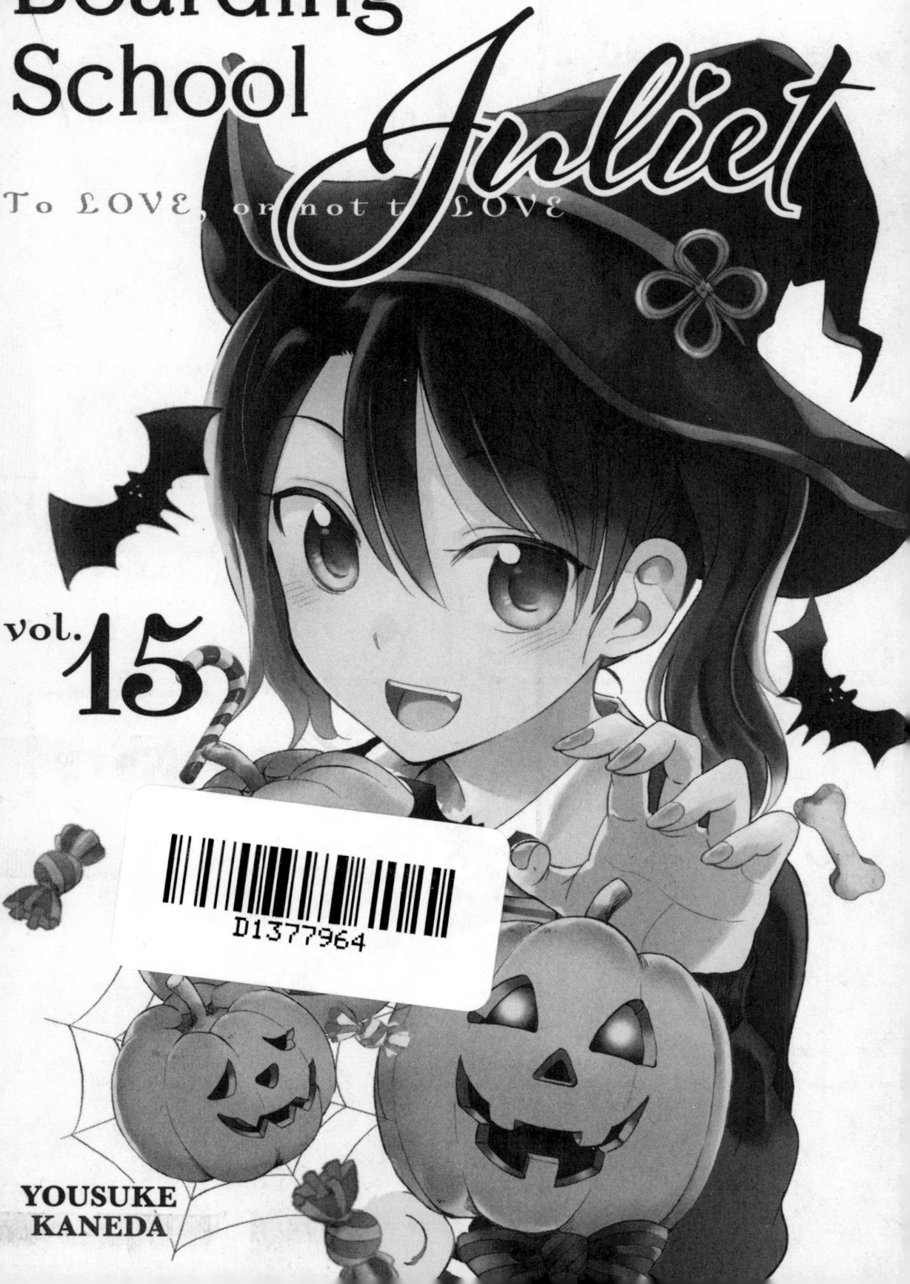



YOUSUKE KANEDA

# THE PLAYERS

character

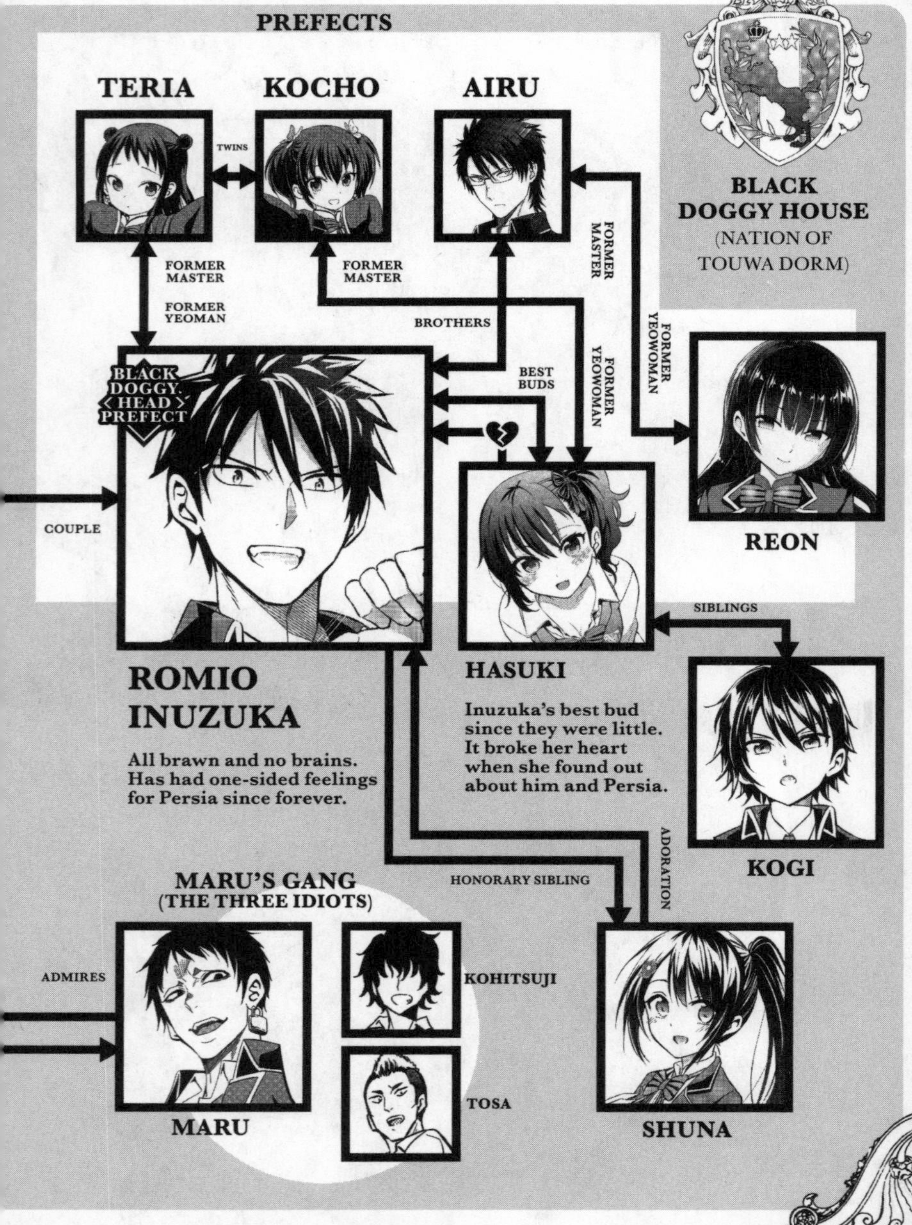
PREFECTS
TERIA
KOCHO
AIRU
TWINS
BLACK DOGGY HOUSE
(NATION OF TOUWA DORM)
FORMER MASTER
FORMER YEOMAN
FORMER MASTER
BROTHERS
FORMER MASTER
FORMER YEOWOMAN
FORMER YEOWOMAN
BEST BUDS
BLACK DOGGY <HEAD> PREFECT
COUPLE
REON
SIBLINGS
ROMIO INUZUKA
All brawn and no brains. Has had one-sided feelings for Persia since forever.
HASUKI
Inuzuka's best bud since they were little. It broke her heart when she found out about him and Persia.
KOGI
ADORATION
HONORARY SIBLING
MARU'S GANG
(THE THREE IDIOTS)
ADMIRES
KOHITSUJI
TOSA
MARU
SHUNA

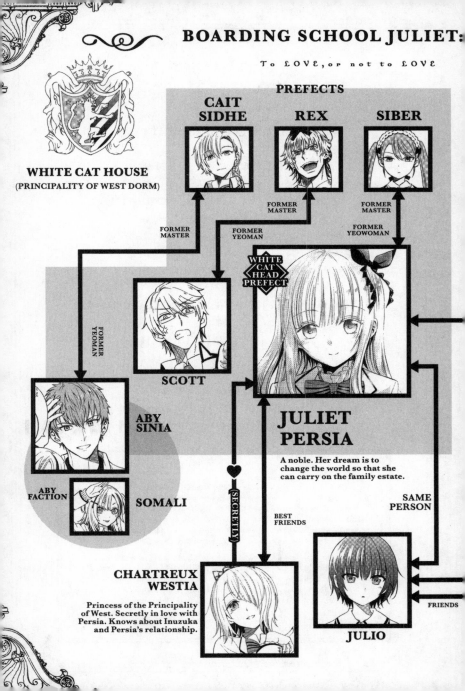

# BOARDING SCHOOL JULIET:

To £OV£, or not to £OV£

## PREFECTS

**CAIT SIDHE**

**REX**

**SIBER**

**WHITE CAT HOUSE**
(PRINCIPALITY OF WEST DORM)

FORMER MASTER

FORMER YEOMAN

FORMER MASTER

FORMER MASTER

FORMER YEOWOMAN

FORMER YEOMAN

WHITE CAT HEAD PREFECT

**SCOTT**

**ABY SINIA**

**JULIET PERSIA**

A noble. Her dream is to change the world so that she can carry on the family estate.

ABY FACTION

**SOMALI**

(SECRETLY)

BEST FRIENDS

SAME PERSON

**CHARTREUX WESTIA**

Princess of the Principality of West. Secretly in love with Persia. Knows about Inuzuka and Persia's relationship.

FRIENDS

**JULIO**

# contents

## story

At boarding school Dahlia Academy, attended by students from two feuding countries, one first-year longs for a forbidden love. His name: Romio Inuzuka, leader of the Black Doggy House first-years. The apple of his eye: Juliet Persia, leader of the White Cat House first-years. It all begins when Inuzuka confesses his feelings to her. This is Inuzuka and Persia's star-crossed, secret love story...

Now as second-years, Inuzuka and Persia's first big job as prefects was a combined Black and White class trip to West. While there, the White Cats stood up to locals who discriminated against the Black Doggies, thus indicating major progress toward mutual friendship. But in the meantime, Hasuki gets lost all alone on the first day and...

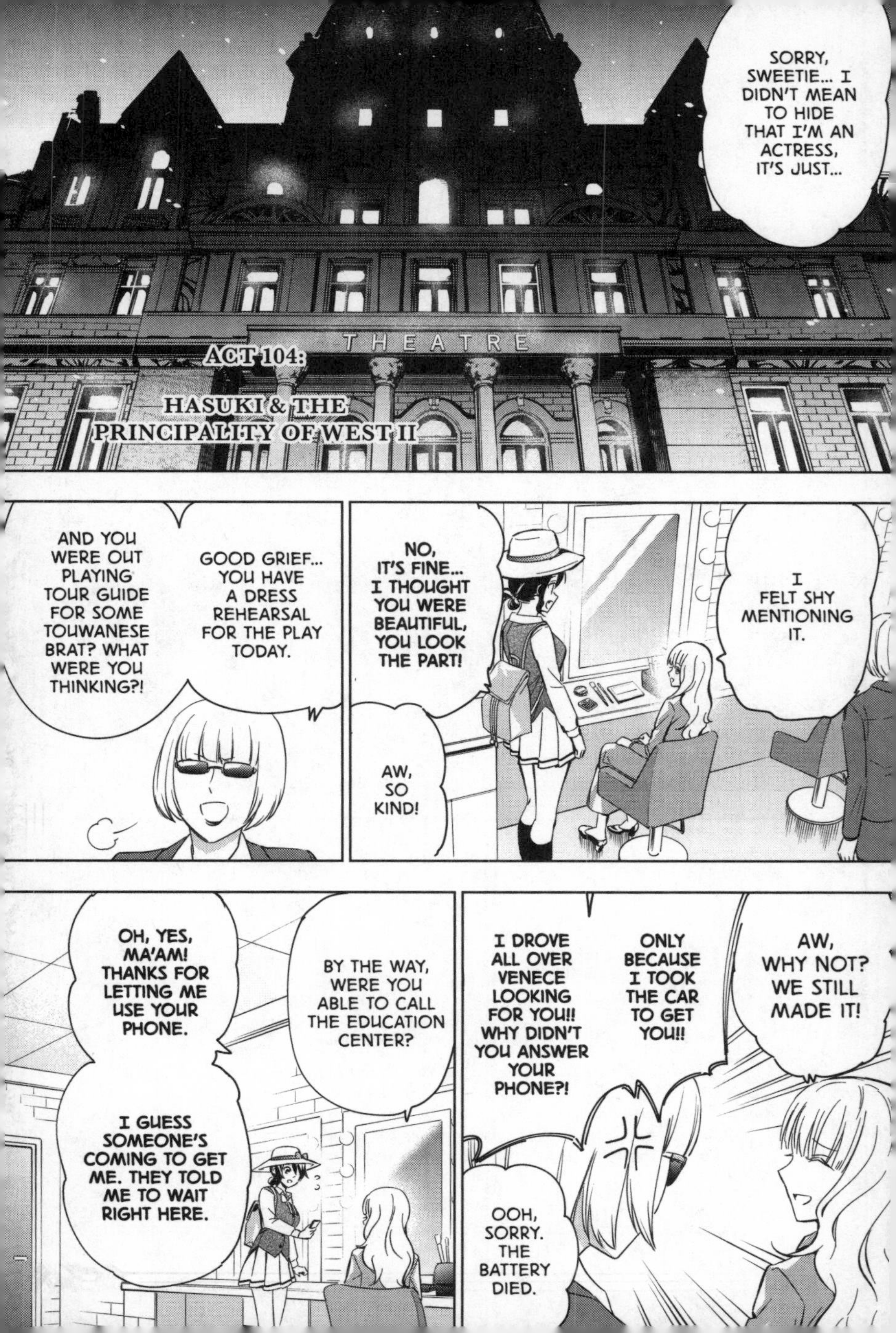
SORRY, SWEETIE... I DIDN'T MEAN TO HIDE THAT I'M AN ACTRESS, IT'S JUST...
THEATRE
ACT 104:
HASUKI & THE PRINCIPALITY OF WEST II
I FELT SHY MENTIONING IT.
NO, IT'S FINE... I THOUGHT YOU WERE BEAUTIFUL, YOU LOOK THE PART!
AW, SO KIND!
GOOD GRIEF... YOU HAVE A DRESS REHEARSAL FOR THE PLAY TODAY.
AND YOU WERE OUT PLAYING TOUR GUIDE FOR SOME TOUWANESE BRAT? WHAT WERE YOU THINKING?!
AW, WHY NOT? WE STILL MADE IT!
ONLY BECAUSE I TOOK THE CAR TO GET YOU!!
I DROVE ALL OVER VENECE LOOKING FOR YOU!! WHY DIDN'T YOU ANSWER YOUR PHONE?!
OOH, SORRY. THE BATTERY DIED.
BY THE WAY, WERE YOU ABLE TO CALL THE EDUCATION CENTER?
OH, YES, MA'AM! THANKS FOR LETTING ME USE YOUR PHONE.
I GUESS SOMEONE'S COMING TO GET ME. THEY TOLD ME TO WAIT RIGHT HERE.

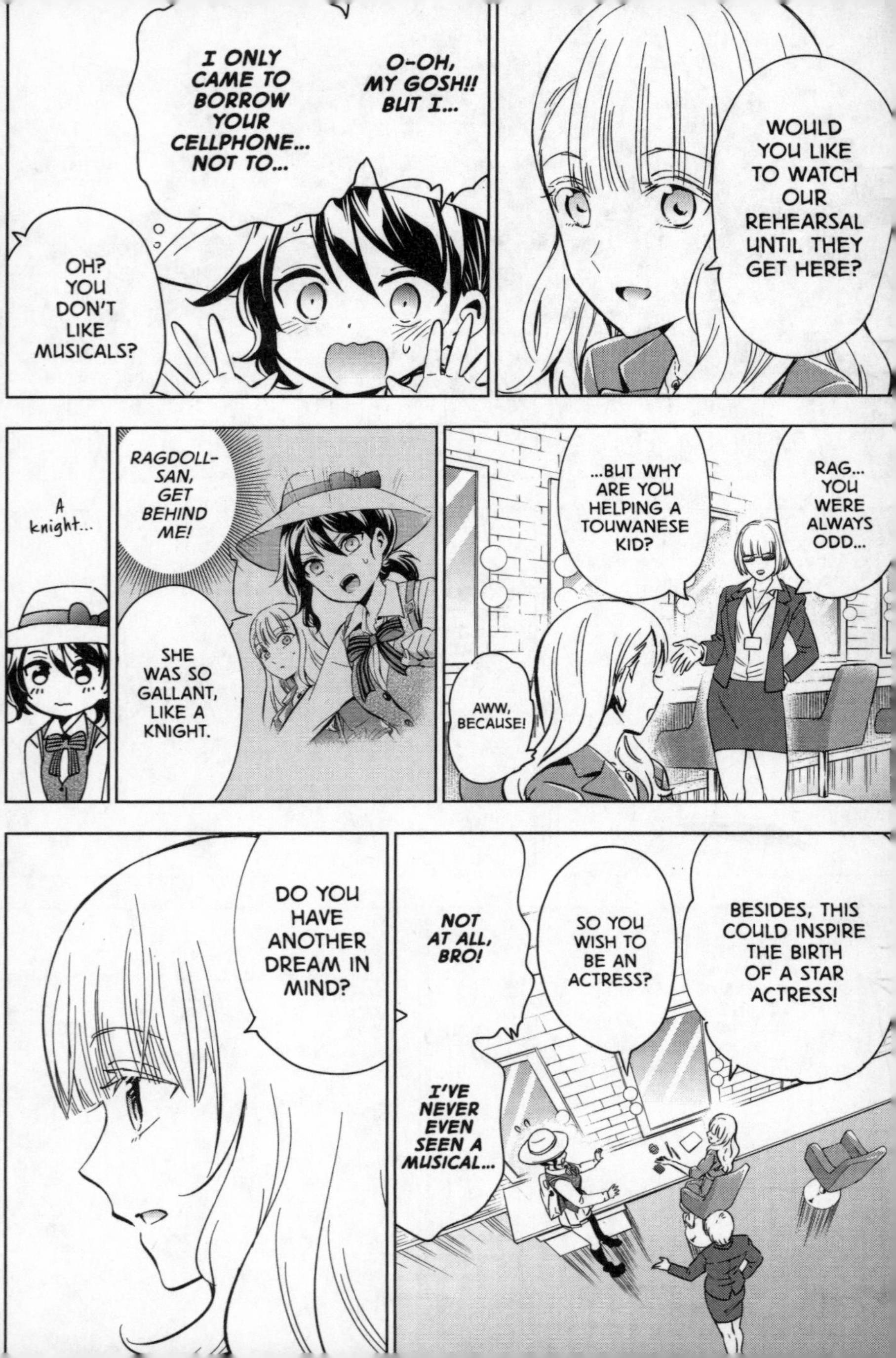
WOULD YOU LIKE TO WATCH OUR REHEARSAL UNTIL THEY GET HERE?
O-OH, MY GOSH!! BUT I...
I ONLY CAME TO BORROW YOUR CELLPHONE... NOT TO...
OH? YOU DON'T LIKE MUSICALS?
RAG... YOU WERE ALWAYS ODD...
...BUT WHY ARE YOU HELPING A TOUWANESE KID?
AWW, BECAUSE!
RAGDOLL-SAN, GET BEHIND ME!
SHE WAS SO GALLANT, LIKE A KNIGHT.
A knight...
BESIDES, THIS COULD INSPIRE THE BIRTH OF A STAR ACTRESS!
SO YOU WISH TO BE AN ACTRESS?
NOT AT ALL, BRO!
I'VE NEVER EVEN SEEN A MUSICAL...
DO YOU HAVE ANOTHER DREAM IN MIND?

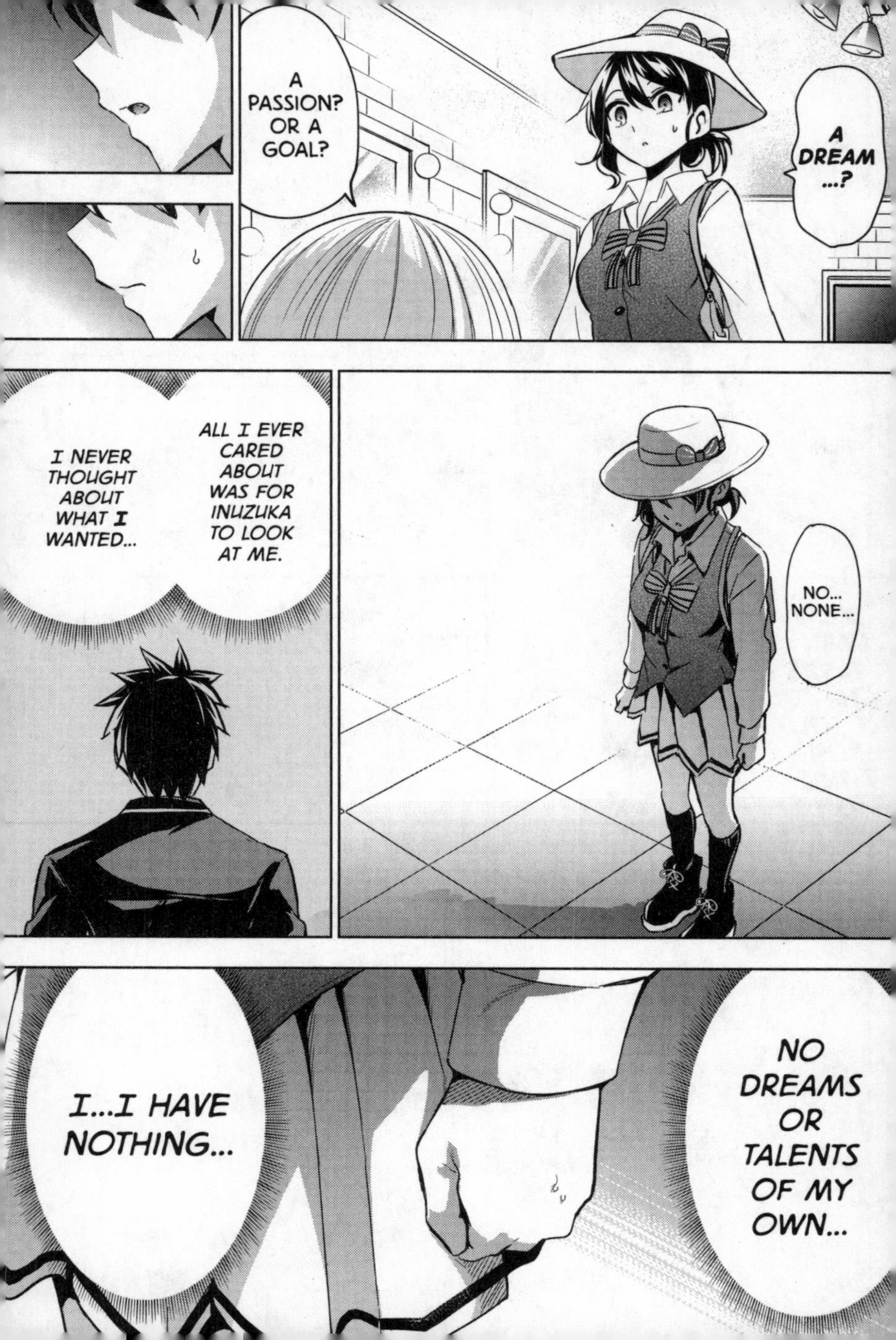
A DREAM...?
A PASSION? OR A GOAL?
NO... NONE...
ALL I EVER CARED ABOUT WAS FOR INUZUKA TO LOOK AT ME.
I NEVER THOUGHT ABOUT WHAT **I** WANTED...
NO DREAMS OR TALENTS OF MY OWN...
I...I HAVE NOTHING...

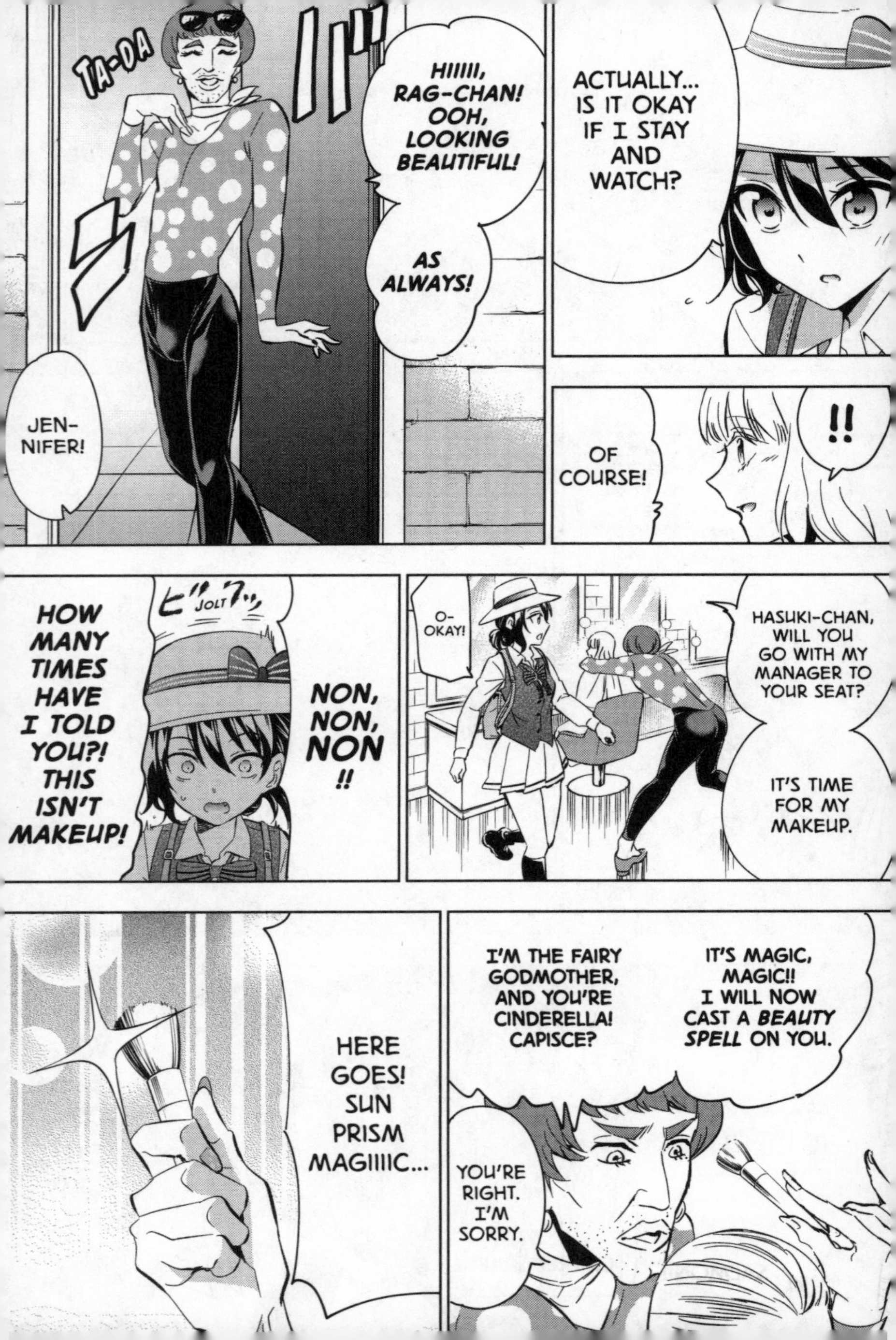

ACTUALLY... IS IT OKAY IF I STAY AND WATCH?
!!
OF COURSE!
TA-DA
HIIIII, RAG-CHAN! OOH, LOOKING BEAUTIFUL!
AS ALWAYS!
JEN-NIFER!
HASUKI-CHAN, WILL YOU GO WITH MY MANAGER TO YOUR SEAT?
IT'S TIME FOR MY MAKEUP.
O-OKAY!
JOLT
NON, NON, NON!!
HOW MANY TIMES HAVE I TOLD YOU?! THIS ISN'T MAKEUP!
IT'S MAGIC, MAGIC!! I WILL NOW CAST A *BEAUTY SPELL* ON YOU.
I'M THE FAIRY GODMOTHER, AND YOU'RE CINDERELLA! CAPISCE?
YOU'RE RIGHT. I'M SORRY.
HERE GOES! SUN PRISM MAGIIIIC...

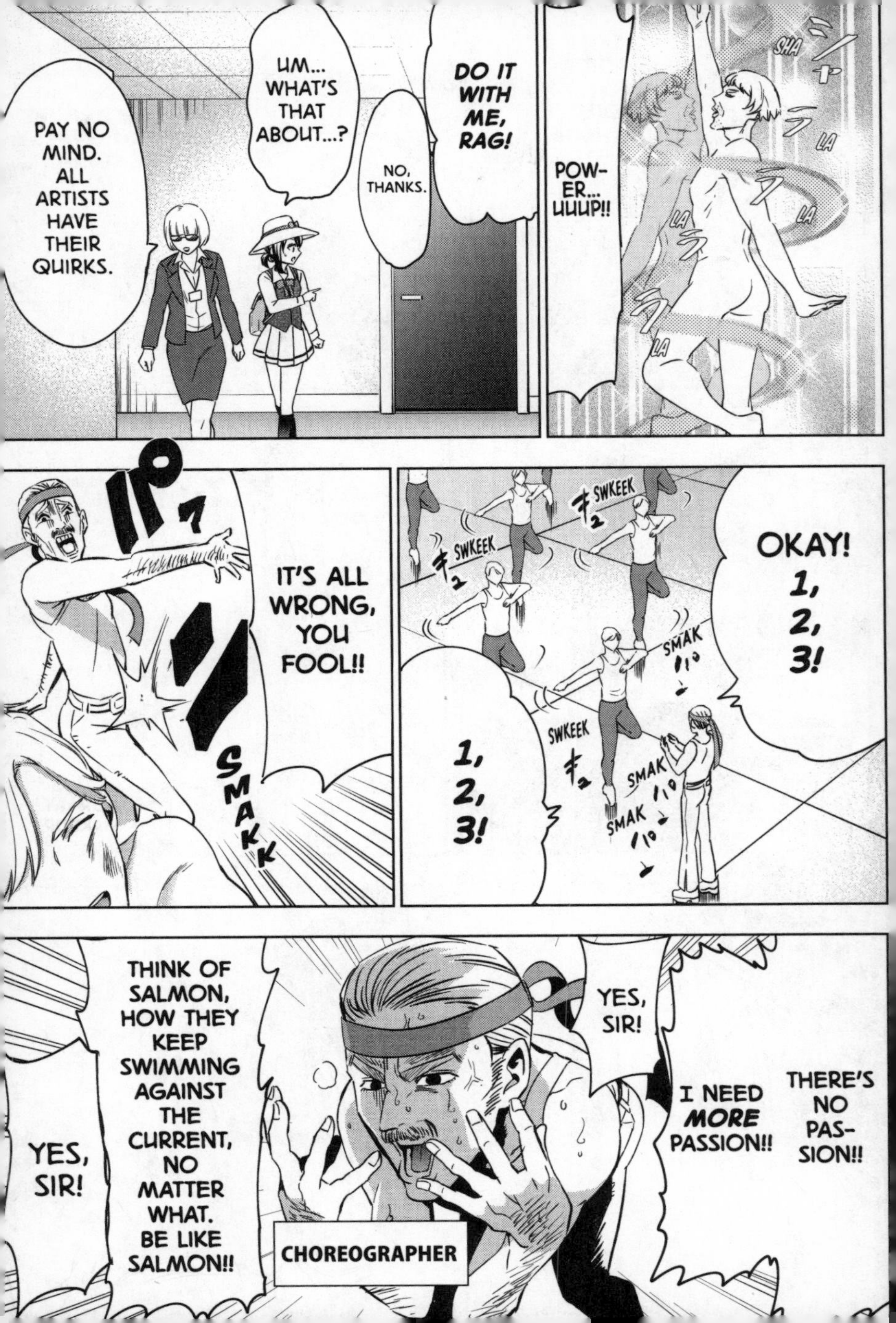
SHA
LA
LA
LA
LA
POW-ER... UUUP!!
DO IT WITH ME, RAG!
NO, THANKS.
UM... WHAT'S THAT ABOUT...?
PAY NO MIND. ALL ARTISTS HAVE THEIR QUIRKS.
OKAY! 1, 2, 3!
SWKEEK
SWKEEK
SMAK
SWKEEK
SMAK
SMAK
1, 2, 3!
IT'S ALL WRONG, YOU FOOL!!
SMAKK
THERE'S NO PAS-SION!!
I NEED MORE PASSION!!
YES, SIR!
THINK OF SALMON, HOW THEY KEEP SWIMMING AGAINST THE CURRENT, NO MATTER WHAT. BE LIKE SALMON!!
YES, SIR!
CHOREOGRAPHER

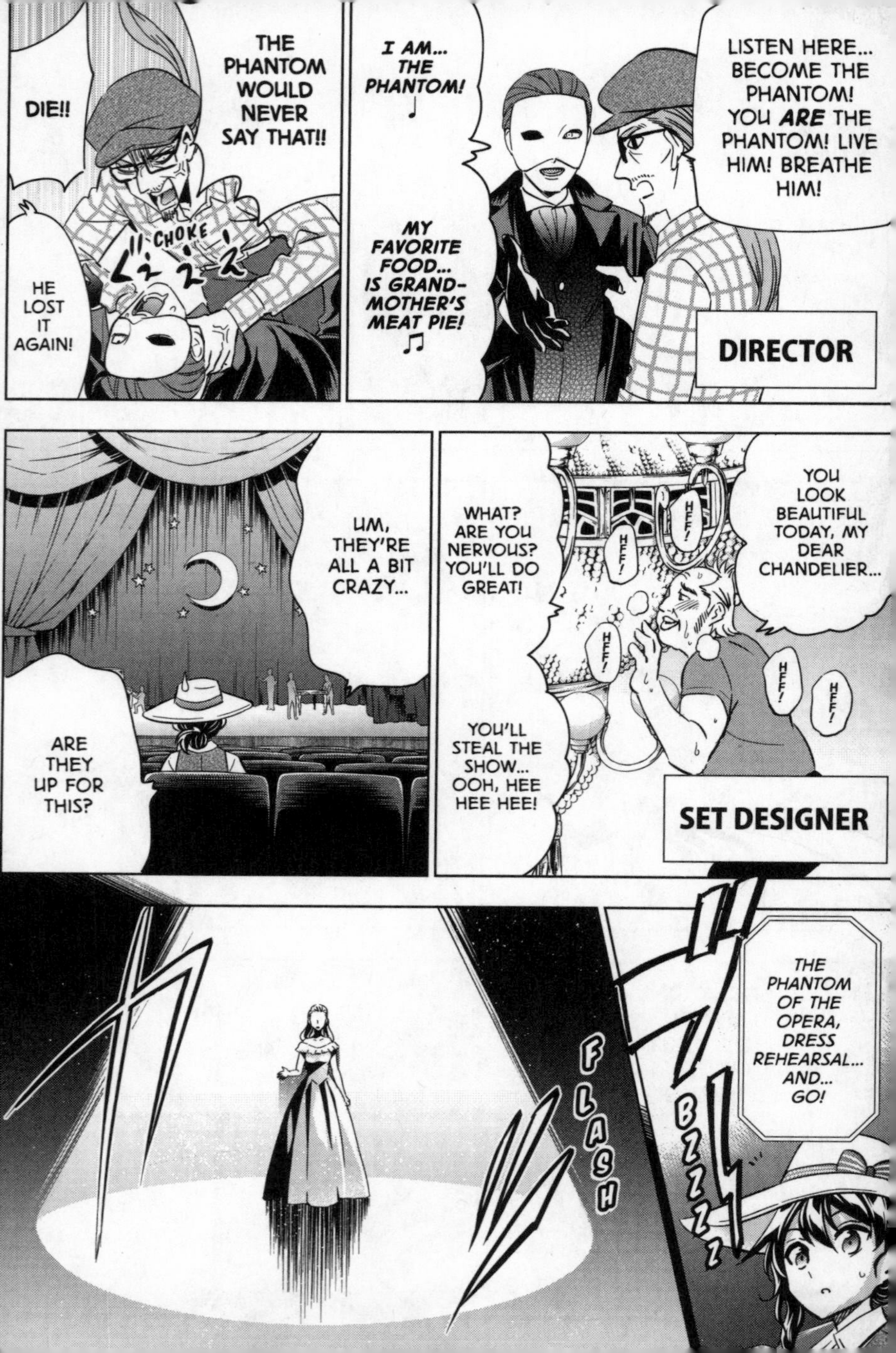
LISTEN HERE... BECOME THE PHANTOM! YOU ARE THE PHANTOM! LIVE HIM! BREATHE HIM!
DIRECTOR
I AM... THE PHANTOM! ♪
MY FAVORITE FOOD... IS GRAND-MOTHER'S MEAT PIE! ♫
THE PHANTOM WOULD NEVER SAY THAT!!
DIE!!
CHOKE
HE LOST IT AGAIN!
YOU LOOK BEAUTIFUL TODAY, MY DEAR CHANDELIER...
HFF! HFF!
HFF! HFF!
HFF! HFF!
SET DESIGNER
WHAT? ARE YOU NERVOUS? YOU'LL DO GREAT!
YOU'LL STEAL THE SHOW... OOH, HEE HEE HEE!
UM, THEY'RE ALL A BIT CRAZY...
ARE THEY UP FOR THIS?
THE PHANTOM OF THE OPERA, DRESS REHEARSAL... AND... GO!
BZZZZ
FLASH

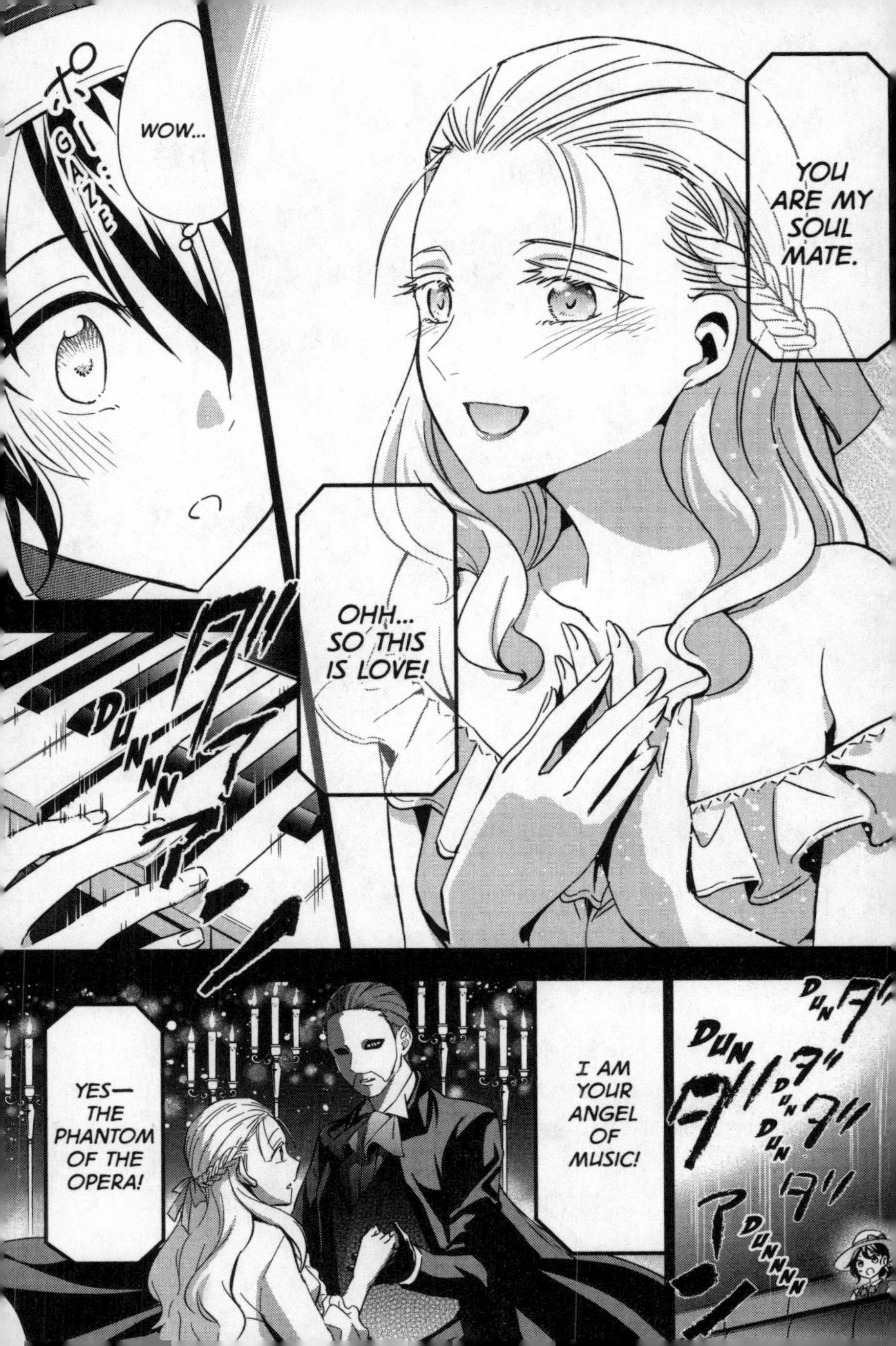

YOU ARE MY SOUL MATE.
OHH... SO THIS IS LOVE!
WOW...
GAZE
DUNNN
DUN
DUN
DUN
DUN
DUNNN
I AM YOUR ANGEL OF MUSIC!
YES— THE PHANTOM OF THE OPERA!

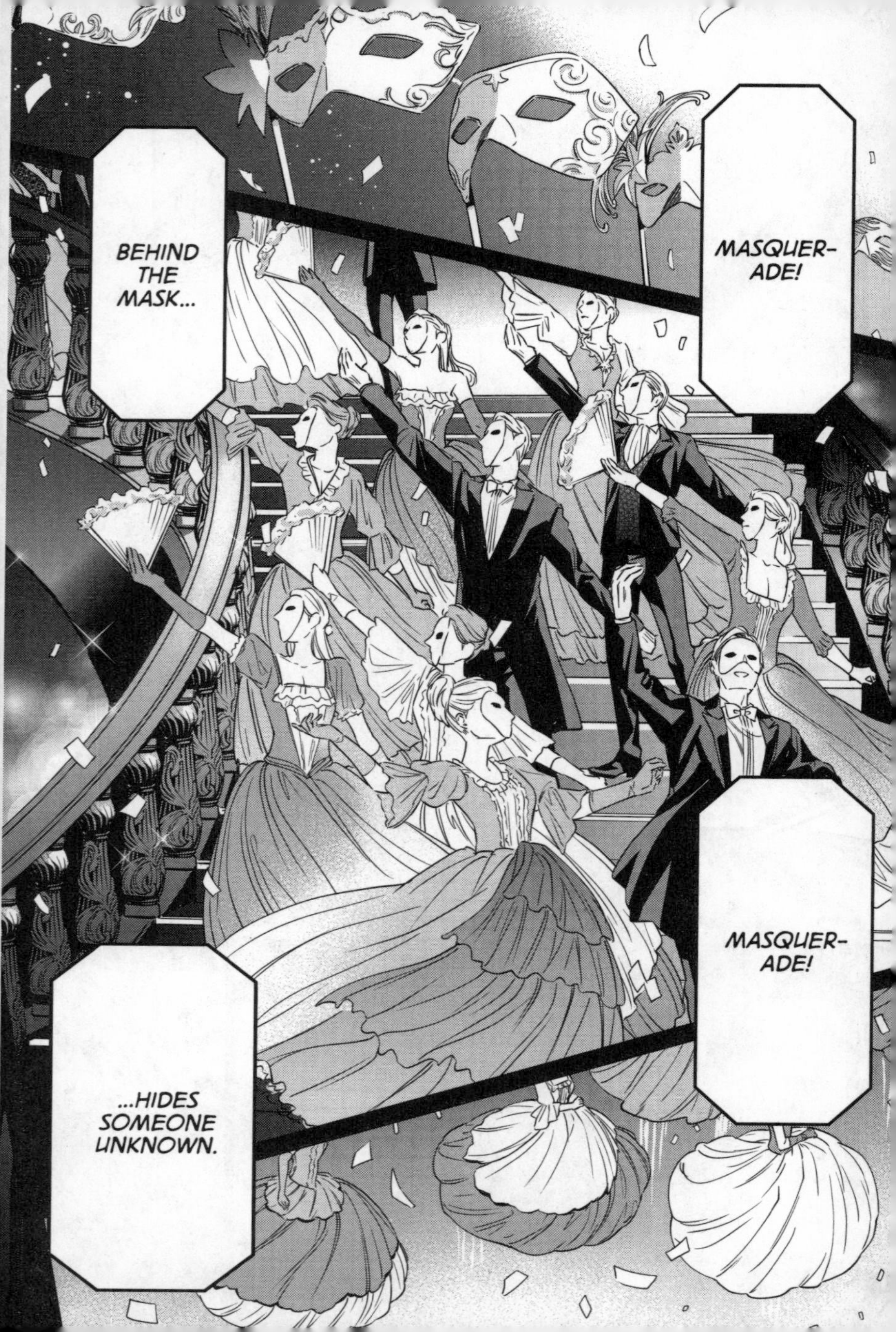
MASQUER-ADE!
BEHIND THE MASK...
MASQUER-ADE!
...HIDES SOMEONE UNKNOWN.

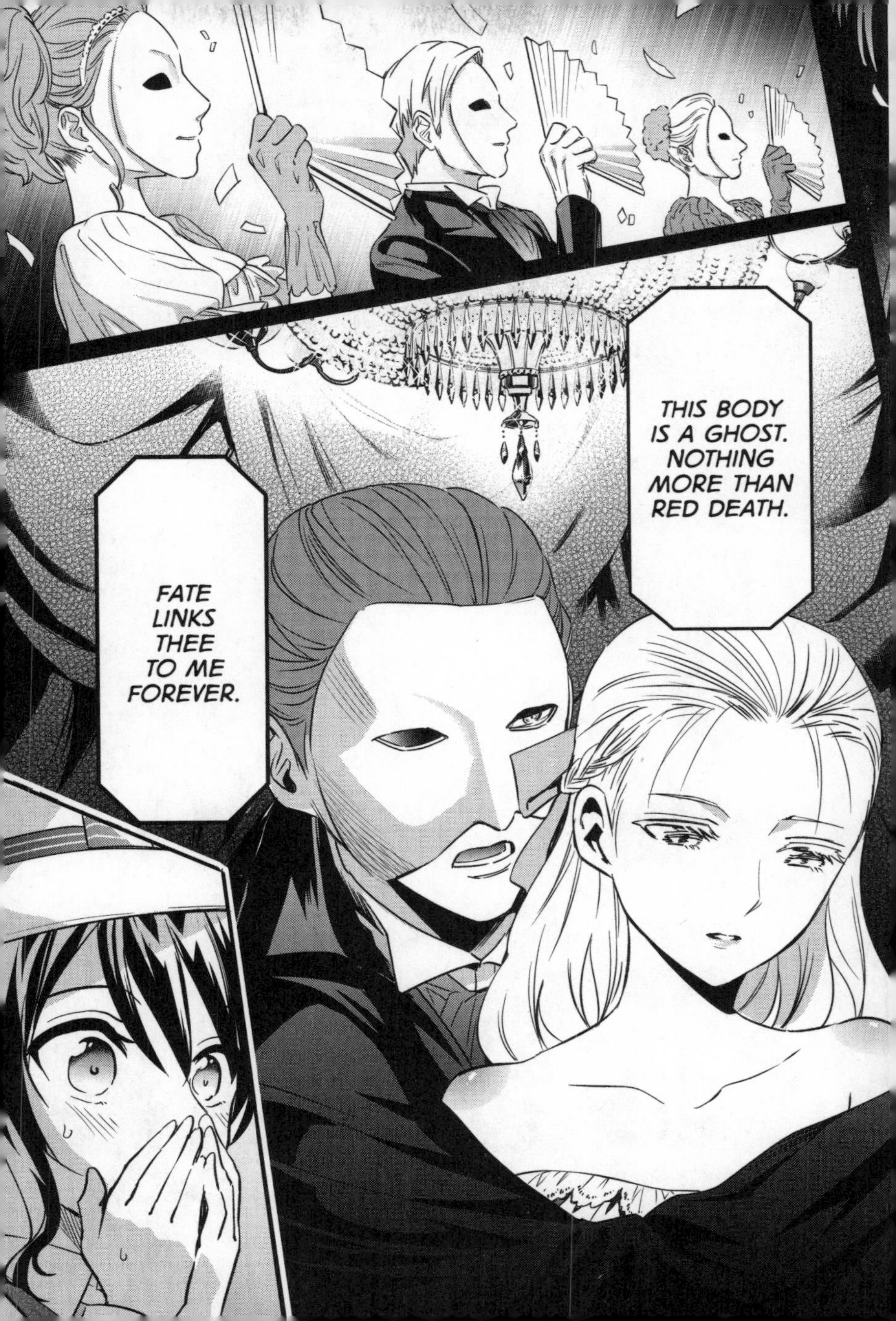
THIS BODY IS A GHOST. NOTHING MORE THAN RED DEATH.
FATE LINKS THEE TO ME FOREVER.

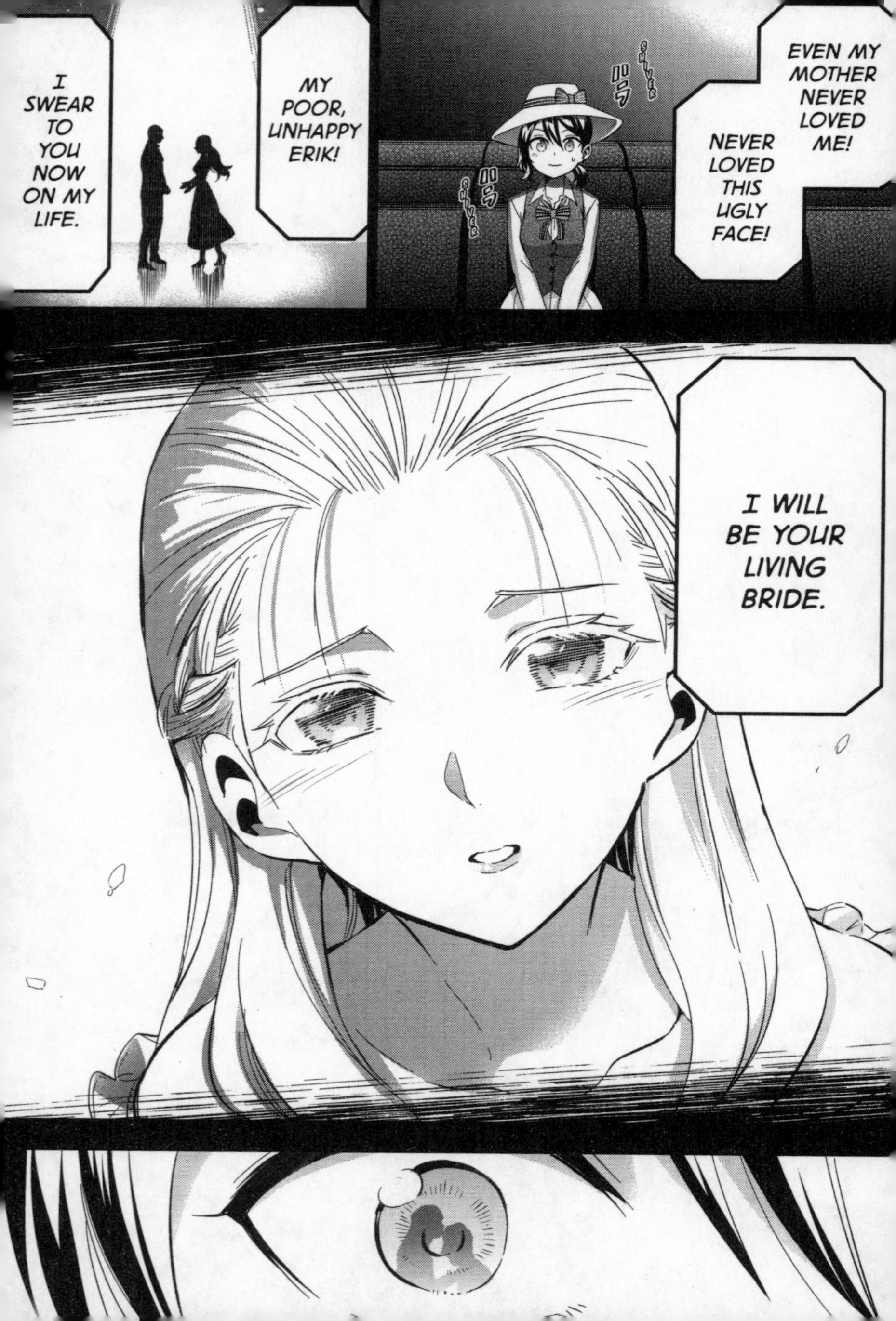
EVEN MY MOTHER NEVER LOVED ME!
NEVER LOVED THIS UGLY FACE!
SHIVER
SHIVER
MY POOR, UNHAPPY ERIK!
I SWEAR TO YOU NOW ON MY LIFE.
I WILL BE YOUR LIVING BRIDE.

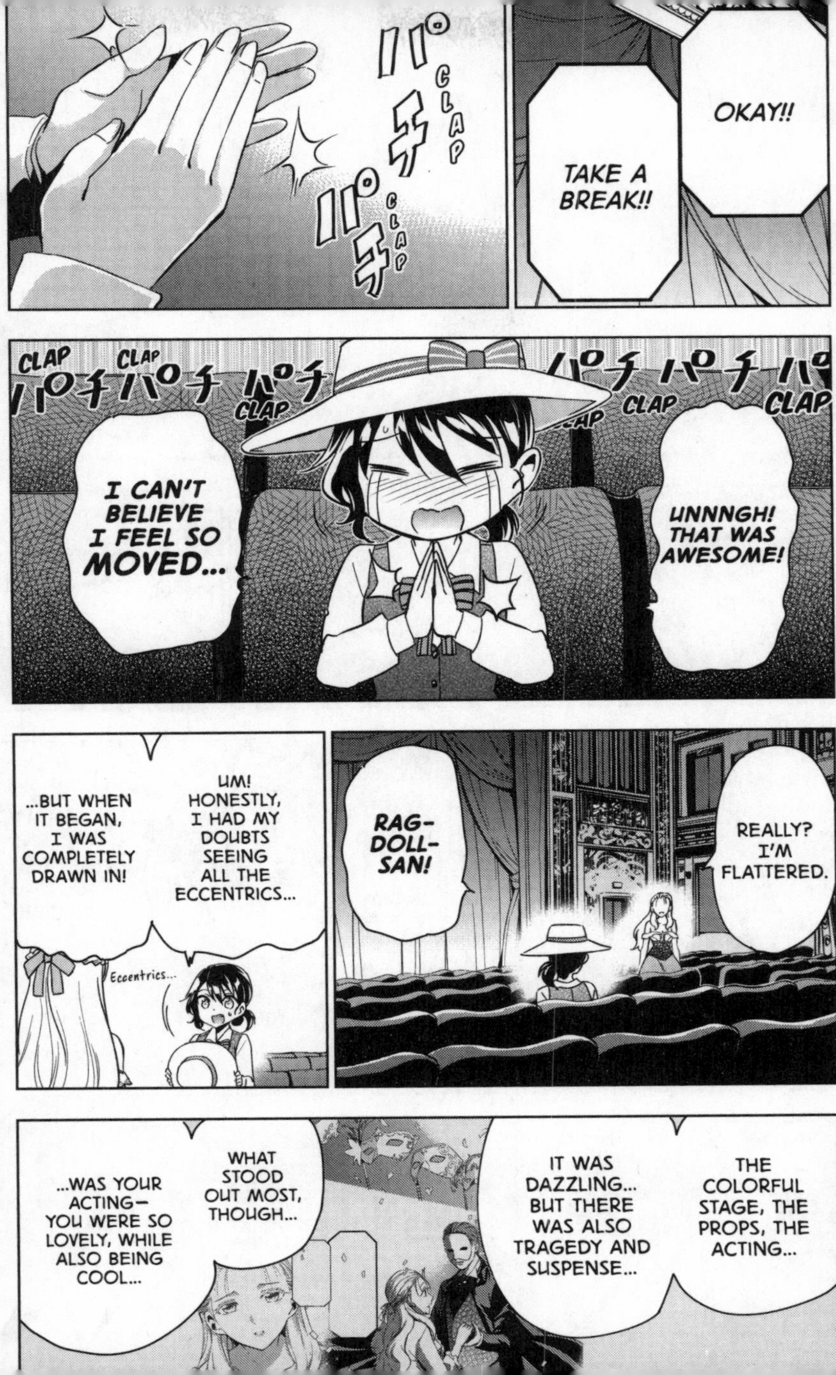
OKAY!!
TAKE A BREAK!!
パチ
CLAP
パチ
CLAP
パチパチパ
CLAP CLAP CLAP
UNNNGH! THAT WAS AWESOME!
I CAN'T BELIEVE I FEEL SO MOVED...
パチパチパチ
CLAP CLAP CLAP
REALLY? I'M FLATTERED.
RAG-DOLL-SAN!
UM! HONESTLY, I HAD MY DOUBTS SEEING ALL THE ECCENTRICS...
...BUT WHEN IT BEGAN, I WAS COMPLETELY DRAWN IN!
Eccentrics...
THE COLORFUL STAGE, THE PROPS, THE ACTING...
IT WAS DAZZLING... BUT THERE WAS ALSO TRAGEDY AND SUSPENSE...
WHAT STOOD OUT MOST, THOUGH...
...WAS YOUR ACTING— YOU WERE SO LOVELY, WHILE ALSO BEING COOL...

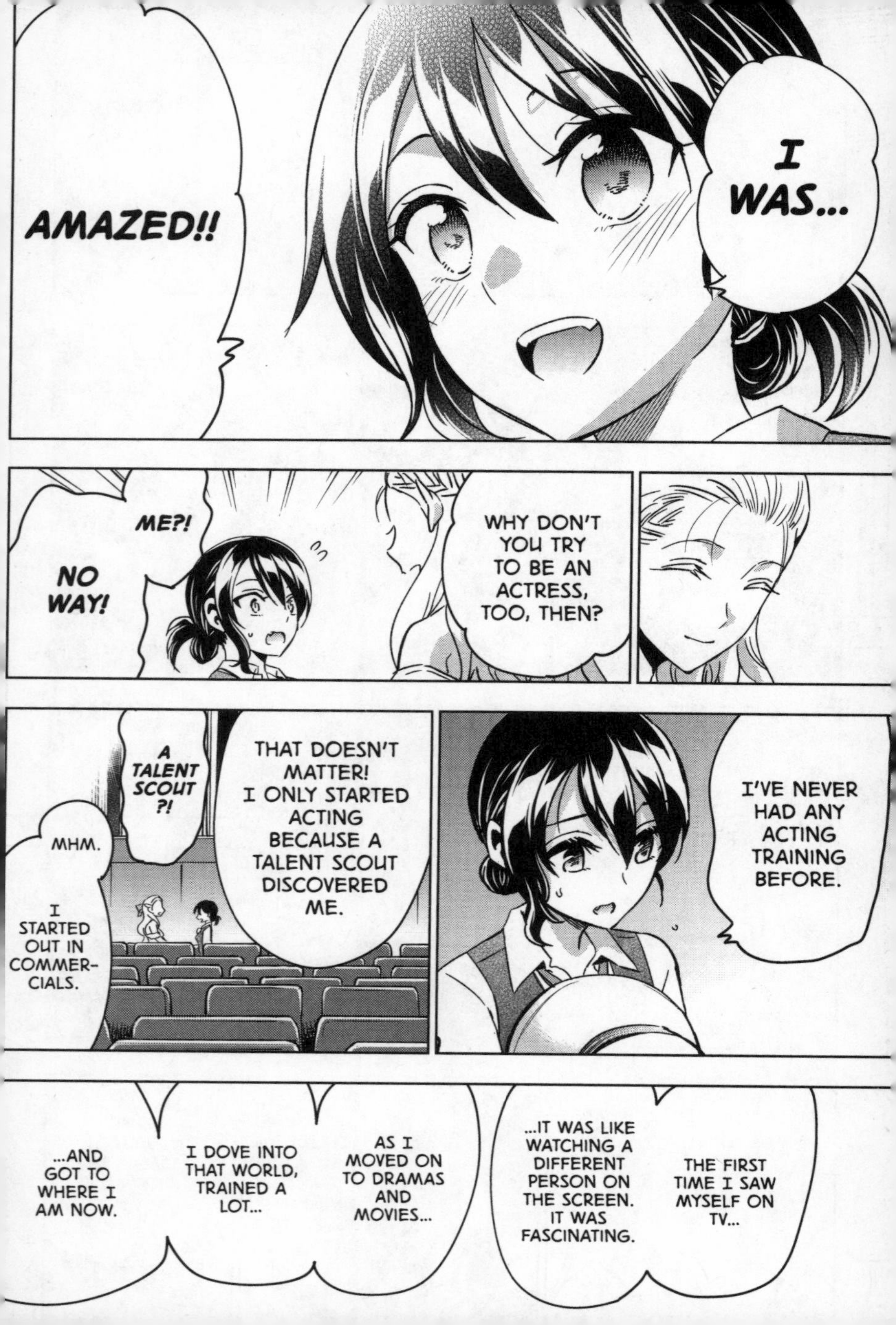
I WAS...
AMAZED!!
WHY DON'T YOU TRY TO BE AN ACTRESS, TOO, THEN?
ME?!
NO WAY!
I'VE NEVER HAD ANY ACTING TRAINING BEFORE.
THAT DOESN'T MATTER! I ONLY STARTED ACTING BECAUSE A TALENT SCOUT DISCOVERED ME.
A TALENT SCOUT ?!
MHM.
I STARTED OUT IN COMMER-CIALS.
THE FIRST TIME I SAW MYSELF ON TV...
...IT WAS LIKE WATCHING A DIFFERENT PERSON ON THE SCREEN. IT WAS FASCINATING.
AS I MOVED ON TO DRAMAS AND MOVIES...
I DOVE INTO THAT WORLD, TRAINED A LOT...
...AND GOT TO WHERE I AM NOW.

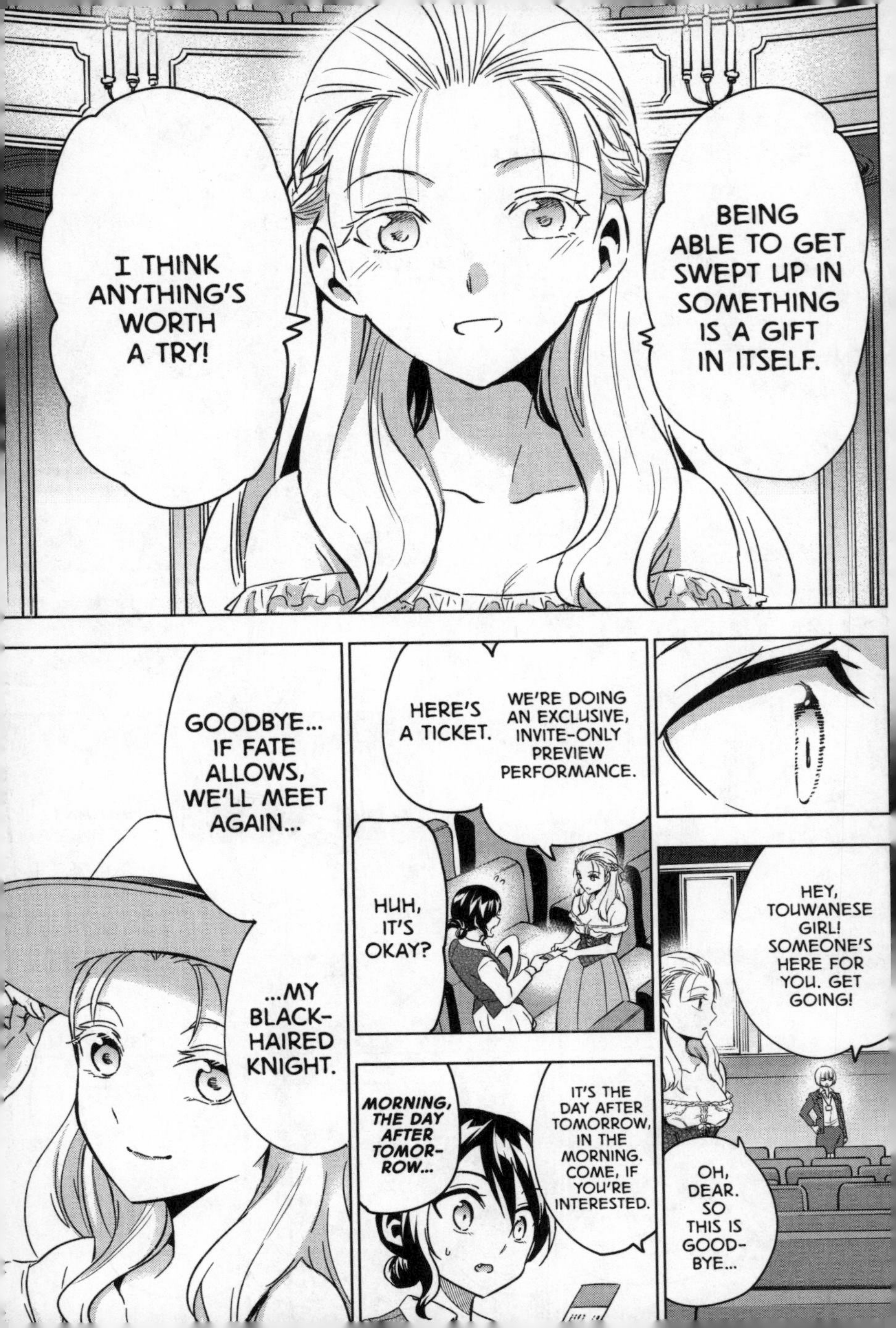
BEING ABLE TO GET SWEPT UP IN SOMETHING IS A GIFT IN ITSELF.
I THINK ANYTHING'S WORTH A TRY!
WE'RE DOING AN EXCLUSIVE, INVITE-ONLY PREVIEW PERFORMANCE.
HERE'S A TICKET.
HUH, IT'S OKAY?
HEY, TOUWANESE GIRL! SOMEONE'S HERE FOR YOU. GET GOING!
OH, DEAR. SO THIS IS GOOD-BYE...
IT'S THE DAY AFTER TOMORROW, IN THE MORNING. COME, IF YOU'RE INTERESTED.
MORNING, THE DAY AFTER TOMOR-ROW...
GOODBYE... IF FATE ALLOWS, WE'LL MEET AGAIN...
...MY BLACK-HAIRED KNIGHT.

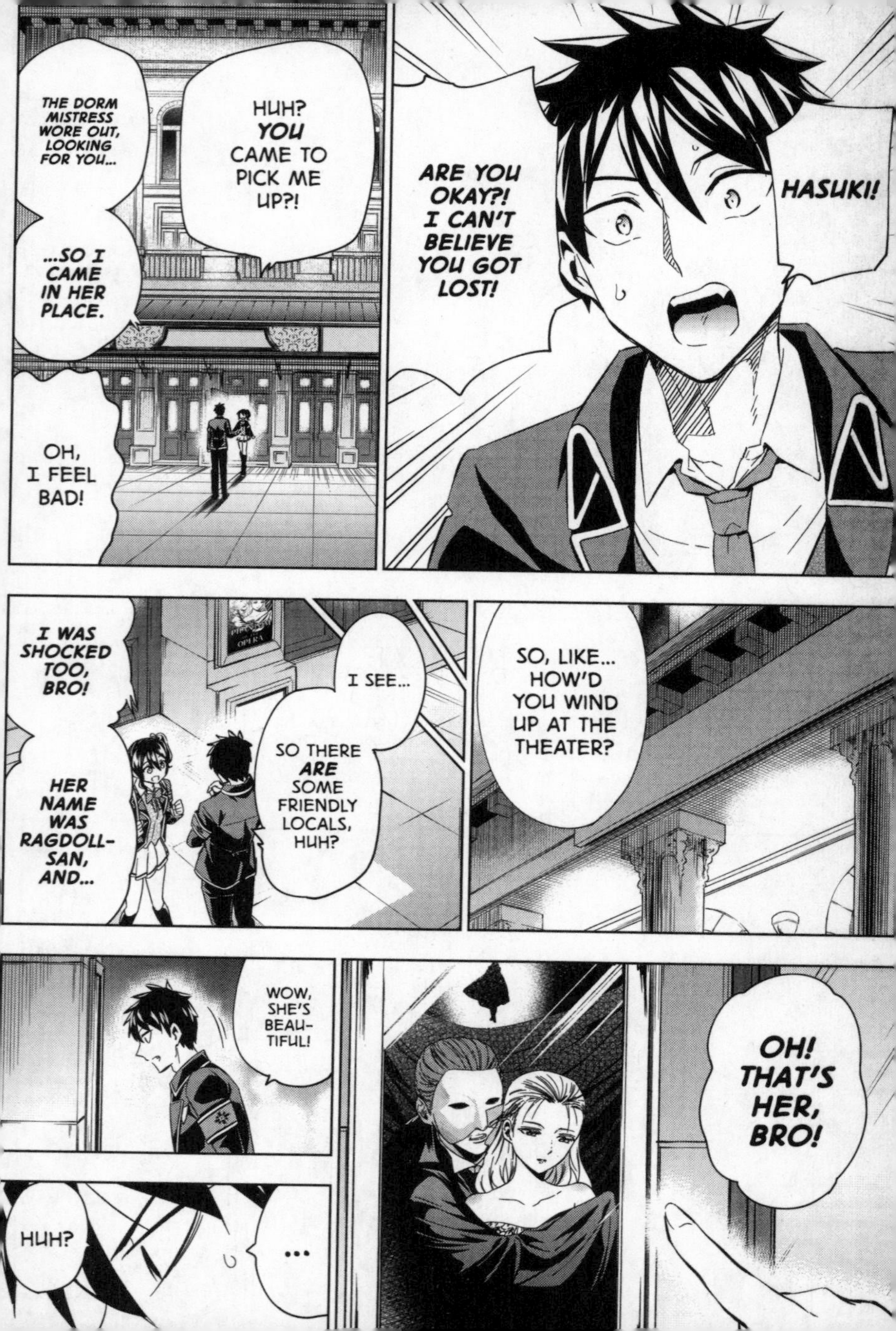
HASUKI!
ARE YOU OKAY?! I CAN'T BELIEVE YOU GOT LOST!
HUH? YOU CAME TO PICK ME UP?!
THE DORM MISTRESS WORE OUT, LOOKING FOR YOU...
...SO I CAME IN HER PLACE.
OH, I FEEL BAD!
SO, LIKE... HOW'D YOU WIND UP AT THE THEATER?
OPERA
I WAS SHOCKED TOO, BRO!
HER NAME WAS RAGDOLL-SAN, AND...
I SEE...
SO THERE ARE SOME FRIENDLY LOCALS, HUH?
OH! THAT'S HER, BRO!
WOW, SHE'S BEAU-TIFUL!
HUH?
...

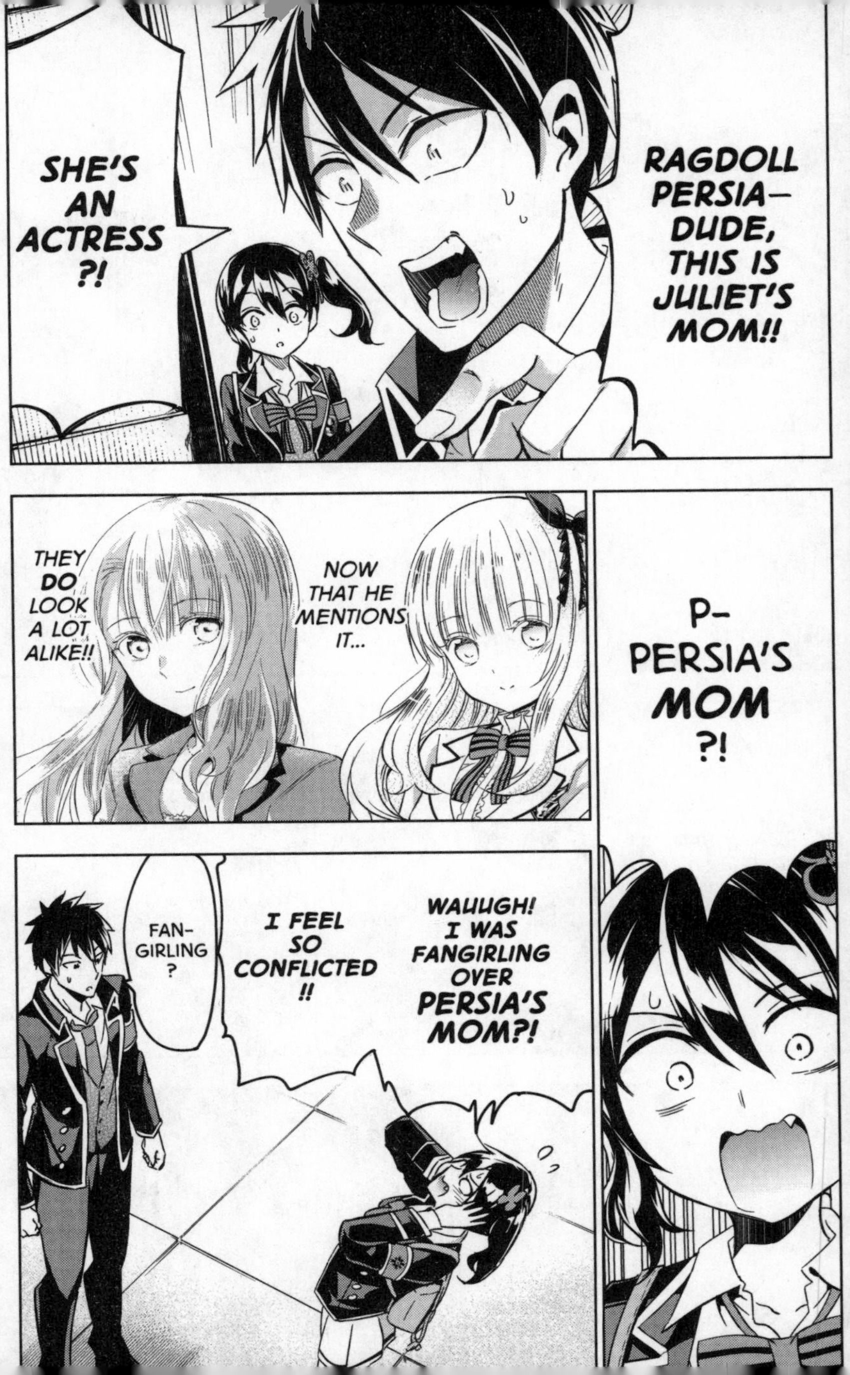
RAGDOLL PERSIA—DUDE, THIS IS JULIET'S MOM!!
SHE'S AN ACTRESS?!
P-PERSIA'S MOM?!
NOW THAT HE MENTIONS IT...
THEY DO LOOK A LOT ALIKE!!
WAUUGH! I WAS FANGIRLING OVER PERSIA'S MOM?!
I FEEL SO CONFLICTED!!
FAN-GIRLING?

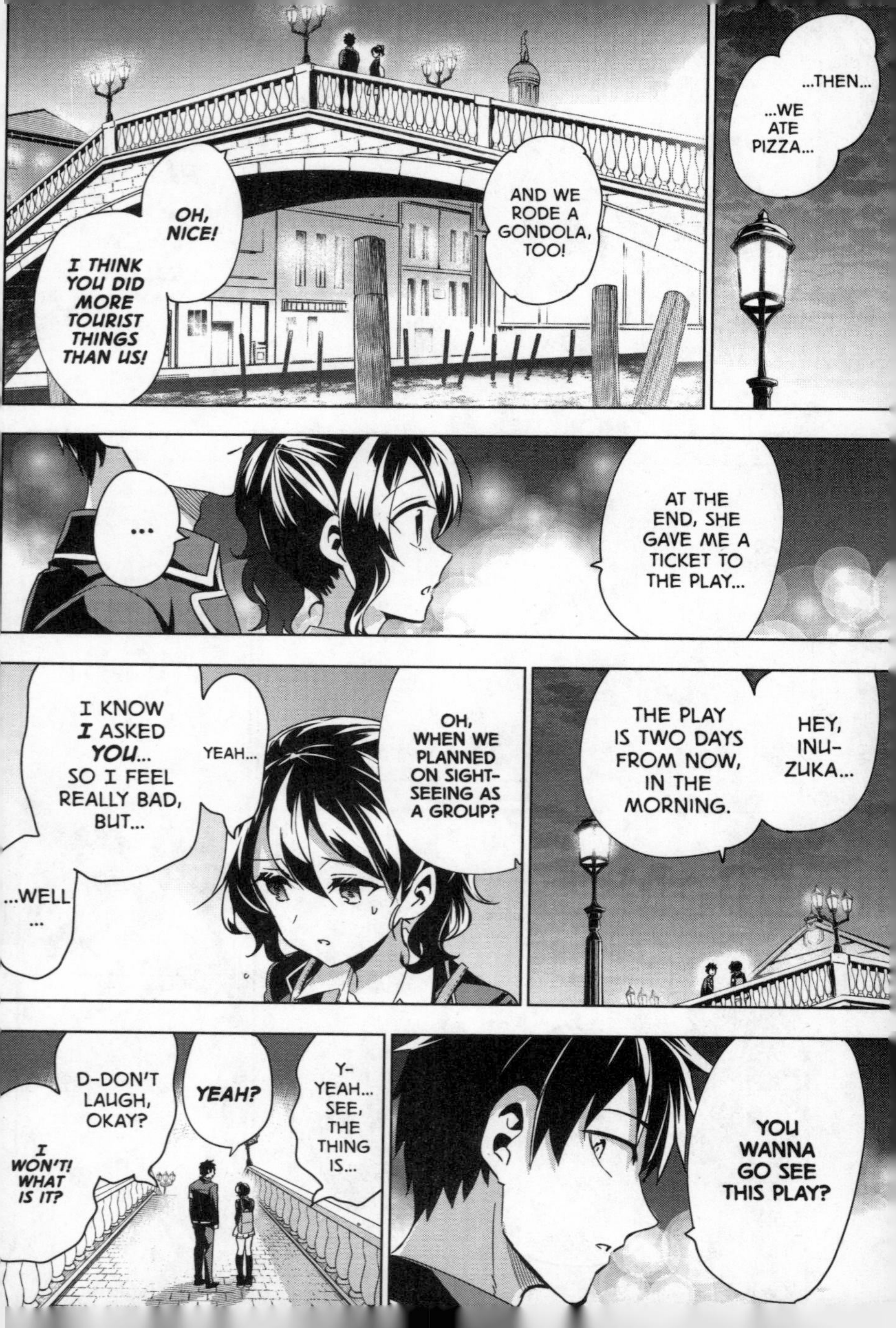
...THEN...
...WE ATE PIZZA...
AND WE RODE A GONDOLA, TOO!
OH, NICE!
I THINK YOU DID MORE TOURIST THINGS THAN US!
AT THE END, SHE GAVE ME A TICKET TO THE PLAY...
...
HEY, INU-ZUKA...
THE PLAY IS TWO DAYS FROM NOW, IN THE MORNING.
OH, WHEN WE PLANNED ON SIGHT-SEEING AS A GROUP?
YEAH...
I KNOW I ASKED YOU... SO I FEEL REALLY BAD, BUT...
...WELL ...
YOU WANNA GO SEE THIS PLAY?
Y-YEAH... SEE, THE THING IS...
YEAH?
D-DON'T LAUGH, OKAY?
I WON'T! WHAT IS IT?

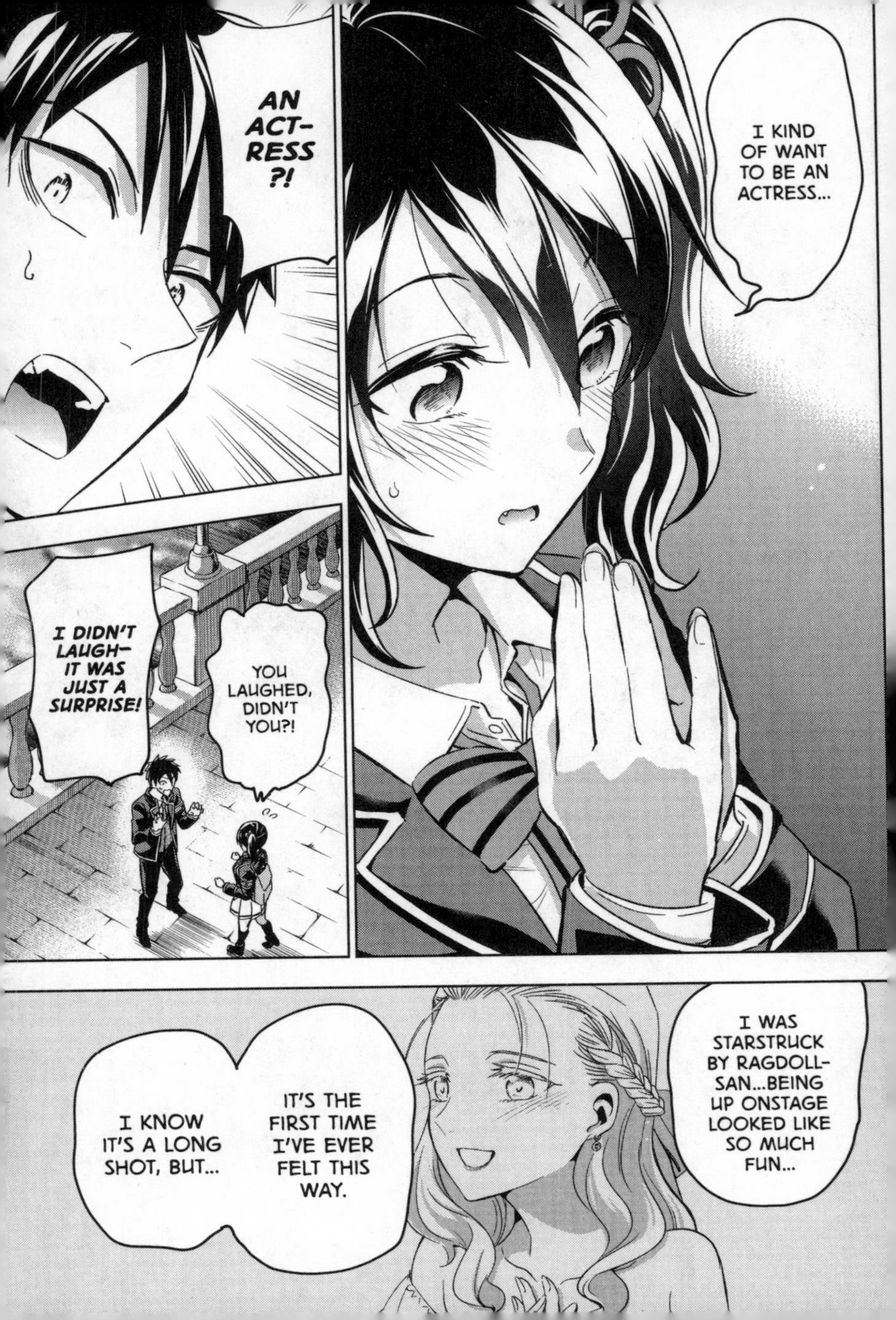
I KIND OF WANT TO BE AN ACTRESS...
AN ACT-RESS?!
YOU LAUGHED, DIDN'T YOU?!
I DIDN'T LAUGH—IT WAS JUST A SURPRISE!
I WAS STARSTRUCK BY RAGDOLL-SAN...BEING UP ONSTAGE LOOKED LIKE SO MUCH FUN...
IT'S THE FIRST TIME I'VE EVER FELT THIS WAY.
I KNOW IT'S A LONG SHOT, BUT...

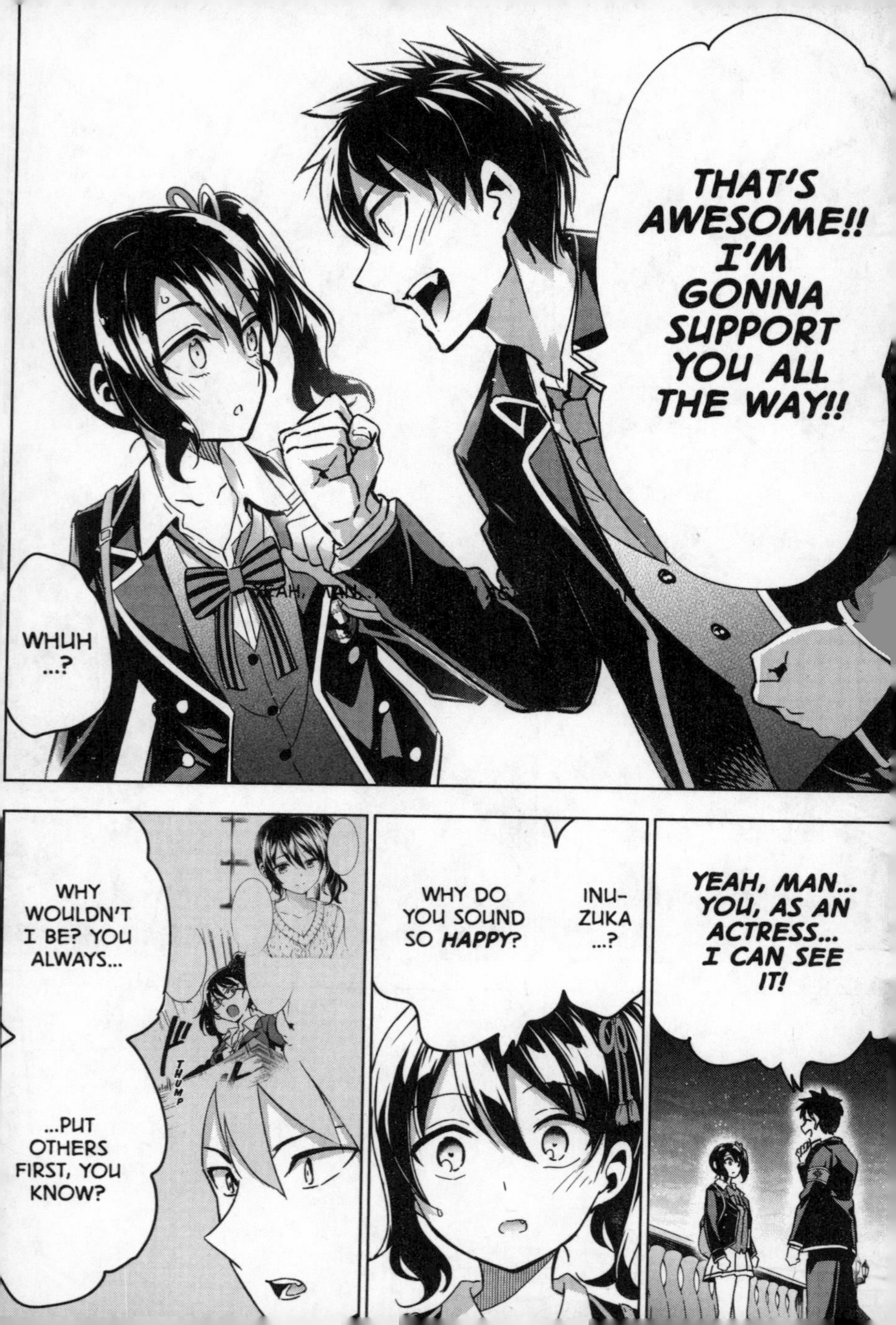
THAT'S AWESOME!! I'M GONNA SUPPORT YOU ALL THE WAY!!
WHUH ...?
YEAH, MAN... YOU, AS AN ACTRESS... I CAN SEE IT!
INU-ZUKA ...?
WHY DO YOU SOUND SO HAPPY?
WHY WOULDN'T I BE? YOU ALWAYS...
THUMP
...PUT OTHERS FIRST, YOU KNOW?

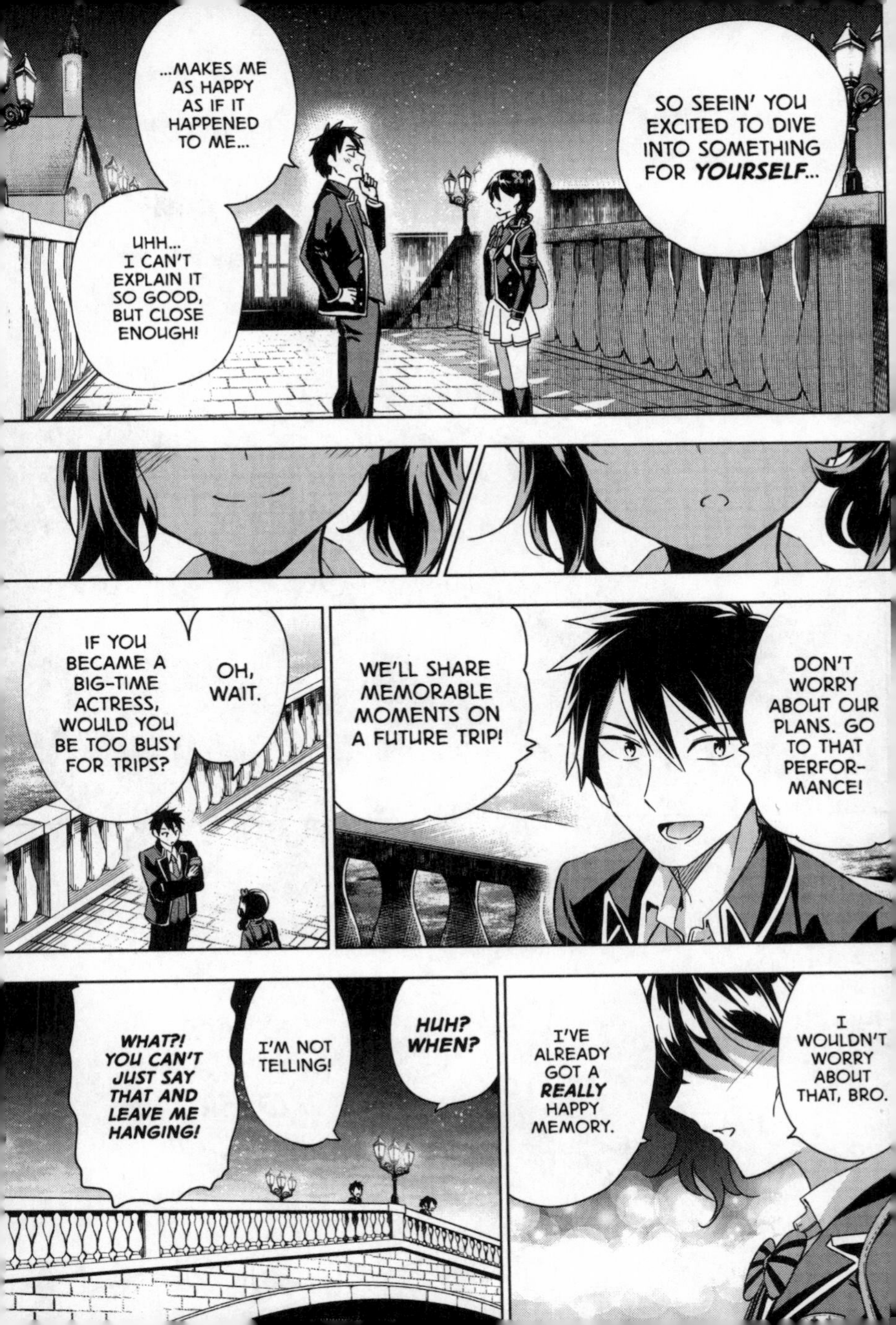
SO SEEIN' YOU EXCITED TO DIVE INTO SOMETHING FOR YOURSELF...
...MAKES ME AS HAPPY AS IF IT HAPPENED TO ME...
UHH... I CAN'T EXPLAIN IT SO GOOD, BUT CLOSE ENOUGH!
DON'T WORRY ABOUT OUR PLANS. GO TO THAT PERFORMANCE!
WE'LL SHARE MEMORABLE MOMENTS ON A FUTURE TRIP!
OH, WAIT.
IF YOU BECAME A BIG-TIME ACTRESS, WOULD YOU BE TOO BUSY FOR TRIPS?
I WOULDN'T WORRY ABOUT THAT, BRO.
I'VE ALREADY GOT A REALLY HAPPY MEMORY.
HUH? WHEN?
I'M NOT TELLING!
WHAT?! YOU CAN'T JUST SAY THAT AND LEAVE ME HANGING!

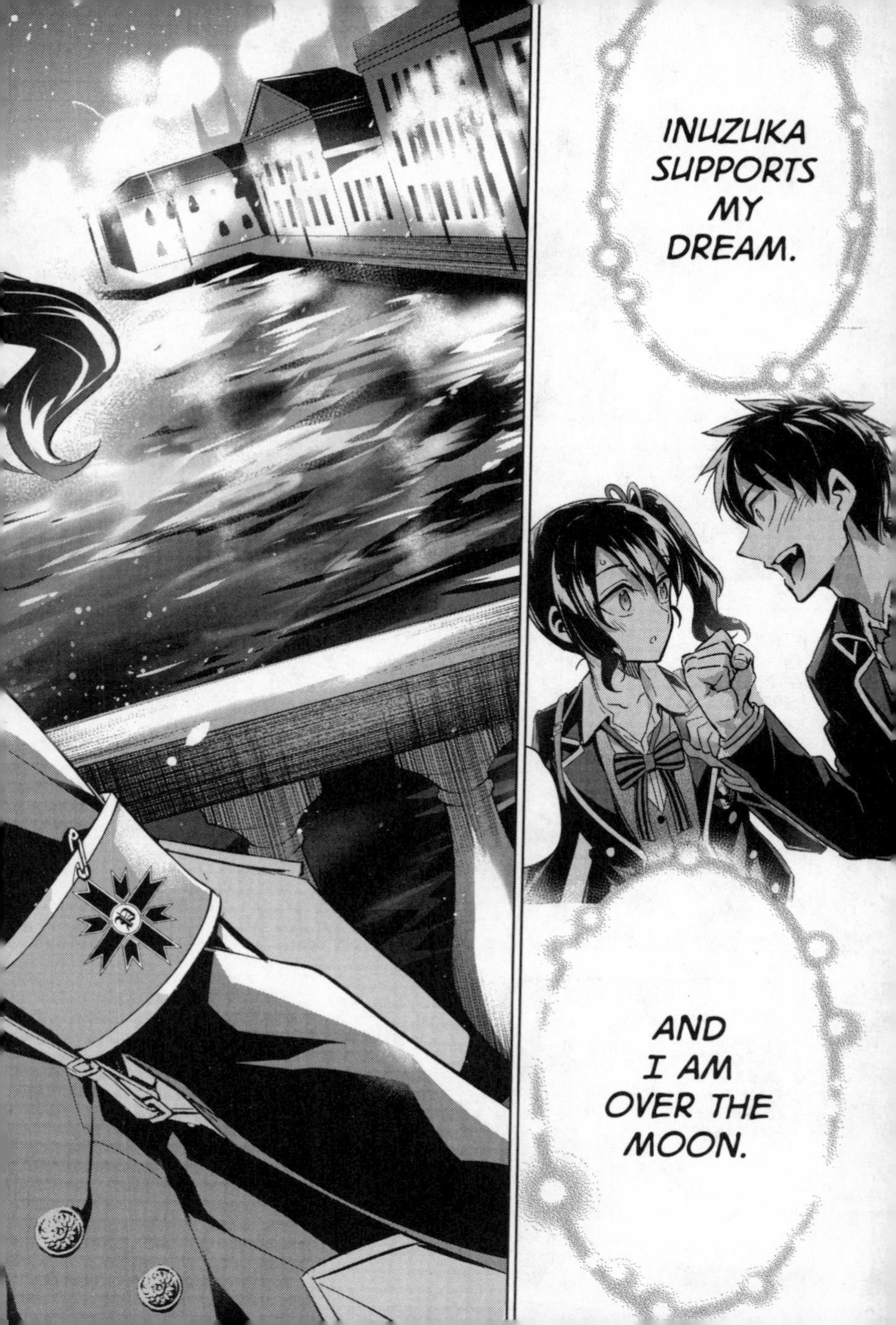
INUZUKA SUPPORTS MY DREAM.
AND I AM OVER THE MOON.

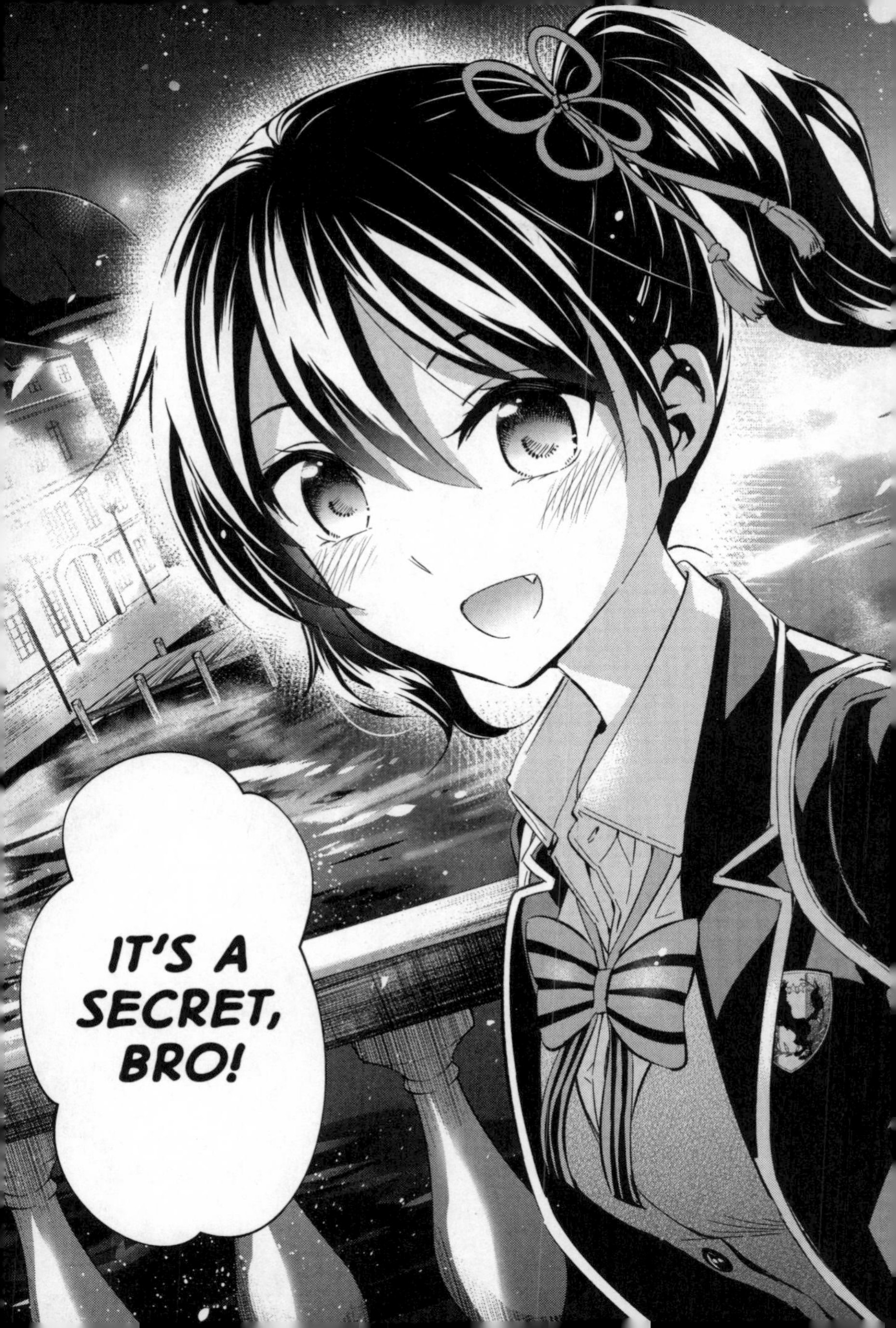
IT'S A SECRET, BRO!

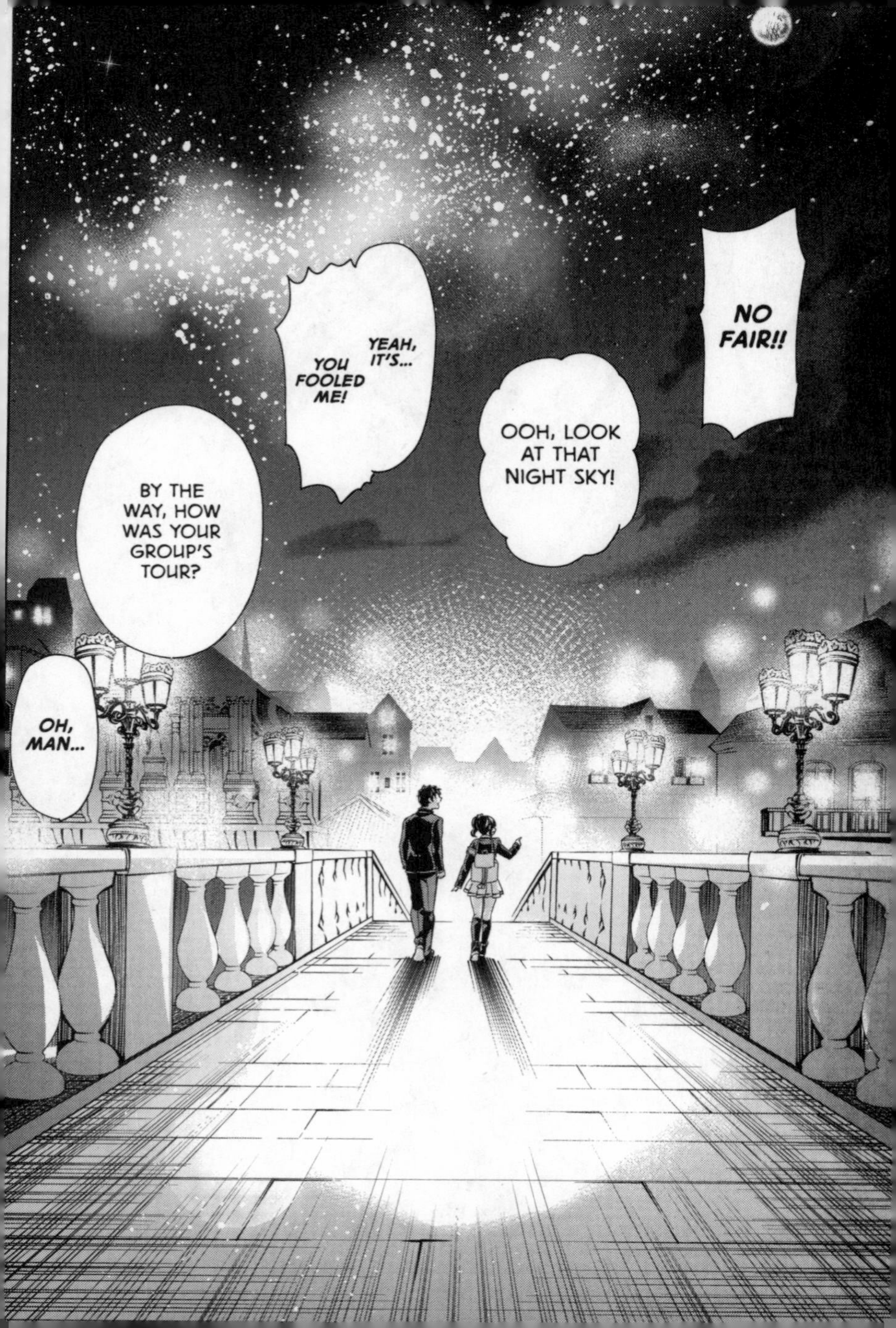
NO FAIR!!
OOH, LOOK AT THAT NIGHT SKY!
YEAH, IT'S...
YOU FOOLED ME!
BY THE WAY, HOW WAS YOUR GROUP'S TOUR?
OH, MAN...

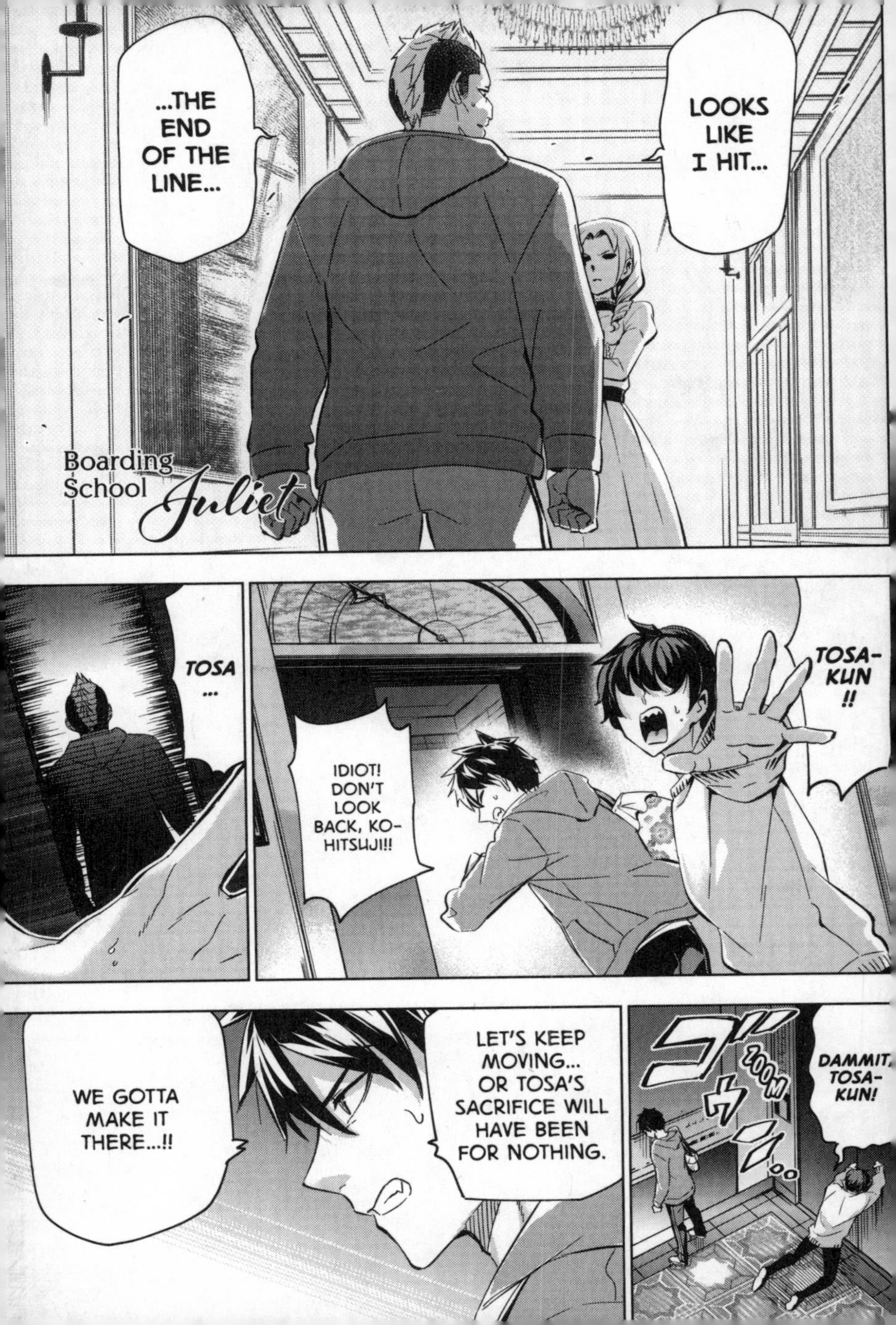
LOOKS LIKE I HIT...
...THE END OF THE LINE...
Boarding School Juliet
TOSA-KUN!!
IDIOT! DON'T LOOK BACK, KO-HITSUJI!!
TOSA ...
DAMMIT, TOSA-KUN!
ZOOM
LET'S KEEP MOVING... OR TOSA'S SACRIFICE WILL HAVE BEEN FOR NOTHING.
WE GOTTA MAKE IT THERE...!!

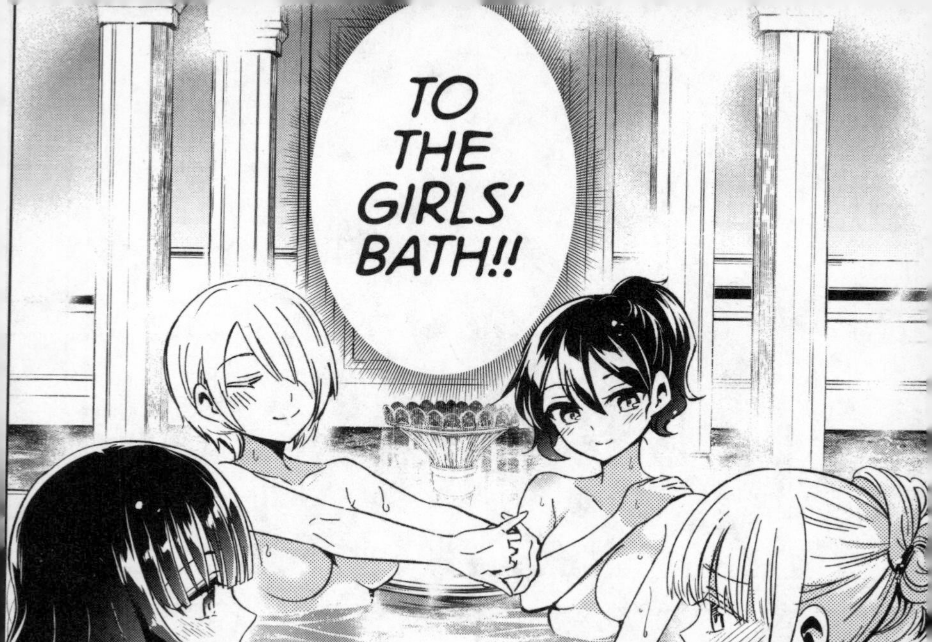
TO THE GIRLS' BATH!!

## ACT 105:

## ROMIO & THE HOT SPRING I

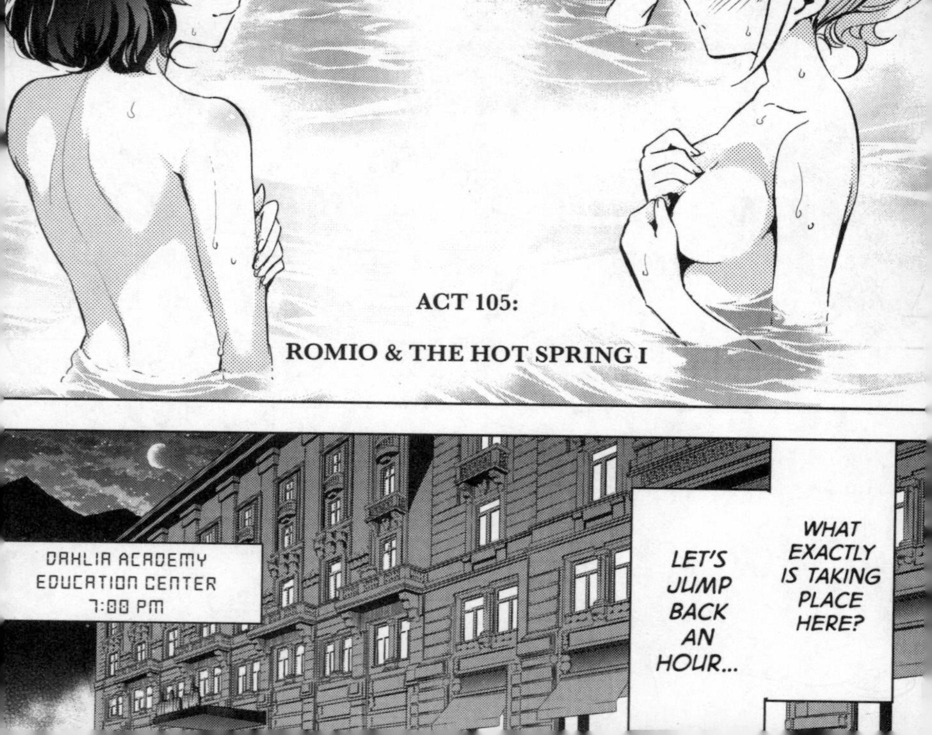
WHAT EXACTLY IS TAKING PLACE HERE?
LET'S JUMP BACK AN HOUR...
DAHLIA ACADEMY EDUCATION CENTER 7:00 PM

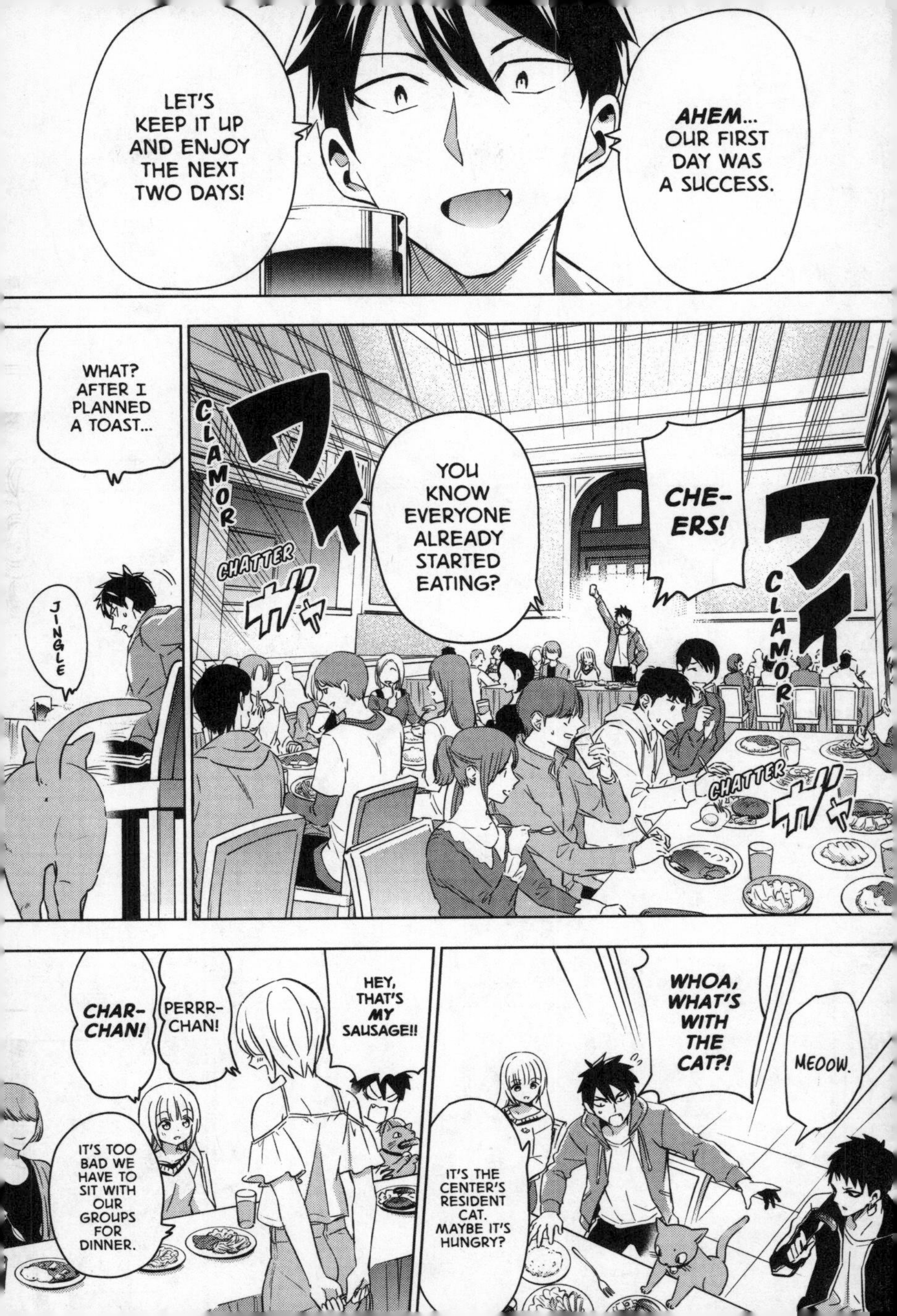
*AHEM*... OUR FIRST DAY WAS A SUCCESS.
LET'S KEEP IT UP AND ENJOY THE NEXT TWO DAYS!
CHE- ERS!
ワイ
CLAMOR
YOU KNOW EVERYONE ALREADY STARTED EATING?
ワイ
CLAMOR
CHATTER
ガヤ
CHATTER
ガヤ
WHAT? AFTER I PLANNED A TOAST...
JINGLE
WHOA, WHAT'S WITH THE CAT?!
MEOOW.
IT'S THE CENTER'S RESIDENT CAT. MAYBE IT'S HUNGRY?
HEY, THAT'S *MY* SAUSAGE!!
PERRR- CHAN!
CHAR- CHAN!
IT'S TOO BAD WE HAVE TO SIT WITH OUR GROUPS FOR DINNER.

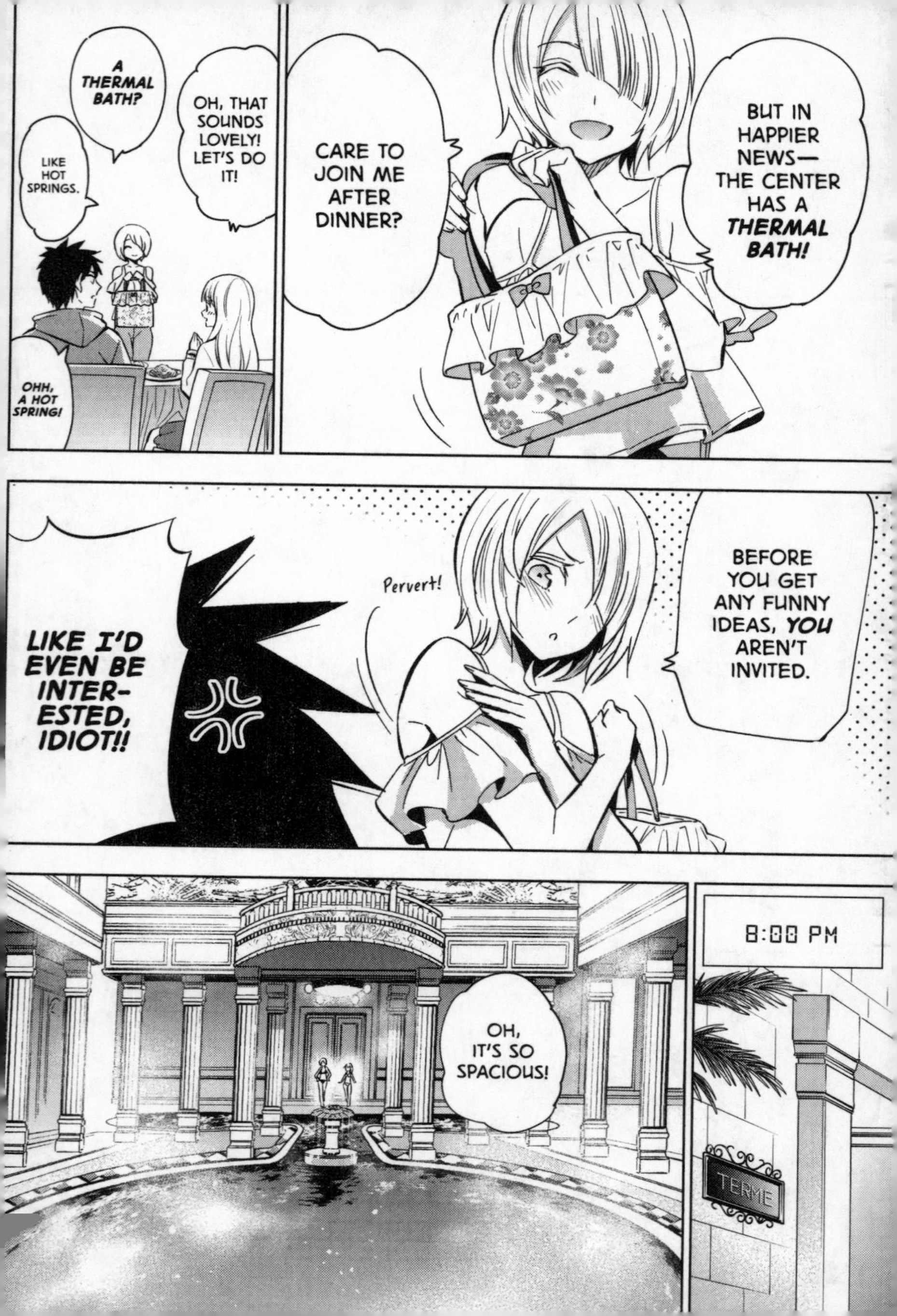
BUT IN HAPPIER NEWS— THE CENTER HAS A THERMAL BATH!
CARE TO JOIN ME AFTER DINNER?
A THERMAL BATH?
OH, THAT SOUNDS LOVELY! LET'S DO IT!
LIKE HOT SPRINGS.
OHH, A HOT SPRING!
BEFORE YOU GET ANY FUNNY IDEAS, YOU AREN'T INVITED.
Pervert!
LIKE I'D EVEN BE INTER- ESTED, IDIOT!!
8:00 PM
TERME
OH, IT'S SO SPACIOUS!

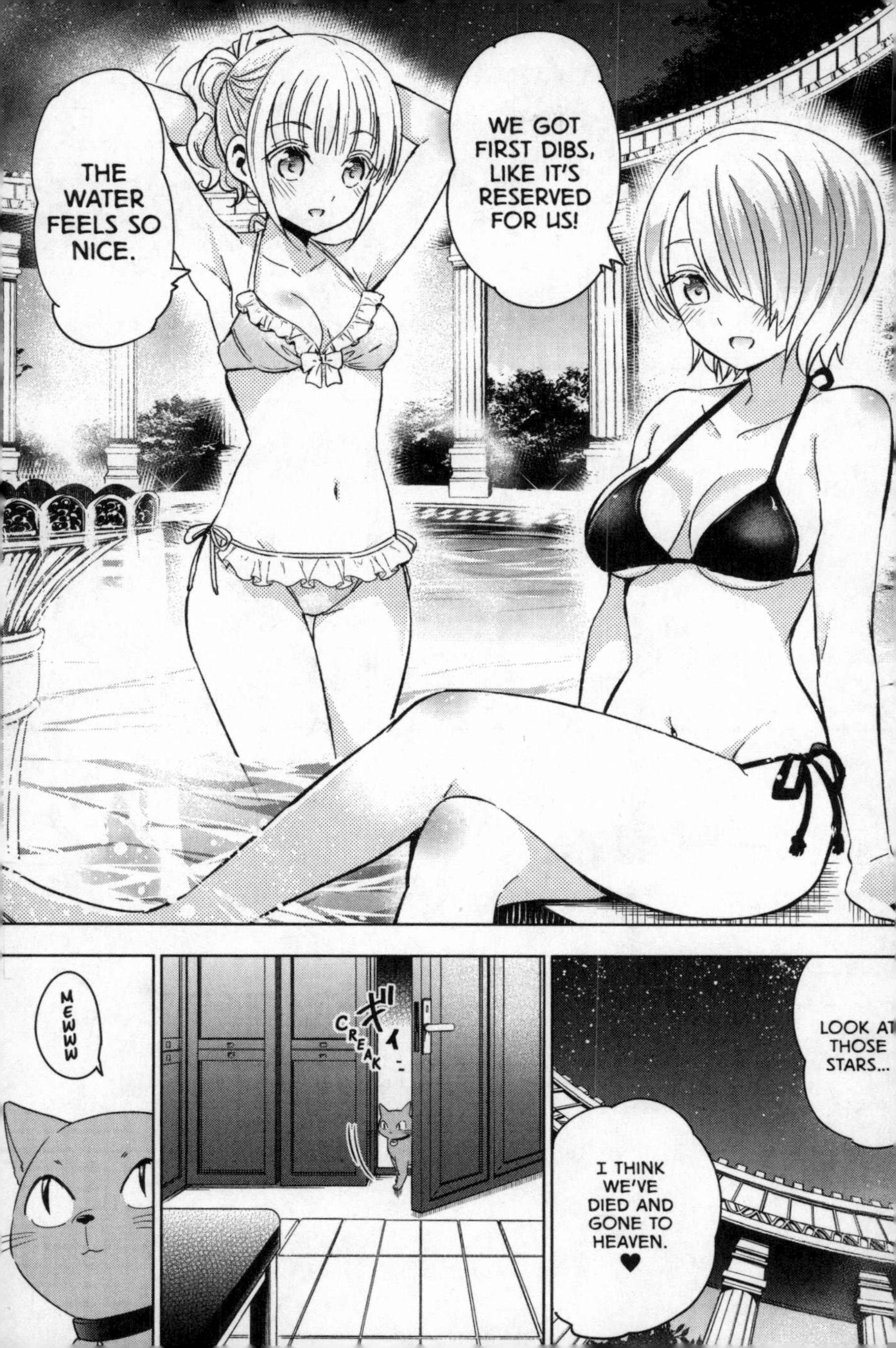
WE GOT FIRST DIBS, LIKE IT'S RESERVED FOR US!
THE WATER FEELS SO NICE.
LOOK AT THOSE STARS...
I THINK WE'VE DIED AND GONE TO HEAVEN. ♥
CREAK
MEWWW

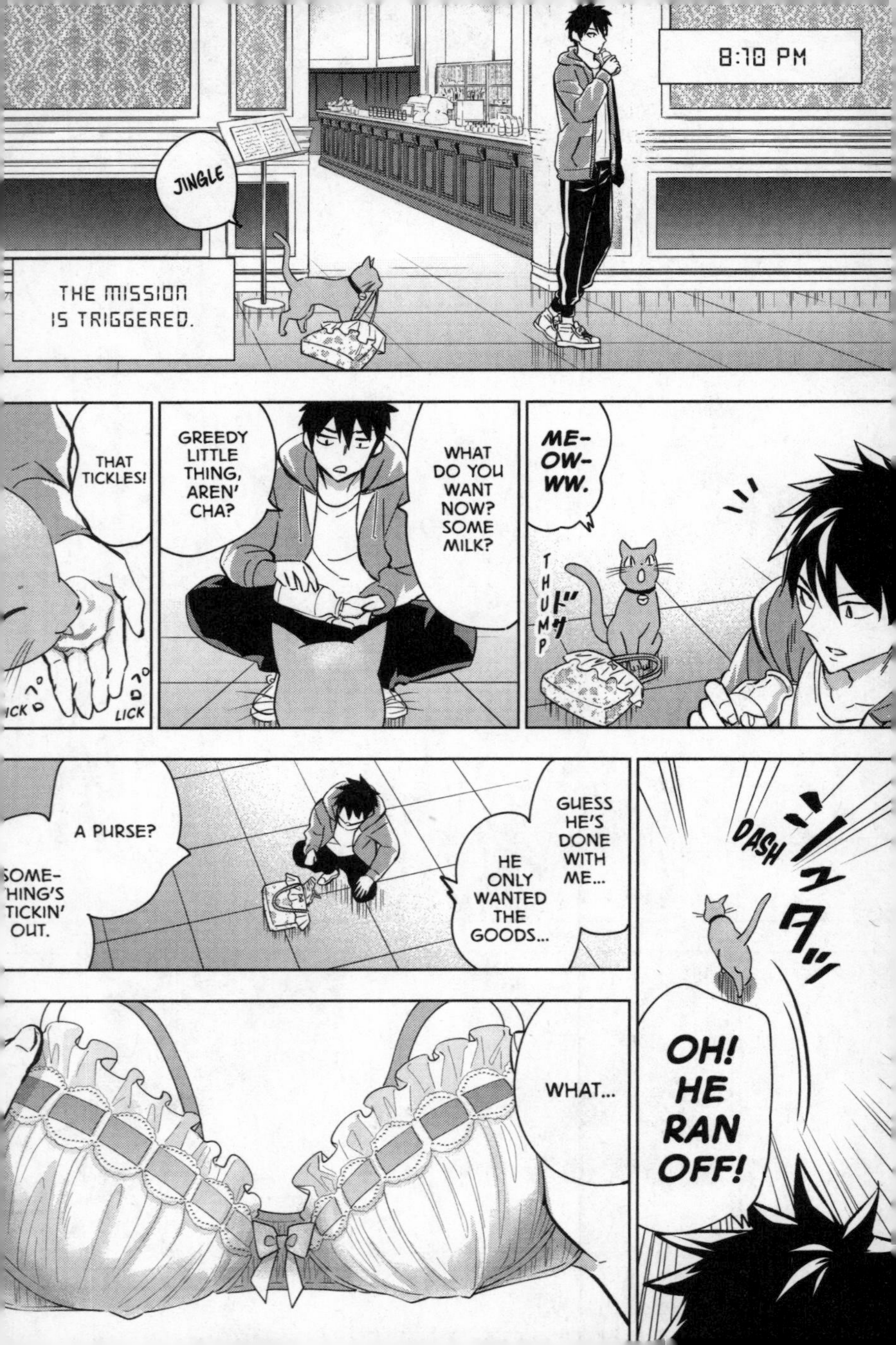
8:10 PM
JINGLE
THE MISSION IS TRIGGERED.
ME-OW-WW.
THUMP
WHAT DO YOU WANT NOW? SOME MILK?
GREEDY LITTLE THING, AREN'CHA?
THAT TICKLES!
LICK
LICK
DASH
OH! HE RAN OFF!
GUESS HE'S DONE WITH ME...
HE ONLY WANTED THE GOODS...
A PURSE?
SOME-HING'S TICKIN' OUT.
WHAT...

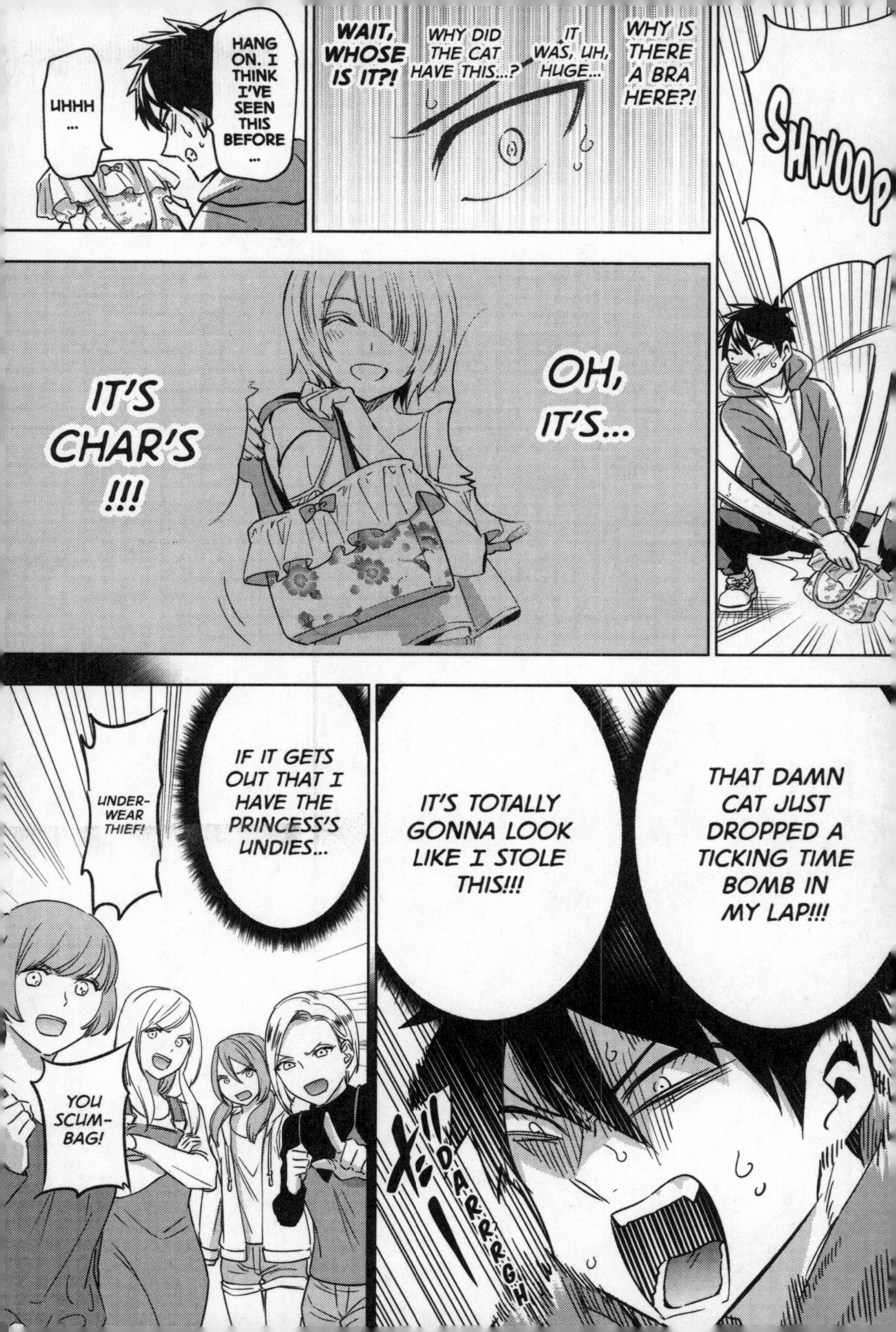
SHWOOP
WHY IS THERE A BRA HERE?!
IT WAS, UH, HUGE...
WHY DID THE CAT HAVE THIS...?
WAIT, WHOSE IS IT?!
HANG ON. I THINK I'VE SEEN THIS BEFORE ...
UHHH ...
OH, IT'S...
IT'S CHAR'S !!!
THAT DAMN CAT JUST DROPPED A TICKING TIME BOMB IN MY LAP!!!
IT'S TOTALLY GONNA LOOK LIKE I STOLE THIS!!!
DARRRRGH
IF IT GETS OUT THAT I HAVE THE PRINCESS'S UNDIES...
UNDER-WEAR THIEF!
YOU SCUM-BAG!

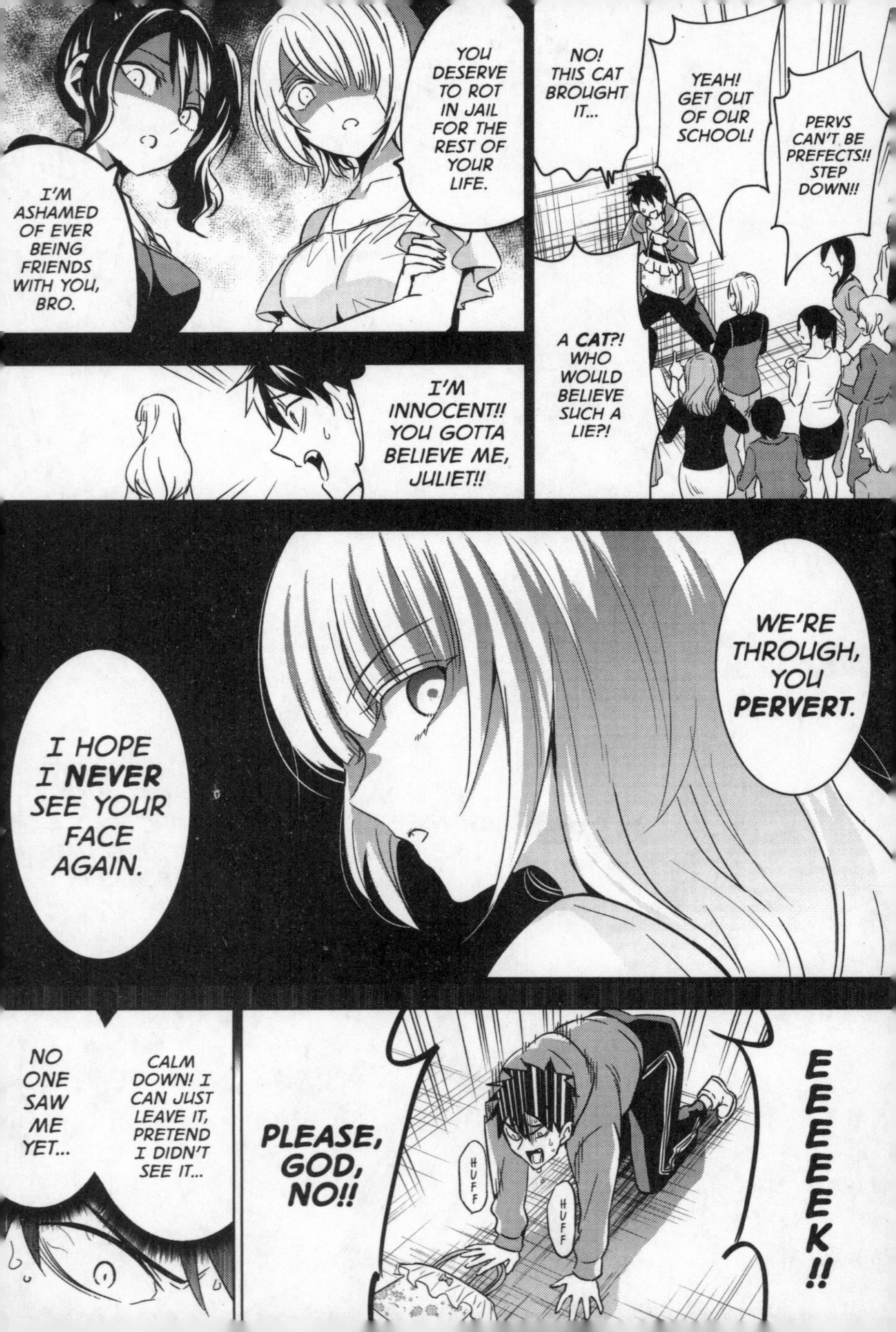
PERVS CAN'T BE PREFECTS!! STEP DOWN!!
YEAH! GET OUT OF OUR SCHOOL!
NO! THIS CAT BROUGHT IT...
A CAT?! WHO WOULD BELIEVE SUCH A LIE?!
YOU DESERVE TO ROT IN JAIL FOR THE REST OF YOUR LIFE.
I'M ASHAMED OF EVER BEING FRIENDS WITH YOU, BRO.
I'M INNOCENT!! YOU GOTTA BELIEVE ME, JULIET!!
WE'RE THROUGH, YOU PERVERT.
I HOPE I NEVER SEE YOUR FACE AGAIN.
EEEEEK!!
PLEASE, GOD, NO!!
HUFF
HUFF
CALM DOWN! I CAN JUST LEAVE IT, PRETEND I DIDN'T SEE IT...
NO ONE SAW ME YET...

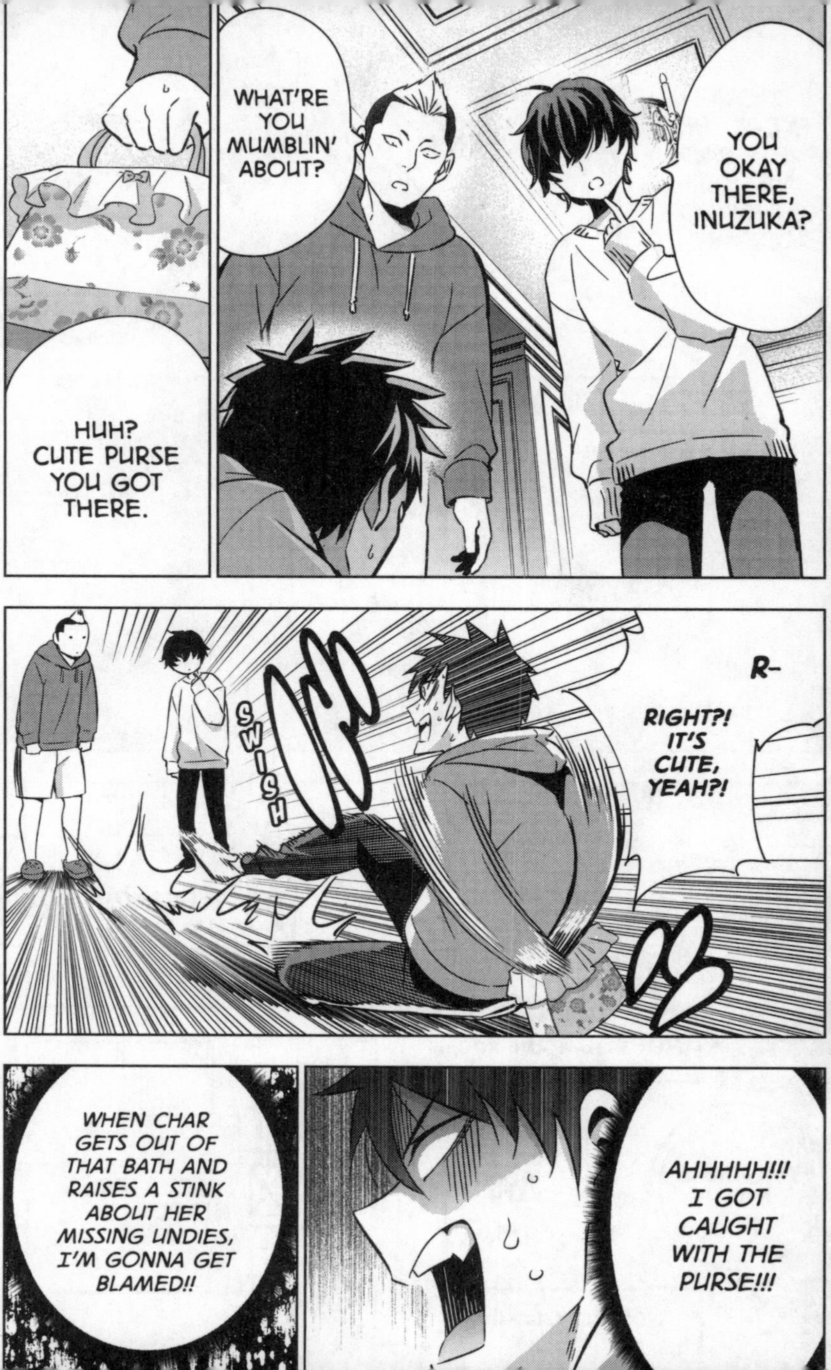
YOU OKAY THERE, INUZUKA?
WHAT'RE YOU MUMBLIN' ABOUT?
HUH? CUTE PURSE YOU GOT THERE.
R-
RIGHT?! IT'S CUTE, YEAH?!
SWISH
AHHHHH!!! I GOT CAUGHT WITH THE PURSE!!!
WHEN CHAR GETS OUT OF THAT BATH AND RAISES A STINK ABOUT HER MISSING UNDIES, I'M GONNA GET BLAMED!!

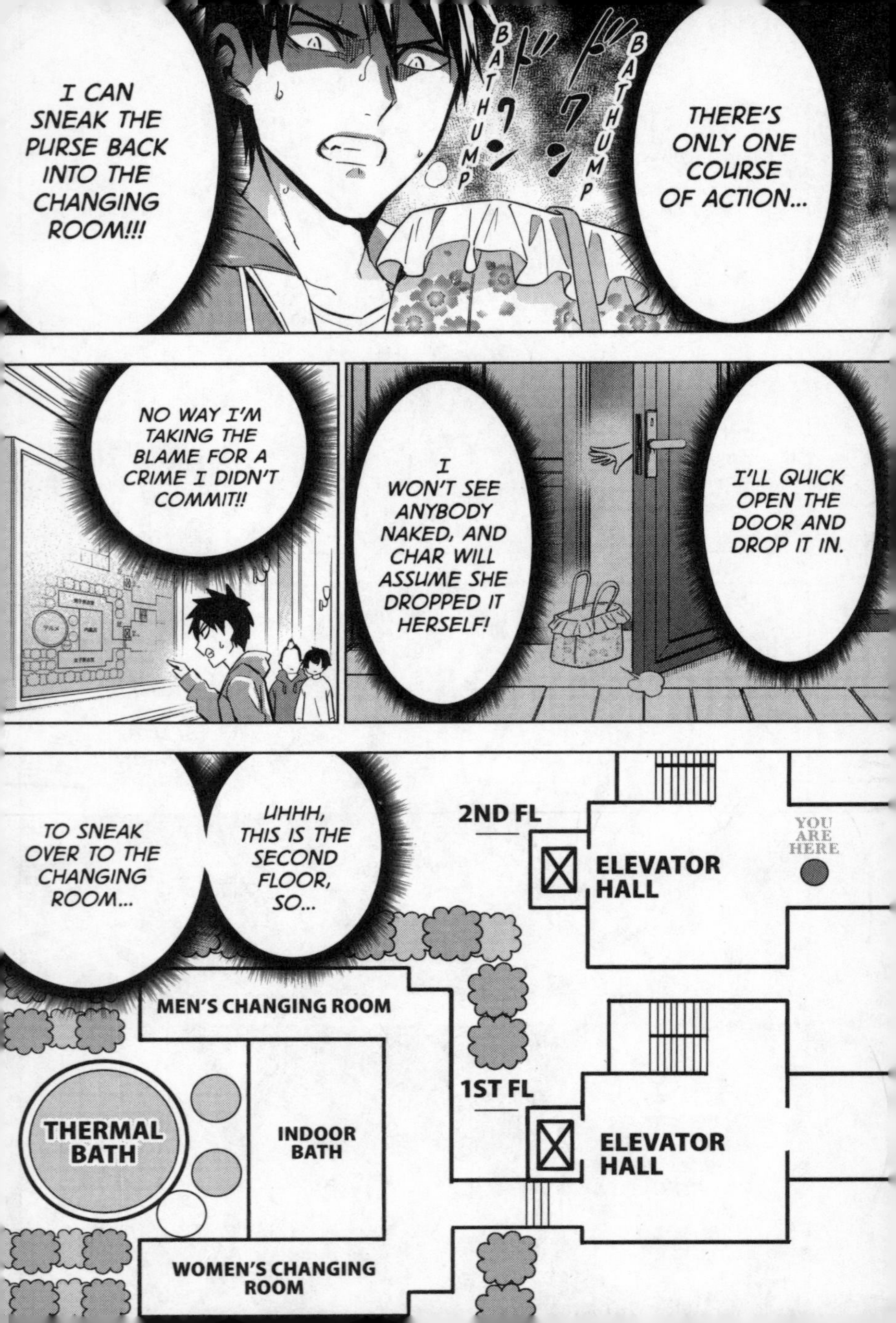
THERE'S ONLY ONE COURSE OF ACTION...
BATHUMP
BATHUMP
I CAN SNEAK THE PURSE BACK INTO THE CHANGING ROOM!!!
I'LL QUICK OPEN THE DOOR AND DROP IT IN.
I WON'T SEE ANYBODY NAKED, AND CHAR WILL ASSUME SHE DROPPED IT HERSELF!
NO WAY I'M TAKING THE BLAME FOR A CRIME I DIDN'T COMMIT!!
YOU ARE HERE
2ND FL
ELEVATOR HALL
1ST FL
ELEVATOR HALL
UHHH, THIS IS THE SECOND FLOOR, SO...
TO SNEAK OVER TO THE CHANGING ROOM...
MEN'S CHANGING ROOM
THERMAL BATH
INDOOR BATH
WOMEN'S CHANGING ROOM

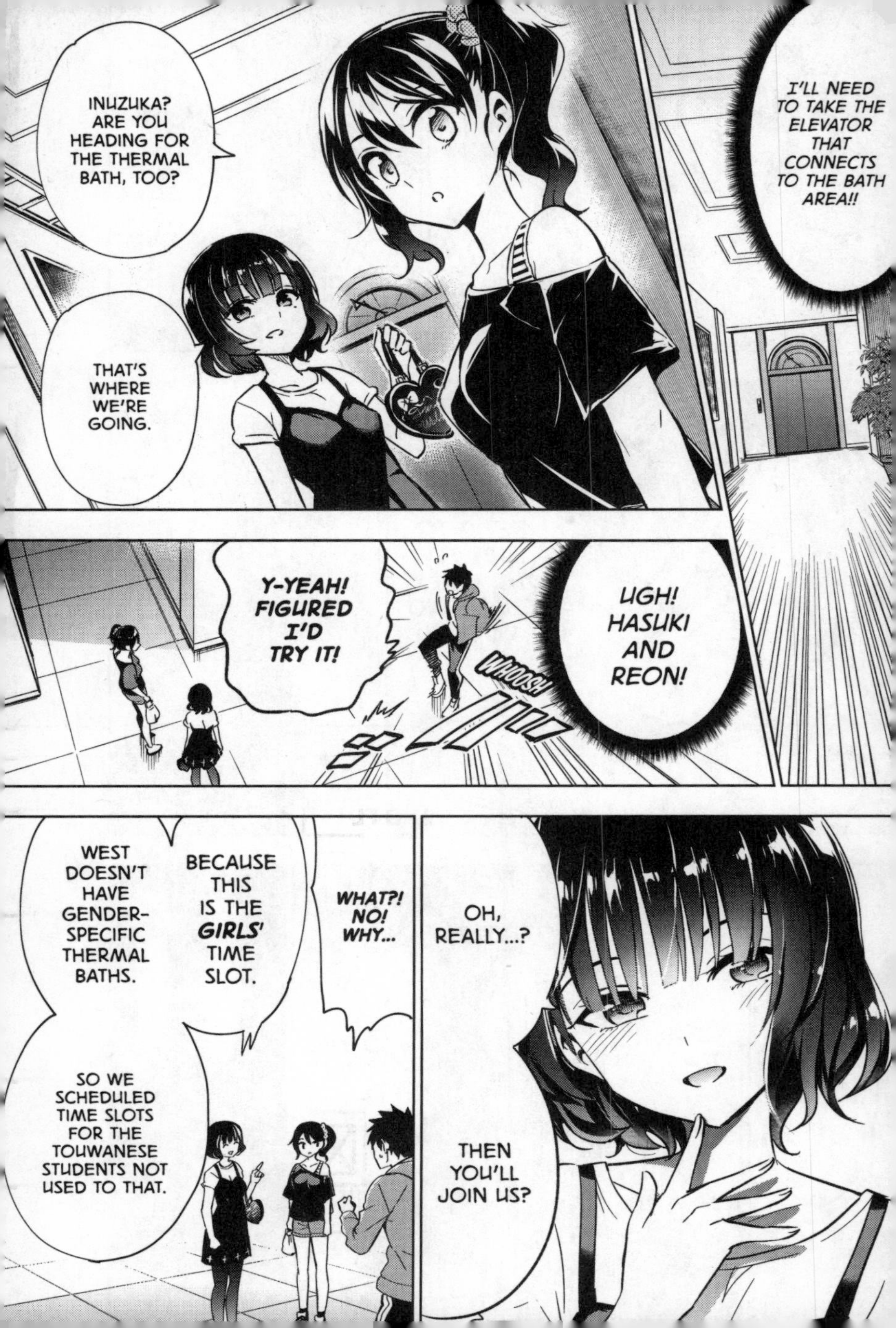
I'LL NEED TO TAKE THE ELEVATOR THAT CONNECTS TO THE BATH AREA!!
INUZUKA? ARE YOU HEADING FOR THE THERMAL BATH, TOO?
THAT'S WHERE WE'RE GOING.
UGH! HASUKI AND REON!
WHOOSH
Y-YEAH! FIGURED I'D TRY IT!
OH, REALLY...?
THEN YOU'LL JOIN US?
WHAT?! NO! WHY...
BECAUSE THIS IS THE GIRLS' TIME SLOT.
WEST DOESN'T HAVE GENDER-SPECIFIC THERMAL BATHS.
SO WE SCHEDULED TIME SLOTS FOR THE TOUWANESE STUDENTS NOT USED TO THAT.

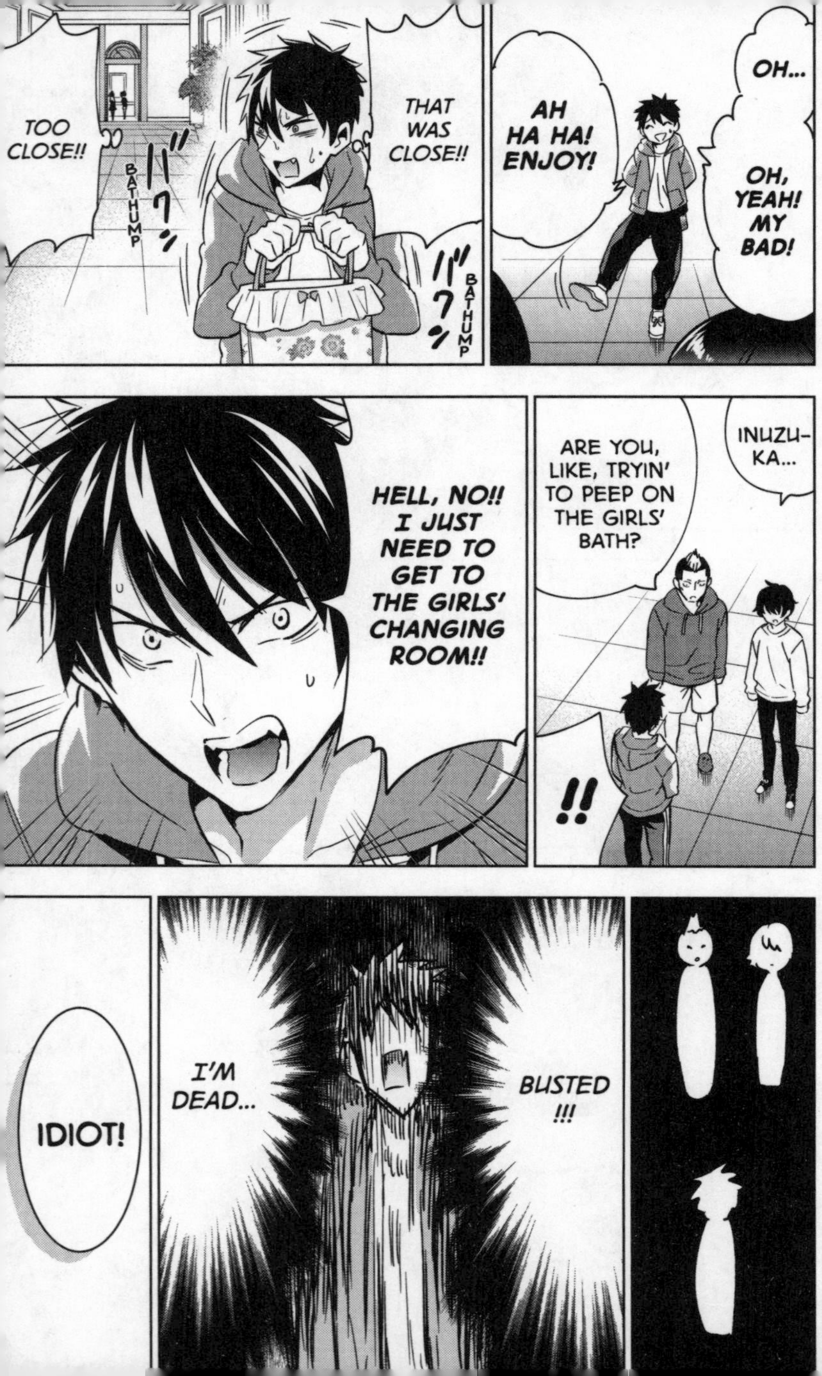
OH...
OH, YEAH! MY BAD!
AH HA HA! ENJOY!
THAT WAS CLOSE!!
BATHUMP
BATHUMP
TOO CLOSE!!
INUZU-KA...
ARE YOU, LIKE, TRYIN' TO PEEP ON THE GIRLS' BATH?
!!
HELL, NO!! I JUST NEED TO GET TO THE GIRLS' CHANGING ROOM!!
BUSTED !!!
I'M DEAD...
IDIOT!

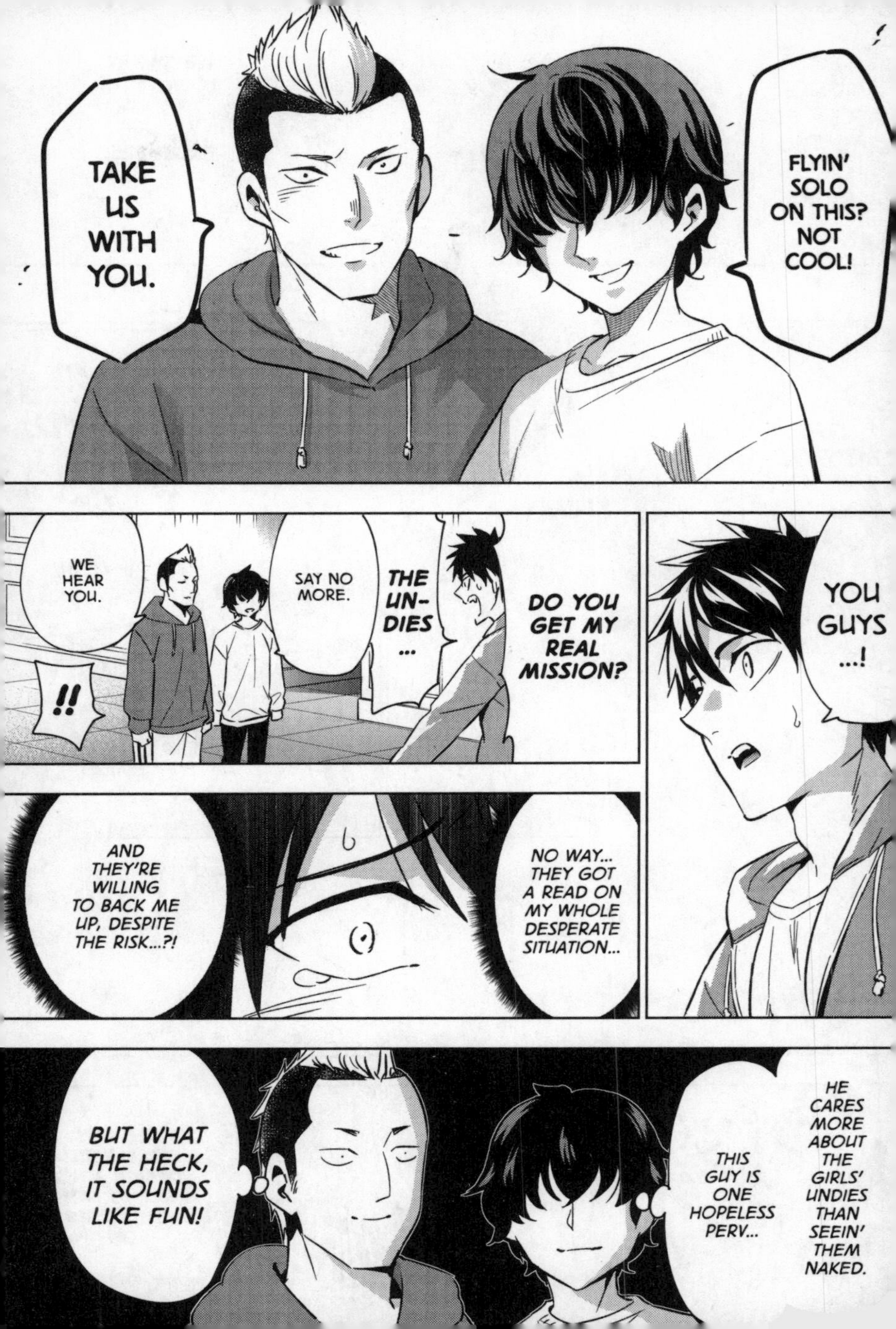
FLYIN' SOLO ON THIS? NOT COOL!
TAKE US WITH YOU.
YOU GUYS ...!
DO YOU GET MY REAL MISSION?
THE UN-DIES ...
SAY NO MORE.
WE HEAR YOU.
!!
NO WAY... THEY GOT A READ ON MY WHOLE DESPERATE SITUATION...
AND THEY'RE WILLING TO BACK ME UP, DESPITE THE RISK...?!
HE CARES MORE ABOUT THE GIRLS' UNDIES THAN SEEIN' THEM NAKED.
THIS GUY IS ONE HOPELESS PERV...
BUT WHAT THE HECK, IT SOUNDS LIKE FUN!

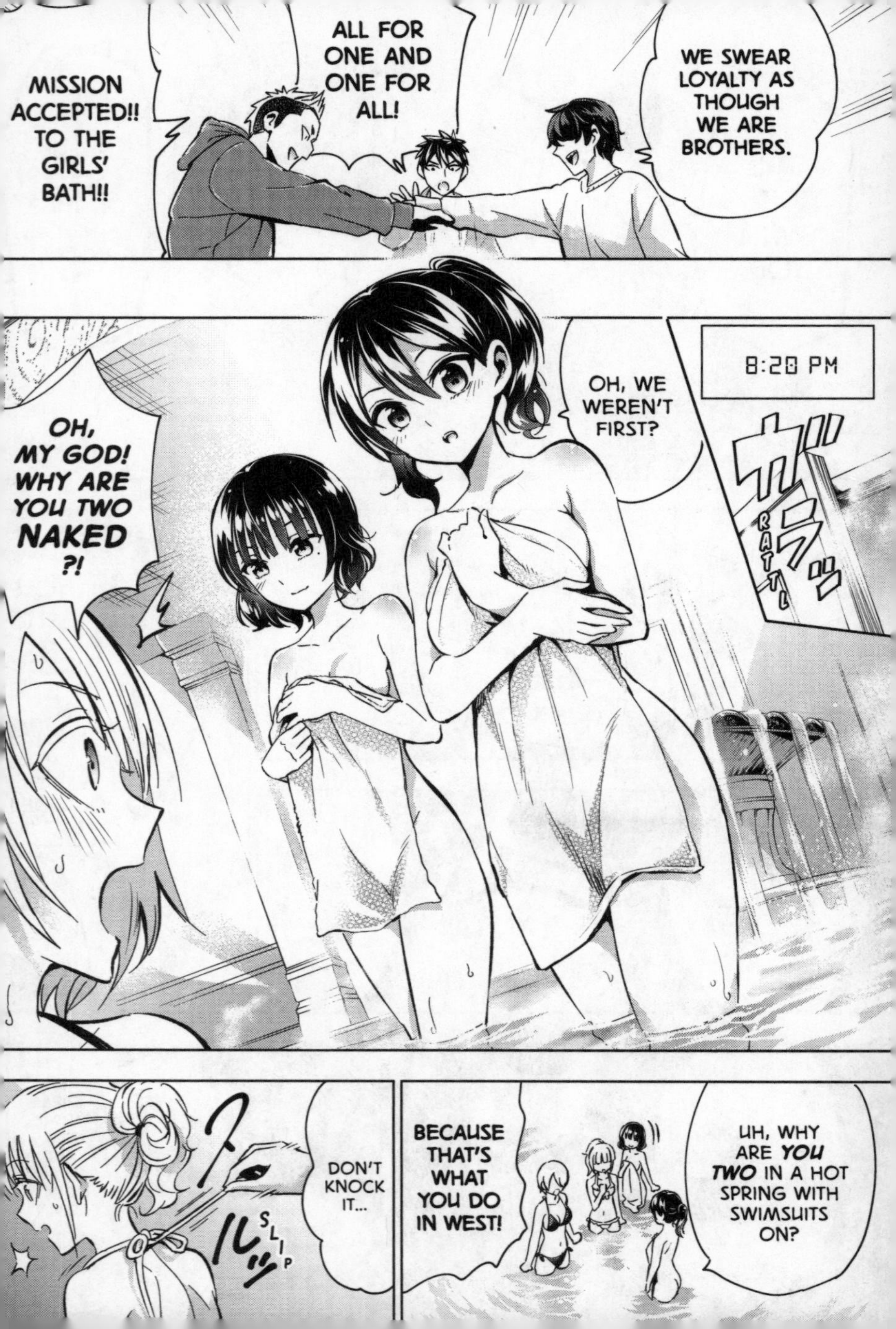
WE SWEAR LOYALTY AS THOUGH WE ARE BROTHERS.
ALL FOR ONE AND ONE FOR ALL!
MISSION ACCEPTED!! TO THE GIRLS' BATH!!
8:20 PM
RATTL
OH, WE WEREN'T FIRST?
OH, MY GOD! WHY ARE YOU TWO **NAKED** ?!
UH, WHY ARE ***YOU TWO*** IN A HOT SPRING WITH SWIMSUITS ON?
BECAUSE THAT'S WHAT YOU DO IN WEST!
DON'T KNOCK IT...
?
SLIP

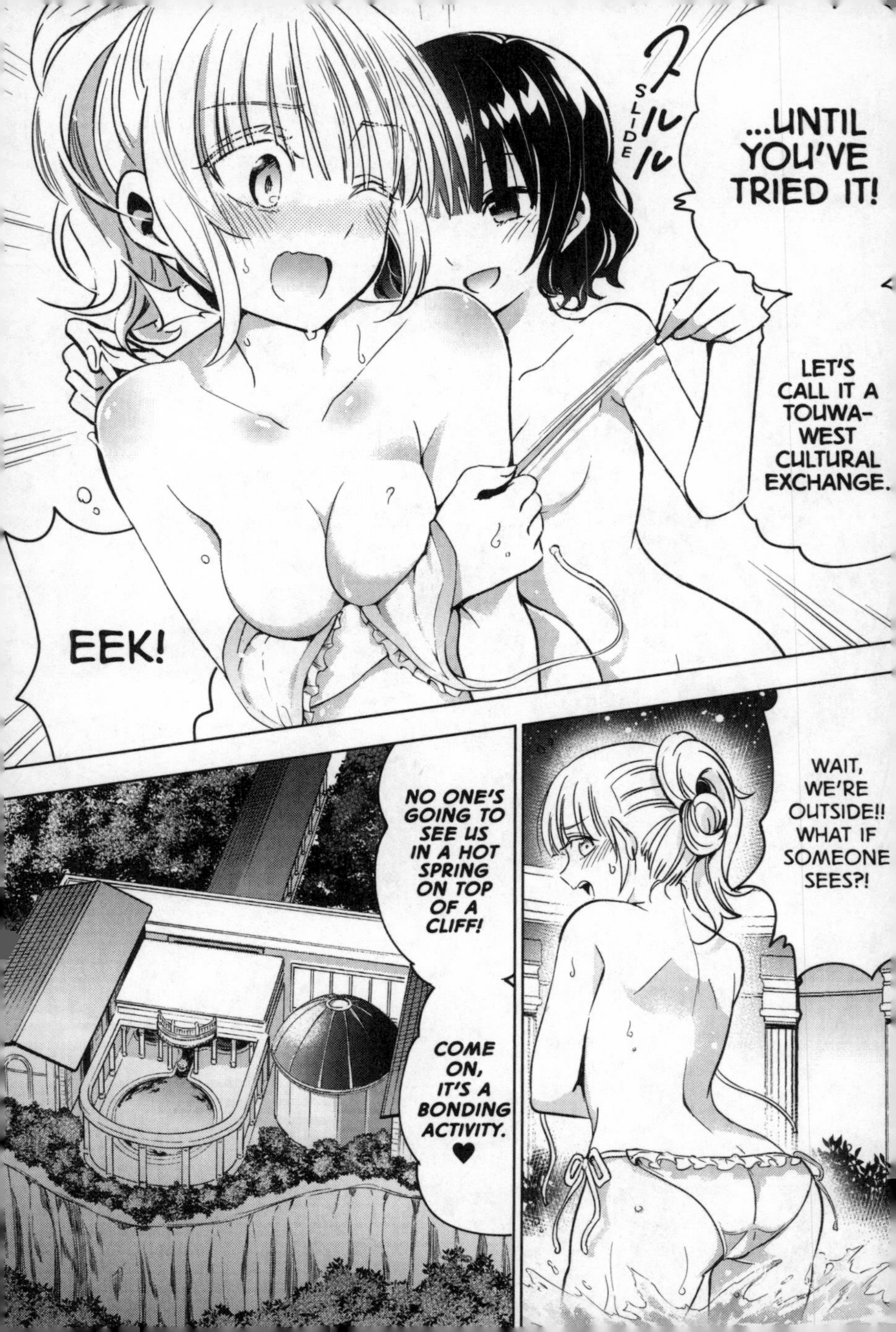
...UNTIL YOU'VE TRIED IT!
SLIDE
LET'S CALL IT A TOUWA-WEST CULTURAL EXCHANGE.
EEK!
WAIT, WE'RE OUTSIDE!! WHAT IF SOMEONE SEES?!
NO ONE'S GOING TO SEE US IN A HOT SPRING ON TOP OF A CLIFF!
COME ON, IT'S A BONDING ACTIVITY. ♥

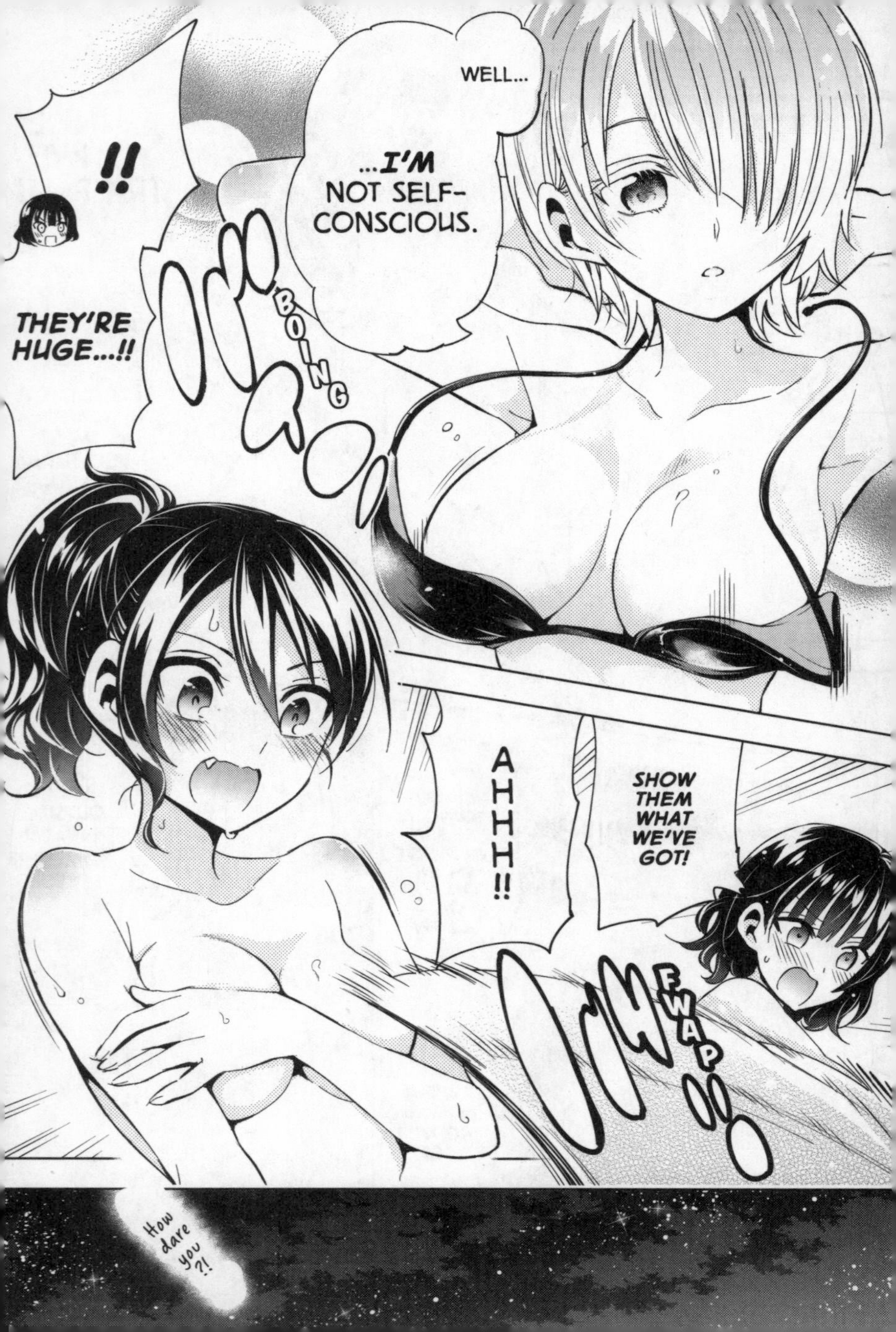
WELL...
...I'M NOT SELF-CONSCIOUS.
BOING
!!
THEY'RE HUGE...!!
SHOW THEM WHAT WE'VE GOT!
FWAP!!
AHHH!!
How dare you?!

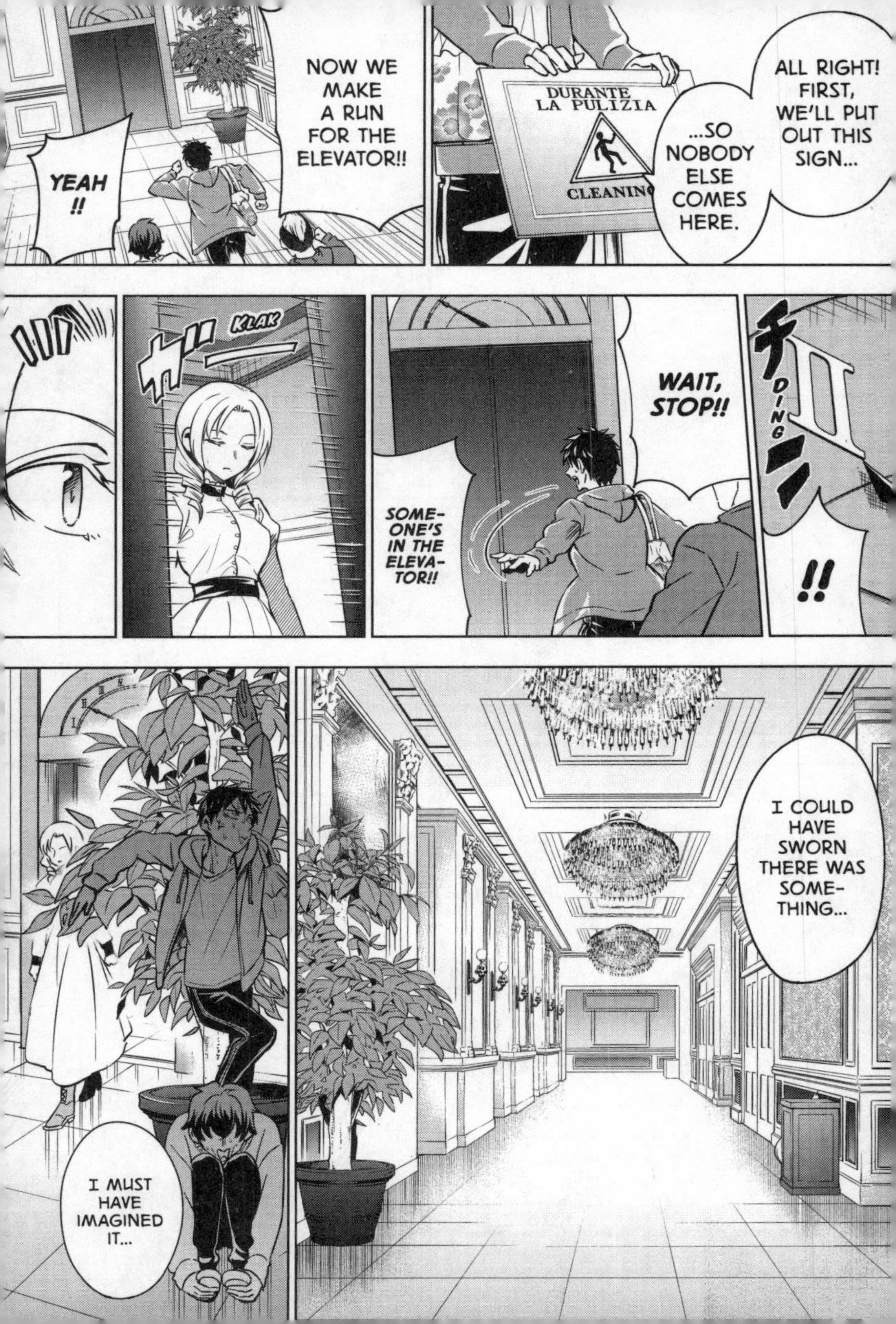

ALL RIGHT! FIRST, WE'LL PUT OUT THIS SIGN...
...SO NOBODY ELSE COMES HERE.
DURANTE LA PULIZIA
CLEANIN
NOW WE MAKE A RUN FOR THE ELEVATOR!!
YEAH!!
DING
!!
WAIT, STOP!!
SOME-ONE'S IN THE ELEVA-TOR!!
KLAK
I COULD HAVE SWORN THERE WAS SOME-THING...
I MUST HAVE IMAGINED IT...

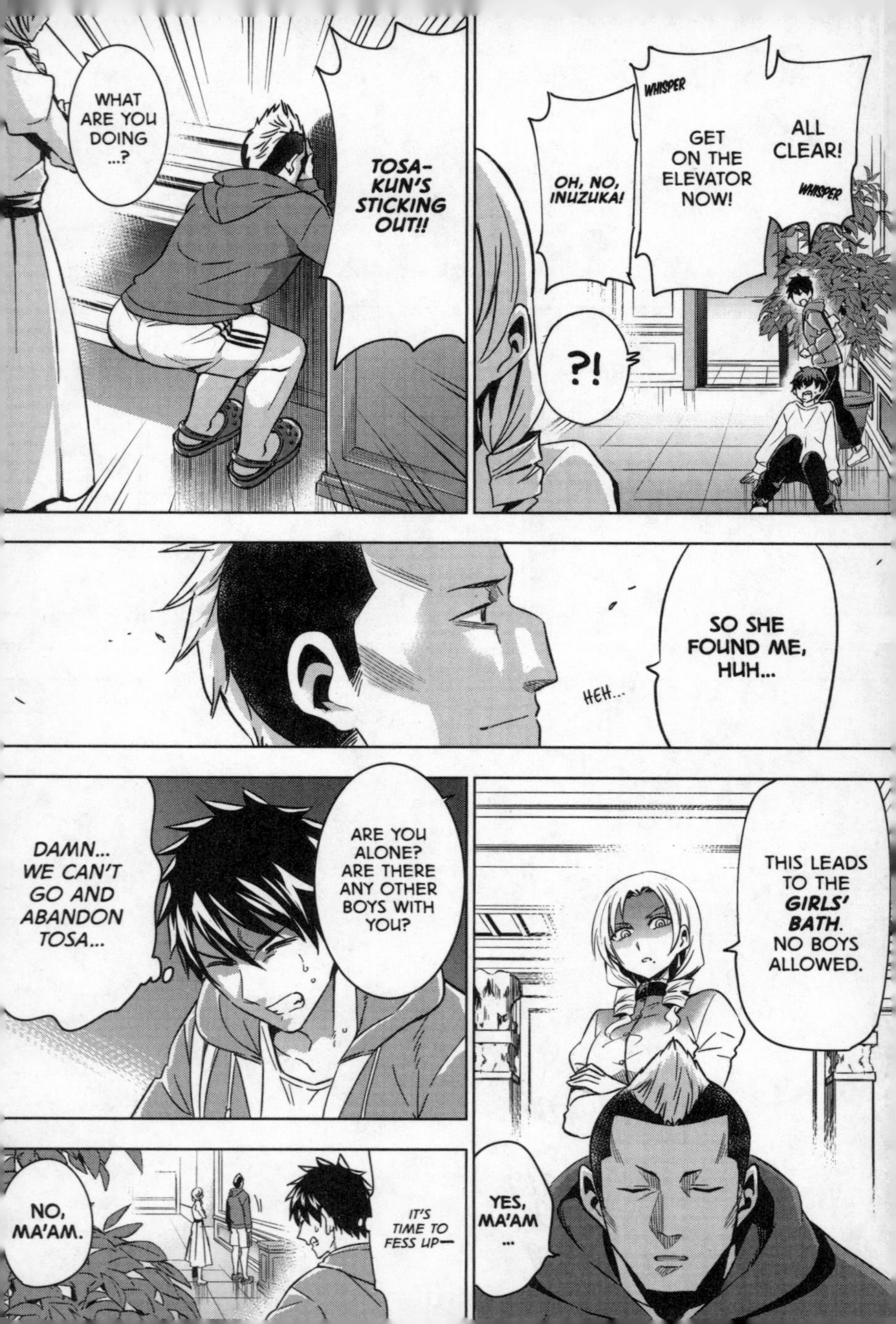
WHISPER
ALL CLEAR!
GET ON THE ELEVATOR NOW!
WHISPER
OH, NO, INUZUKA!
?!
TOSA-KUN'S STICKING OUT!!
WHAT ARE YOU DOING ...?
SO SHE FOUND ME, HUH...
HEH...
THIS LEADS TO THE GIRLS' BATH. NO BOYS ALLOWED.
YES, MA'AM ...
ARE YOU ALONE? ARE THERE ANY OTHER BOYS WITH YOU?
DAMN... WE CAN'T GO AND ABANDON TOSA...
IT'S TIME TO FESS UP—
NO, MA'AM.

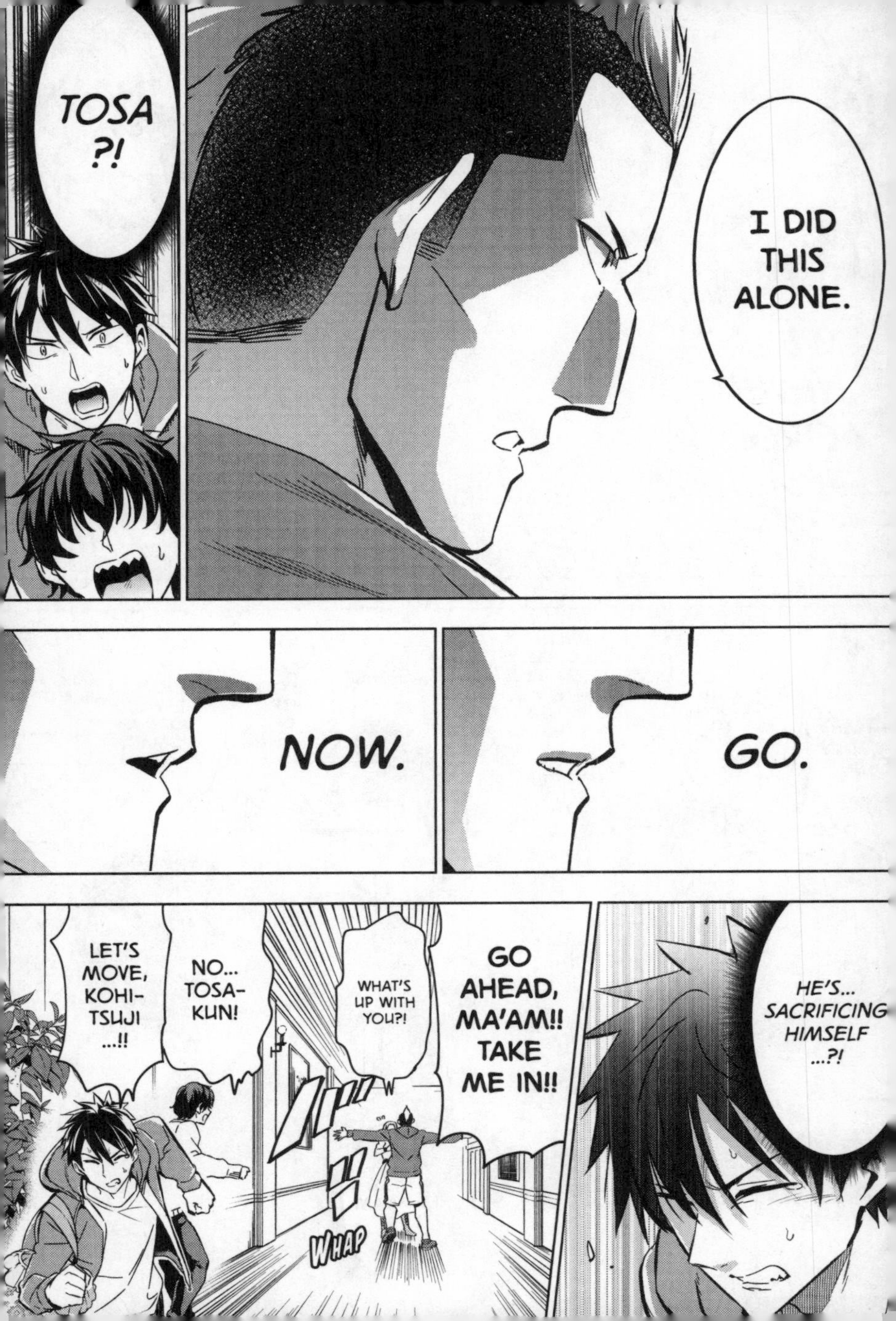
I DID THIS ALONE.
TOSA ?!
GO.
NOW.
HE'S... SACRIFICING HIMSELF ...?!
GO AHEAD, MA'AM!! TAKE ME IN!!
WHAT'S UP WITH YOU?!
NO... TOSA-KUN!
LET'S MOVE, KOHI-TSUJI ...!!
WHAP

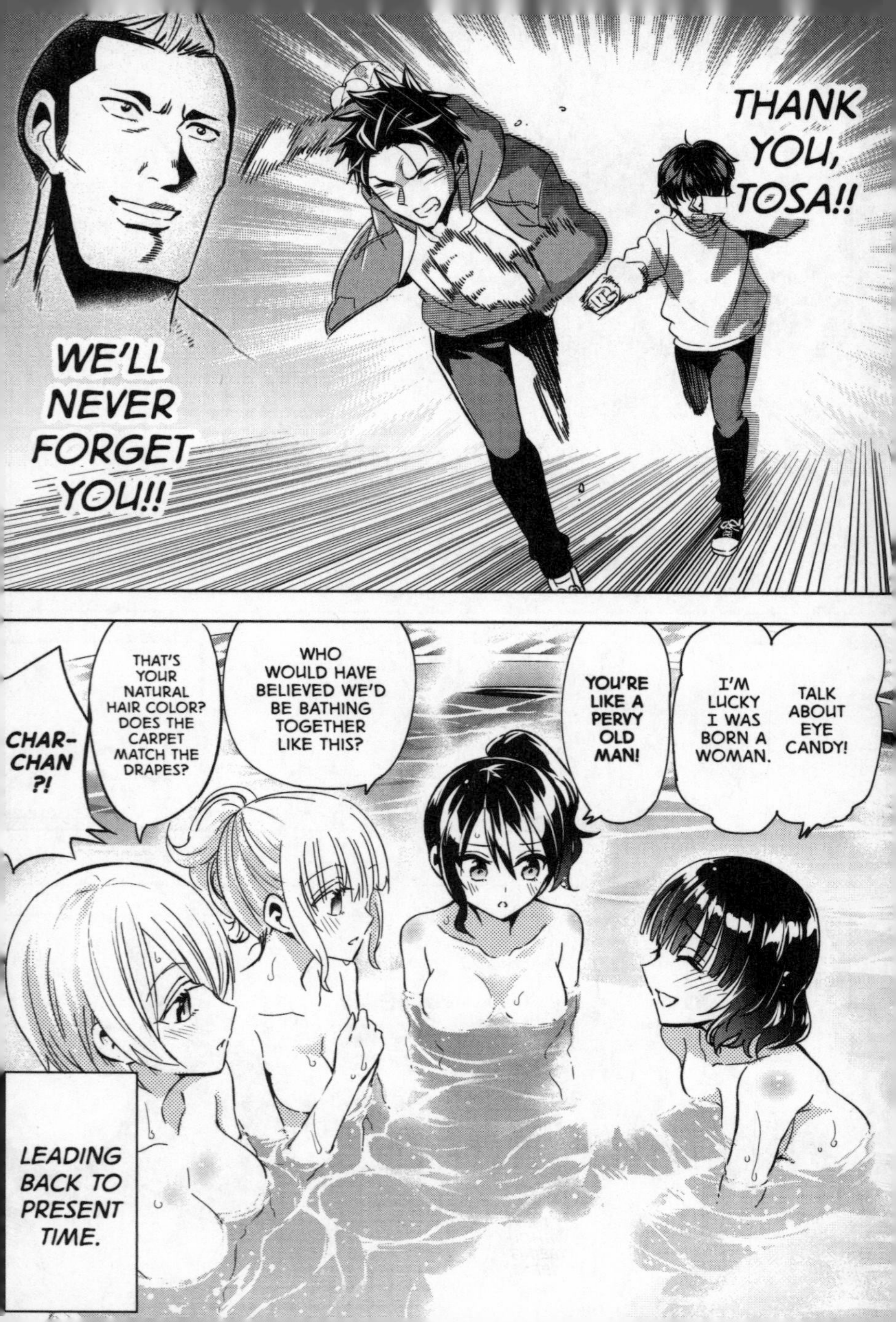
THANK YOU, TOSA!!
WE'LL NEVER FORGET YOU!!
TALK ABOUT EYE CANDY!
I'M LUCKY I WAS BORN A WOMAN.
YOU'RE LIKE A PERVY OLD MAN!
WHO WOULD HAVE BELIEVED WE'D BE BATHING TOGETHER LIKE THIS?
THAT'S YOUR NATURAL HAIR COLOR? DOES THE CARPET MATCH THE DRAPES?
CHAR-CHAN?!
LEADING BACK TO PRESENT TIME.

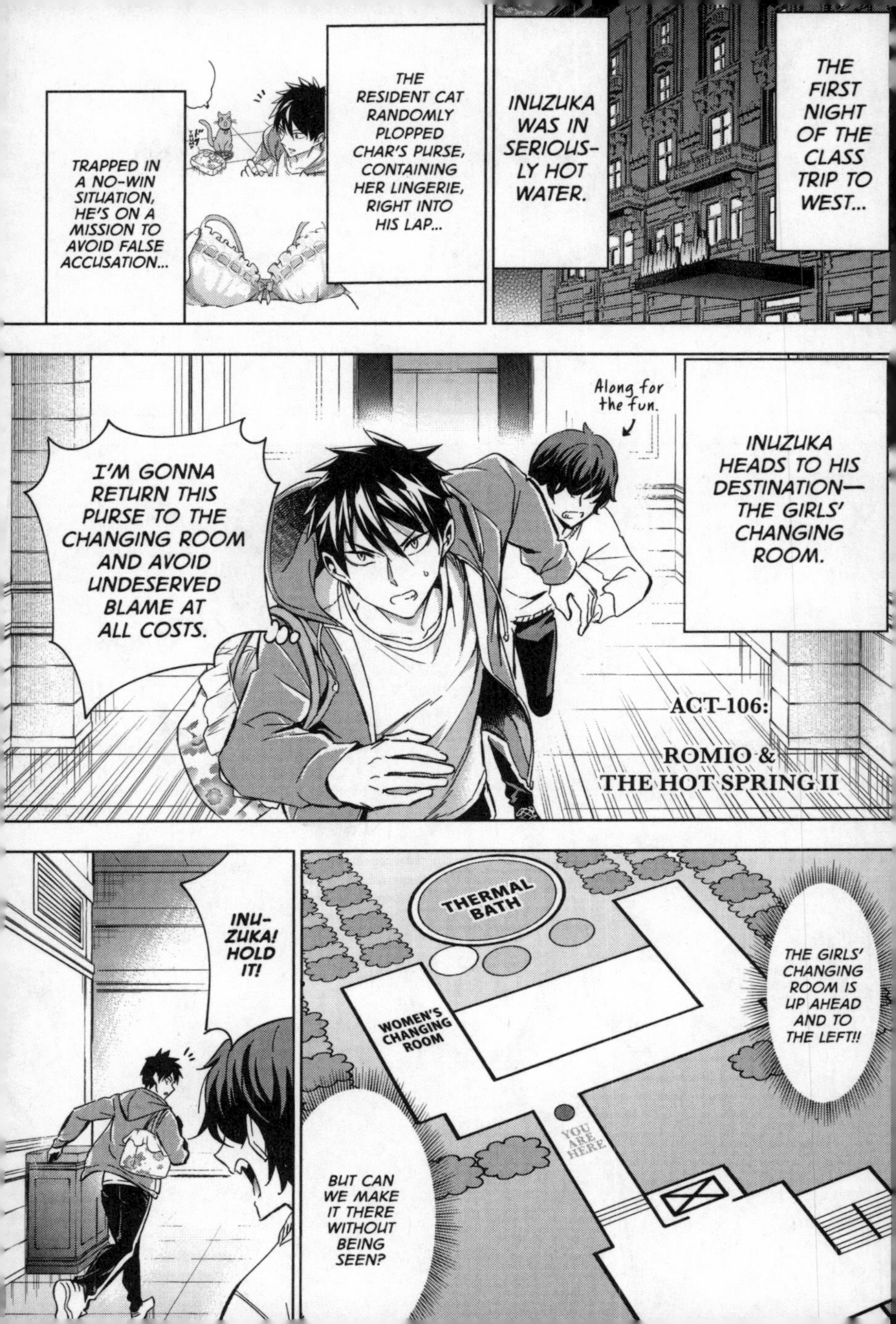
THE FIRST NIGHT OF THE CLASS TRIP TO WEST...
INUZUKA WAS IN SERIOUSLY HOT WATER.
THE RESIDENT CAT RANDOMLY PLOPPED CHAR'S PURSE, CONTAINING HER LINGERIE, RIGHT INTO HIS LAP...
TRAPPED IN A NO-WIN SITUATION, HE'S ON A MISSION TO AVOID FALSE ACCUSATION...
INUZUKA HEADS TO HIS DESTINATION—THE GIRLS' CHANGING ROOM.
Along for the fun.
I'M GONNA RETURN THIS PURSE TO THE CHANGING ROOM AND AVOID UNDESERVED BLAME AT ALL COSTS.
ACT-106:
ROMIO & THE HOT SPRING II
THE GIRLS' CHANGING ROOM IS UP AHEAD AND TO THE LEFT!!
THERMAL BATH
WOMEN'S CHANGING ROOM
YOU ARE HERE
BUT CAN WE MAKE IT THERE WITHOUT BEING SEEN?
INUZUKA! HOLD IT!

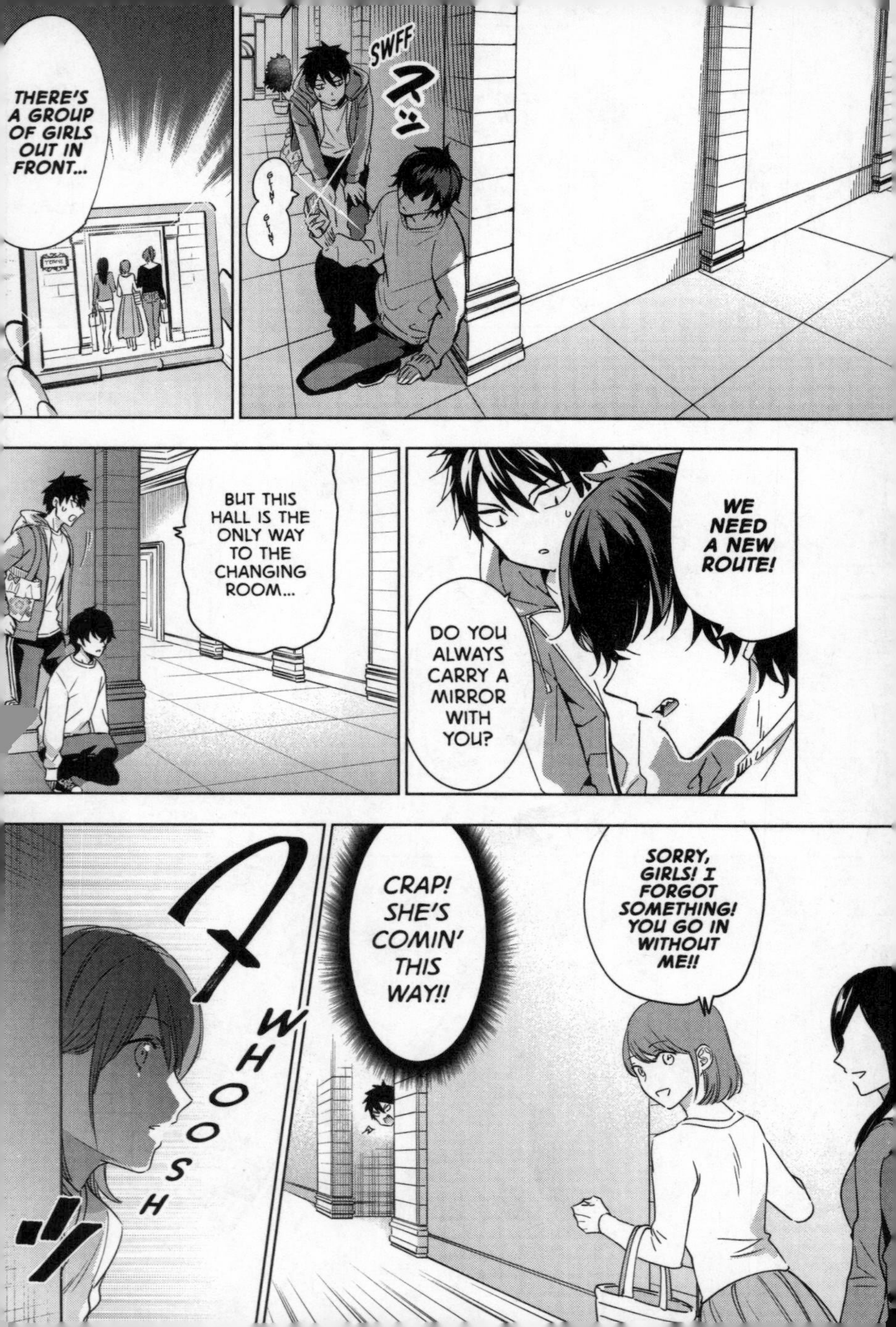
SWFF
GLINT GLINT
THERE'S A GROUP OF GIRLS OUT IN FRONT...
WE NEED A NEW ROUTE!
DO YOU ALWAYS CARRY A MIRROR WITH YOU?
BUT THIS HALL IS THE ONLY WAY TO THE CHANGING ROOM...
SORRY, GIRLS! I FORGOT SOMETHING! YOU GO IN WITHOUT ME!!
CRAP! SHE'S COMIN' THIS WAY!!
WHOOSH

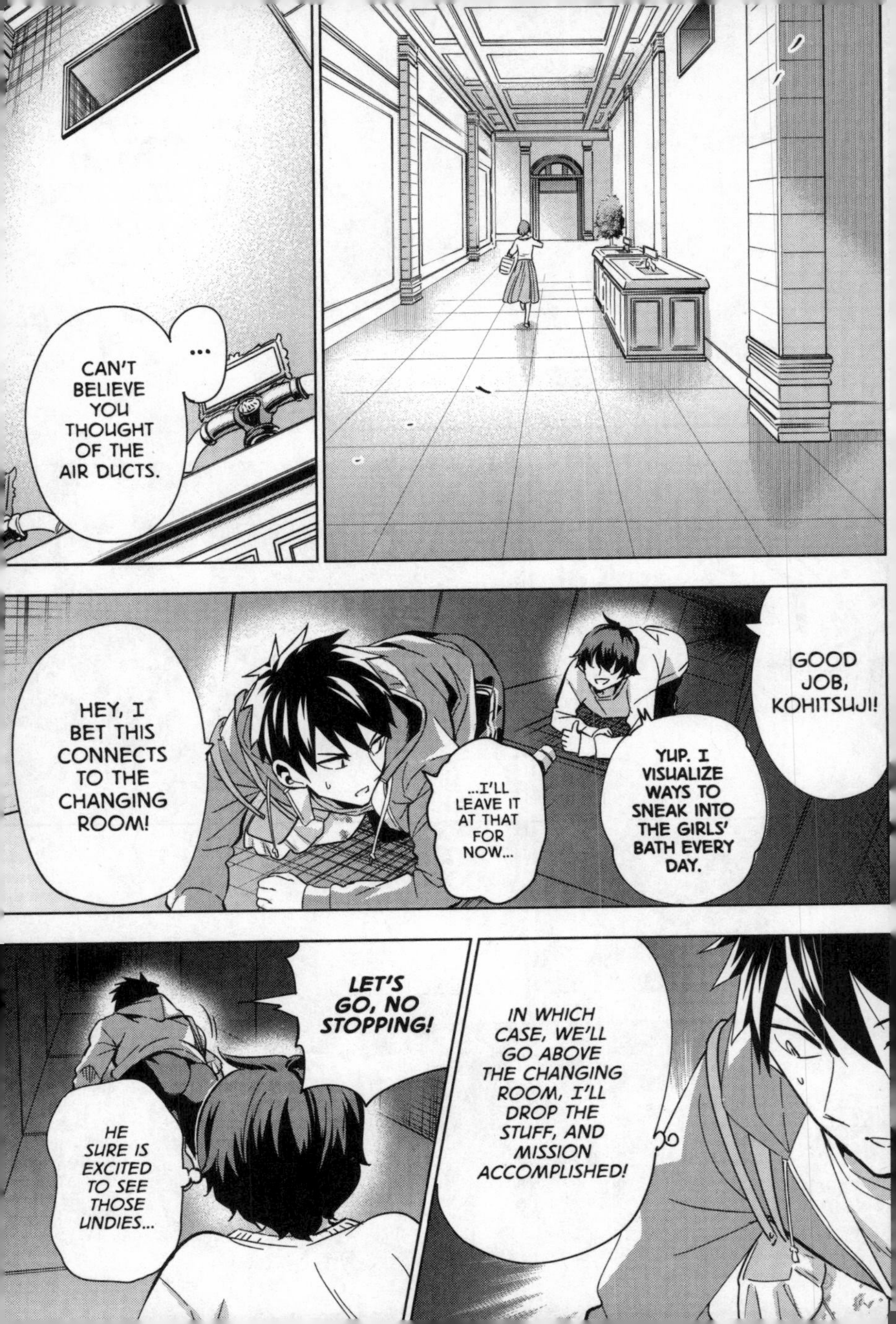
...
CAN'T BELIEVE YOU THOUGHT OF THE AIR DUCTS.
GOOD JOB, KOHITSUJI!
YUP. I VISUALIZE WAYS TO SNEAK INTO THE GIRLS' BATH EVERY DAY.
...I'LL LEAVE IT AT THAT FOR NOW...
HEY, I BET THIS CONNECTS TO THE CHANGING ROOM!
IN WHICH CASE, WE'LL GO ABOVE THE CHANGING ROOM, I'LL DROP THE STUFF, AND MISSION ACCOMPLISHED!
LET'S GO, NO STOPPING!
HE SURE IS EXCITED TO SEE THOSE UNDIES...

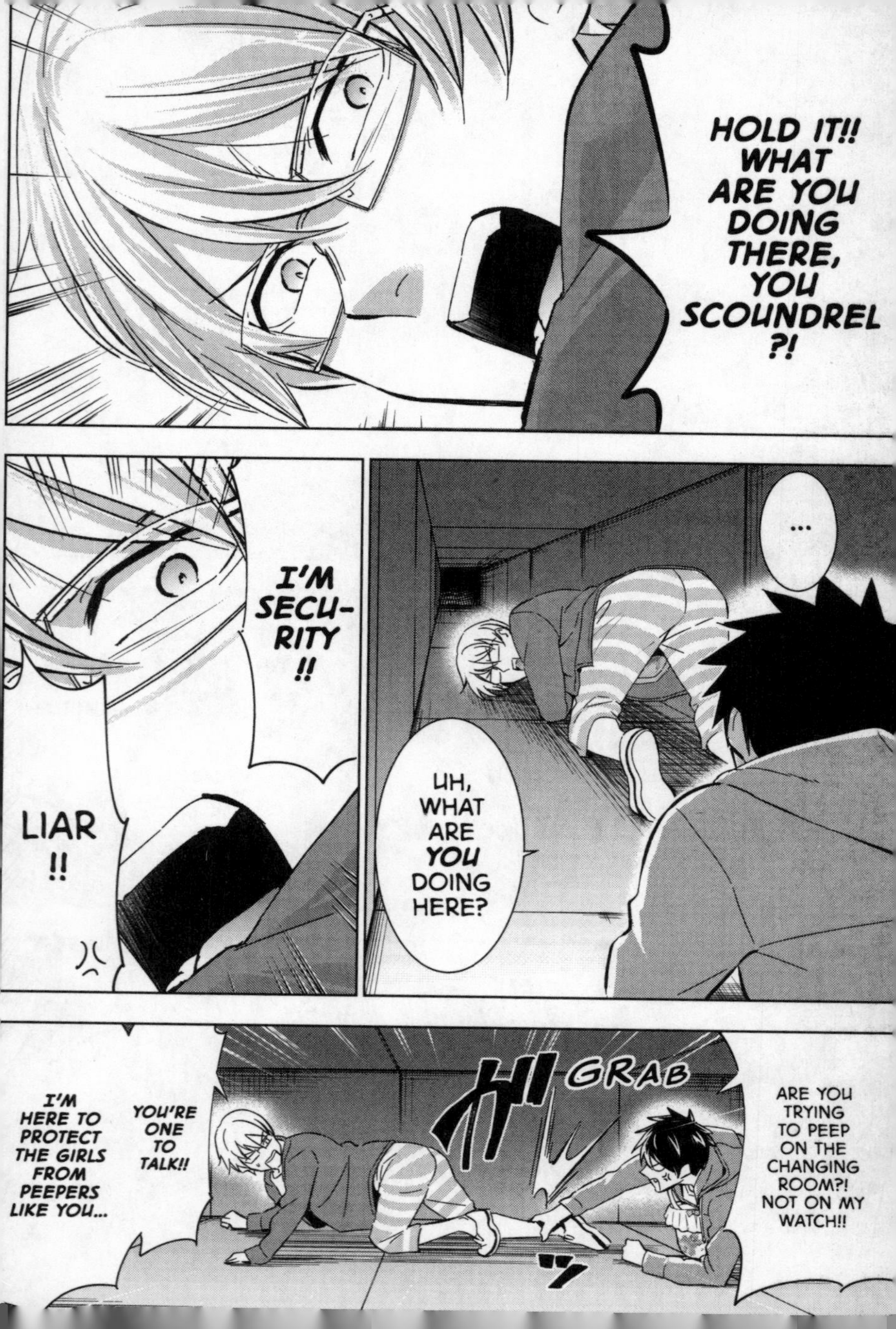
HOLD IT!! WHAT ARE YOU DOING THERE, YOU SCOUNDREL ?!
...
UH, WHAT ARE YOU DOING HERE?
I'M SECU-RITY !!
LIAR !!
ARE YOU TRYING TO PEEP ON THE CHANGING ROOM?! NOT ON MY WATCH!!
GRAB
YOU'RE ONE TO TALK!!
I'M HERE TO PROTECT THE GIRLS FROM PEEPERS LIKE YOU...

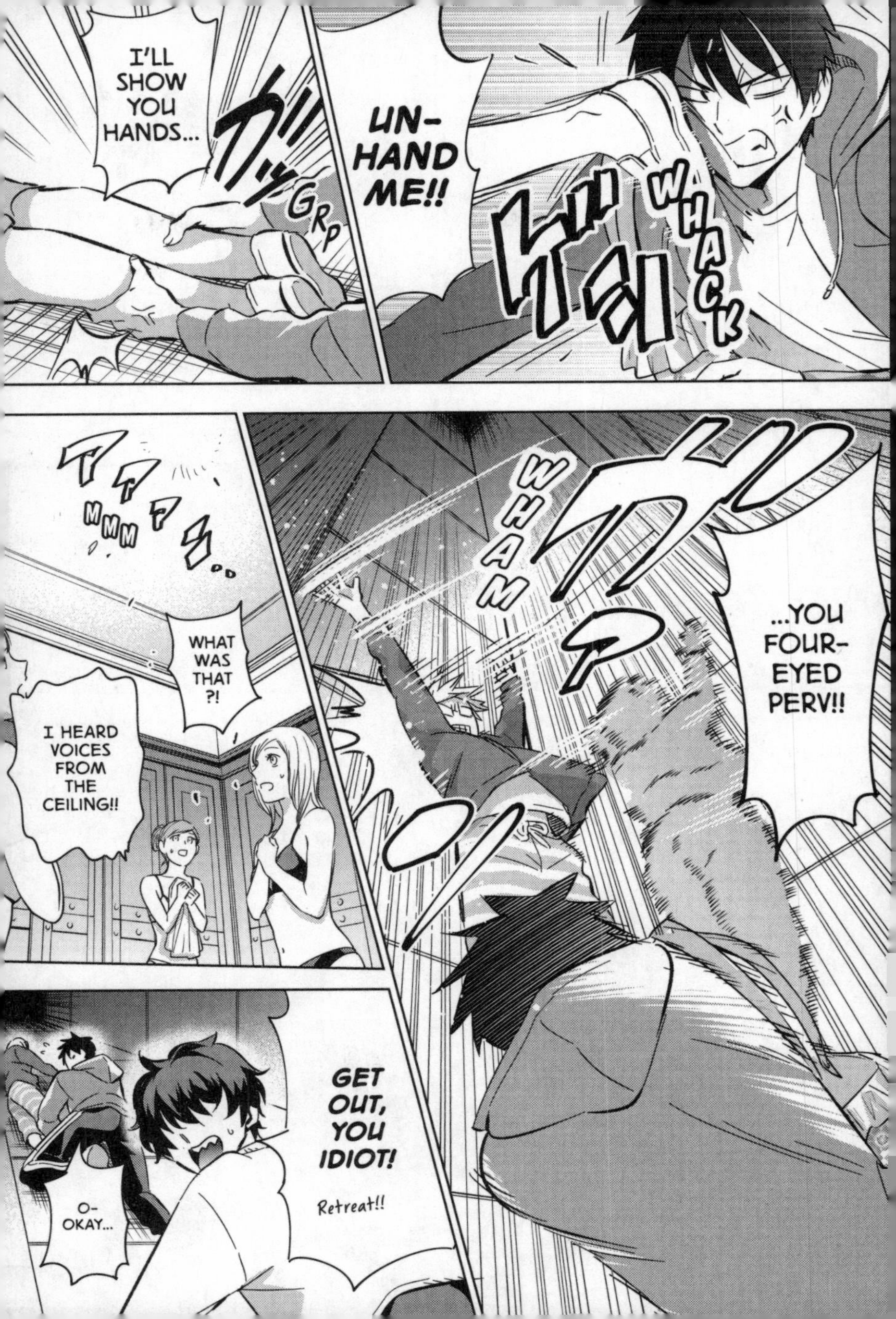
UN-HAND ME!!
WHACK
I'LL SHOW YOU HANDS...
GRP
WHAM
...YOU FOUR-EYED PERV!!
MMM
WHAT WAS THAT?!
I HEARD VOICES FROM THE CEILING!!
GET OUT, YOU IDIOT!
Retreat!!
O-OKAY...

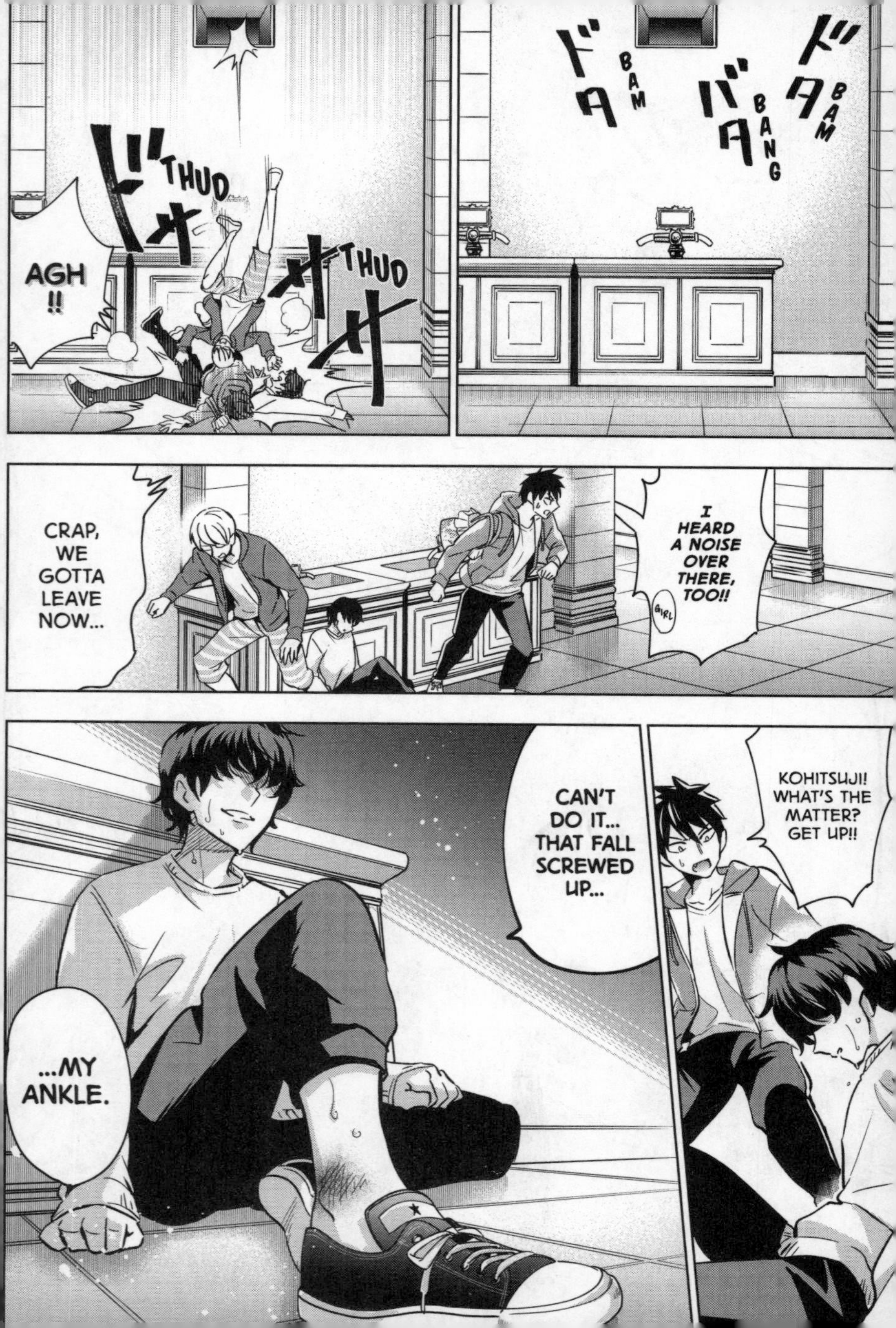
ドタ
BAM
バタ
BANG
ドタ
BAM
AGH!!
ドサ
THUD
ドサ
THUD
I HEARD A NOISE OVER THERE, TOO!!
CRAP, WE GOTTA LEAVE NOW...
KOHITSUJI! WHAT'S THE MATTER? GET UP!!
CAN'T DO IT... THAT FALL SCREWED UP...
...MY ANKLE.

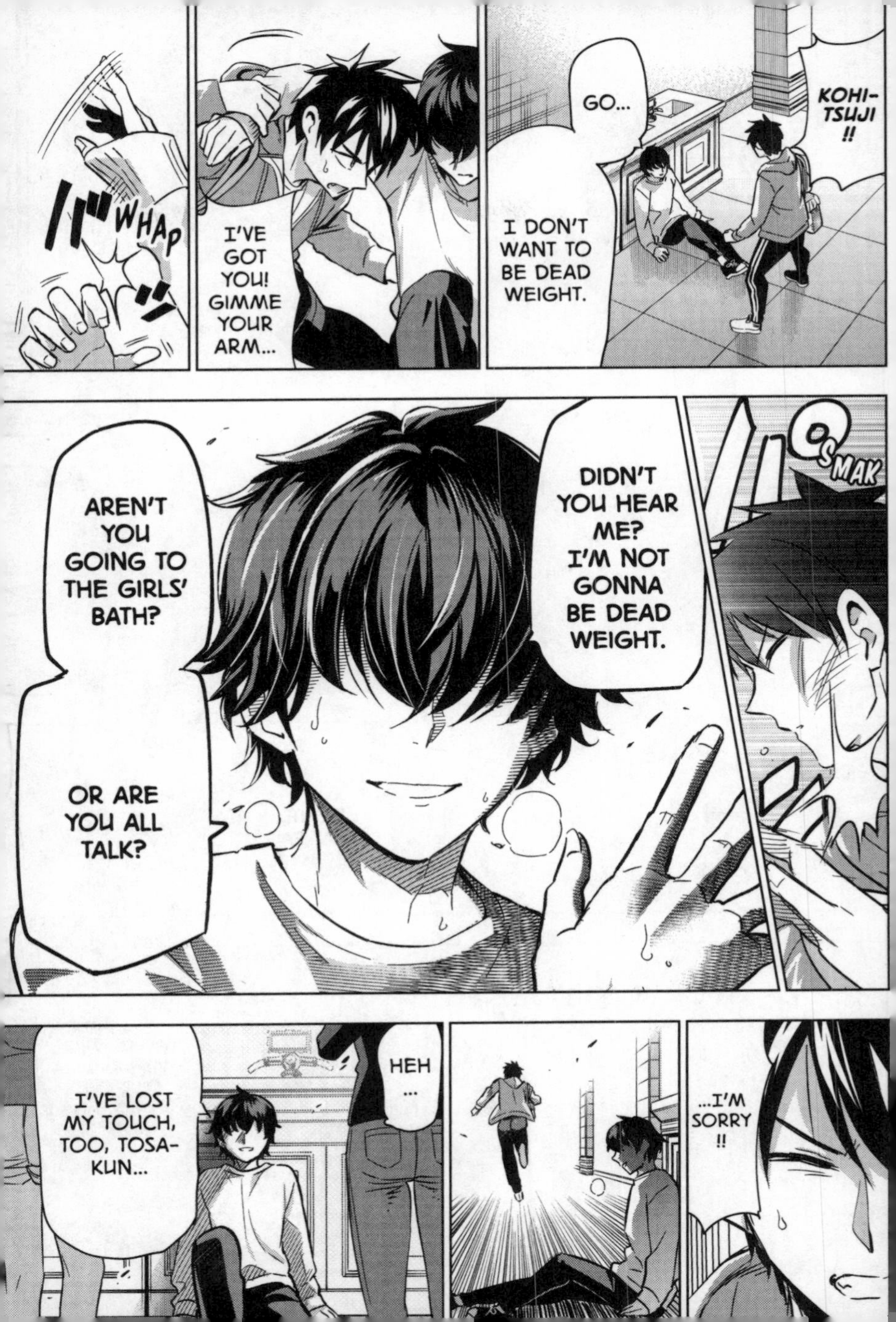
KOHI-TSUJI !!
GO...
I DON'T WANT TO BE DEAD WEIGHT.
I'VE GOT YOU! GIMME YOUR ARM...
WHAP
SMAK
DIDN'T YOU HEAR ME? I'M NOT GONNA BE DEAD WEIGHT.
AREN'T YOU GOING TO THE GIRLS' BATH?
OR ARE YOU ALL TALK?
...I'M SORRY !!
HEH ...
I'VE LOST MY TOUCH, TOO, TOSA-KUN...

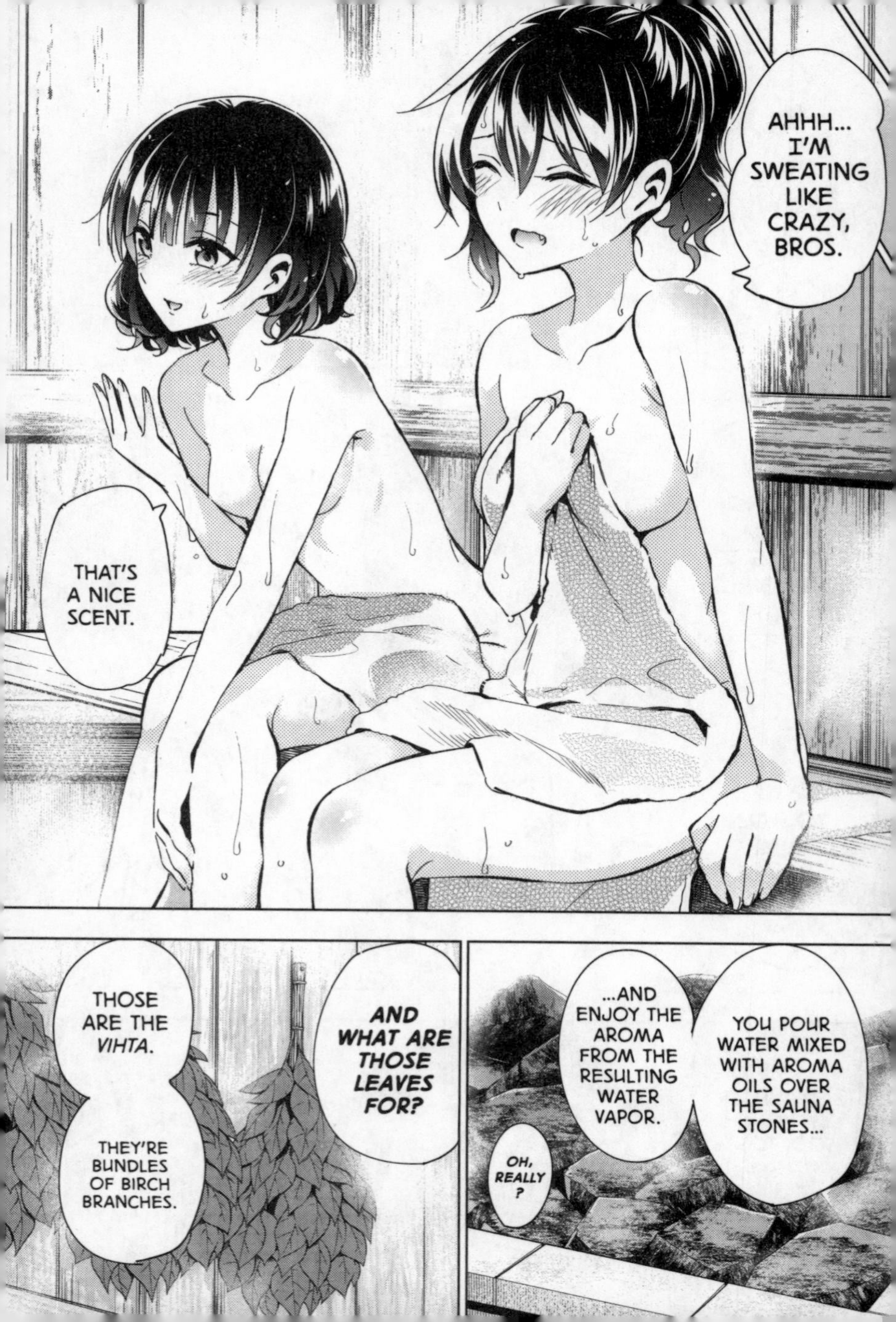
AHHH... I'M SWEATING LIKE CRAZY, BROS.
THAT'S A NICE SCENT.
YOU POUR WATER MIXED WITH AROMA OILS OVER THE SAUNA STONES...
...AND ENJOY THE AROMA FROM THE RESULTING WATER VAPOR.
OH, REALLY?
AND WHAT ARE THOSE LEAVES FOR?
THOSE ARE THE *VIHTA*.
THEY'RE BUNDLES OF BIRCH BRANCHES.

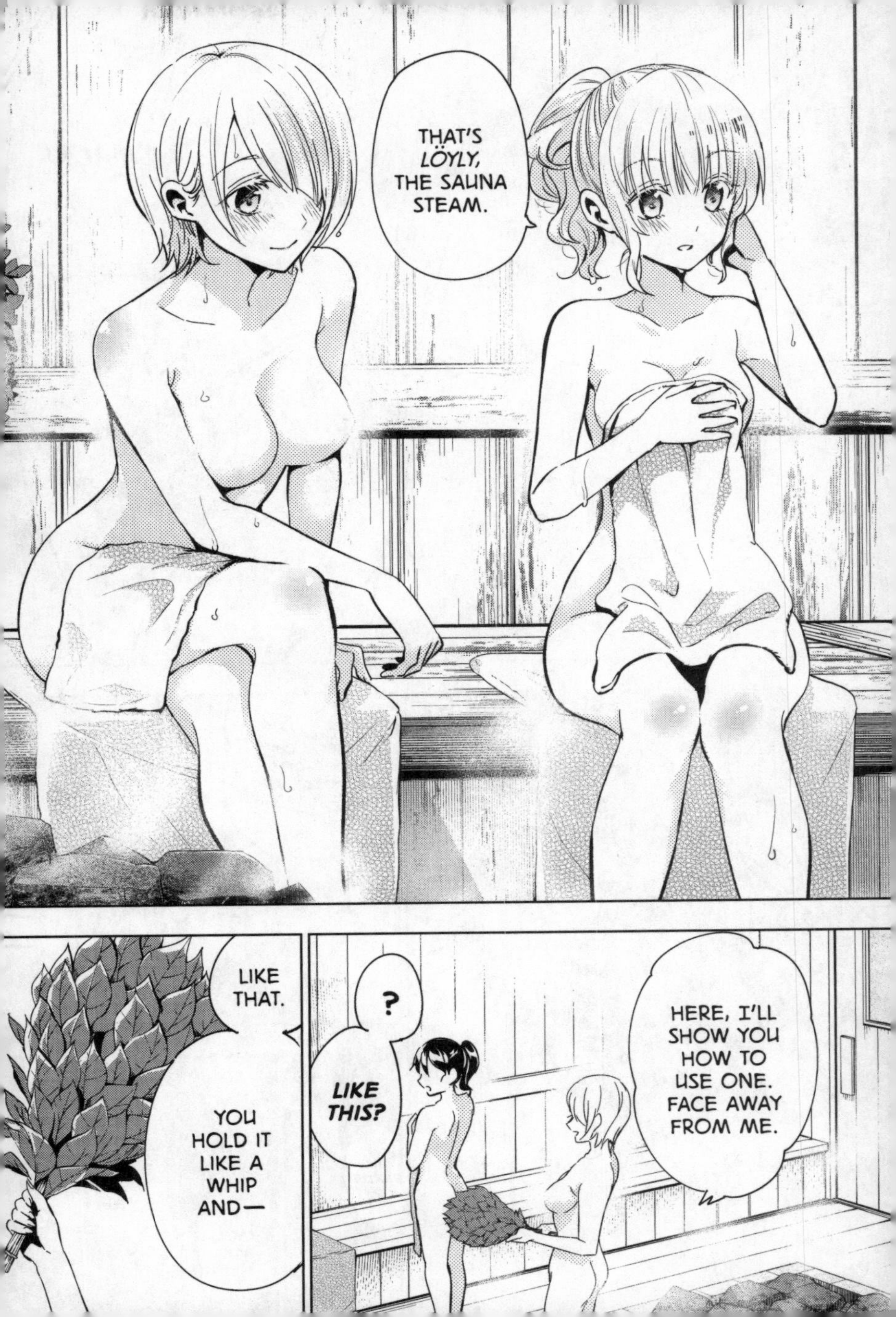
THAT'S *LÖYLY*, THE SAUNA STEAM.
HERE, I'LL SHOW YOU HOW TO USE ONE. FACE AWAY FROM ME.
?
*LIKE THIS?*
LIKE THAT.
YOU HOLD IT LIKE A WHIP AND—

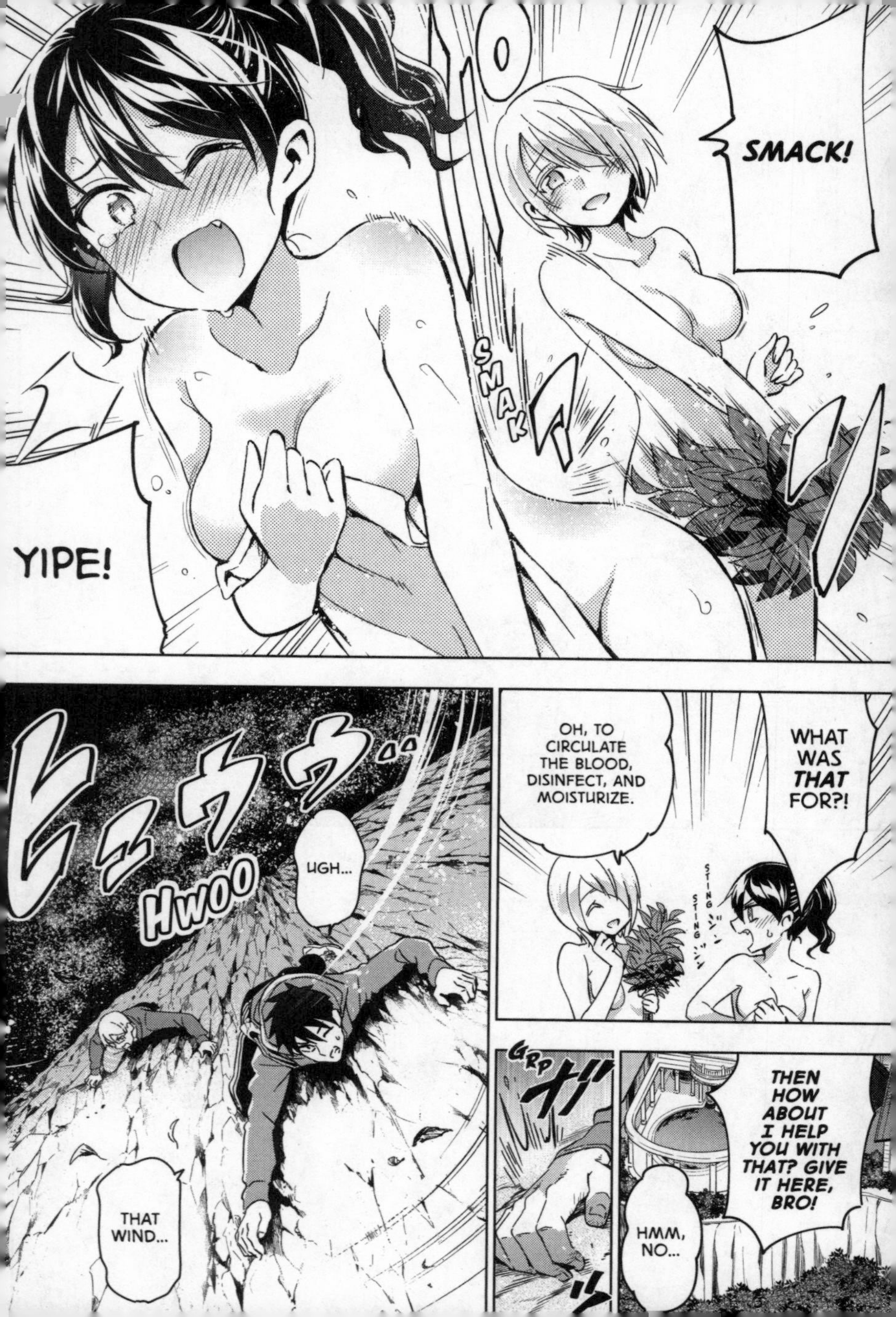
SMACK!
SMAK
YIPE!
WHAT WAS THAT FOR?!
OH, TO CIRCULATE THE BLOOD, DISINFECT, AND MOISTURIZE.
STING STING
THEN HOW ABOUT I HELP YOU WITH THAT? GIVE IT HERE, BRO!
HMM, NO...
GRP
HWOO
UGH...
THAT WIND...

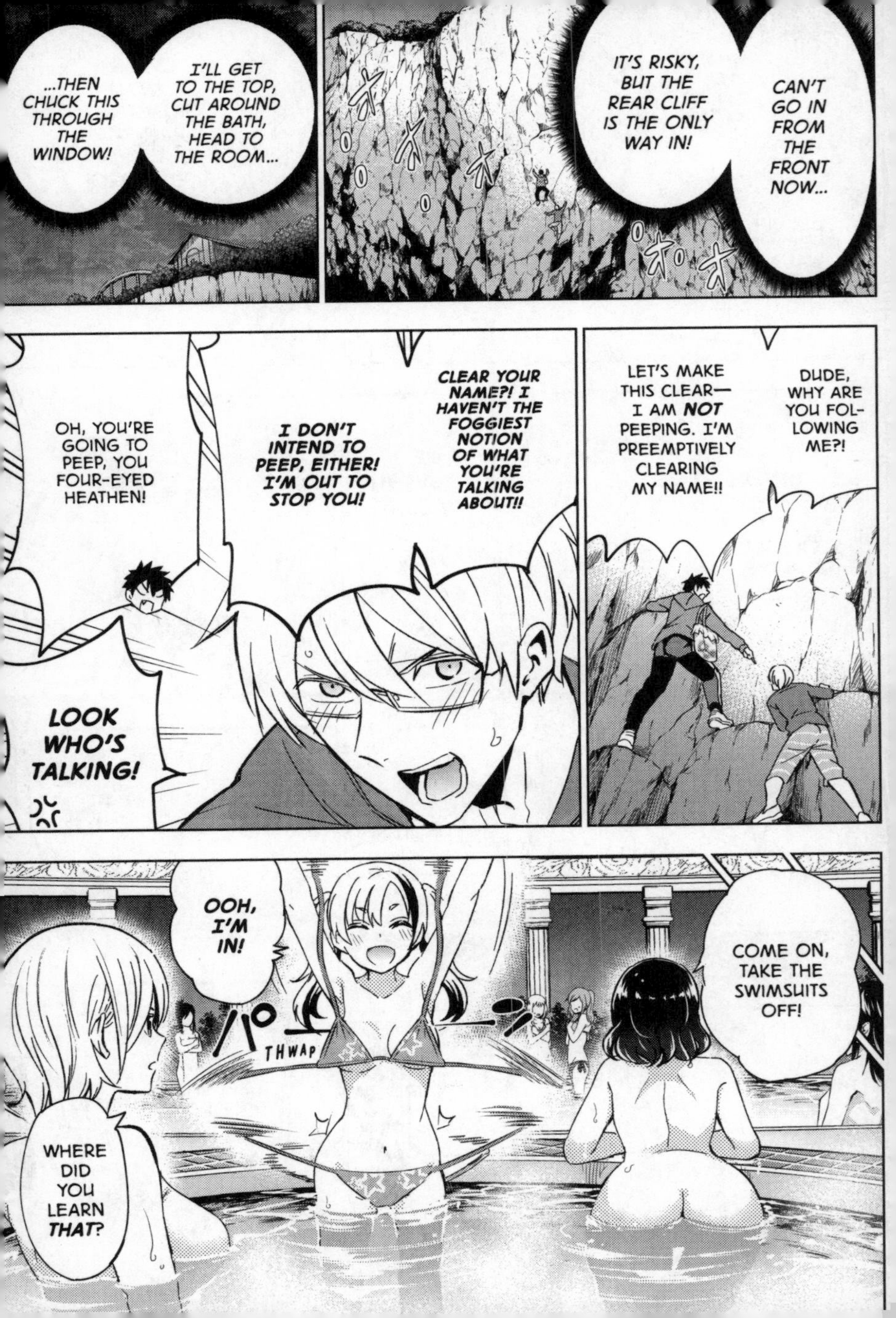

CAN'T GO IN FROM THE FRONT NOW...
IT'S RISKY, BUT THE REAR CLIFF IS THE ONLY WAY IN!
I'LL GET TO THE TOP, CUT AROUND THE BATH, HEAD TO THE ROOM...
...THEN CHUCK THIS THROUGH THE WINDOW!
DUDE, WHY ARE YOU FOL-LOWING ME?!
LET'S MAKE THIS CLEAR— I AM NOT PEEPING. I'M PREEMPTIVELY CLEARING MY NAME!!
CLEAR YOUR NAME?! I HAVEN'T THE FOGGIEST NOTION OF WHAT YOU'RE TALKING ABOUT!!
I DON'T INTEND TO PEEP, EITHER! I'M OUT TO STOP YOU!
OH, YOU'RE GOING TO PEEP, YOU FOUR-EYED HEATHEN!
LOOK WHO'S TALKING!
COME ON, TAKE THE SWIMSUITS OFF!
OOH, I'M IN!
パ—
THWAP
WHERE DID YOU LEARN THAT?

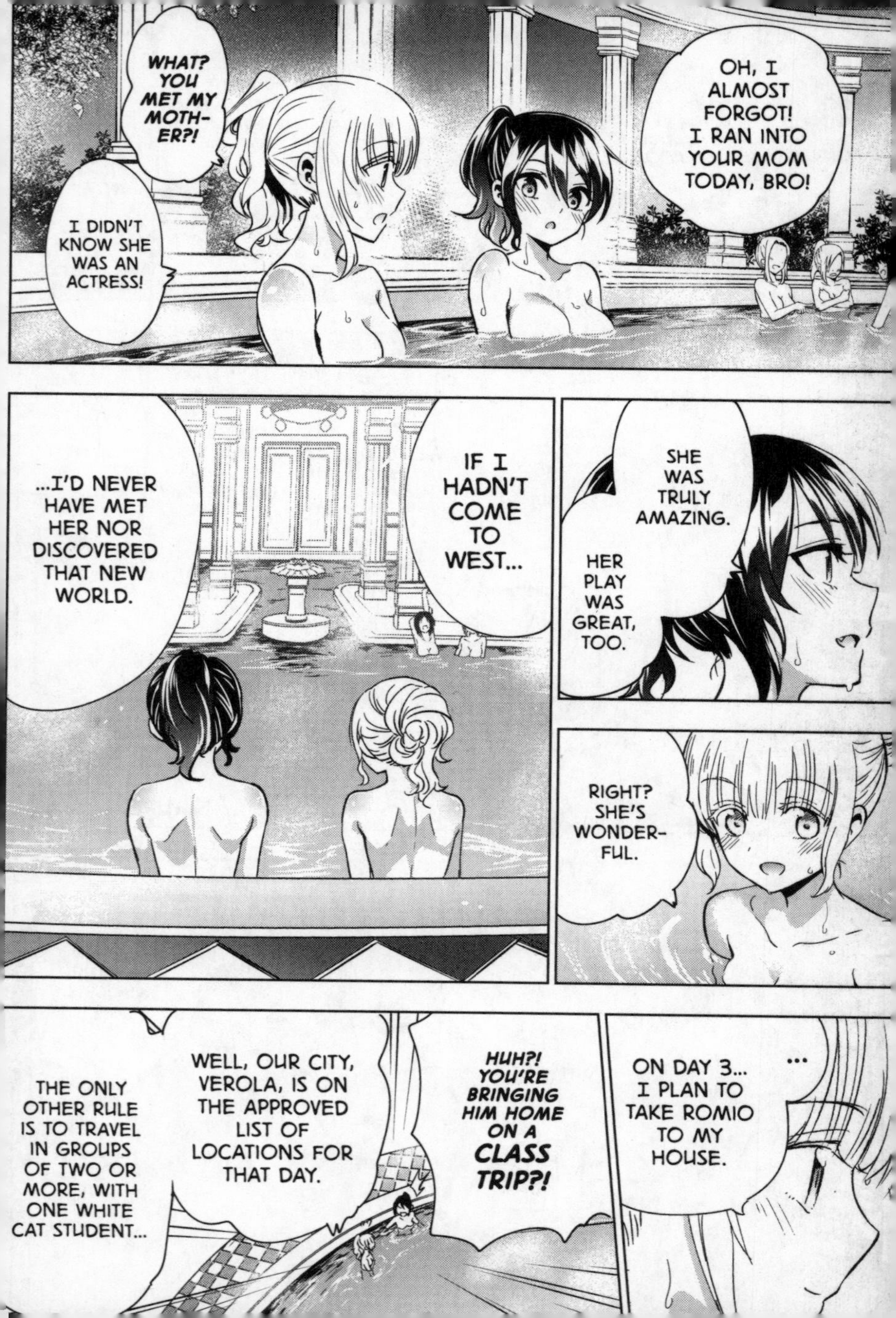
OH, I ALMOST FORGOT! I RAN INTO YOUR MOM TODAY, BRO!
WHAT? YOU MET MY MOTH-ER?!
I DIDN'T KNOW SHE WAS AN ACTRESS!
SHE WAS TRULY AMAZING.
HER PLAY WAS GREAT, TOO.
RIGHT? SHE'S WONDER-FUL.
IF I HADN'T COME TO WEST...
...I'D NEVER HAVE MET HER NOR DISCOVERED THAT NEW WORLD.
...
ON DAY 3... I PLAN TO TAKE ROMIO TO MY HOUSE.
HUH?! YOU'RE BRINGING HIM HOME ON A CLASS TRIP?!
WELL, OUR CITY, VEROLA, IS ON THE APPROVED LIST OF LOCATIONS FOR THAT DAY.
THE ONLY OTHER RULE IS TO TRAVEL IN GROUPS OF TWO OR MORE, WITH ONE WHITE CAT STUDENT...

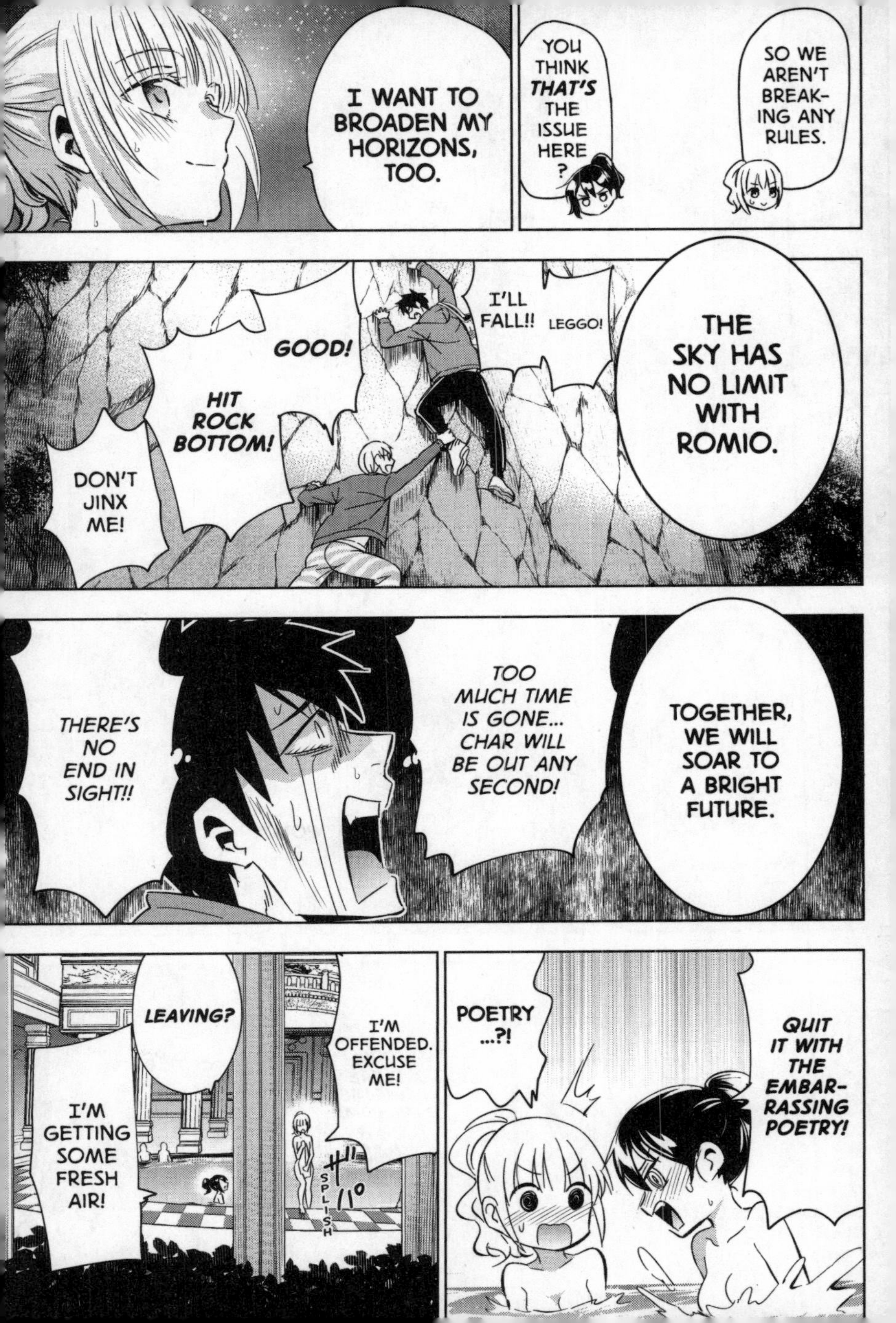
SO WE AREN'T BREAKING ANY RULES.
YOU THINK THAT'S THE ISSUE HERE?
I WANT TO BROADEN MY HORIZONS, TOO.
THE SKY HAS NO LIMIT WITH ROMIO.
LEGGO!
I'LL FALL!!
GOOD!
HIT ROCK BOTTOM!
DON'T JINX ME!
TOGETHER, WE WILL SOAR TO A BRIGHT FUTURE.
TOO MUCH TIME IS GONE... CHAR WILL BE OUT ANY SECOND!
THERE'S NO END IN SIGHT!!
QUIT IT WITH THE EMBARRASSING POETRY!
POETRY ...?!
I'M OFFENDED. EXCUSE ME!
LEAVING?
I'M GETTING SOME FRESH AIR!
SPLISH

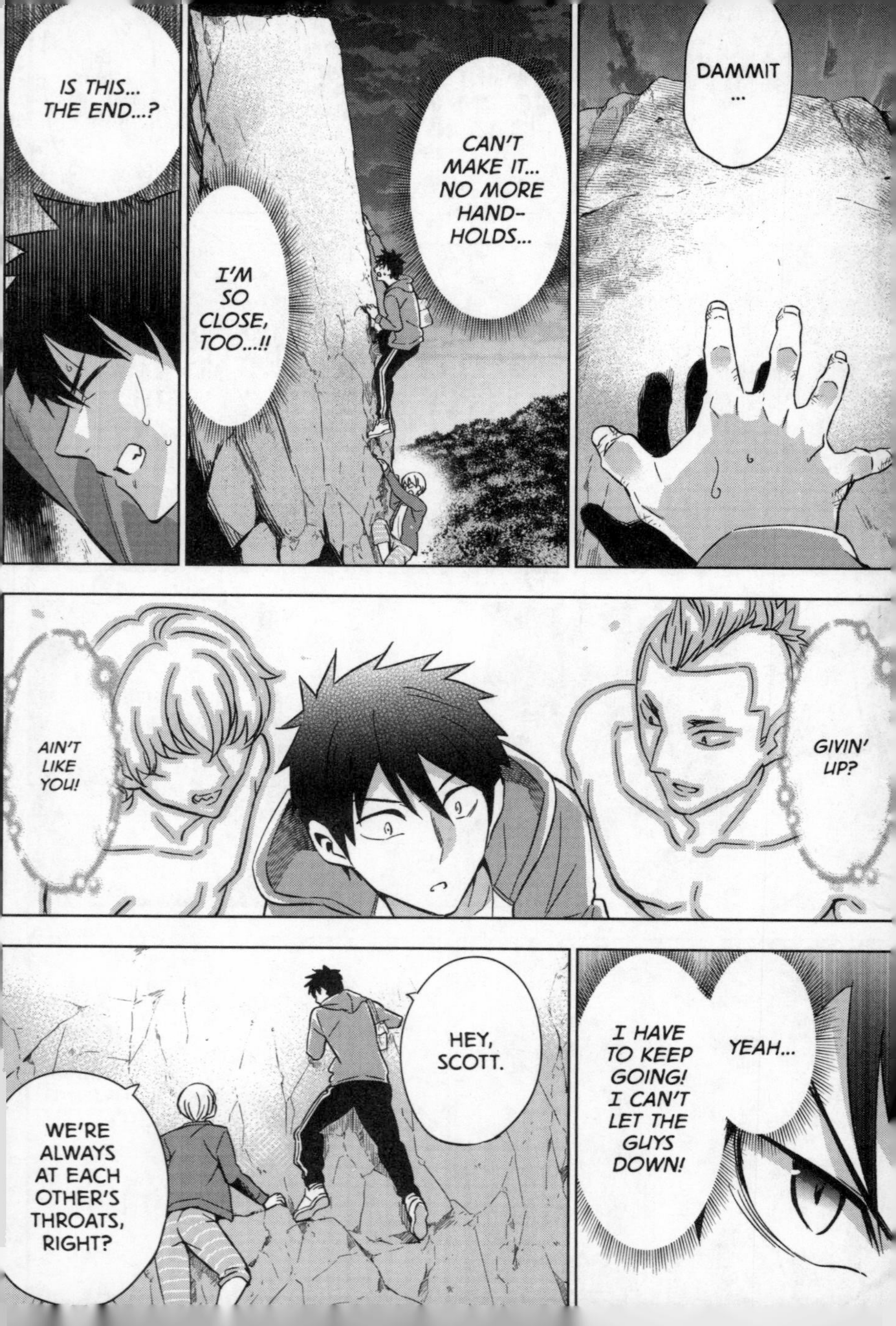
DAMMIT ...
CAN'T MAKE IT... NO MORE HAND-HOLDS...
I'M SO CLOSE, TOO...!!
IS THIS... THE END...?
GIVIN' UP?
AIN'T LIKE YOU!
YEAH...
I HAVE TO KEEP GOING! I CAN'T LET THE GUYS DOWN!
HEY, SCOTT.
WE'RE ALWAYS AT EACH OTHER'S THROATS, RIGHT?

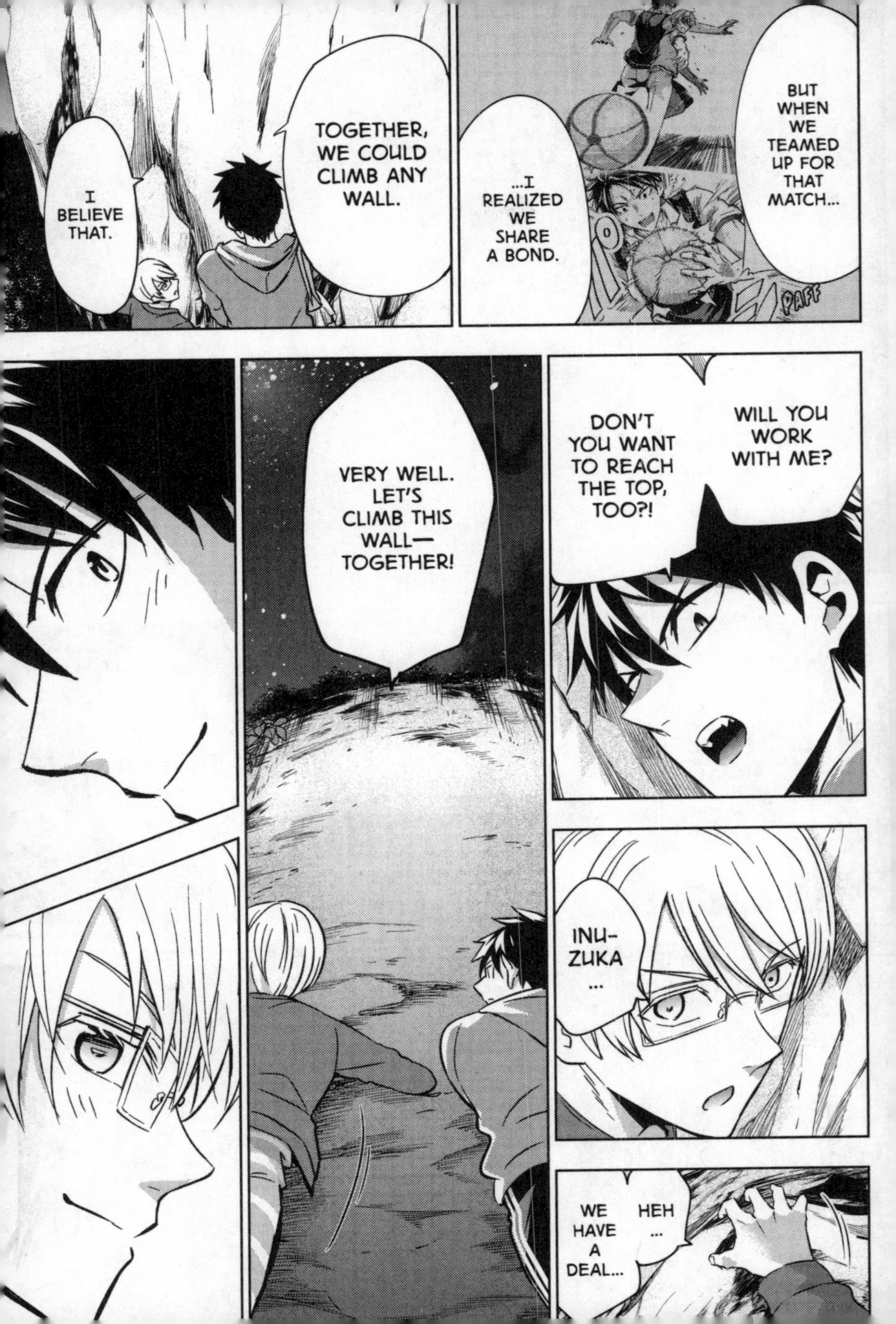
BUT WHEN WE TEAMED UP FOR THAT MATCH...
...I REALIZED WE SHARE A BOND.
PAFF
TOGETHER, WE COULD CLIMB ANY WALL.
I BELIEVE THAT.
WILL YOU WORK WITH ME?
DON'T YOU WANT TO REACH THE TOP, TOO?!
INU-ZUKA ...
HEH ...
WE HAVE A DEAL...
VERY WELL. LET'S CLIMB THIS WALL—TOGETHER!

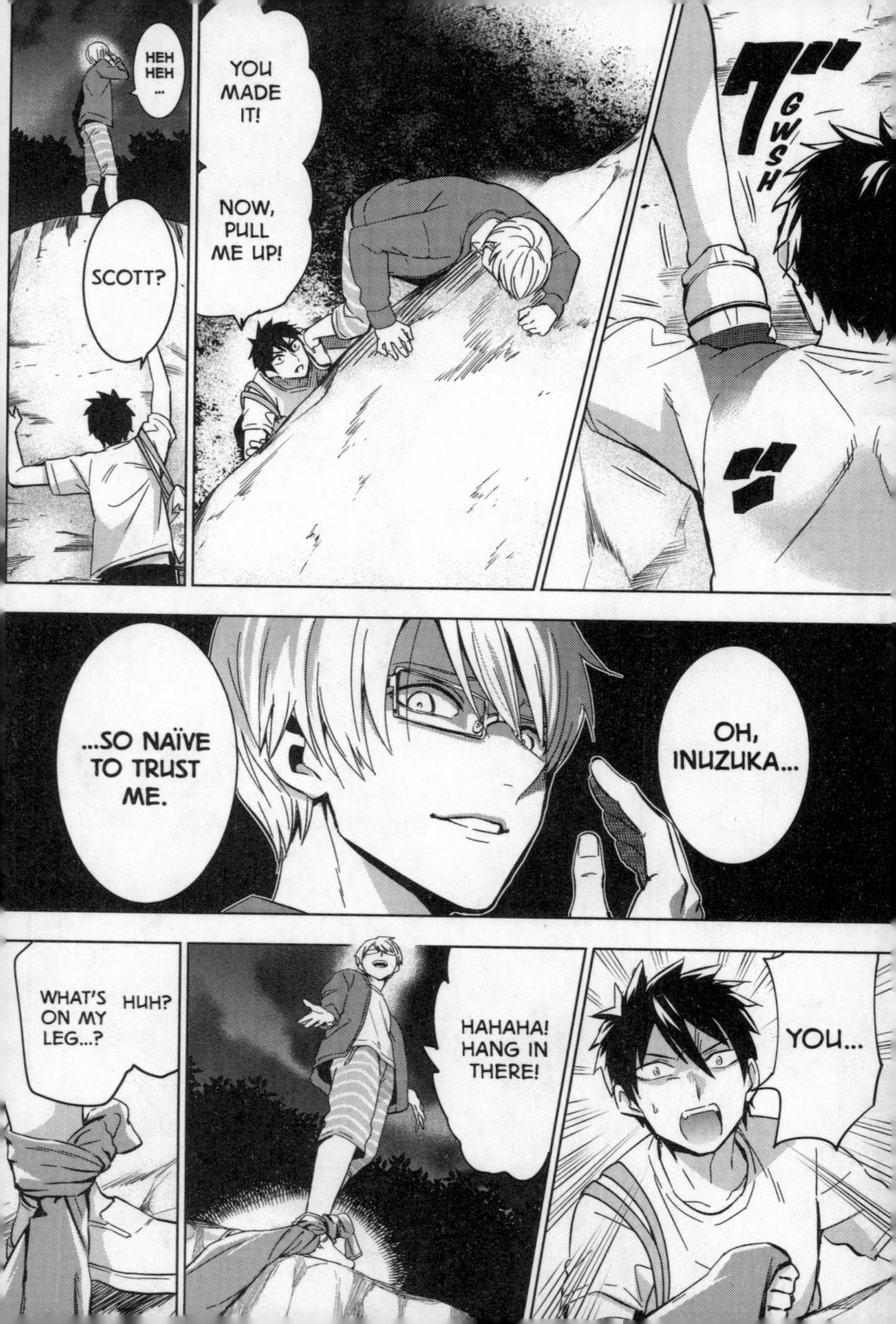
GWSH
YOU MADE IT!
NOW, PULL ME UP!
HEH HEH ...
SCOTT?
OH, INUZUKA...
...SO NAÏVE TO TRUST ME.
YOU...
HAHAHA! HANG IN THERE!
HUH?
WHAT'S ON MY LEG...?

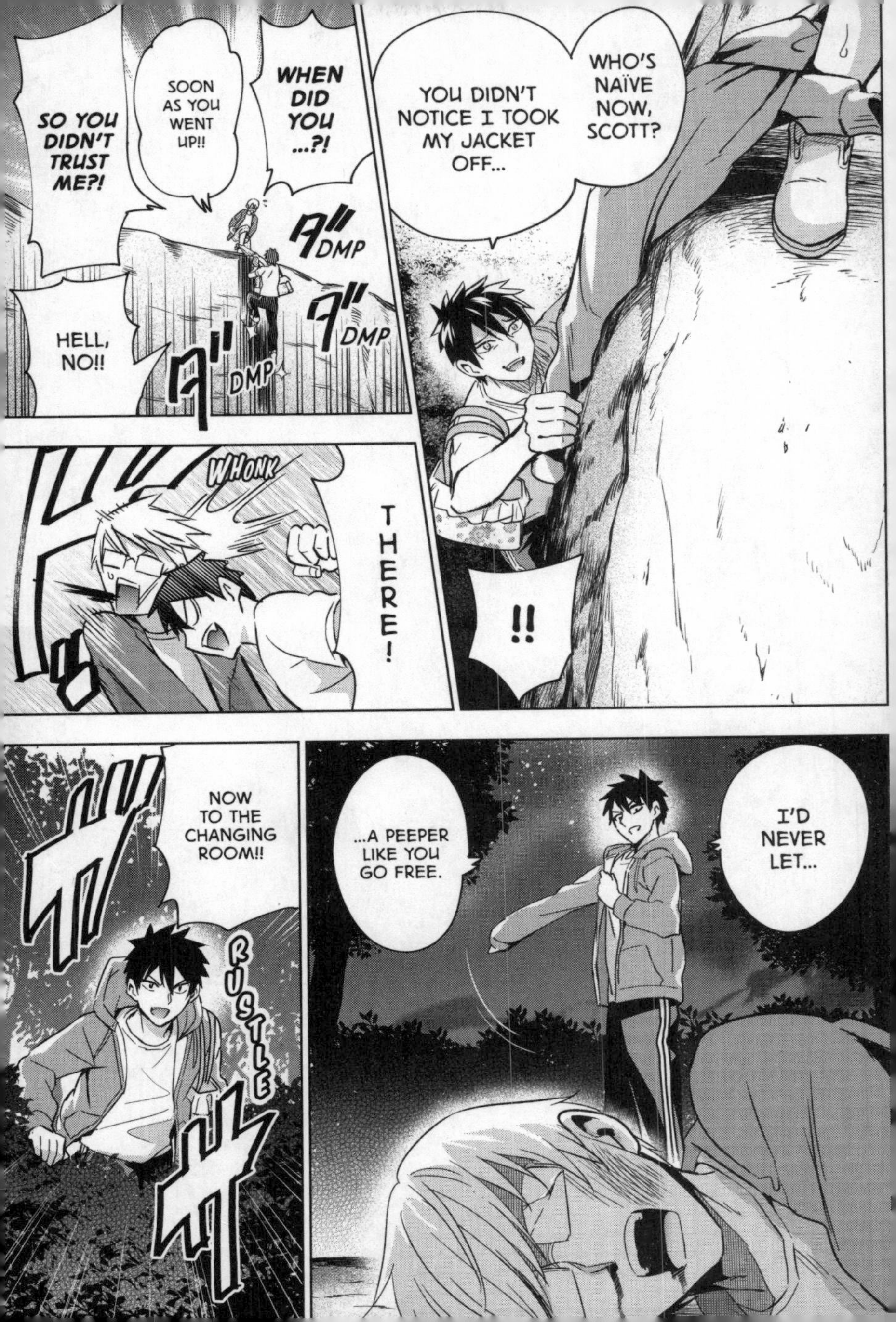
WHO'S NAÏVE NOW, SCOTT?
YOU DIDN'T NOTICE I TOOK MY JACKET OFF...
!!
WHEN DID YOU ...?!
SOON AS YOU WENT UP!!
SO YOU DIDN'T TRUST ME?!
HELL, NO!!
DMP
DMP
DMP
WHONK
THERE!
I'D NEVER LET...
...A PEEPER LIKE YOU GO FREE.
NOW TO THE CHANGING ROOM!!
RUSTLE

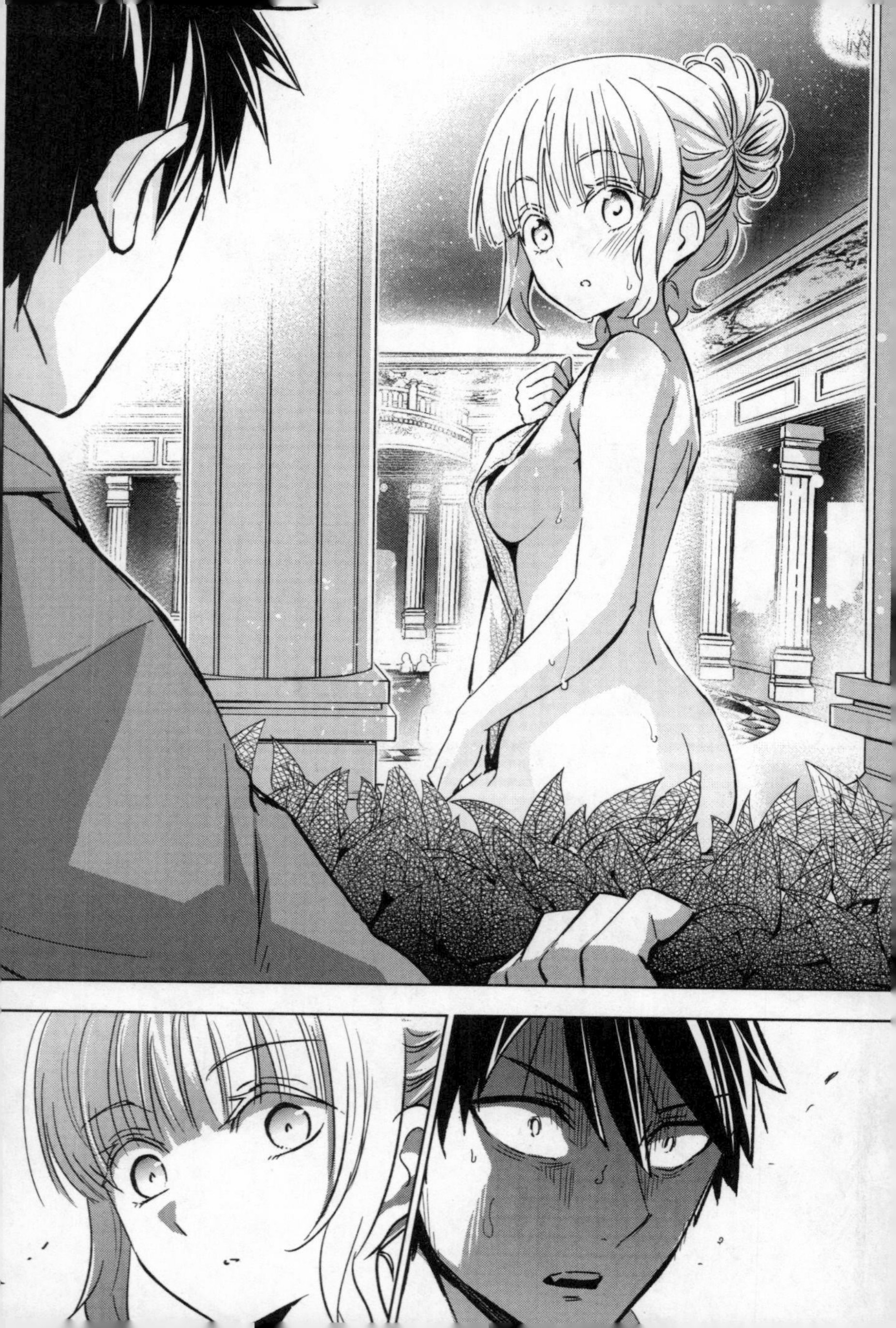

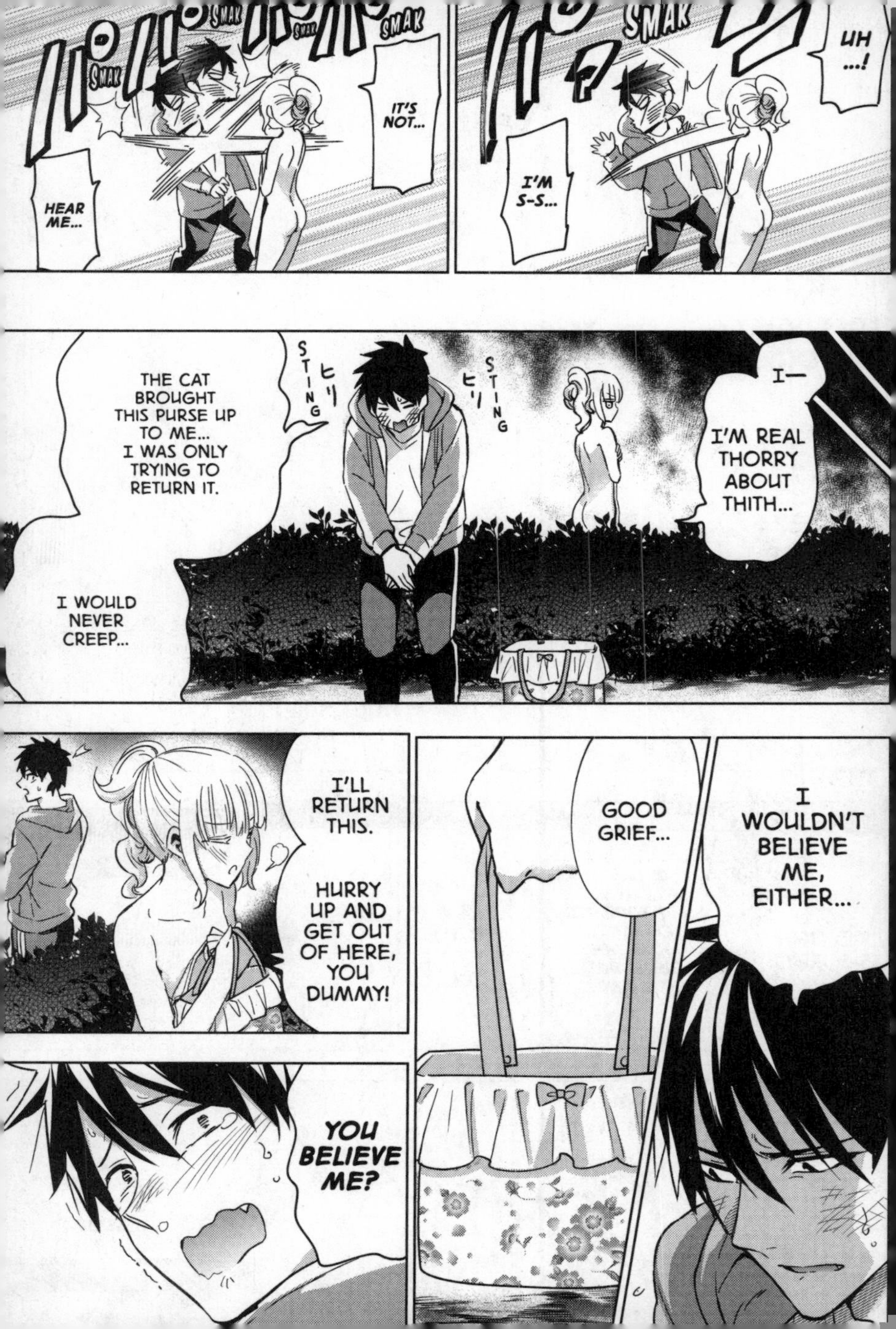
UH ...!
SMAK
I'M S-S...
SMAK
SMAK
SMAK
SMAK
IT'S NOT...
HEAR ME...
I—
I'M REAL THORRY ABOUT THITH...
STING ヒリ
STING ヒリ
THE CAT BROUGHT THIS PURSE UP TO ME... I WAS ONLY TRYING TO RETURN IT.
I WOULD NEVER CREEP...
I WOULDN'T BELIEVE ME, EITHER...
GOOD GRIEF...
I'LL RETURN THIS.
HURRY UP AND GET OUT OF HERE, YOU DUMMY!
YOU BELIEVE ME?

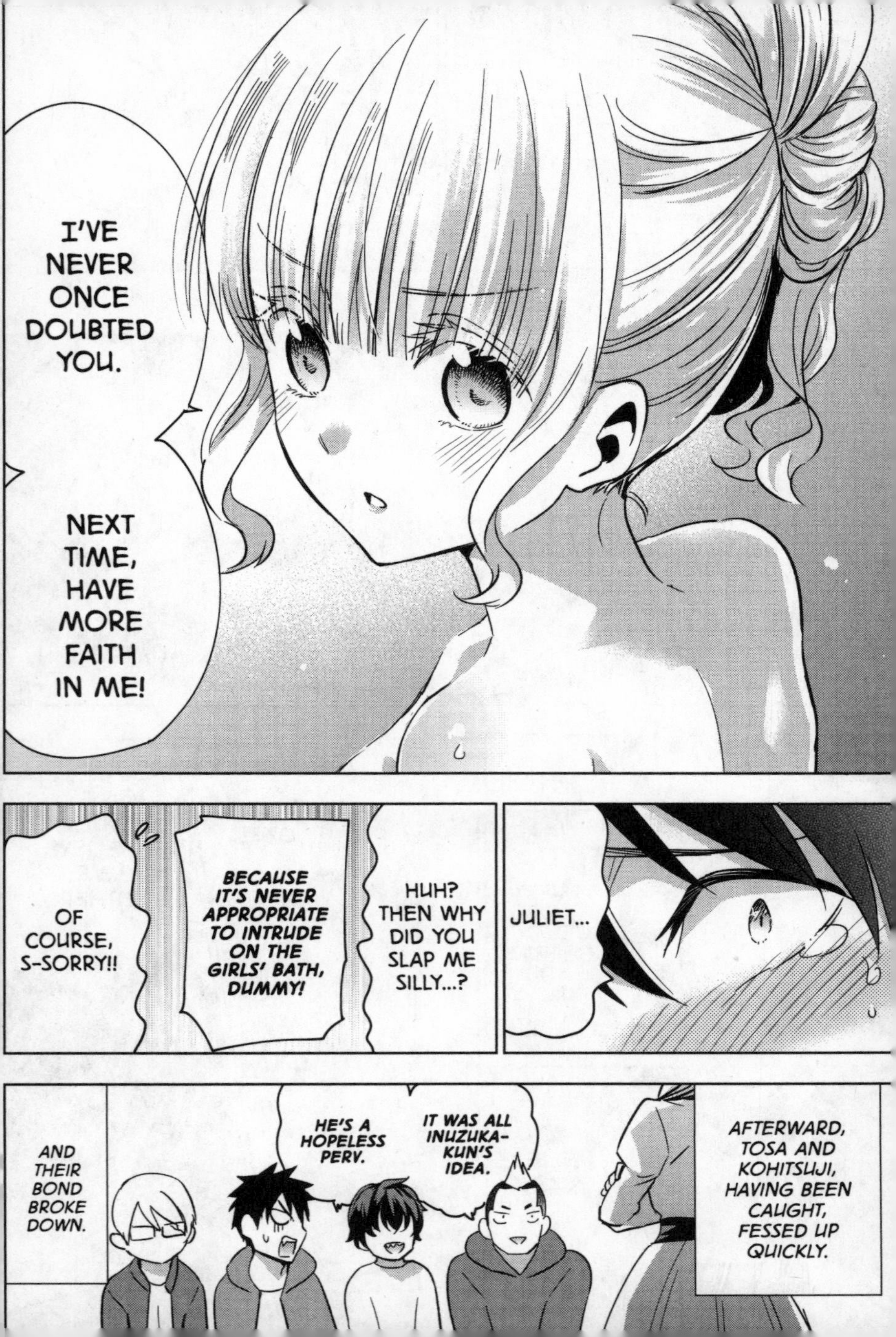
I'VE NEVER ONCE DOUBTED YOU.
NEXT TIME, HAVE MORE FAITH IN ME!
JULIET...
HUH? THEN WHY DID YOU SLAP ME SILLY...?
BECAUSE IT'S NEVER APPROPRIATE TO INTRUDE ON THE GIRLS' BATH, DUMMY!
OF COURSE, S-SORRY!!
AFTERWARD, TOSA AND KOHITSUJI, HAVING BEEN CAUGHT, FESSED UP QUICKLY.
IT WAS ALL INUZUKA-KUN'S IDEA.
HE'S A HOPELESS PERV.
AND THEIR BOND BROKE DOWN.

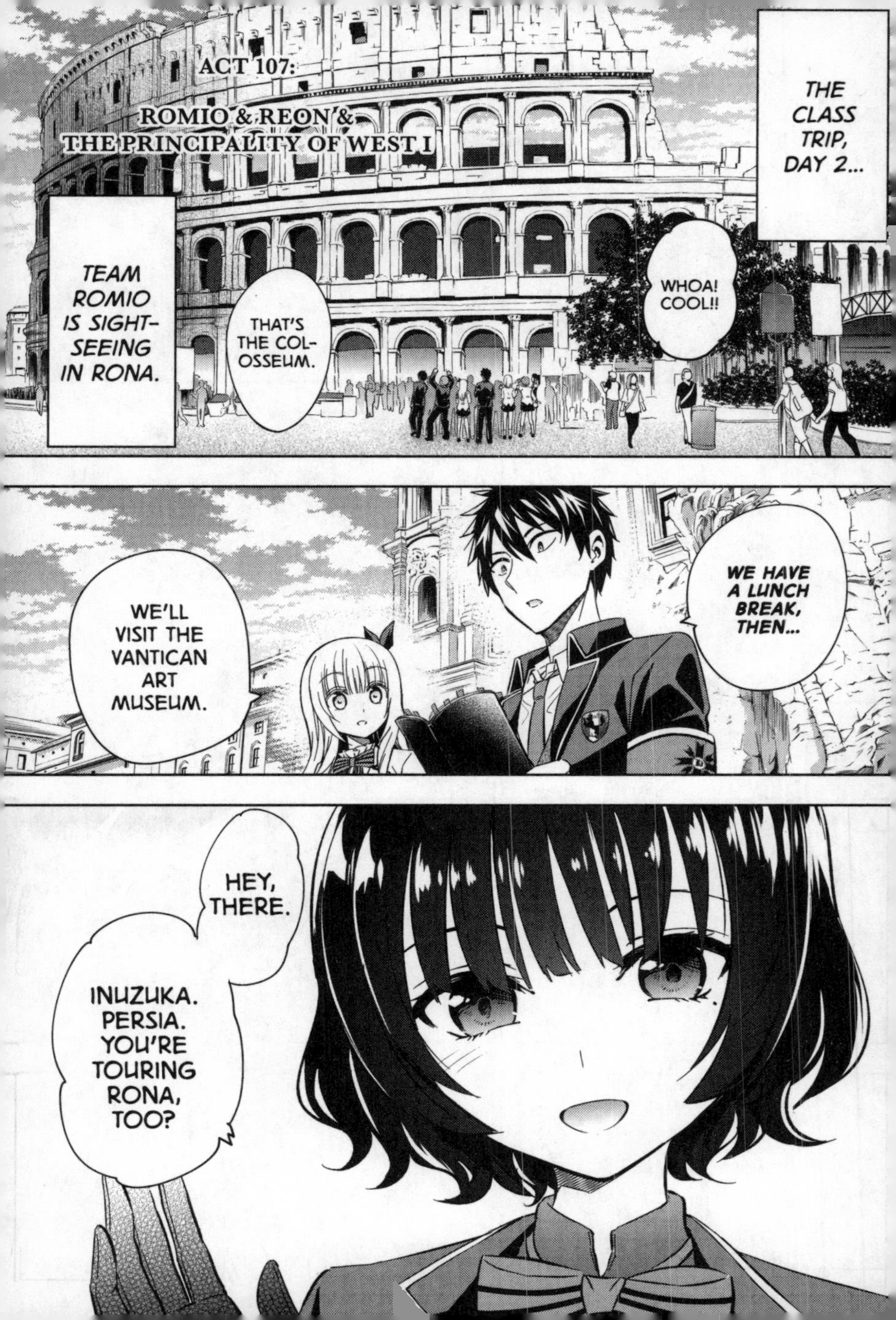
THE CLASS TRIP, DAY 2...
ACT 107:
ROMIO & REON & THE PRINCIPALITY OF WEST I
WHOA! COOL!!
THAT'S THE COL-OSSEUM.
TEAM ROMIO IS SIGHT-SEEING IN RONA.
WE HAVE A LUNCH BREAK, THEN...
WE'LL VISIT THE VANTICAN ART MUSEUM.
HEY, THERE.
INUZUKA. PERSIA. YOU'RE TOURING RONA, TOO?

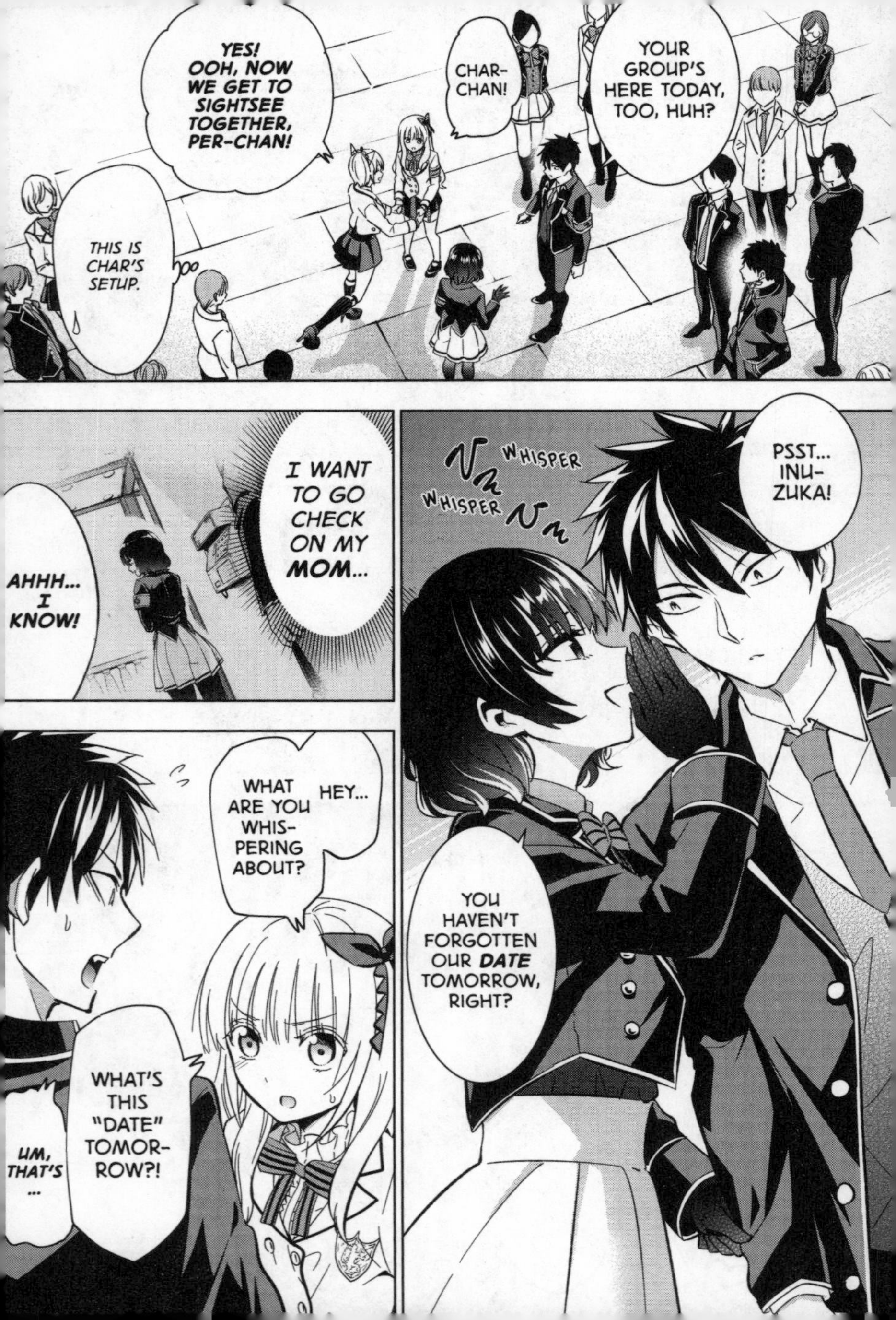
YOUR GROUP'S HERE TODAY, TOO, HUH?
CHAR-CHAN!
YES! OOH, NOW WE GET TO SIGHTSEE TOGETHER, PER-CHAN!
THIS IS CHAR'S SETUP.
PSST... INU-ZUKA!
WHISPER
WHISPER
YOU HAVEN'T FORGOTTEN OUR DATE TOMORROW, RIGHT?
I WANT TO GO CHECK ON MY MOM...
AHHH... I KNOW!
HEY...
WHAT ARE YOU WHIS-PERING ABOUT?
WHAT'S THIS "DATE" TOMOR-ROW?!
UM, THAT'S...

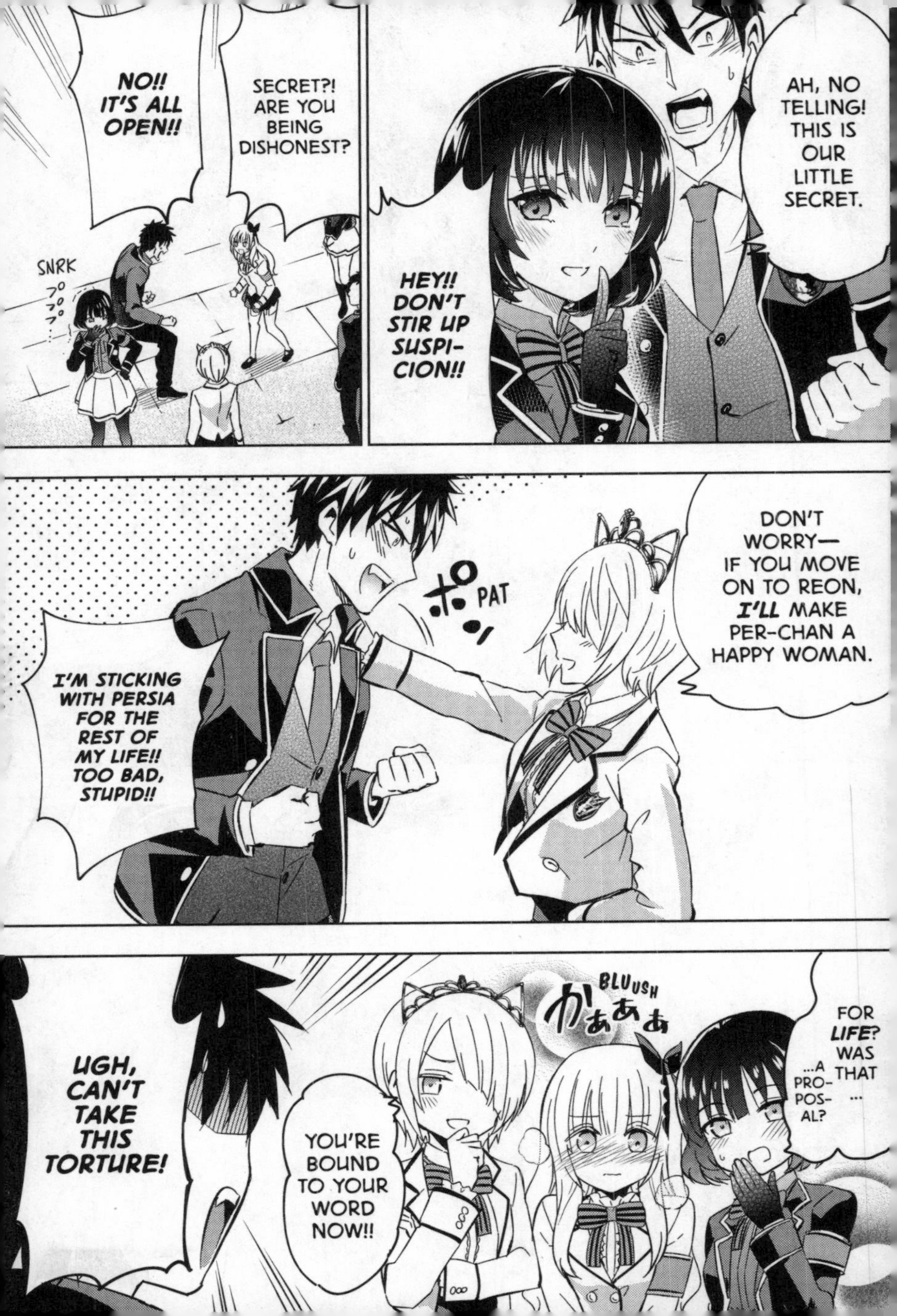
AH, NO TELLING! THIS IS OUR LITTLE SECRET.
HEY!! DON'T STIR UP SUSPICION!!
SECRET?! ARE YOU BEING DISHONEST?
NO!! IT'S ALL OPEN!!
SNRK
DON'T WORRY— IF YOU MOVE ON TO REON, I'LL MAKE PER-CHAN A HAPPY WOMAN.
PAT
I'M STICKING WITH PERSIA FOR THE REST OF MY LIFE!! TOO BAD, STUPID!!
FOR LIFE? WAS THAT...
...A PROPOSAL?
BLUUSH
YOU'RE BOUND TO YOUR WORD NOW!!
UGH, CAN'T TAKE THIS TORTURE!

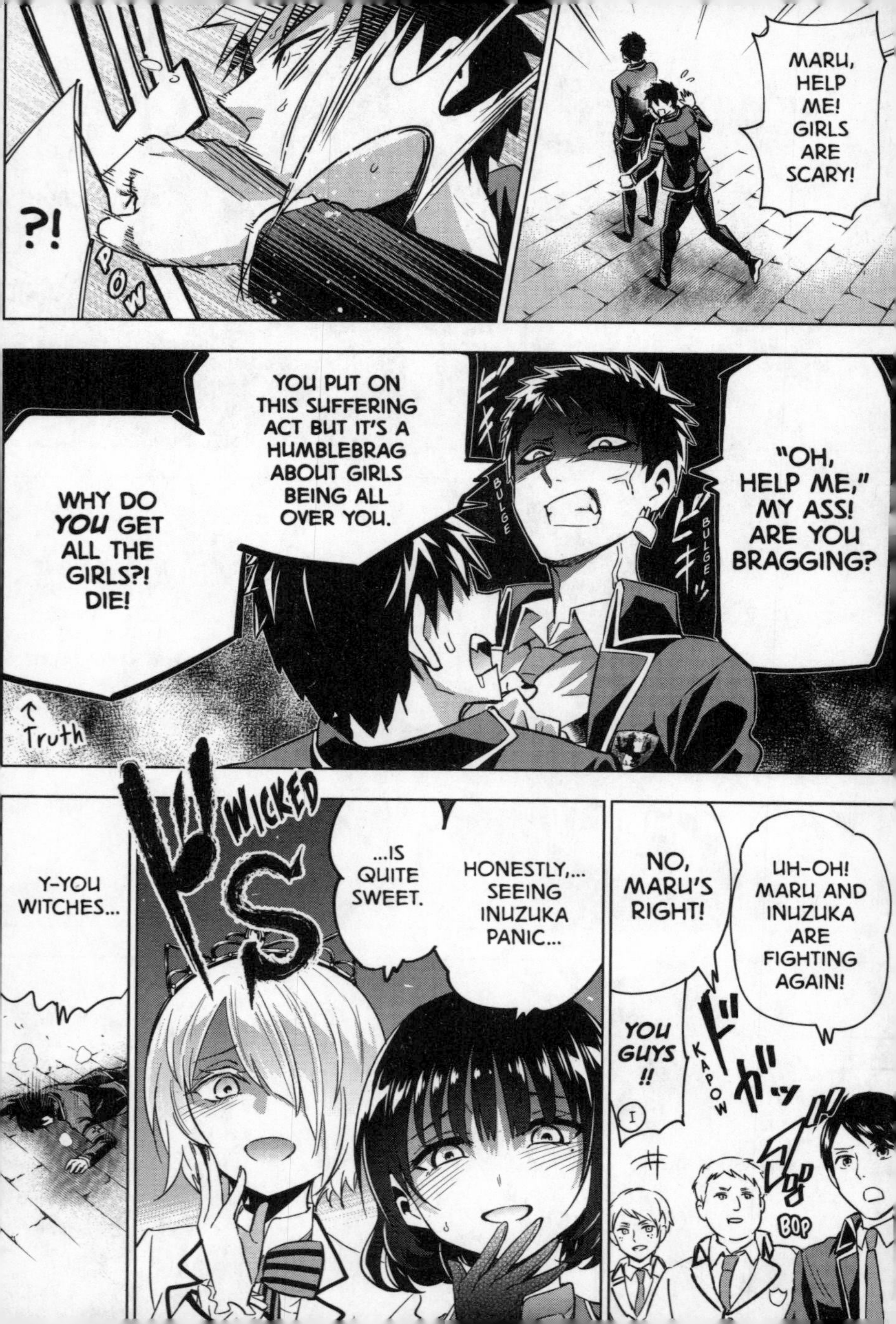

MARU, HELP ME! GIRLS ARE SCARY!
?!
POW
"OH, HELP ME," MY ASS! ARE YOU BRAGGING?
BULGE
BULGE
YOU PUT ON THIS SUFFERING ACT BUT IT'S A HUMBLEBRAG ABOUT GIRLS BEING ALL OVER YOU.
WHY DO *YOU* GET ALL THE GIRLS?! DIE!
↑ Truth
UH-OH! MARU AND INUZUKA ARE FIGHTING AGAIN!
NO, MARU'S RIGHT!
KAPOW
YOU GUYS !!
I
BOP
HONESTLY,... SEEING INUZUKA PANIC...
...IS QUITE SWEET.
WICKED
Y-YOU WITCHES...

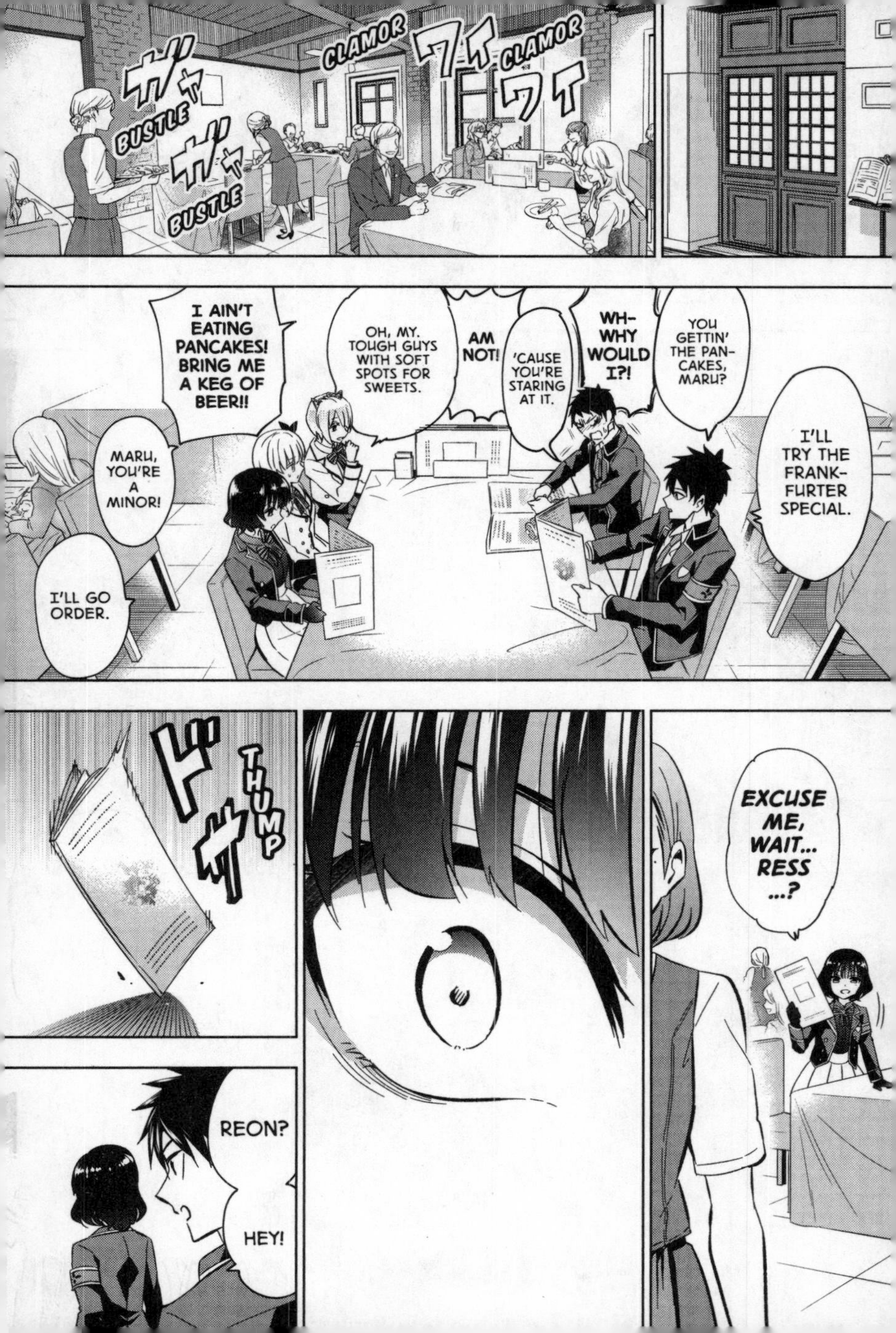

CLAMOR
ワイ
CLAMOR
ワイ
ガヤ
BUSTLE
ガヤ
BUSTLE
YOU GETTIN' THE PAN-CAKES, MARU?
WH-WHY WOULD I?!
'CAUSE YOU'RE STARING AT IT.
AM NOT!
OH, MY. TOUGH GUYS WITH SOFT SPOTS FOR SWEETS.
I AIN'T EATING PANCAKES! BRING ME A KEG OF BEER!!
I'LL TRY THE FRANK-FURTER SPECIAL.
MARU, YOU'RE A MINOR!
I'LL GO ORDER.
EXCUSE ME, WAIT... RESS ...?
ドサ
THUMP
REON?
HEY!

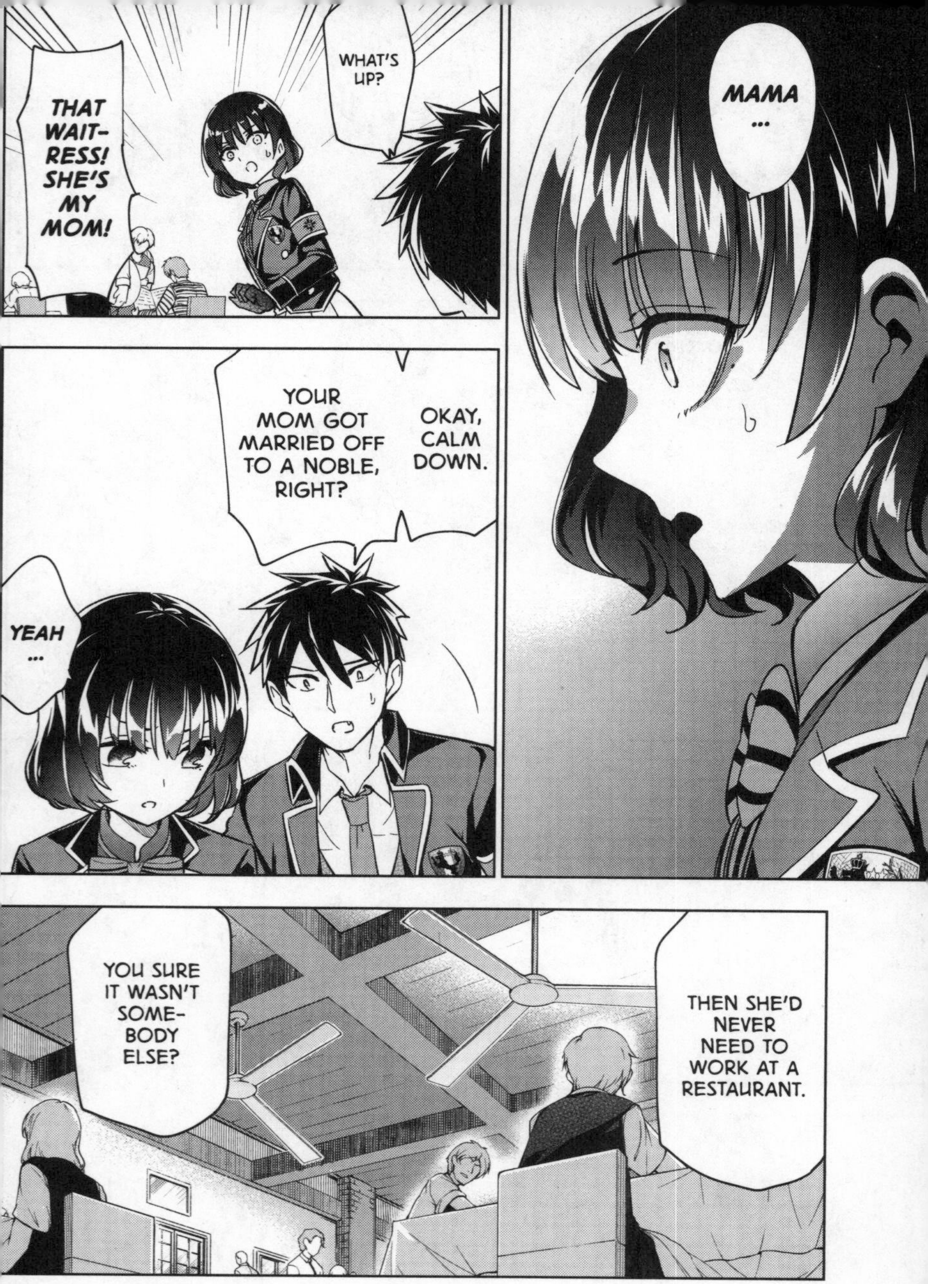
MAMA ...
WHAT'S UP?
THAT WAIT-RESS! SHE'S MY MOM!
OKAY, CALM DOWN.
YOUR MOM GOT MARRIED OFF TO A NOBLE, RIGHT?
YEAH ...
THEN SHE'D NEVER NEED TO WORK AT A RESTAURANT.
YOU SURE IT WASN'T SOME-BODY ELSE?

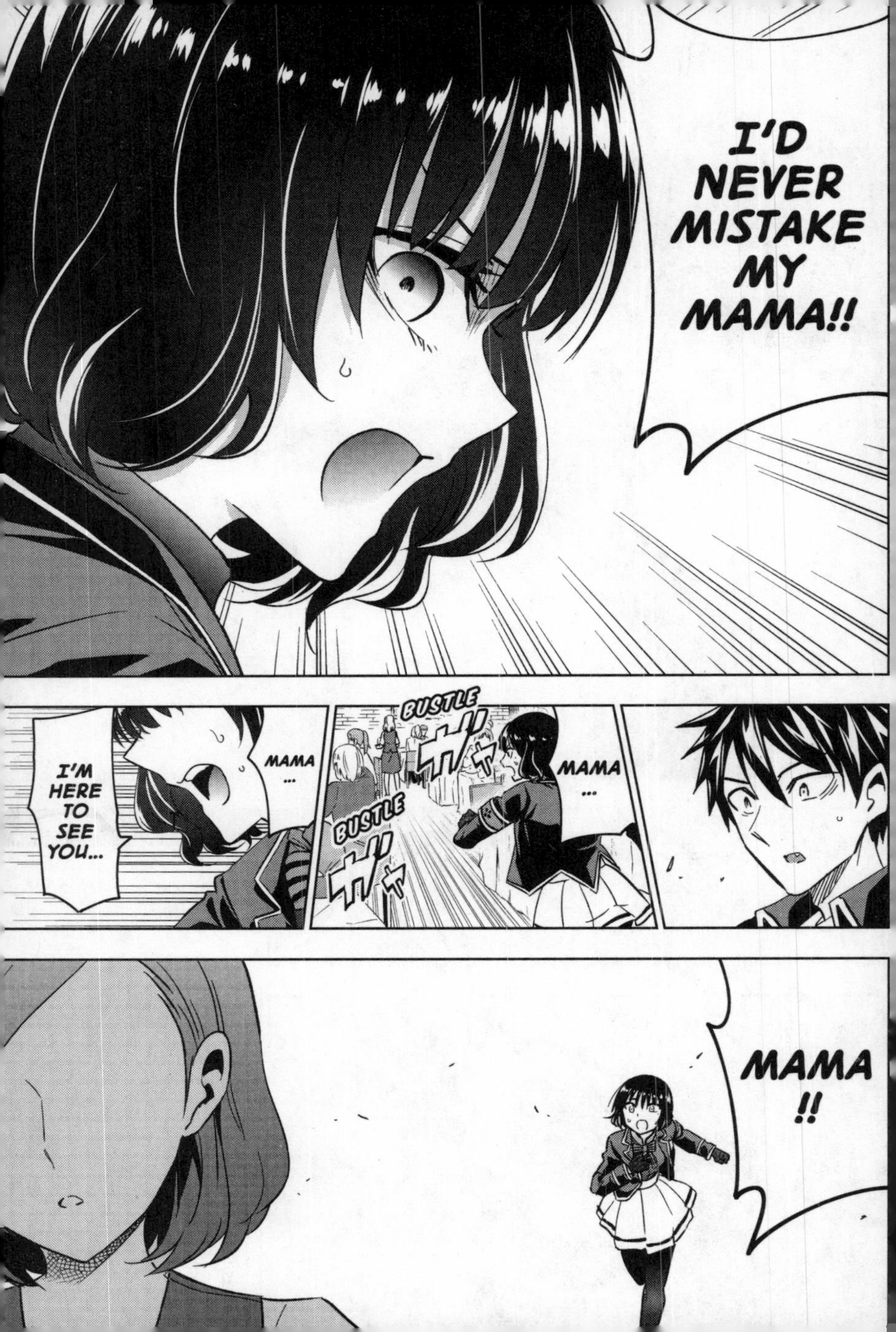
I'D NEVER MISTAKE MY MAMA!!
MAMA ...
BUSTLE
BUSTLE
MAMA ...
I'M HERE TO SEE YOU...
MAMA !!

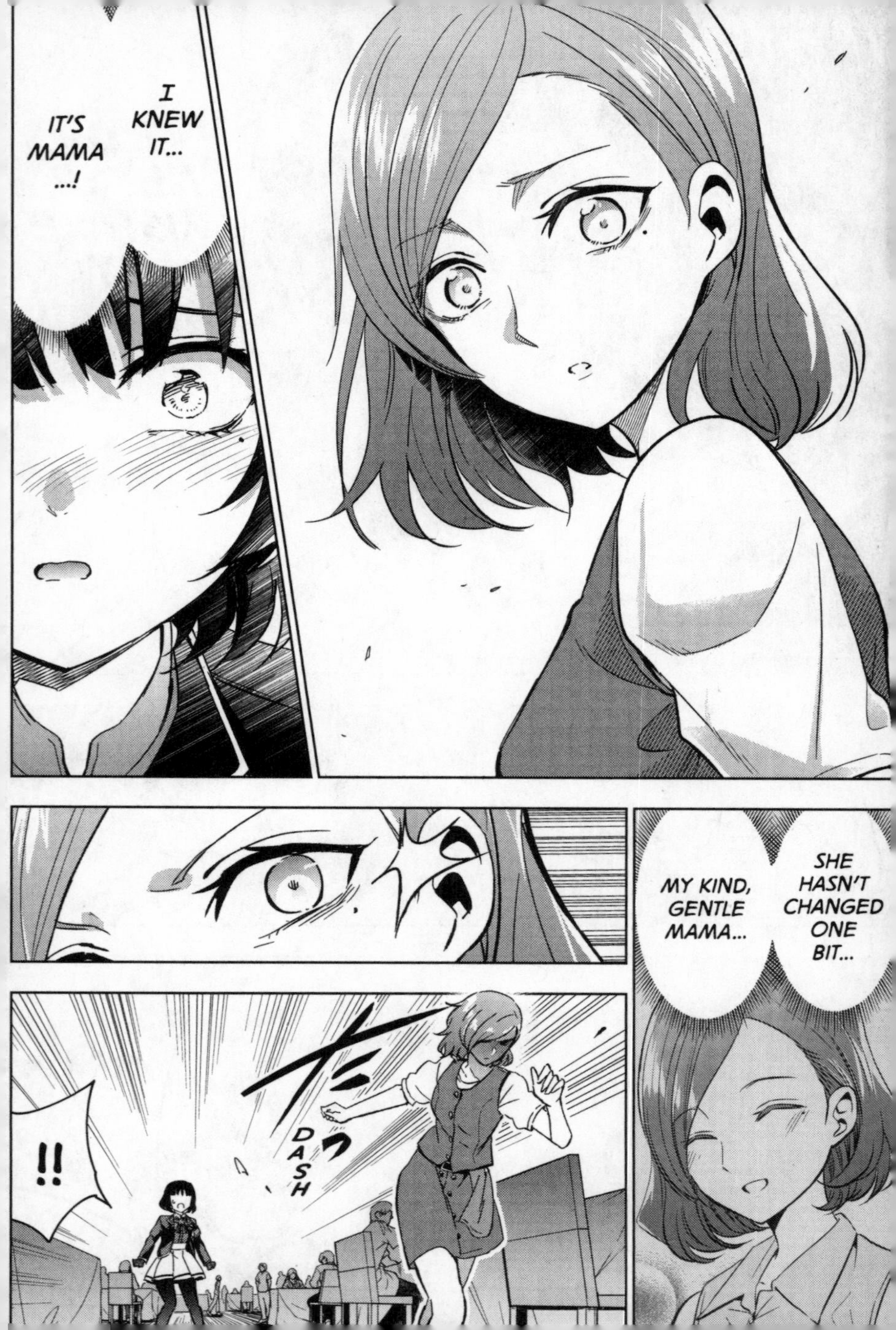

I KNEW IT...
IT'S MAMA ...!
SHE HASN'T CHANGED ONE BIT...
MY KIND, GENTLE MAMA...
DASH
!!

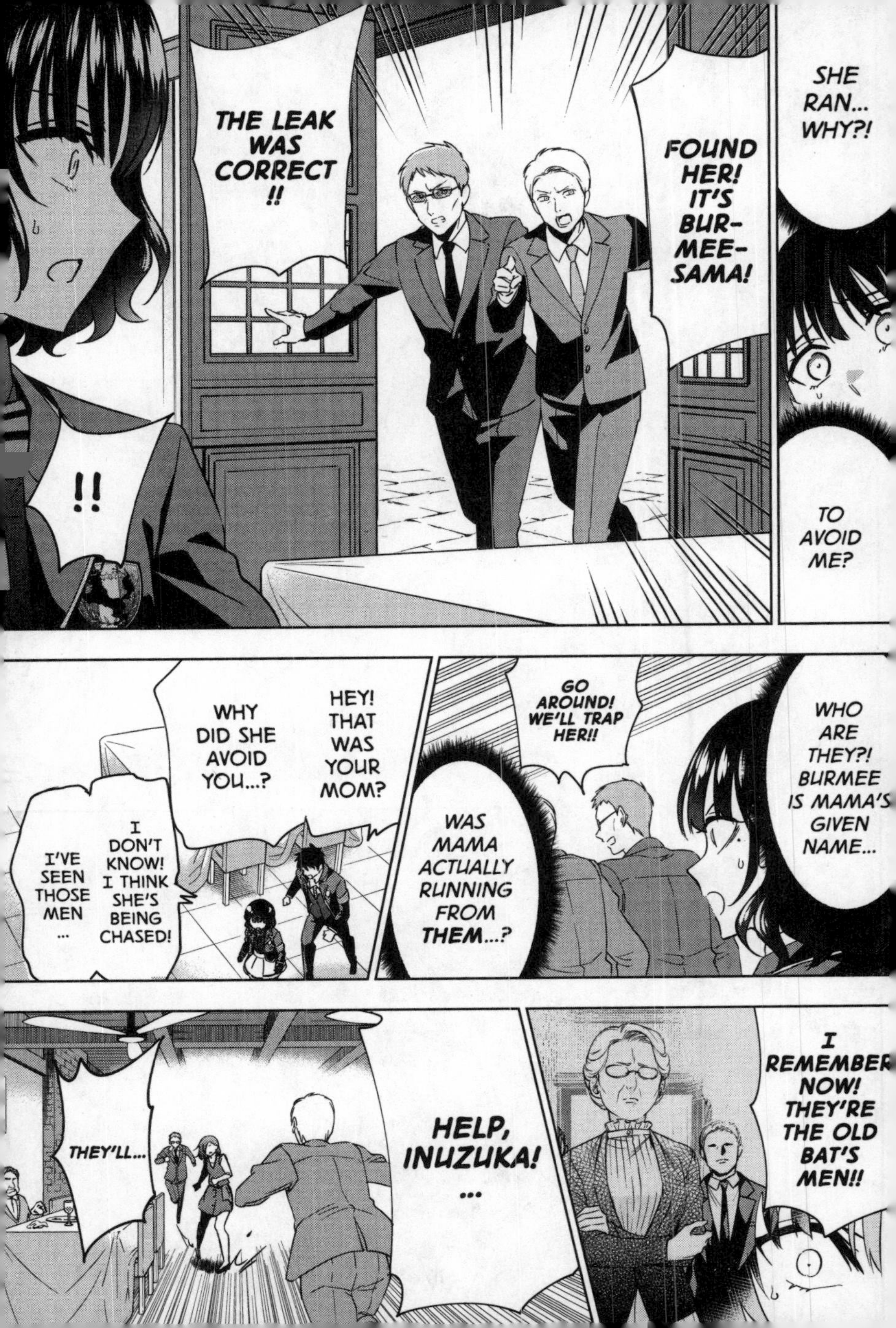
SHE RAN... WHY?!
TO AVOID ME?
FOUND HER! IT'S BURMEE-SAMA!
THE LEAK WAS CORRECT !!
!!
WHO ARE THEY?! BURMEE IS MAMA'S GIVEN NAME...
GO AROUND! WE'LL TRAP HER!!
WAS MAMA ACTUALLY RUNNING FROM THEM...?
HEY! THAT WAS YOUR MOM?
WHY DID SHE AVOID YOU...?
I DON'T KNOW! I THINK SHE'S BEING CHASED!
I'VE SEEN THOSE MEN ...
I REMEMBER NOW! THEY'RE THE OLD BAT'S MEN!!
HELP, INUZUKA! ...
THEY'LL...

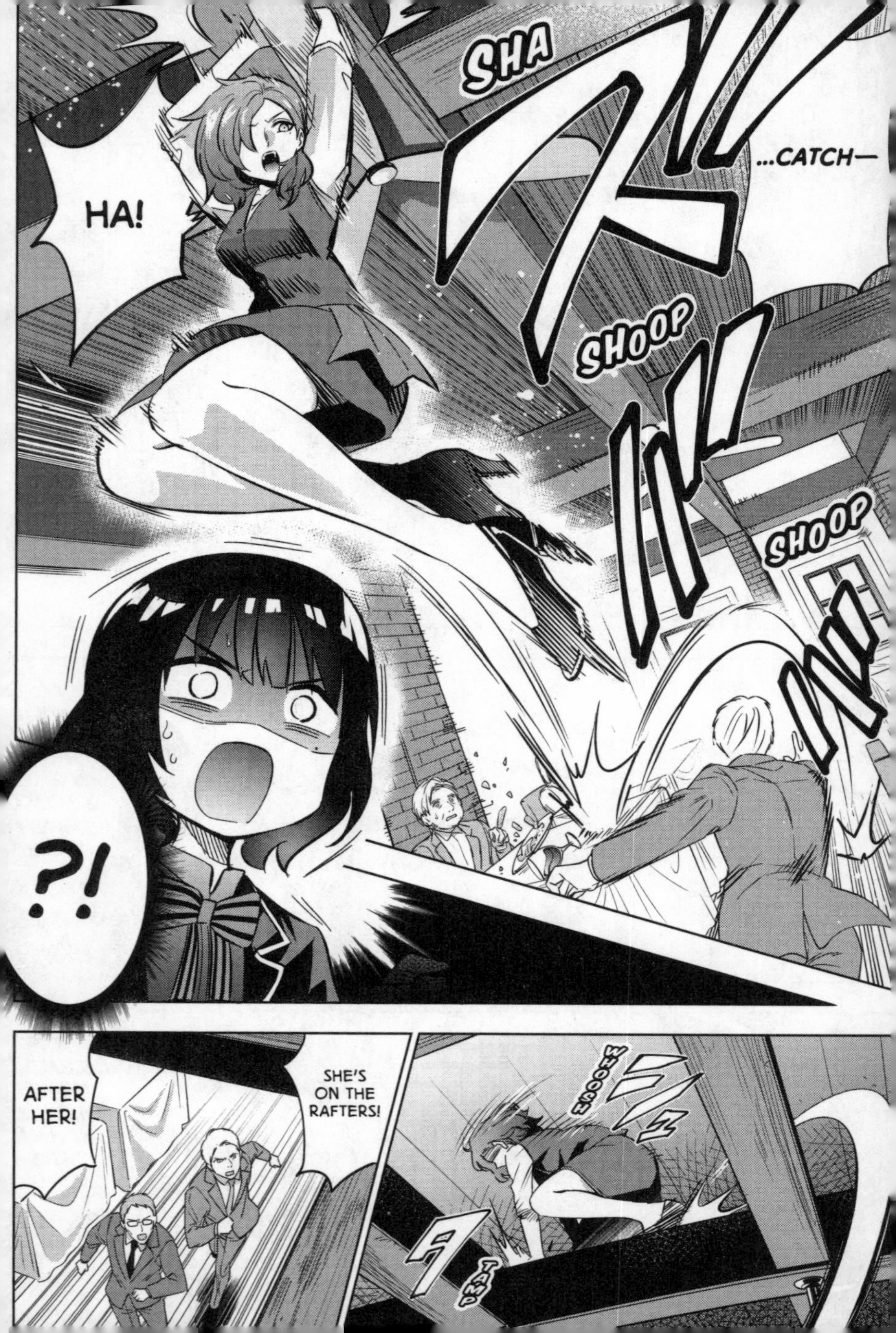
...CATCH—
SHA
HA!
SHOOP
SHOOP
?!
WHOOSH
TAMP
SHE'S ON THE RAFTERS!
AFTER HER!

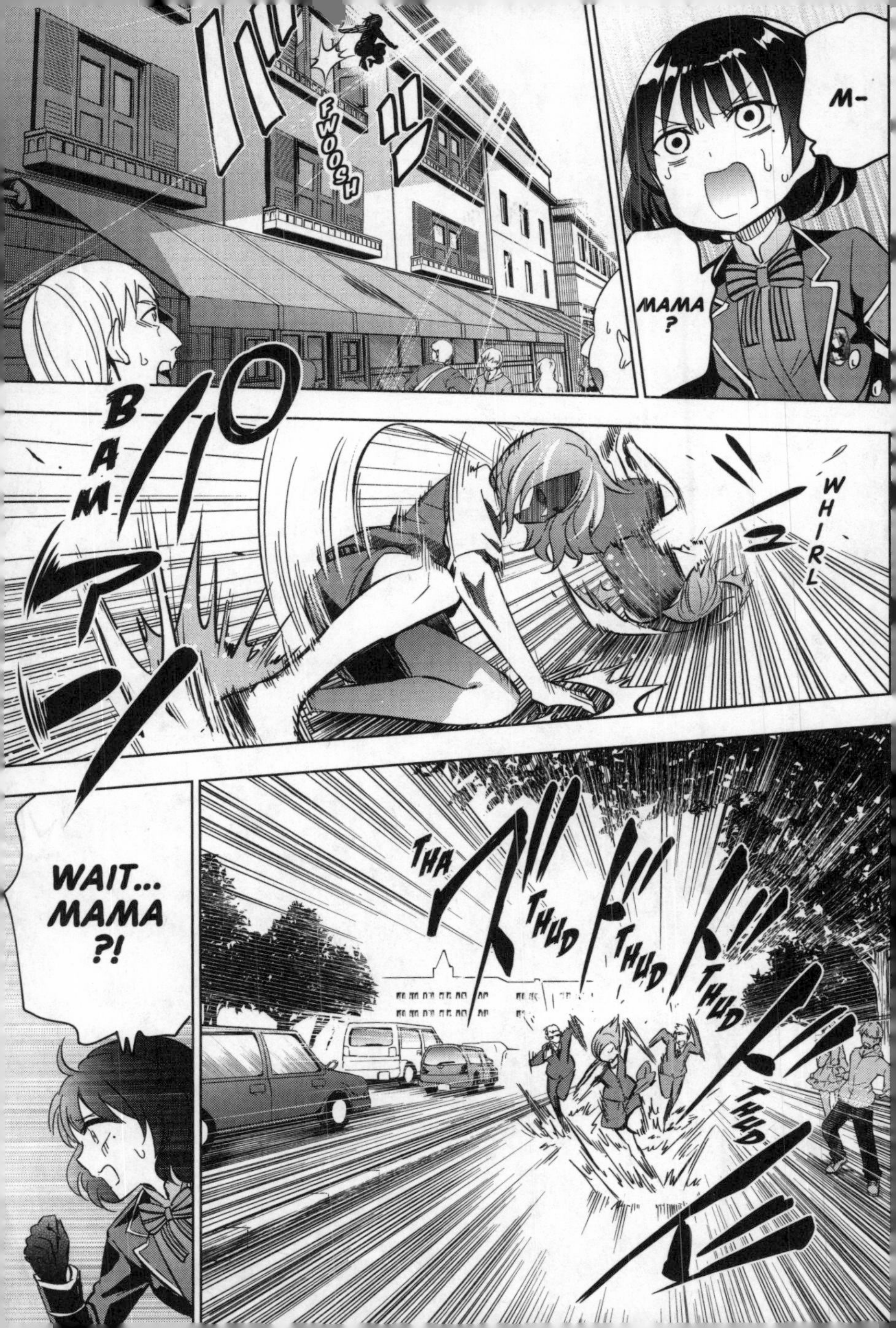
M-
MAMA ?
FWOOSH
WHIRL
BAM
THA
THUD
THUD
THUD
THUD
WAIT... MAMA ?!

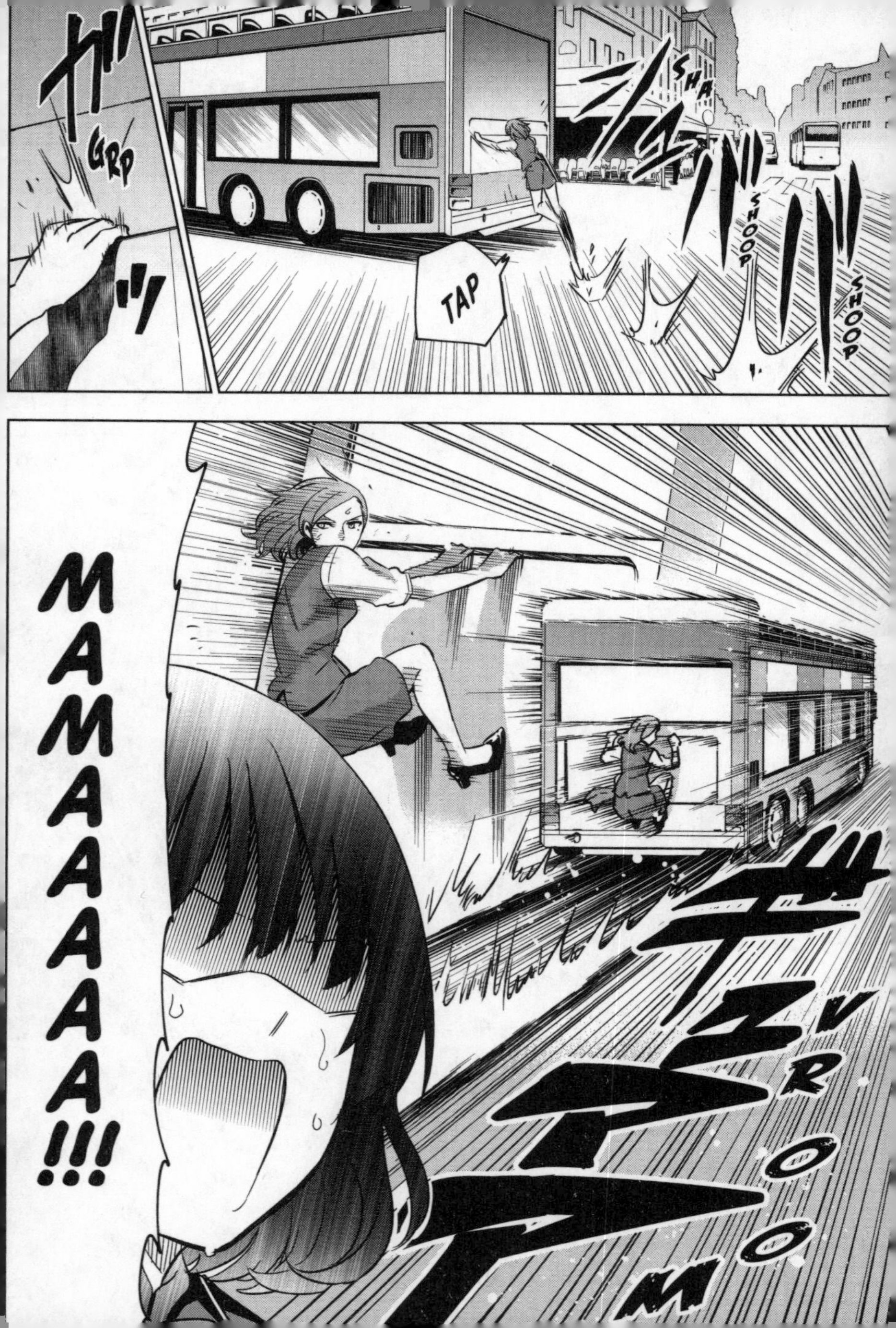

SHOOP
SHOOP
SHA
TAP
GRP
VRROOOM
MAMAAAAAA!!!

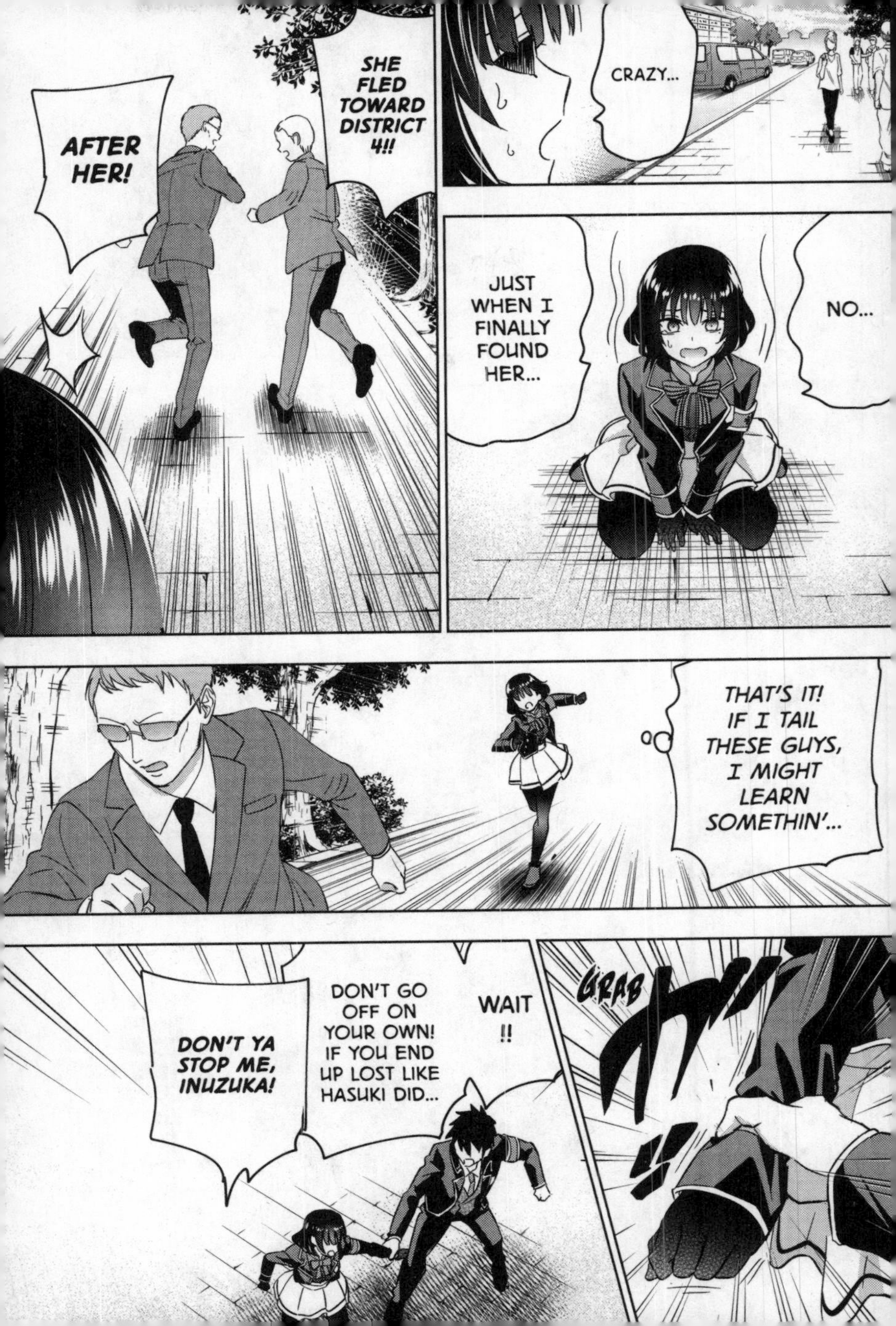

CRAZY...
NO...
JUST WHEN I FINALLY FOUND HER...
SHE FLED TOWARD DISTRICT 4!!
AFTER HER!
THAT'S IT! IF I TAIL THESE GUYS, I MIGHT LEARN SOMETHIN'...
GRAB
WAIT !!
DON'T GO OFF ON YOUR OWN! IF YOU END UP LOST LIKE HASUKI DID...
DON'T YA STOP ME, INUZUKA!

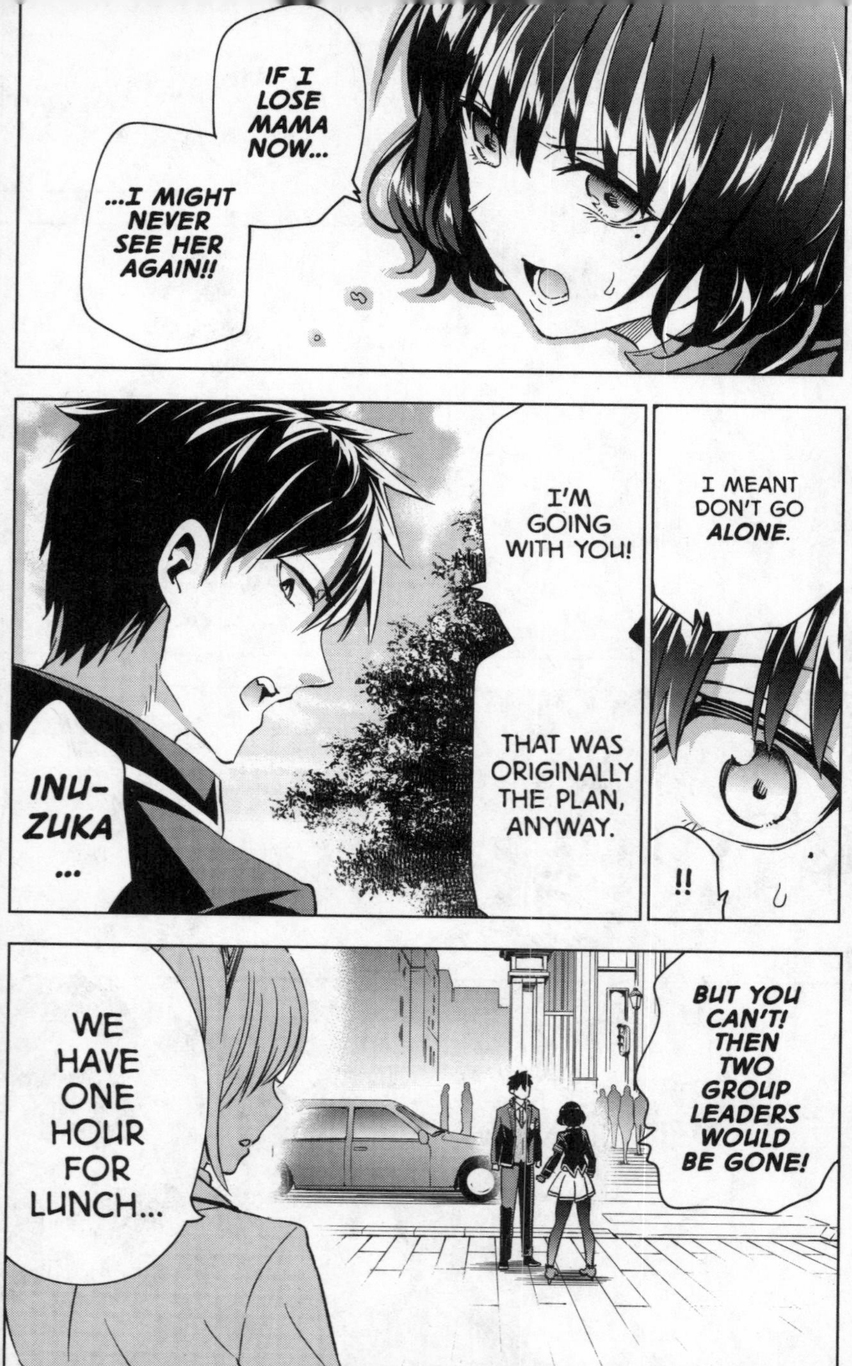
IF I LOSE MAMA NOW...
...I MIGHT NEVER SEE HER AGAIN!!
I MEANT DON'T GO *ALONE*.
!!
I'M GOING WITH YOU!
THAT WAS ORIGINALLY THE PLAN, ANYWAY.
INU-ZUKA...
BUT YOU CAN'T! THEN TWO GROUP LEADERS WOULD BE GONE!
WE HAVE ONE HOUR FOR LUNCH...

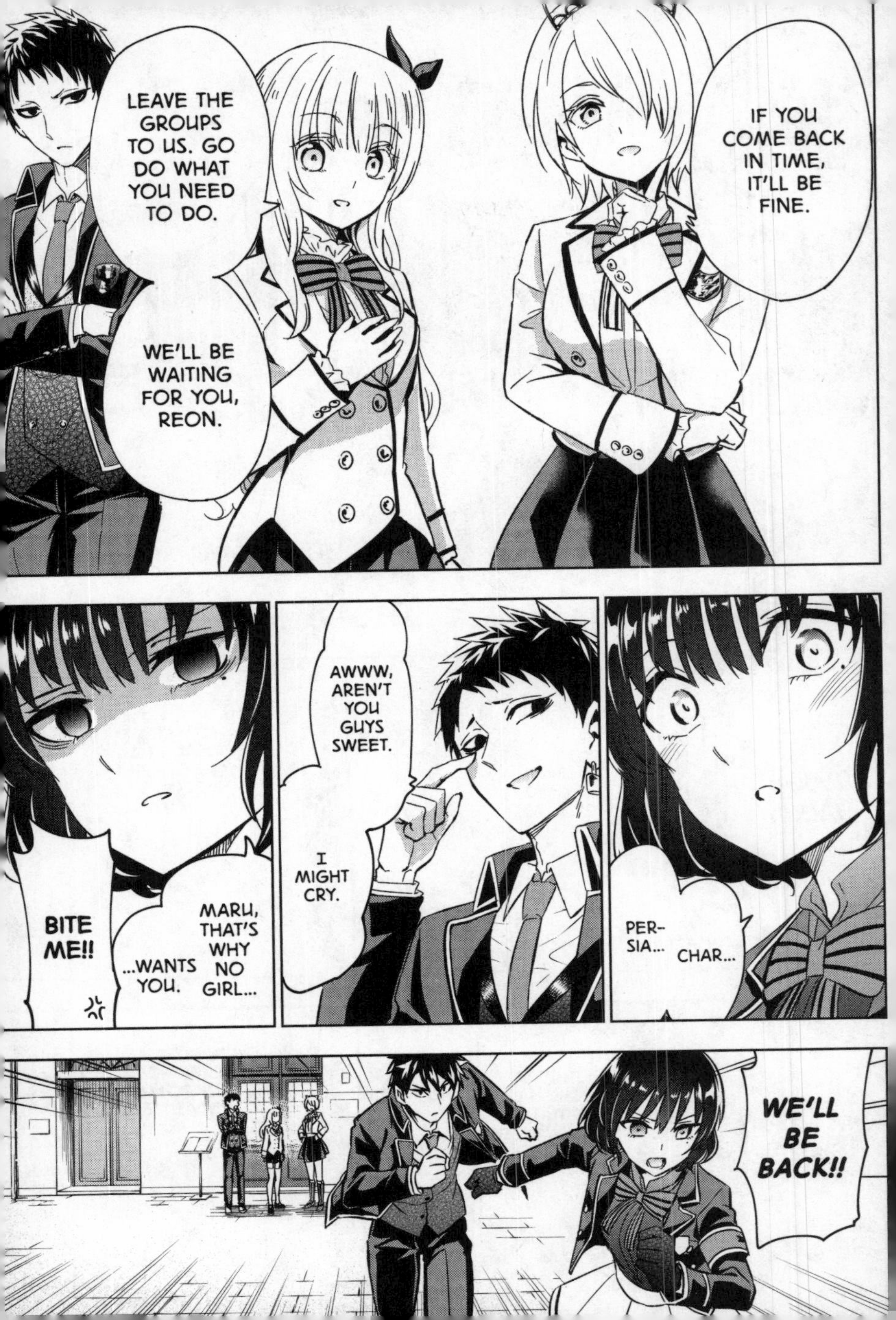
IF YOU COME BACK IN TIME, IT'LL BE FINE.
LEAVE THE GROUPS TO US. GO DO WHAT YOU NEED TO DO.
WE'LL BE WAITING FOR YOU, REON.
CHAR...
PER-SIA...
AWWW, AREN'T YOU GUYS SWEET.
I MIGHT CRY.
MARU, THAT'S WHY NO GIRL...
...WANTS YOU.
BITE ME!!
WE'LL BE BACK!!

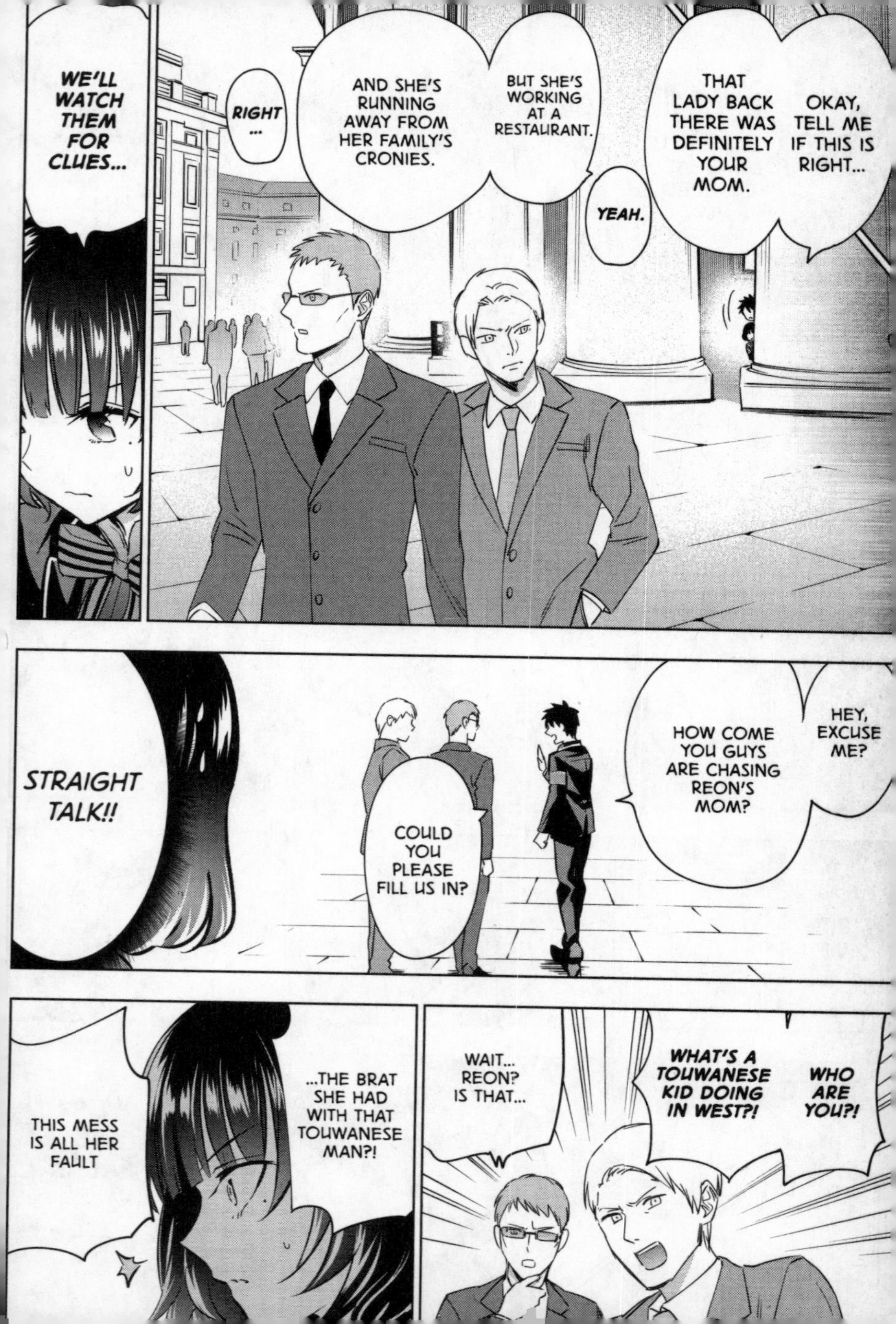
OKAY, TELL ME IF THIS IS RIGHT...
THAT LADY BACK THERE WAS DEFINITELY YOUR MOM.
YEAH.
BUT SHE'S WORKING AT A RESTAURANT.
AND SHE'S RUNNING AWAY FROM HER FAMILY'S CRONIES.
RIGHT...
WE'LL WATCH THEM FOR CLUES...
HEY, EXCUSE ME?
HOW COME YOU GUYS ARE CHASING REON'S MOM?
COULD YOU PLEASE FILL US IN?
STRAIGHT TALK!!
WHO ARE YOU?!
WHAT'S A TOUWANESE KID DOING IN WEST?!
WAIT... REON? IS THAT...
...THE BRAT SHE HAD WITH THAT TOUWANESE MAN?!
THIS MESS IS ALL HER FAULT

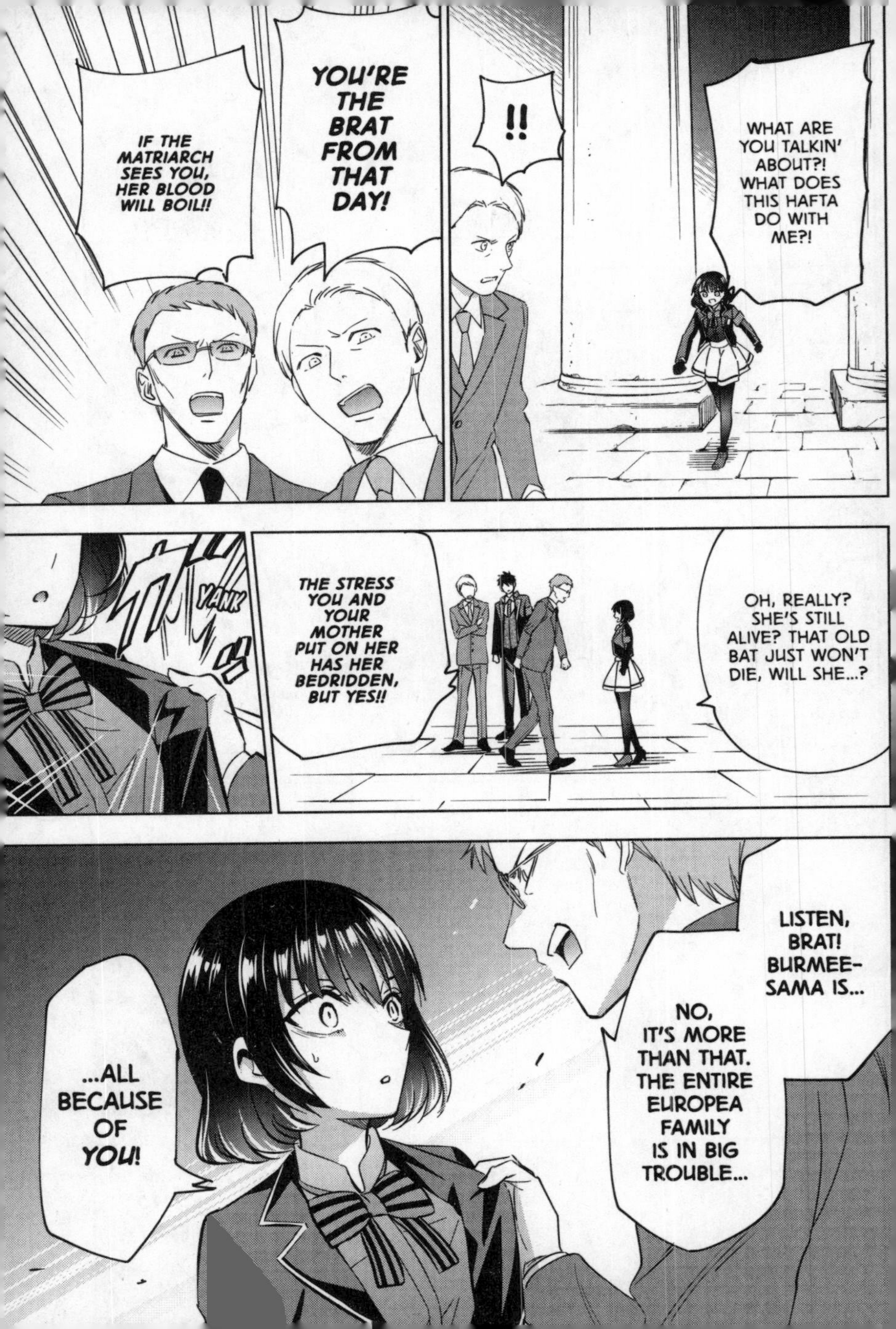
WHAT ARE YOU TALKIN' ABOUT?! WHAT DOES THIS HAFTA DO WITH ME?!
!!
YOU'RE THE BRAT FROM THAT DAY!
IF THE MATRIARCH SEES YOU, HER BLOOD WILL BOIL!!
OH, REALLY? SHE'S STILL ALIVE? THAT OLD BAT JUST WON'T DIE, WILL SHE...?
THE STRESS YOU AND YOUR MOTHER PUT ON HER HAS HER BEDRIDDEN, BUT YES!!
YANK
LISTEN, BRAT! BURMEE-SAMA IS...
NO, IT'S MORE THAN THAT. THE ENTIRE EUROPEA FAMILY IS IN BIG TROUBLE...
...ALL BECAUSE OF YOU!

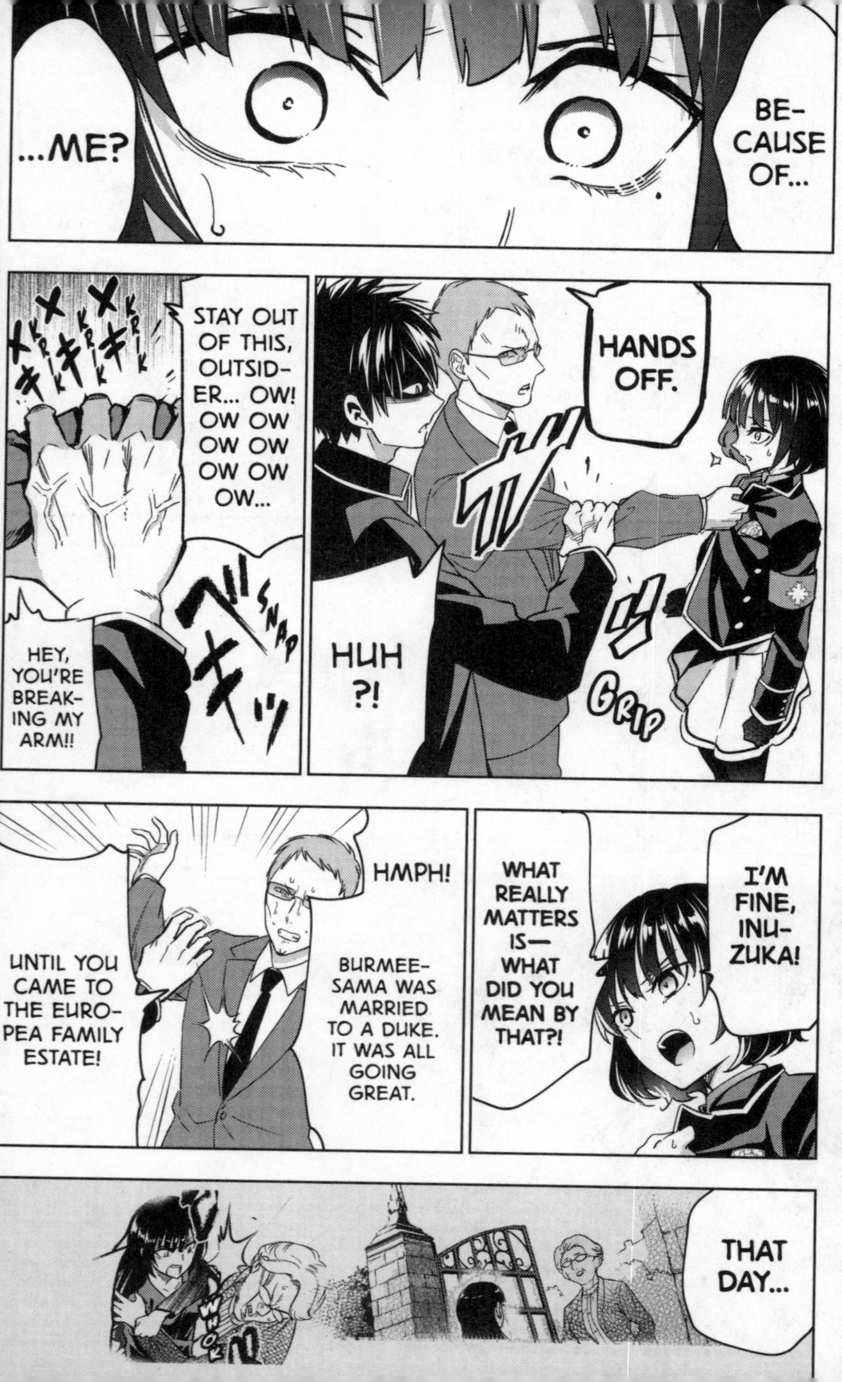
BE-CAUSE OF...
...ME?
HANDS OFF.
GRIP
HUH ?!
STAY OUT OF THIS, OUTSID-ER... OW! OW OW OW OW OW OW OW...
KRIK KRIK KRIK
SNAP
HEY, YOU'RE BREAK-ING MY ARM!!
I'M FINE, INU-ZUKA!
WHAT REALLY MATTERS IS— WHAT DID YOU MEAN BY THAT?!
HMPH!
BURMEE-SAMA WAS MARRIED TO A DUKE. IT WAS ALL GOING GREAT.
UNTIL YOU CAME TO THE EURO-PEA FAMILY ESTATE!
THAT DAY...
WHOK

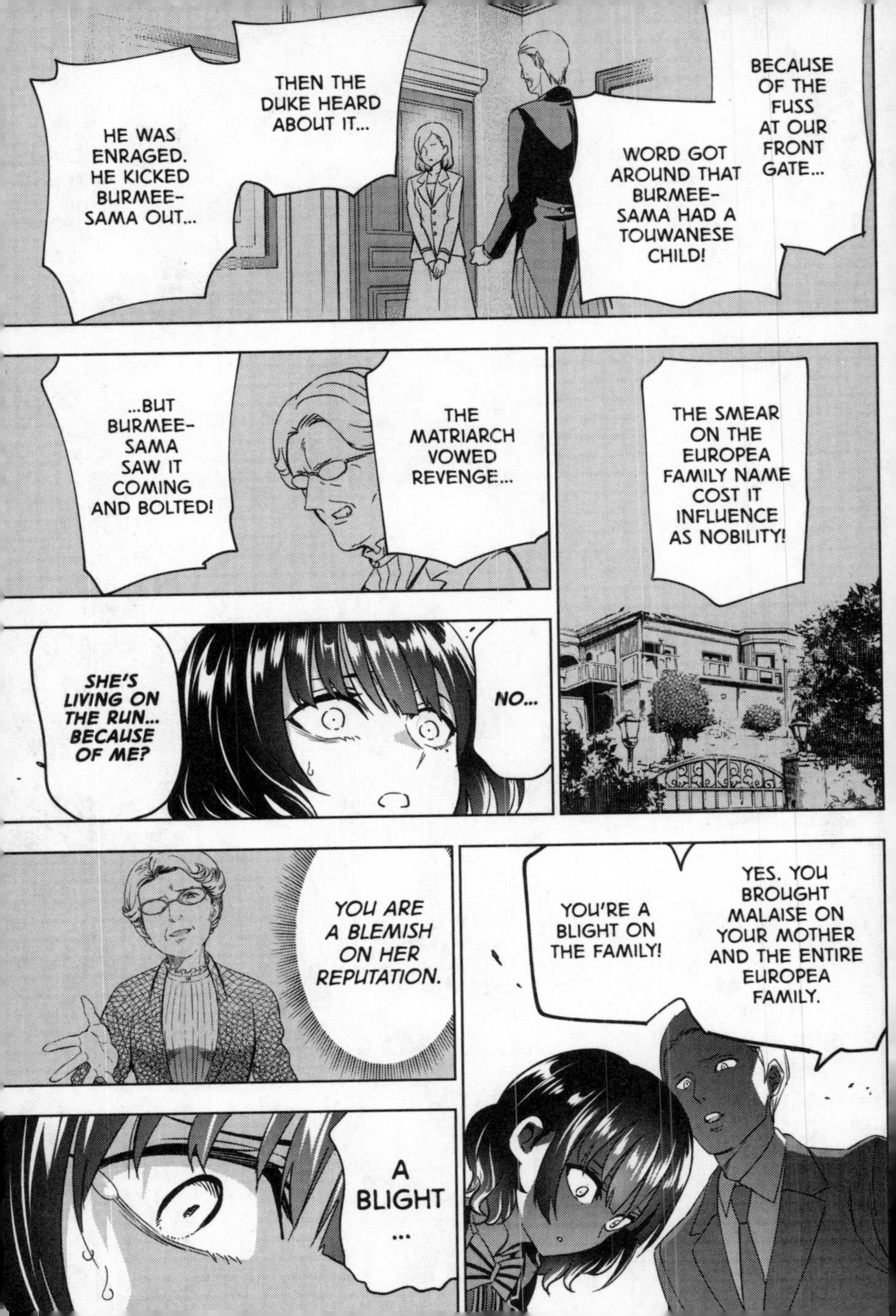
BECAUSE OF THE FUSS AT OUR FRONT GATE...
WORD GOT AROUND THAT BURMEE-SAMA HAD A TOUWANESE CHILD!
THEN THE DUKE HEARD ABOUT IT...
HE WAS ENRAGED. HE KICKED BURMEE-SAMA OUT...
THE SMEAR ON THE EUROPEA FAMILY NAME COST IT INFLUENCE AS NOBILITY!
THE MATRIARCH VOWED REVENGE...
...BUT BURMEE-SAMA SAW IT COMING AND BOLTED!
NO...
SHE'S LIVING ON THE RUN... BECAUSE OF ME?
YES. YOU BROUGHT MALAISE ON YOUR MOTHER AND THE ENTIRE EUROPEA FAMILY.
YOU'RE A BLIGHT ON THE FAMILY!
YOU ARE A BLEMISH ON HER REPUTATION.
A BLIGHT ...

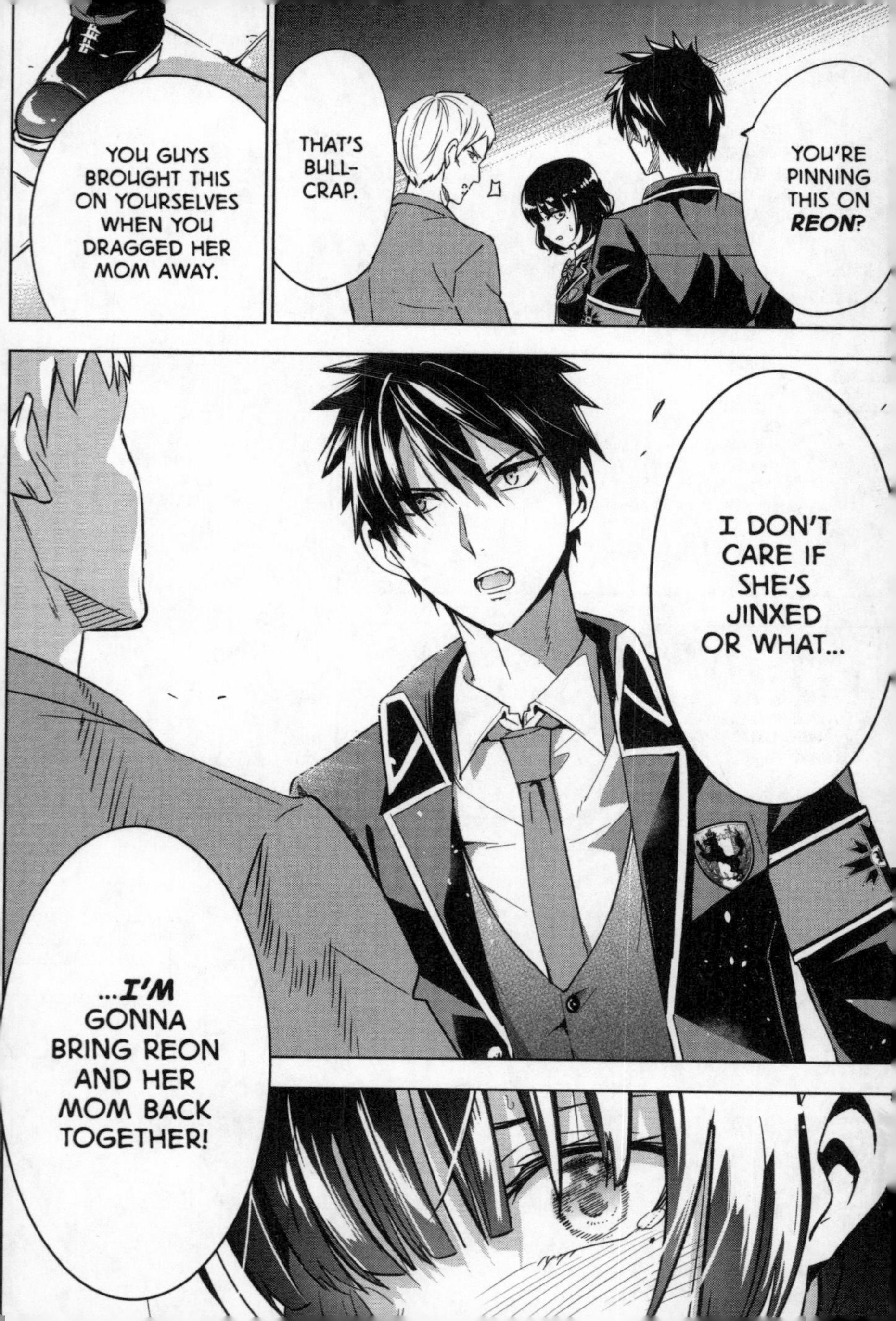
YOU'RE PINNING THIS ON REON?
THAT'S BULL-CRAP.
YOU GUYS BROUGHT THIS ON YOURSELVES WHEN YOU DRAGGED HER MOM AWAY.
I DON'T CARE IF SHE'S JINXED OR WHAT...
...I'M GONNA BRING REON AND HER MOM BACK TOGETHER!

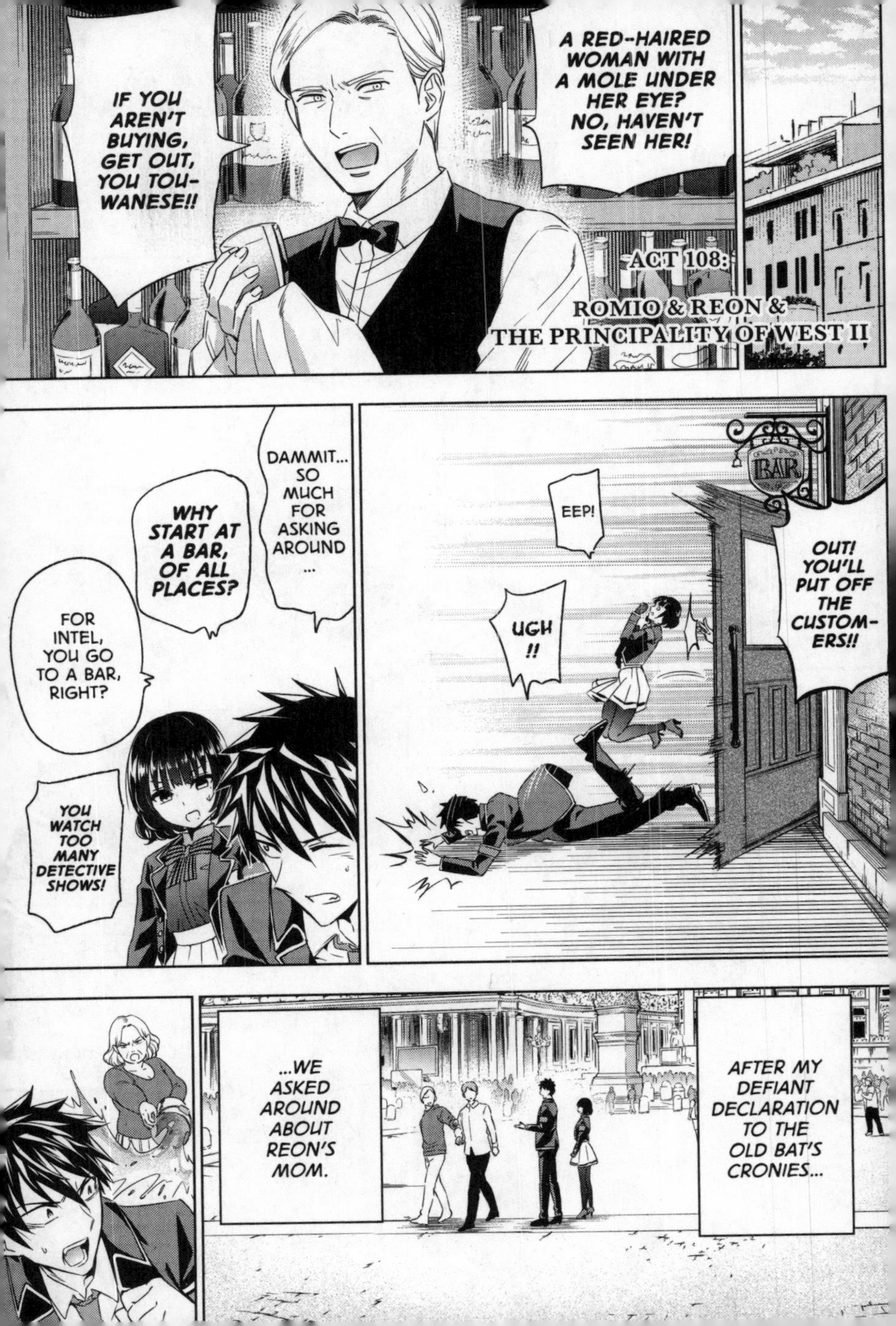
A RED-HAIRED WOMAN WITH A MOLE UNDER HER EYE? NO, HAVEN'T SEEN HER!
IF YOU AREN'T BUYING, GET OUT, YOU TOU-WANESE!!
ACT 108:
ROMIO & REON & THE PRINCIPALITY OF WEST II
OUT! YOU'LL PUT OFF THE CUSTOM-ERS!!
BAR
EEP!
UGH !!
DAMMIT... SO MUCH FOR ASKING AROUND ...
WHY START AT A BAR, OF ALL PLACES?
FOR INTEL, YOU GO TO A BAR, RIGHT?
YOU WATCH TOO MANY DETECTIVE SHOWS!
AFTER MY DEFIANT DECLARATION TO THE OLD BAT'S CRONIES...
...WE ASKED AROUND ABOUT REON'S MOM.

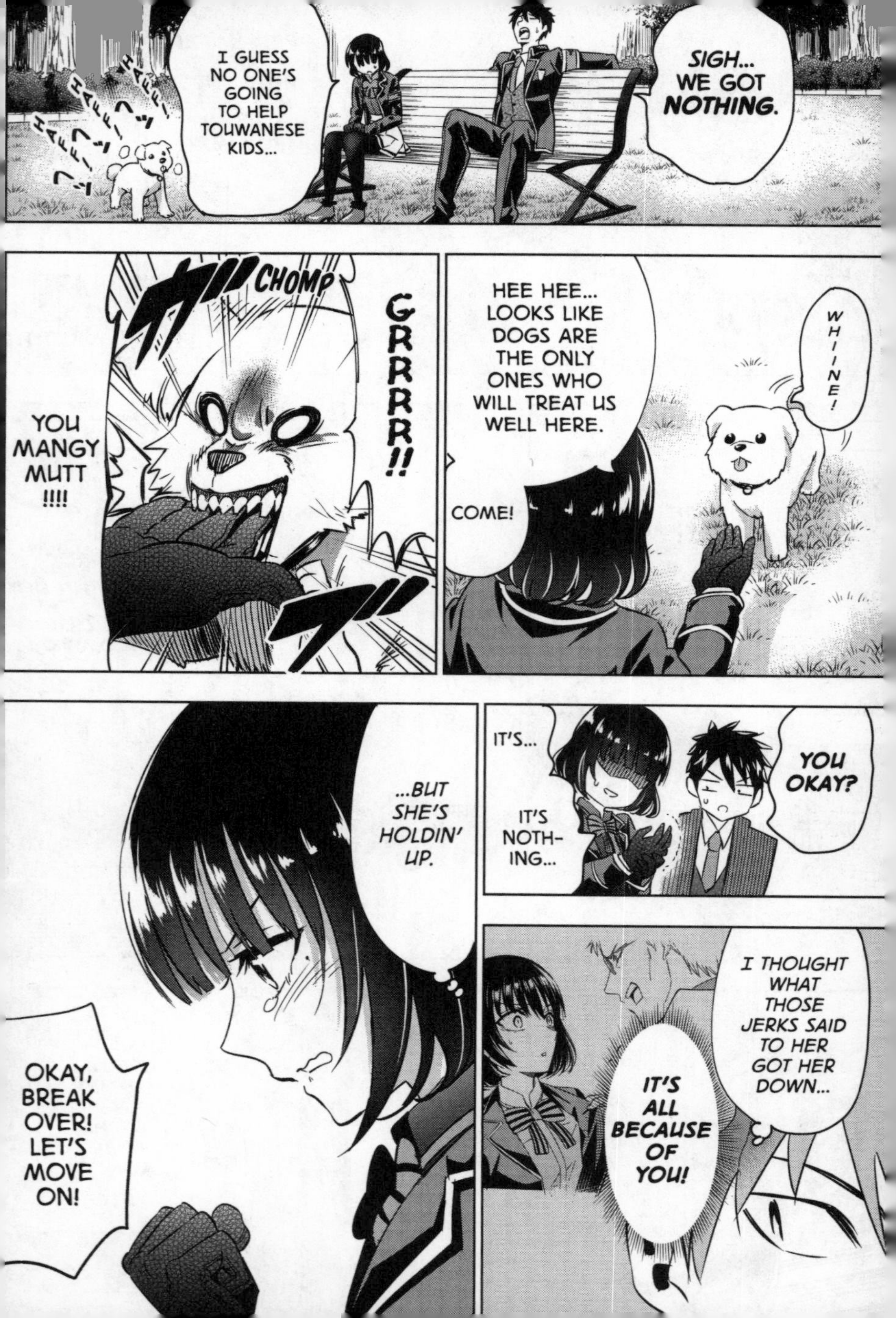
SIGH... WE GOT NOTHING.
I GUESS NO ONE'S GOING TO HELP TOUWANESE KIDS...
WHIINE!
HEE HEE... LOOKS LIKE DOGS ARE THE ONLY ONES WHO WILL TREAT US WELL HERE.
COME!
CHOMP
GRRRRR!!
YOU MANGY MUTT!!!!
YOU OKAY?
IT'S...
IT'S NOTH-ING...
I THOUGHT WHAT THOSE JERKS SAID TO HER GOT HER DOWN...
IT'S ALL BECAUSE OF YOU!
...BUT SHE'S HOLDIN' UP.
OKAY, BREAK OVER! LET'S MOVE ON!

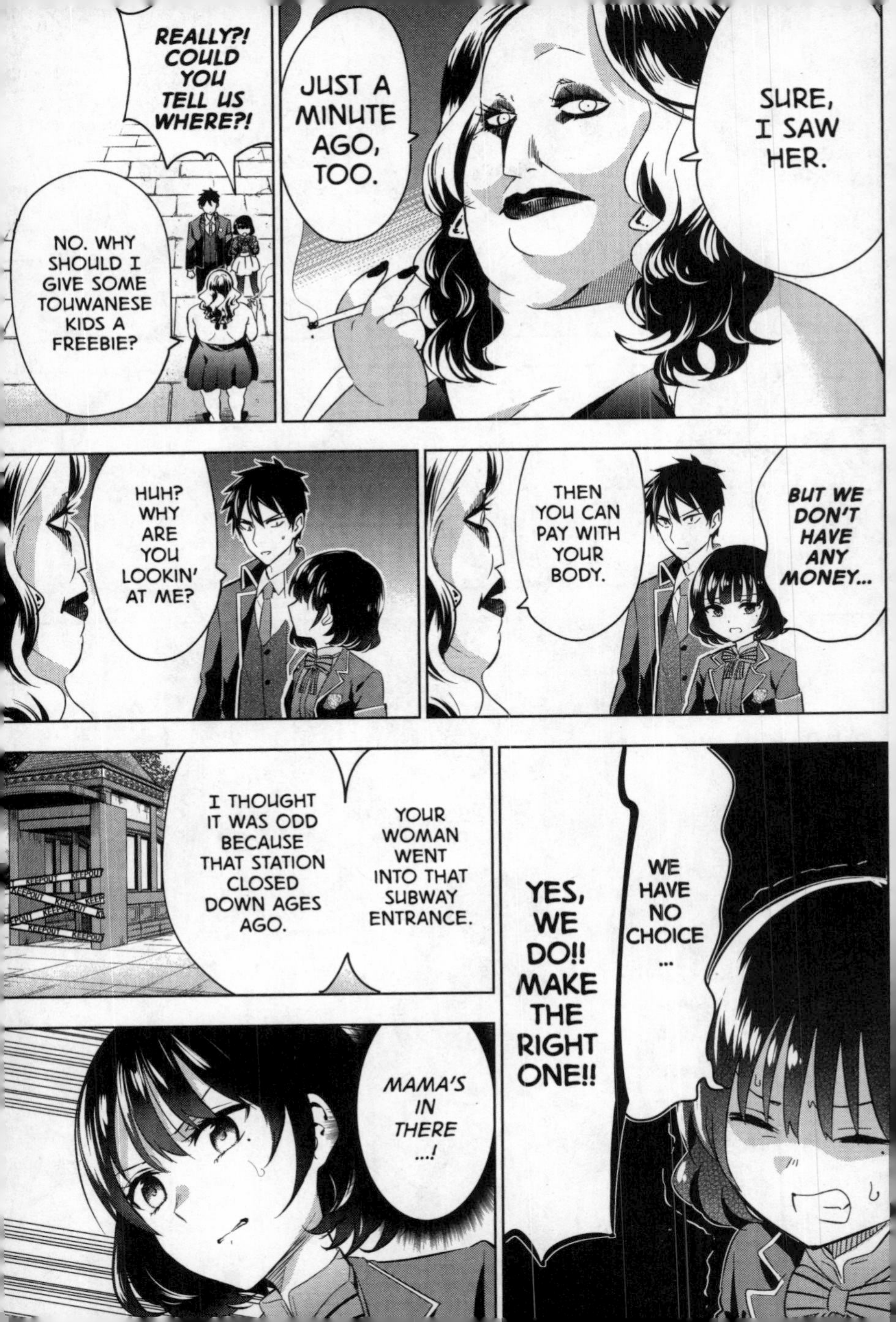
SURE, I SAW HER.
JUST A MINUTE AGO, TOO.
REALLY?! COULD YOU TELL US WHERE?!
NO. WHY SHOULD I GIVE SOME TOUWANESE KIDS A FREEBIE?
BUT WE DON'T HAVE ANY MONEY...
THEN YOU CAN PAY WITH YOUR BODY.
HUH? WHY ARE YOU LOOKIN' AT ME?
WE HAVE NO CHOICE ...
YES, WE DO!! MAKE THE RIGHT ONE!!
YOUR WOMAN WENT INTO THAT SUBWAY ENTRANCE.
I THOUGHT IT WAS ODD BECAUSE THAT STATION CLOSED DOWN AGES AGO.
MAMA'S IN THERE ...!

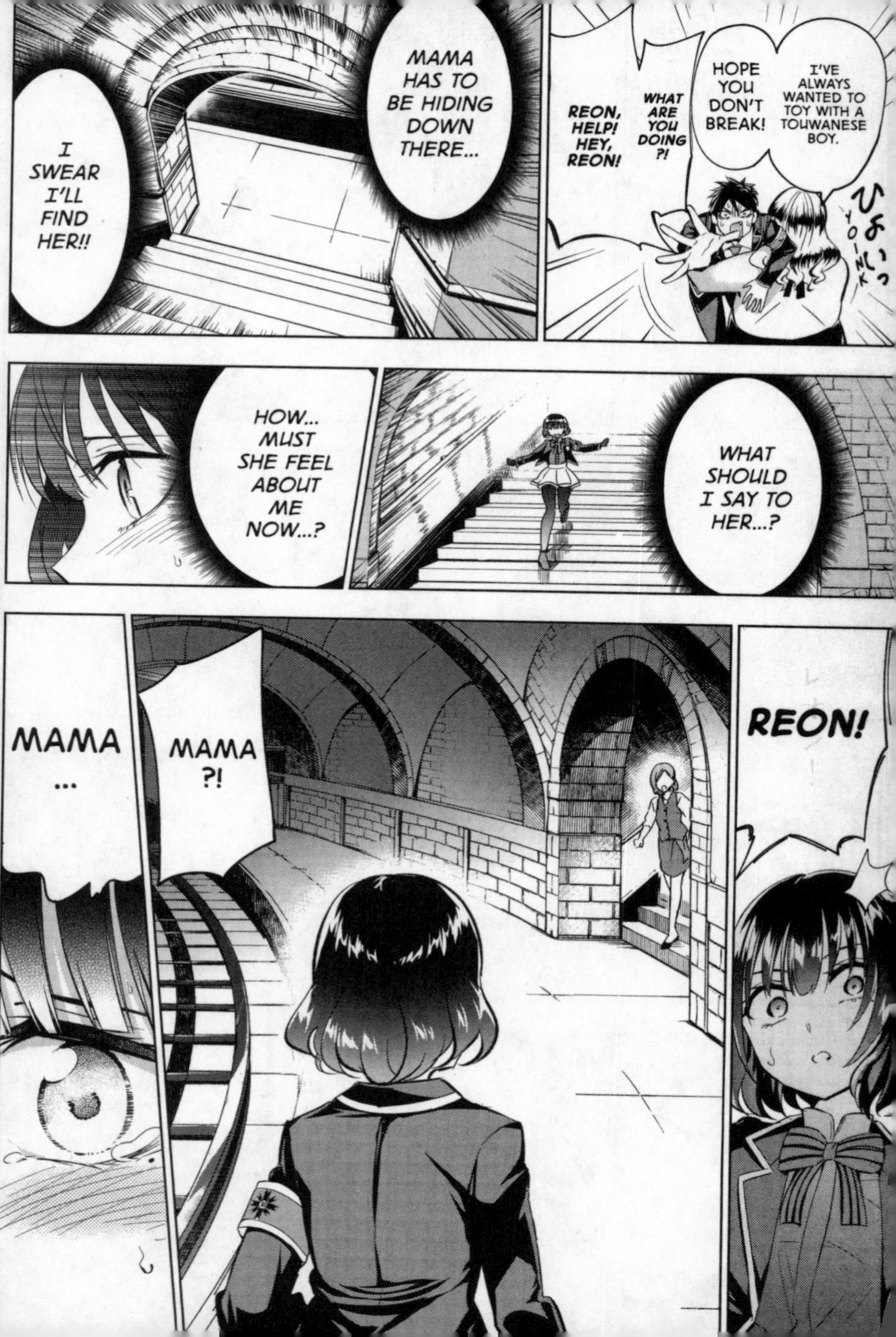
I'VE ALWAYS WANTED TO TOY WITH A TOUWANESE BOY.
HOPE YOU DON'T BREAK!
ひょいっ
YOINK
WHAT ARE YOU DOING ?!
REON, HELP! HEY, REON!
MAMA HAS TO BE HIDING DOWN THERE...
I SWEAR I'LL FIND HER!!
WHAT SHOULD I SAY TO HER...?
HOW... MUST SHE FEEL ABOUT ME NOW...?
REON!
MAMA ?!
MAMA ...

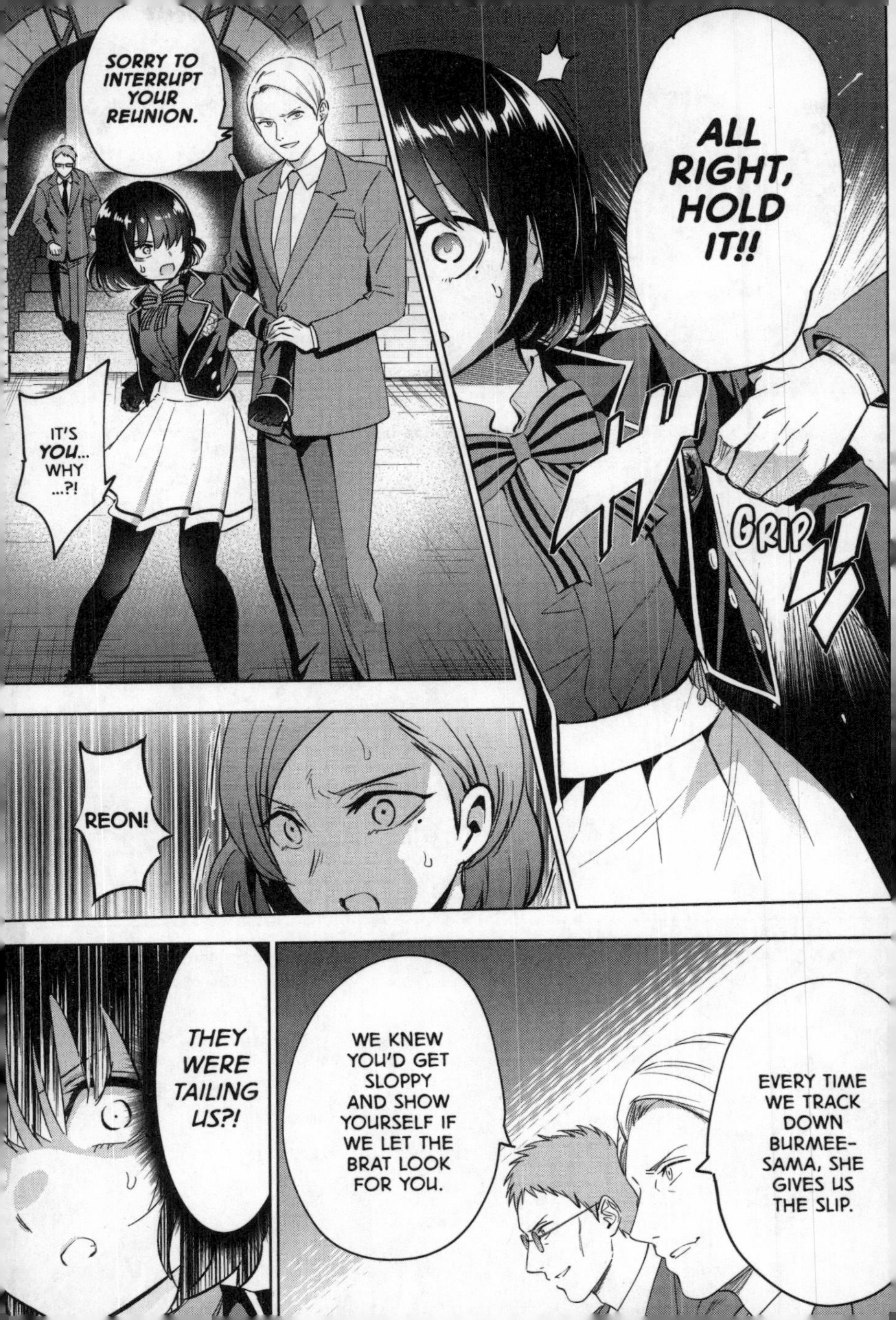
ALL RIGHT, HOLD IT!!
GRIP
SORRY TO INTERRUPT YOUR REUNION.
IT'S *YOU*... WHY ...?!
REON!
EVERY TIME WE TRACK DOWN BURMEE-SAMA, SHE GIVES US THE SLIP.
WE KNEW YOU'D GET SLOPPY AND SHOW YOURSELF IF WE LET THE BRAT LOOK FOR YOU.
*THEY WERE TAILING US?!*

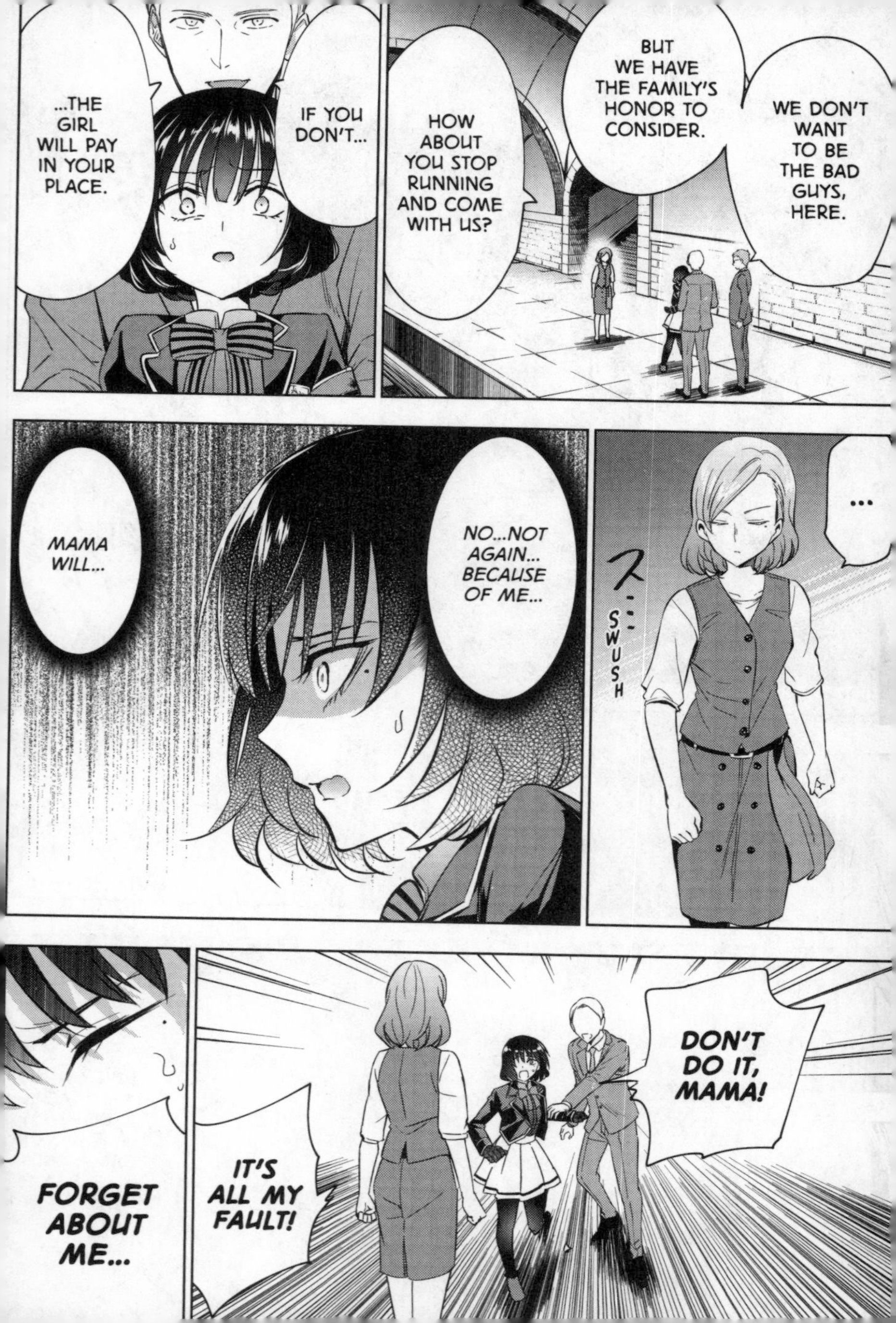
WE DON'T WANT TO BE THE BAD GUYS, HERE.
BUT WE HAVE THE FAMILY'S HONOR TO CONSIDER.
HOW ABOUT YOU STOP RUNNING AND COME WITH US?
IF YOU DON'T...
...THE GIRL WILL PAY IN YOUR PLACE.
...
SWUSH
NO...NOT AGAIN... BECAUSE OF ME...
MAMA WILL...
DON'T DO IT, MAMA!
IT'S ALL MY FAULT!
FORGET ABOUT ME...

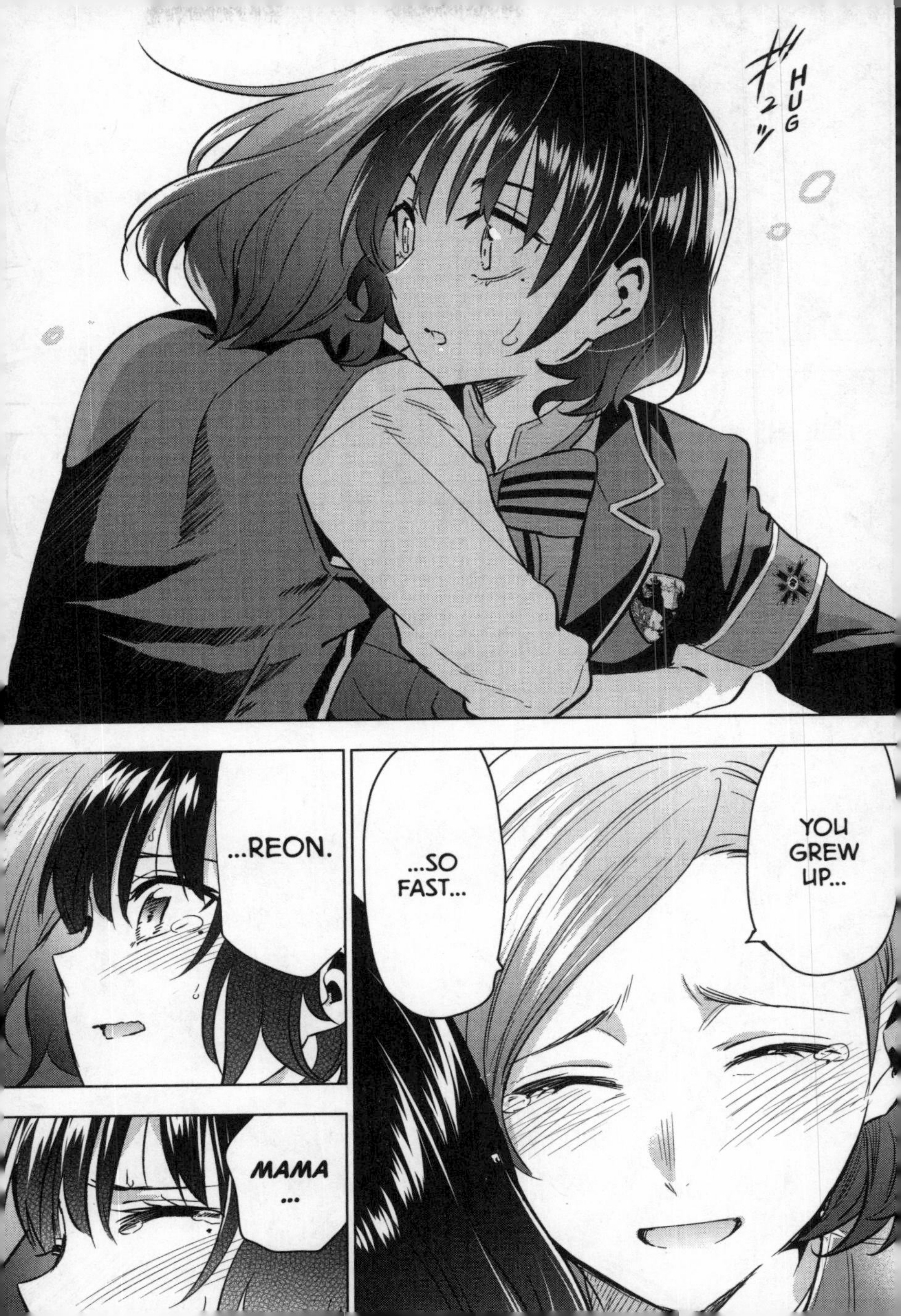
HUG
YOU GREW UP...
...SO FAST...
...REON.
MAMA ...

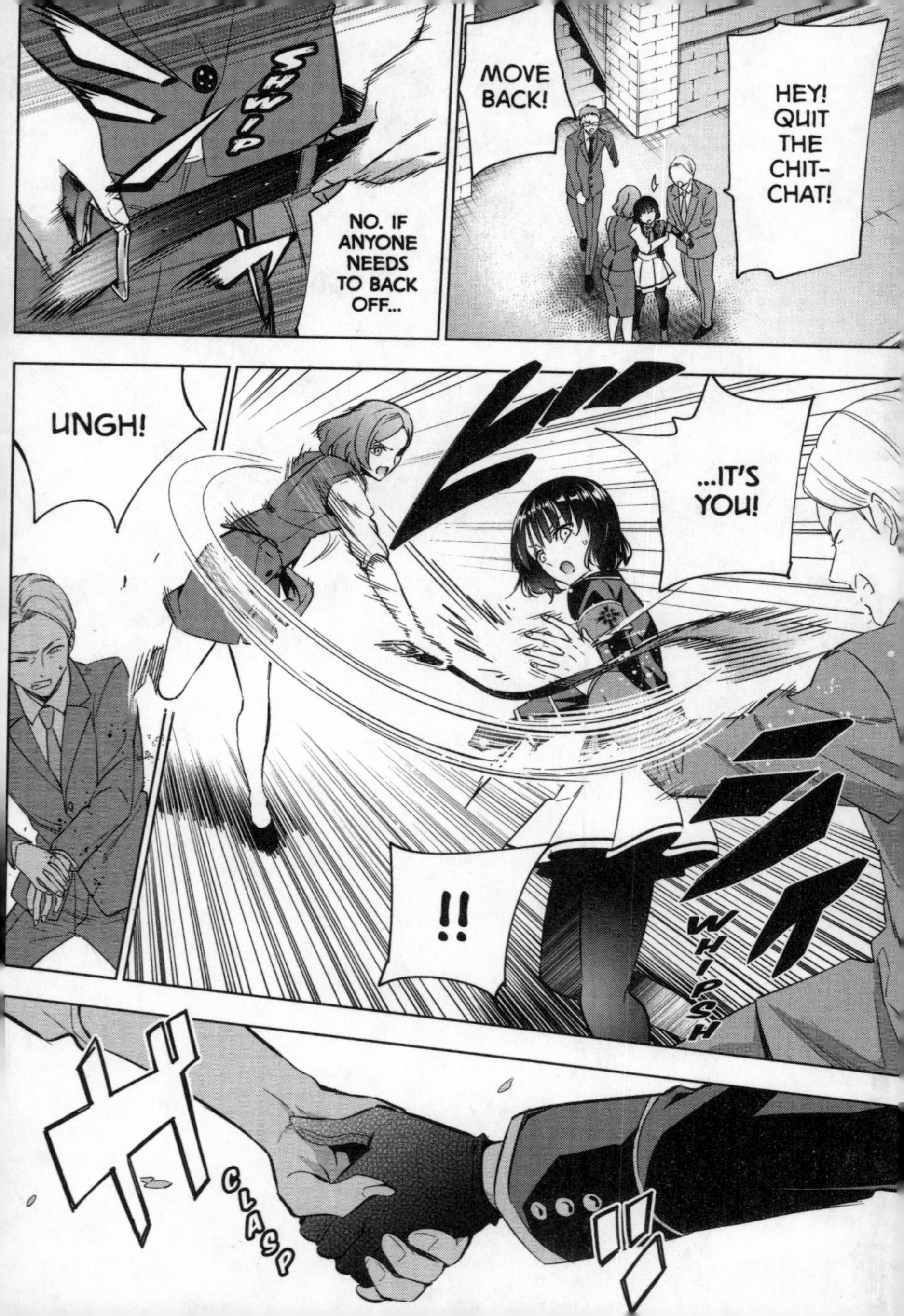
HEY! QUIT THE CHIT-CHAT!
MOVE BACK!
SHWIP
NO. IF ANYONE NEEDS TO BACK OFF...
...IT'S YOU!
UNGH!
!!
WHIPSH
CLASP

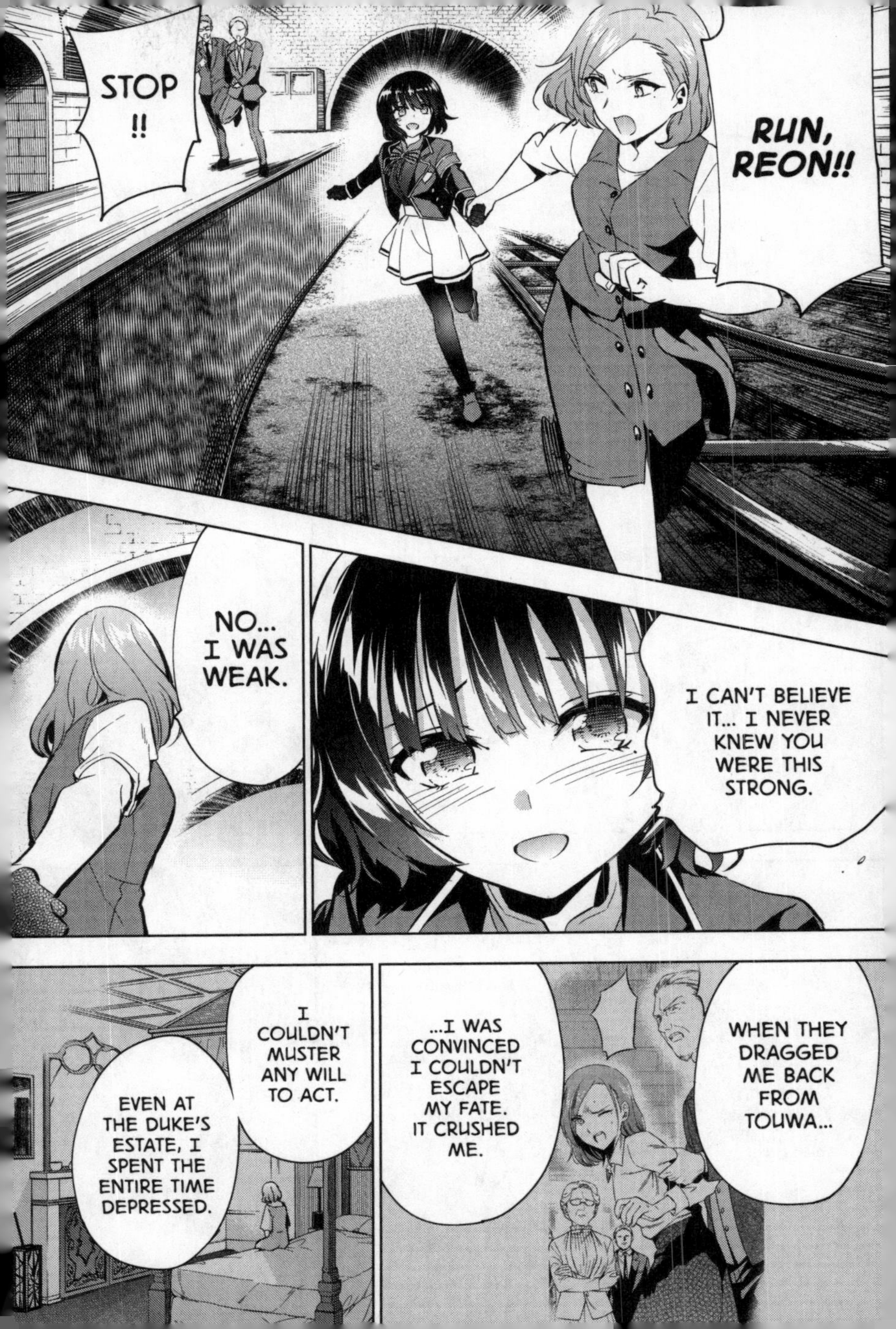
RUN, REON!!
STOP !!
I CAN'T BELIEVE IT... I NEVER KNEW YOU WERE THIS STRONG.
NO... I WAS WEAK.
WHEN THEY DRAGGED ME BACK FROM TOUWA...
...I WAS CONVINCED I COULDN'T ESCAPE MY FATE. IT CRUSHED ME.
I COULDN'T MUSTER ANY WILL TO ACT.
EVEN AT THE DUKE'S ESTATE, I SPENT THE ENTIRE TIME DEPRESSED.

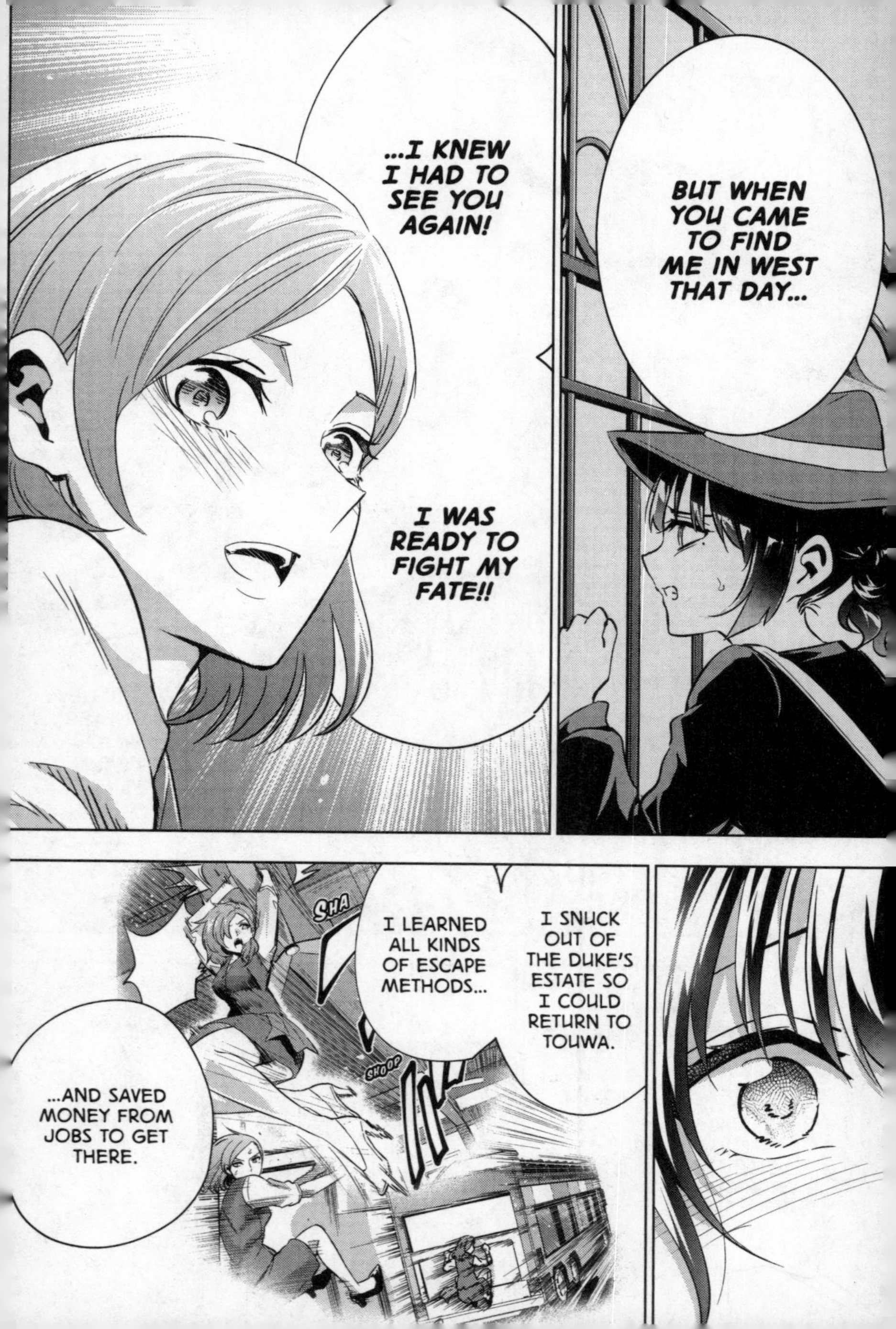
BUT WHEN YOU CAME TO FIND ME IN WEST THAT DAY...
...I KNEW I HAD TO SEE YOU AGAIN!
I WAS READY TO FIGHT MY FATE!!
I SNUCK OUT OF THE DUKE'S ESTATE SO I COULD RETURN TO TOUWA.
I LEARNED ALL KINDS OF ESCAPE METHODS...
SHA
SHOOP
...AND SAVED MONEY FROM JOBS TO GET THERE.

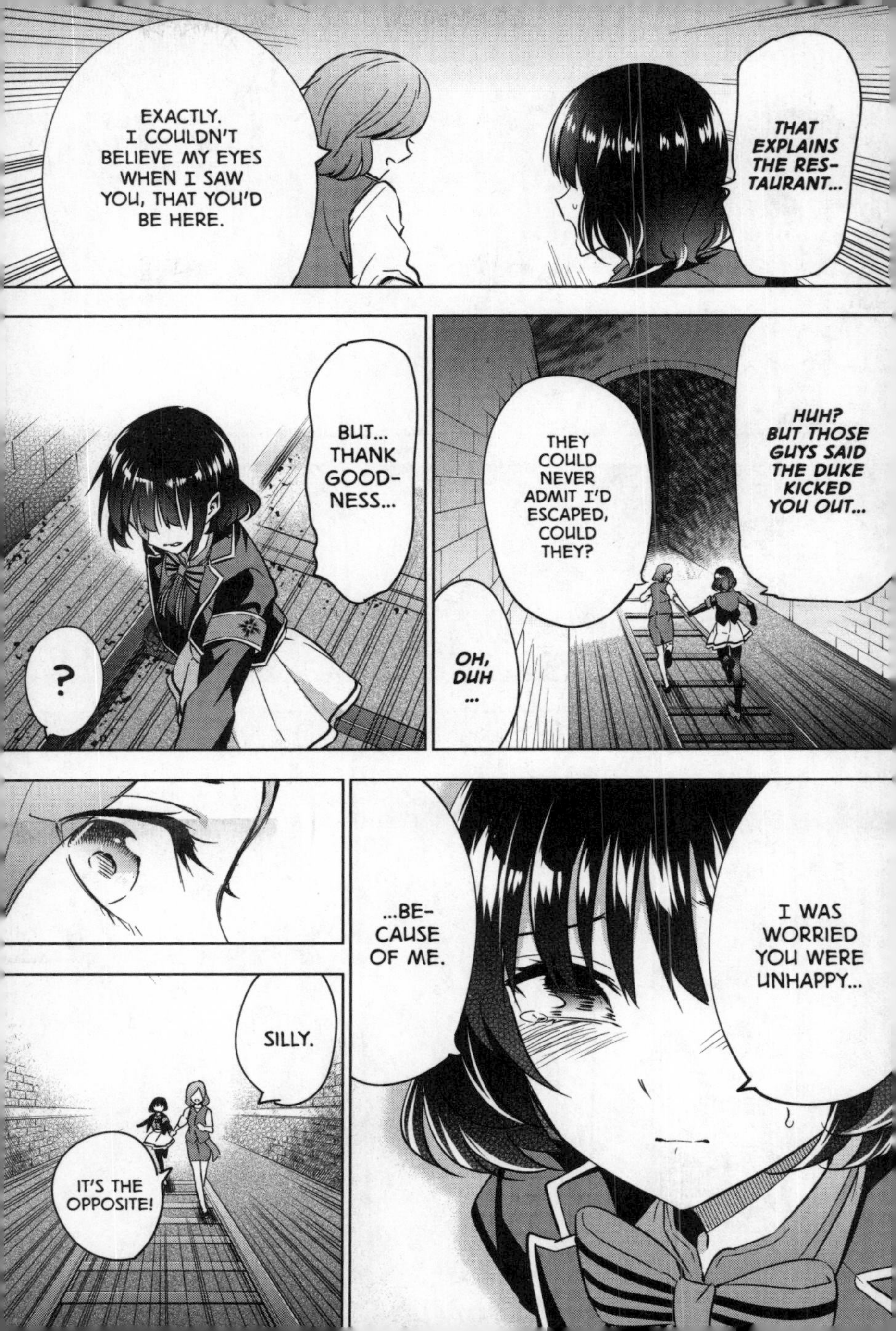
THAT EXPLAINS THE RES-TAURANT...
EXACTLY. I COULDN'T BELIEVE MY EYES WHEN I SAW YOU, THAT YOU'D BE HERE.
HUH? BUT THOSE GUYS SAID THE DUKE KICKED YOU OUT...
THEY COULD NEVER ADMIT I'D ESCAPED, COULD THEY?
OH, DUH ...
BUT... THANK GOOD-NESS...
?
I WAS WORRIED YOU WERE UNHAPPY...
...BE-CAUSE OF ME.
SILLY.
IT'S THE OPPOSITE!

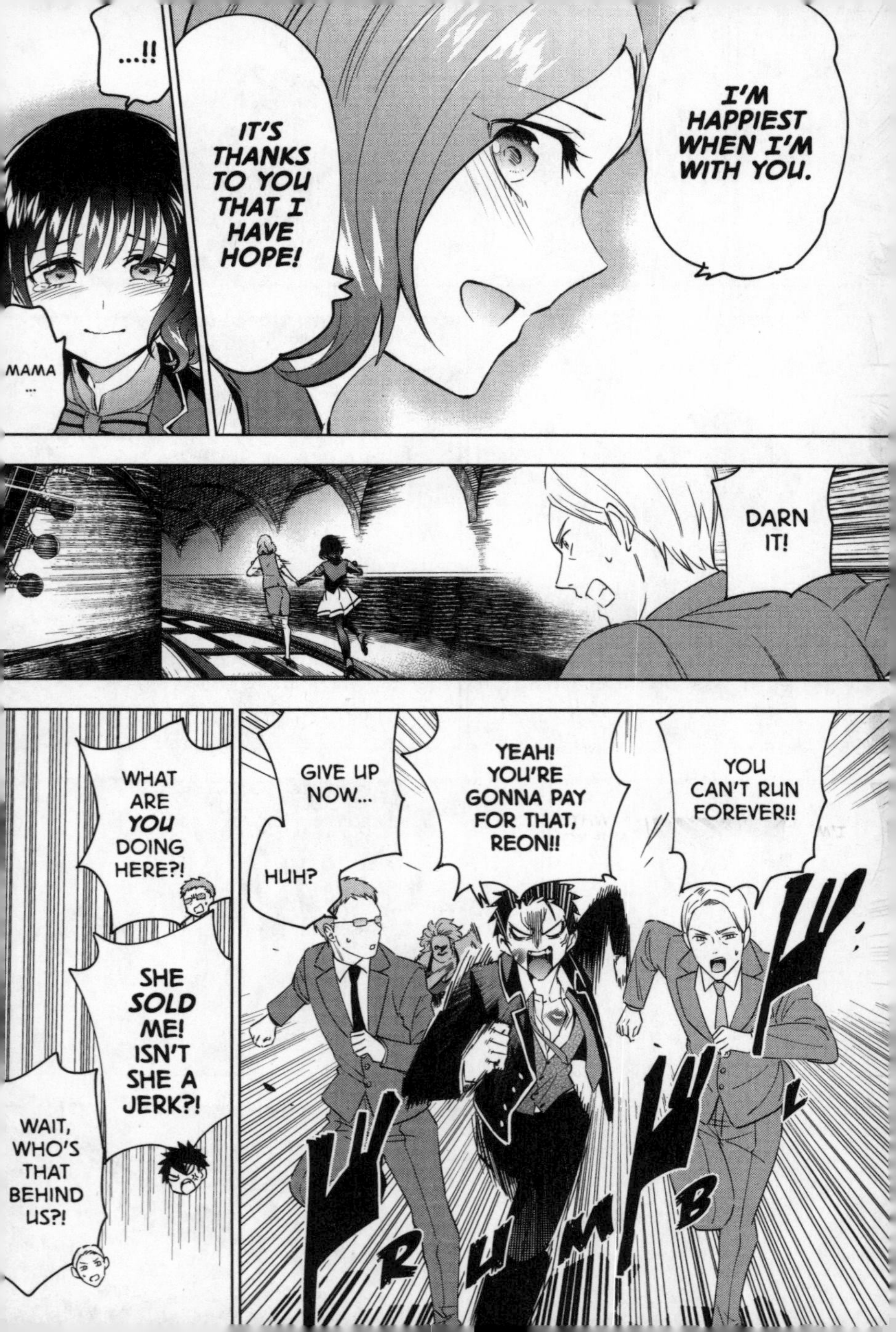
I'M HAPPIEST WHEN I'M WITH YOU.
IT'S THANKS TO YOU THAT I HAVE HOPE!
...!!
MAMA ...
DARN IT!
YOU CAN'T RUN FOREVER!!
YEAH! YOU'RE GONNA PAY FOR THAT, REON!!
GIVE UP NOW...
HUH?
RUMBL
WHAT ARE *YOU* DOING HERE?!
SHE *SOLD* ME! ISN'T SHE A JERK?!
WAIT, WHO'S THAT BEHIND US?!

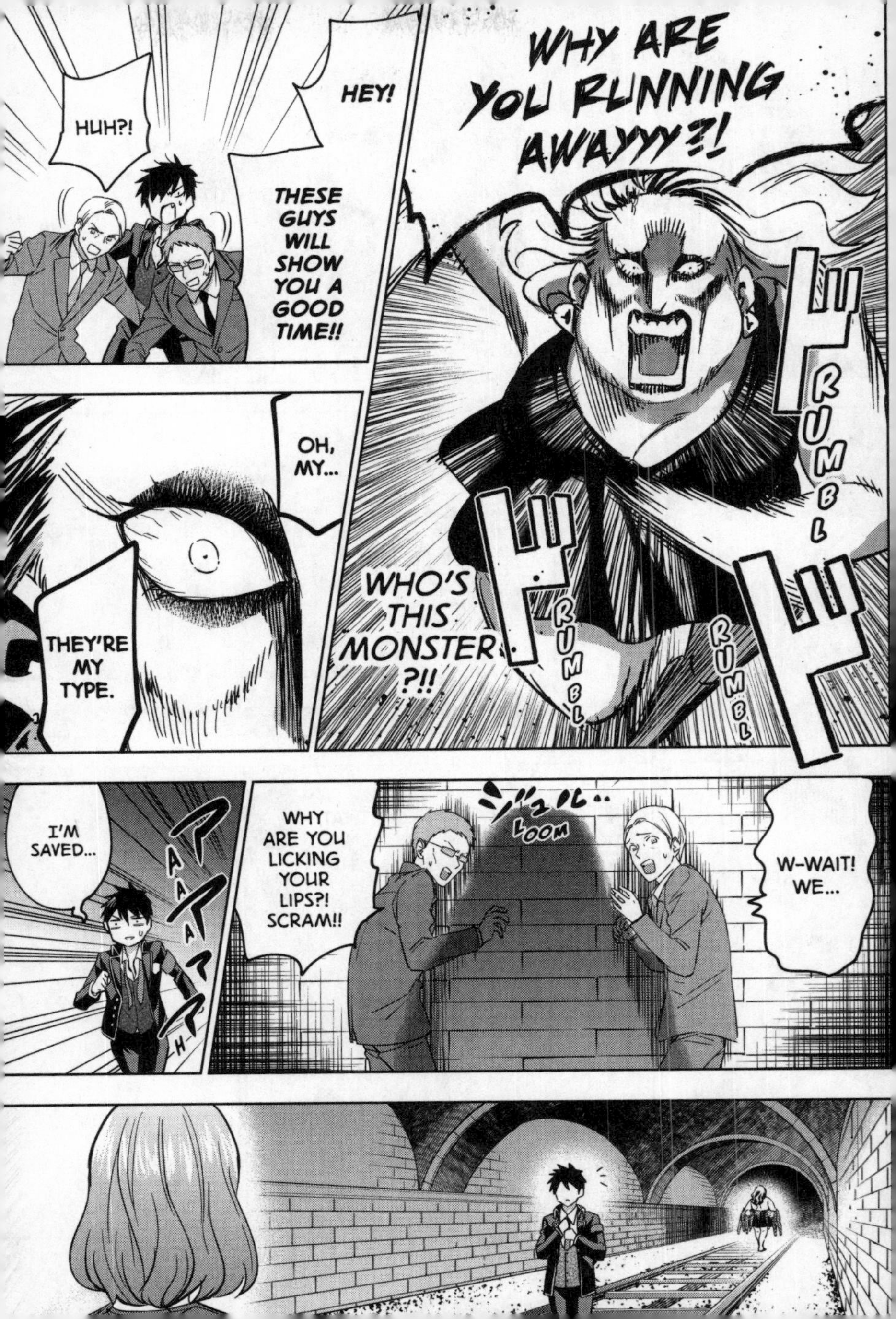

WHY ARE YOU RUNNING AWAYYY?!
RUMBL
WHO'S THIS MONSTER?!!
RUMBL
RUMBL
HEY!
THESE GUYS WILL SHOW YOU A GOOD TIME!!
HUH?!
OH, MY...
THEY'RE MY TYPE.
W-WAIT! WE...
LOOM
WHY ARE YOU LICKING YOUR LIPS?! SCRAM!!
AAAAAH
I'M SAVED...

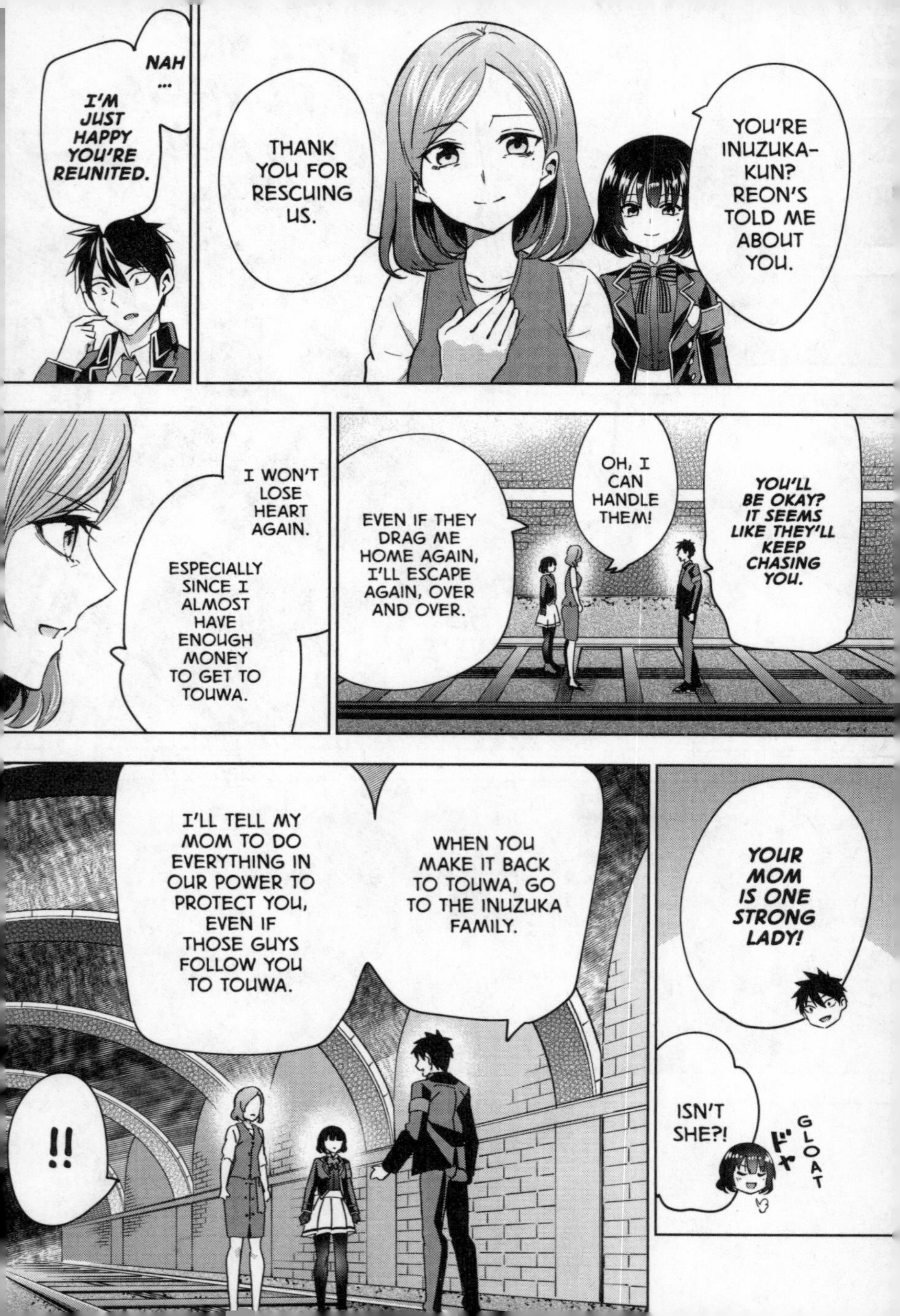
YOU'RE INUZUKA-KUN? REON'S TOLD ME ABOUT YOU.
THANK YOU FOR RESCUING US.
NAH ... I'M JUST HAPPY YOU'RE REUNITED.
YOU'LL BE OKAY? IT SEEMS LIKE THEY'LL KEEP CHASING YOU.
OH, I CAN HANDLE THEM!
EVEN IF THEY DRAG ME HOME AGAIN, I'LL ESCAPE AGAIN, OVER AND OVER.
I WON'T LOSE HEART AGAIN.
ESPECIALLY SINCE I ALMOST HAVE ENOUGH MONEY TO GET TO TOUWA.
YOUR MOM IS ONE STRONG LADY!
ISN'T SHE?!
ドヤ GLOAT
WHEN YOU MAKE IT BACK TO TOUWA, GO TO THE INUZUKA FAMILY.
I'LL TELL MY MOM TO DO EVERYTHING IN OUR POWER TO PROTECT YOU, EVEN IF THOSE GUYS FOLLOW YOU TO TOUWA.
!!

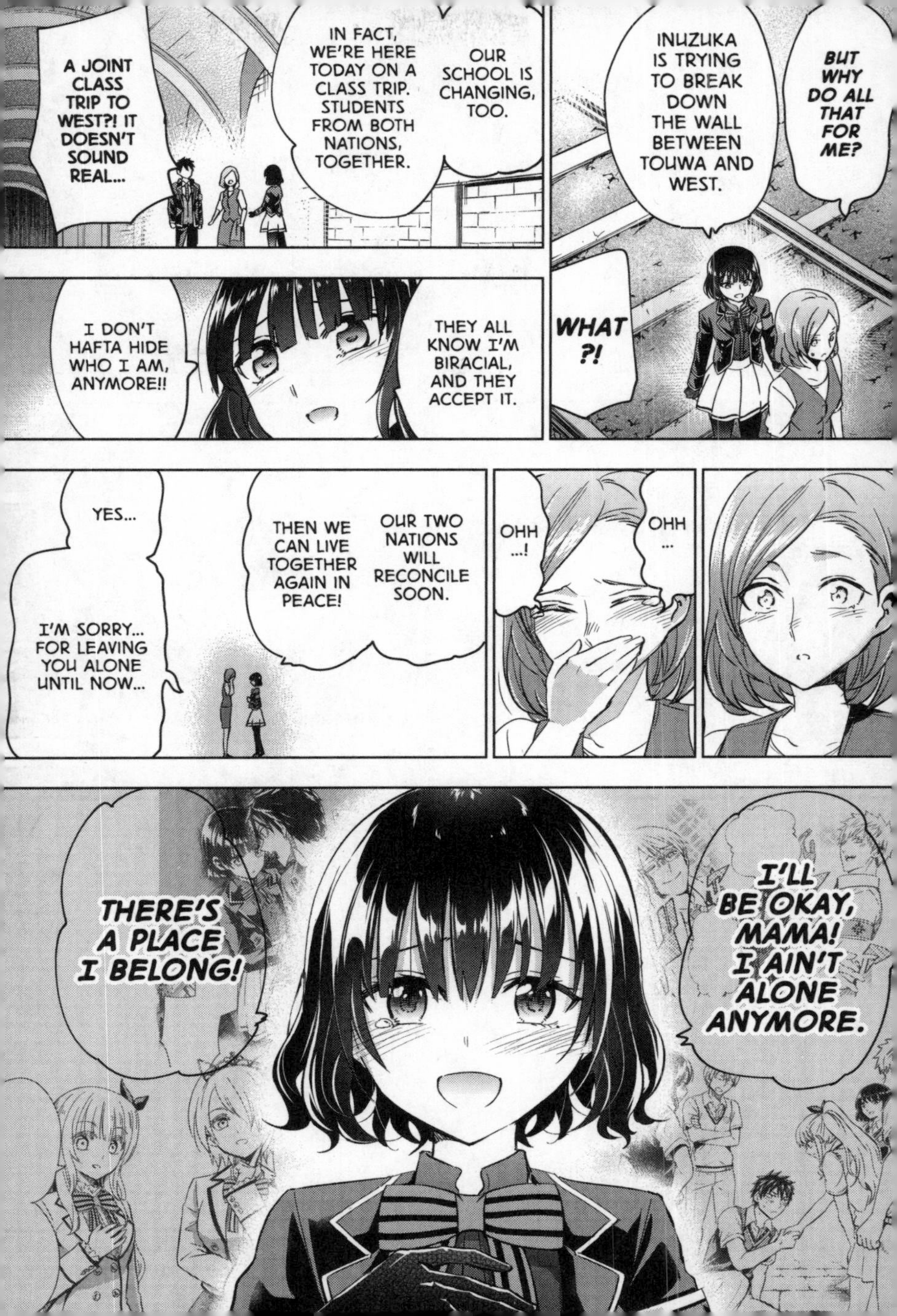
BUT WHY DO ALL THAT FOR ME?
INUZUKA IS TRYING TO BREAK DOWN THE WALL BETWEEN TOUWA AND WEST.
WHAT?!
OUR SCHOOL IS CHANGING, TOO.
IN FACT, WE'RE HERE TODAY ON A CLASS TRIP. STUDENTS FROM BOTH NATIONS, TOGETHER.
A JOINT CLASS TRIP TO WEST?! IT DOESN'T SOUND REAL...
THEY ALL KNOW I'M BIRACIAL, AND THEY ACCEPT IT.
I DON'T HAFTA HIDE WHO I AM, ANYMORE!!
OHH ...
OHH ...!
OUR TWO NATIONS WILL RECONCILE SOON.
THEN WE CAN LIVE TOGETHER AGAIN IN PEACE!
YES...
I'M SORRY... FOR LEAVING YOU ALONE UNTIL NOW...
I'LL BE OKAY, MAMA! I AIN'T ALONE ANYMORE.
THERE'S A PLACE I BELONG!

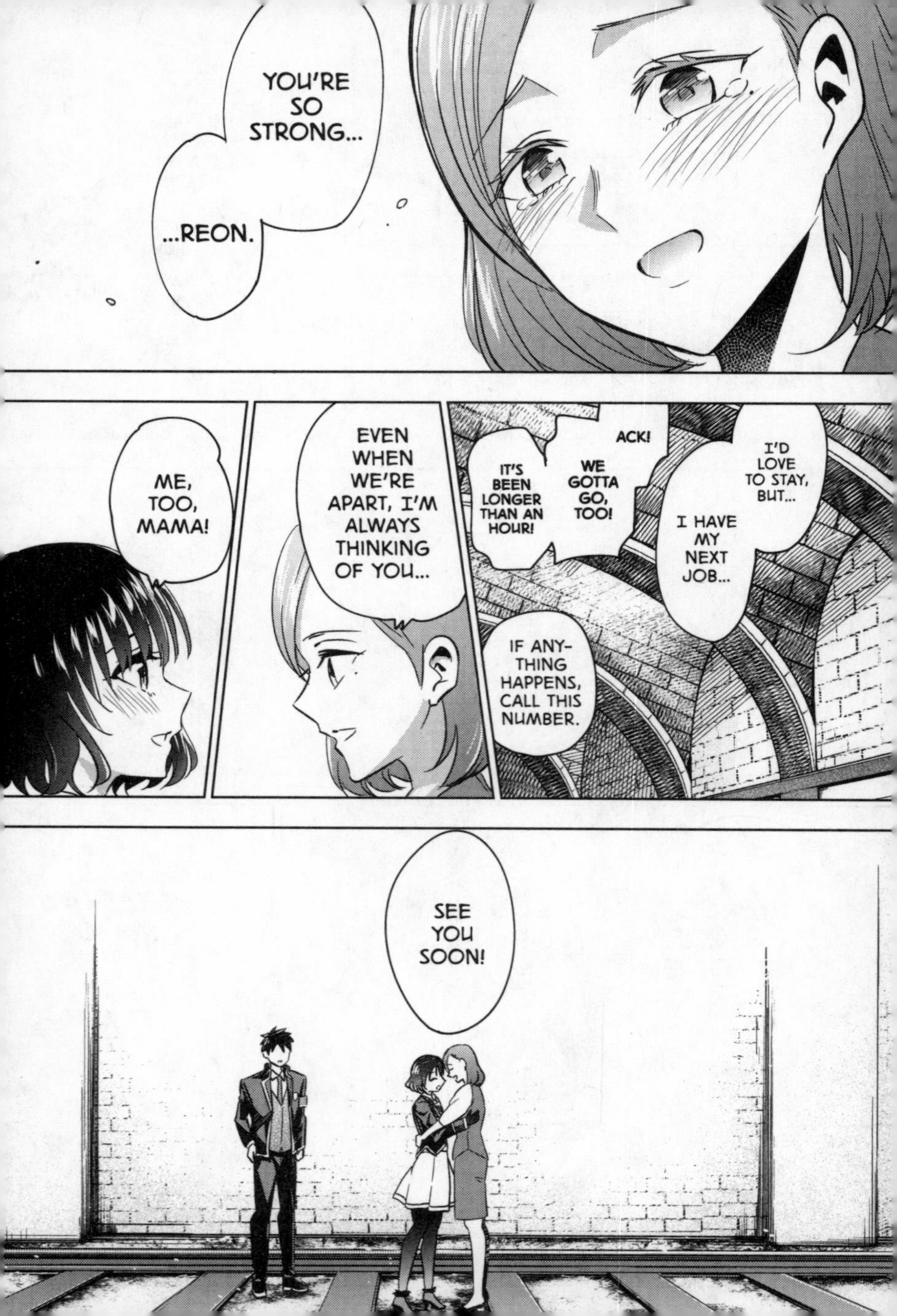
YOU'RE SO STRONG...
...REON.
I'D LOVE TO STAY, BUT...
I HAVE MY NEXT JOB...
ACK!
WE GOTTA GO, TOO!
IT'S BEEN LONGER THAN AN HOUR!
IF ANYTHING HAPPENS, CALL THIS NUMBER.
EVEN WHEN WE'RE APART, I'M ALWAYS THINKING OF YOU...
ME, TOO, MAMA!
SEE YOU SOON!

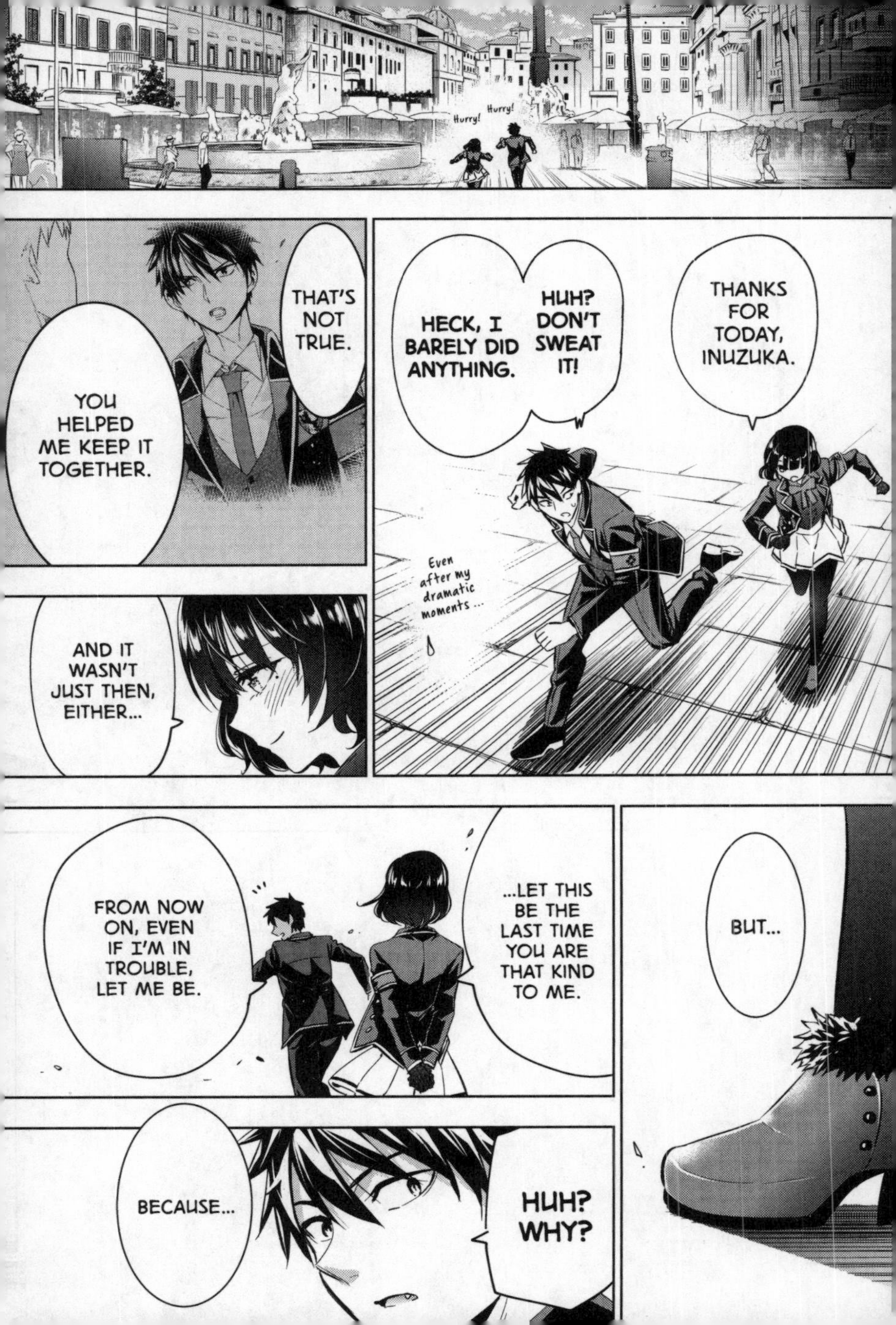
Hurry!
Hurry!
THANKS FOR TODAY, INUZUKA.
HUH? DON'T SWEAT IT!
HECK, I BARELY DID ANYTHING.
Even after my dramatic moments ...
THAT'S NOT TRUE.
YOU HELPED ME KEEP IT TOGETHER.
AND IT WASN'T JUST THEN, EITHER...
BUT...
...LET THIS BE THE LAST TIME YOU ARE THAT KIND TO ME.
FROM NOW ON, EVEN IF I'M IN TROUBLE, LET ME BE.
HUH? WHY?
BECAUSE...

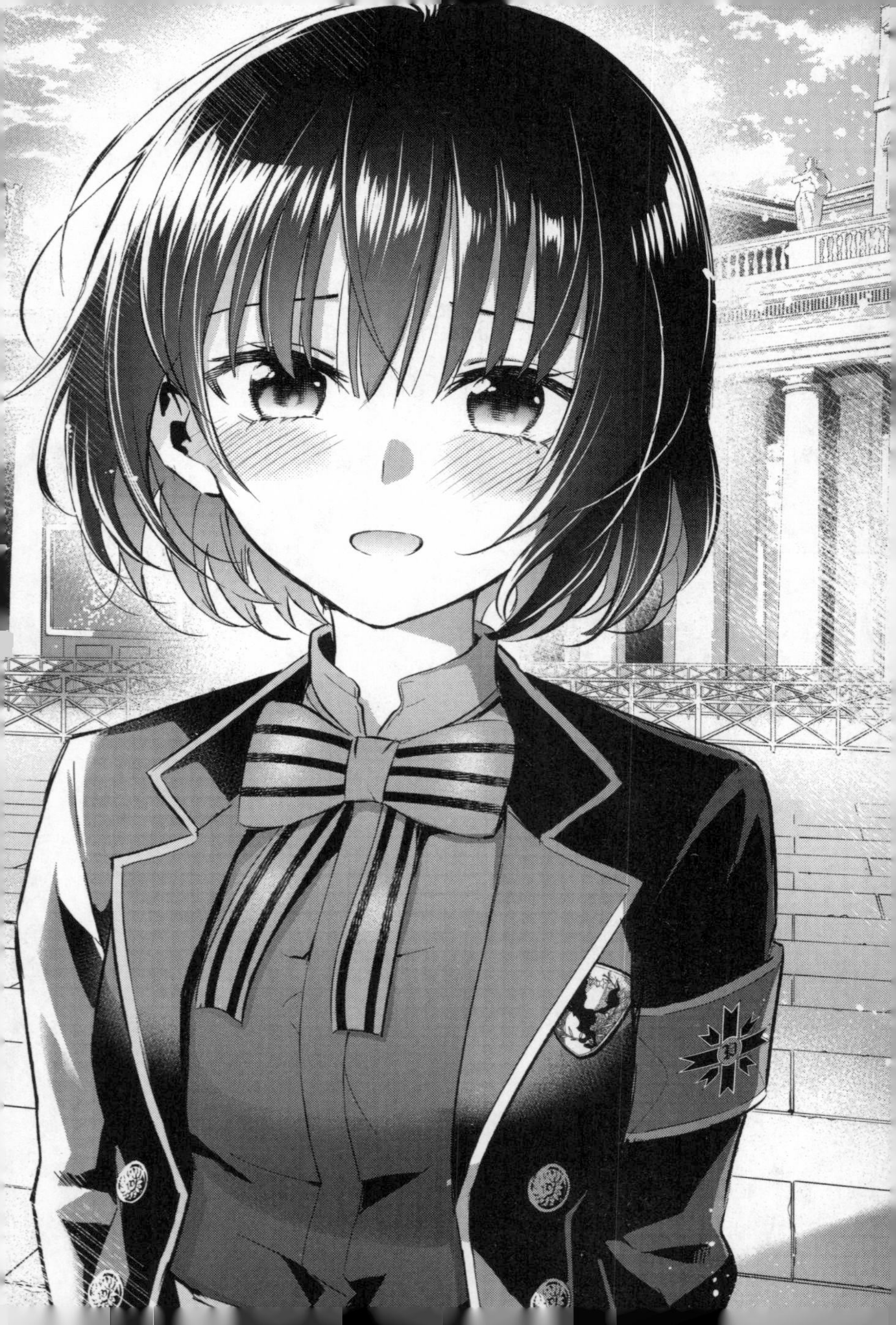

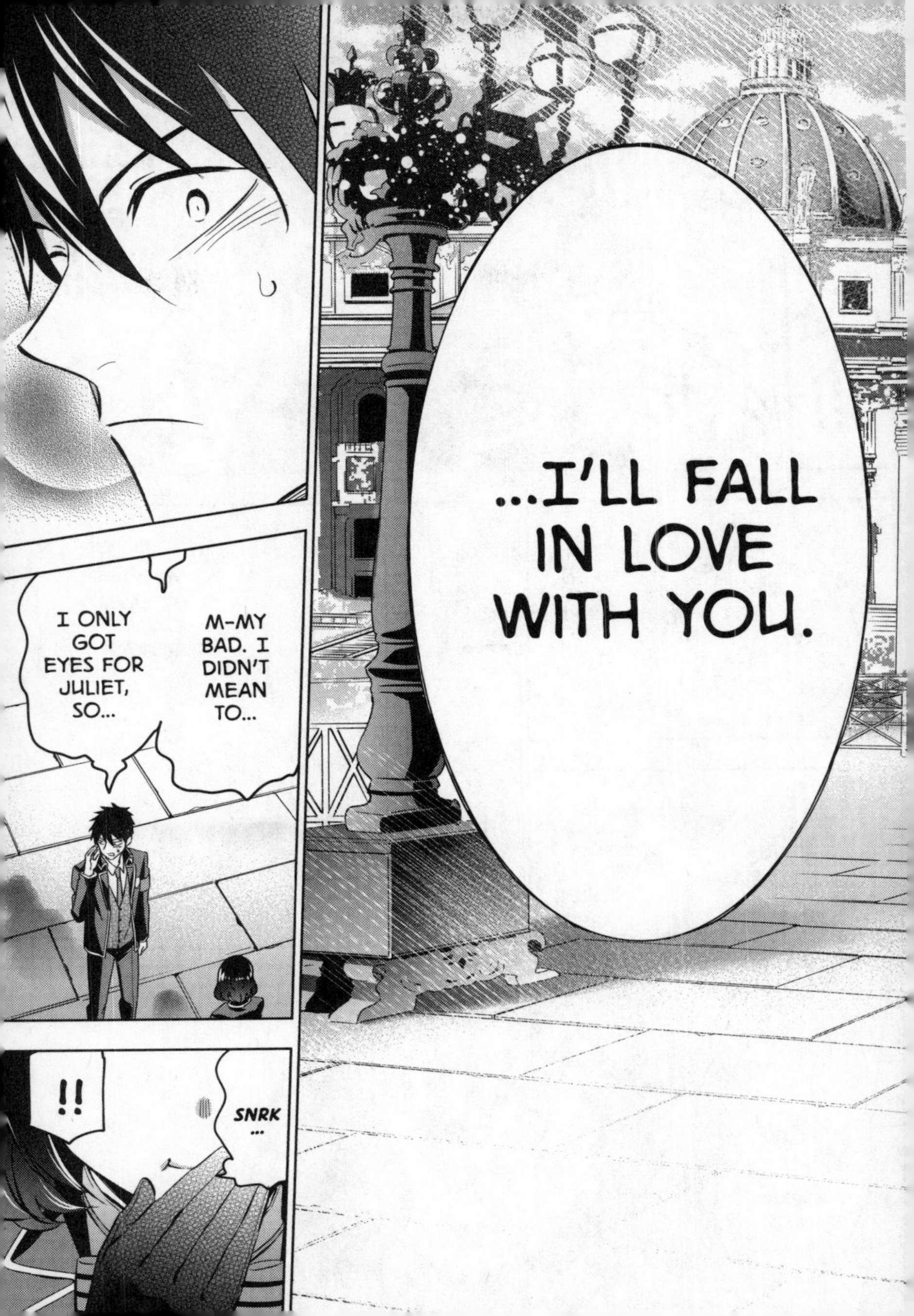
...I'LL FALL IN LOVE WITH YOU.
M-MY BAD. I DIDN'T MEAN TO...
I ONLY GOT EYES FOR JULIET, SO...
SNRK...
!!

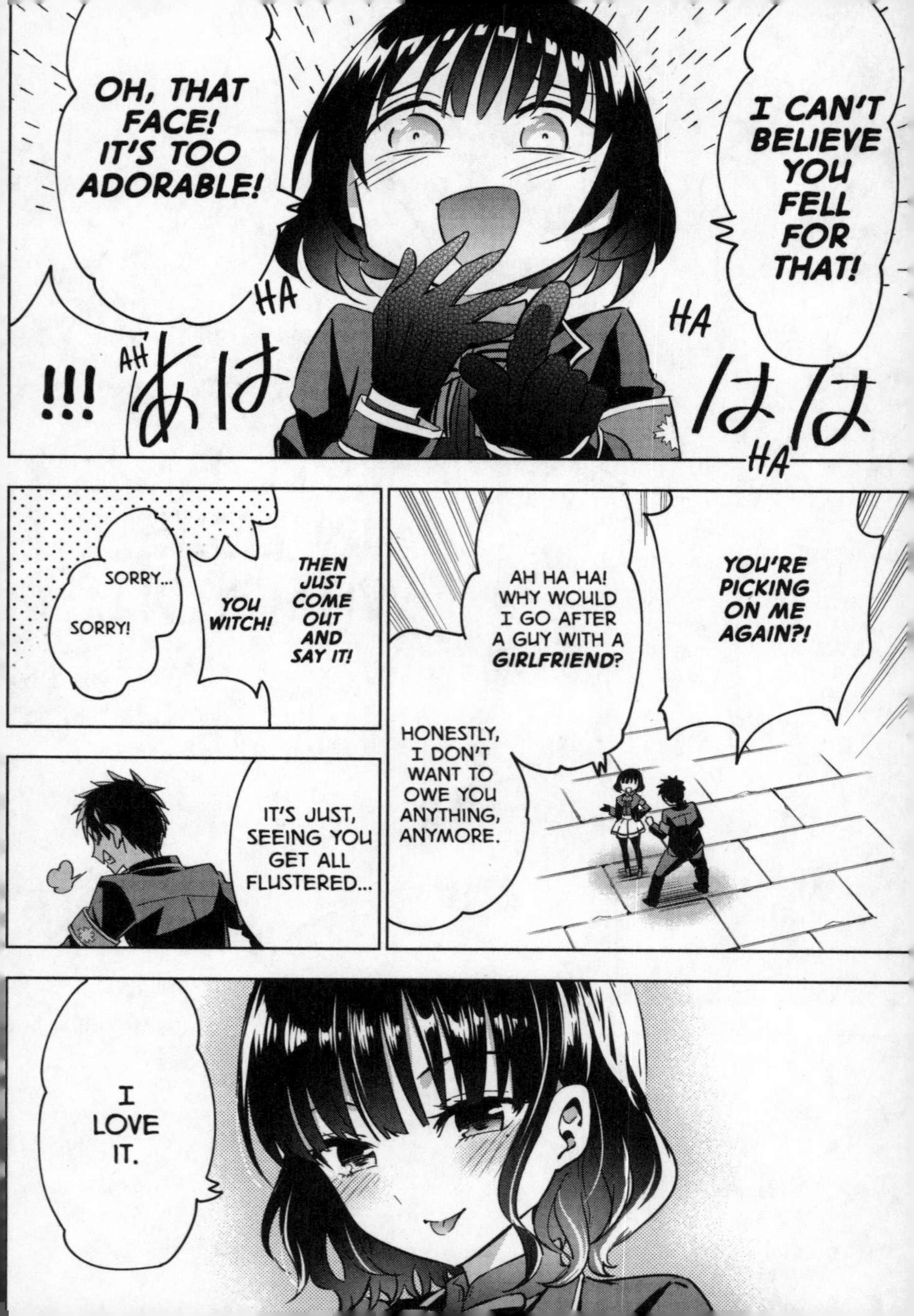
I CAN'T BELIEVE YOU FELL FOR THAT!
OH, THAT FACE! IT'S TOO ADORABLE!
HA はは HA
!!! AH あは HA
YOU'RE PICKING ON ME AGAIN?!
AH HA HA! WHY WOULD I GO AFTER A GUY WITH A GIRLFRIEND?
HONESTLY, I DON'T WANT TO OWE YOU ANYTHING, ANYMORE.
THEN JUST COME OUT AND SAY IT!
YOU WITCH!
SORRY...
SORRY!
IT'S JUST, SEEING YOU GET ALL FLUSTERED...
I LOVE IT.

Boarding
School *Juliet*

To LOVE, or not to LOVE

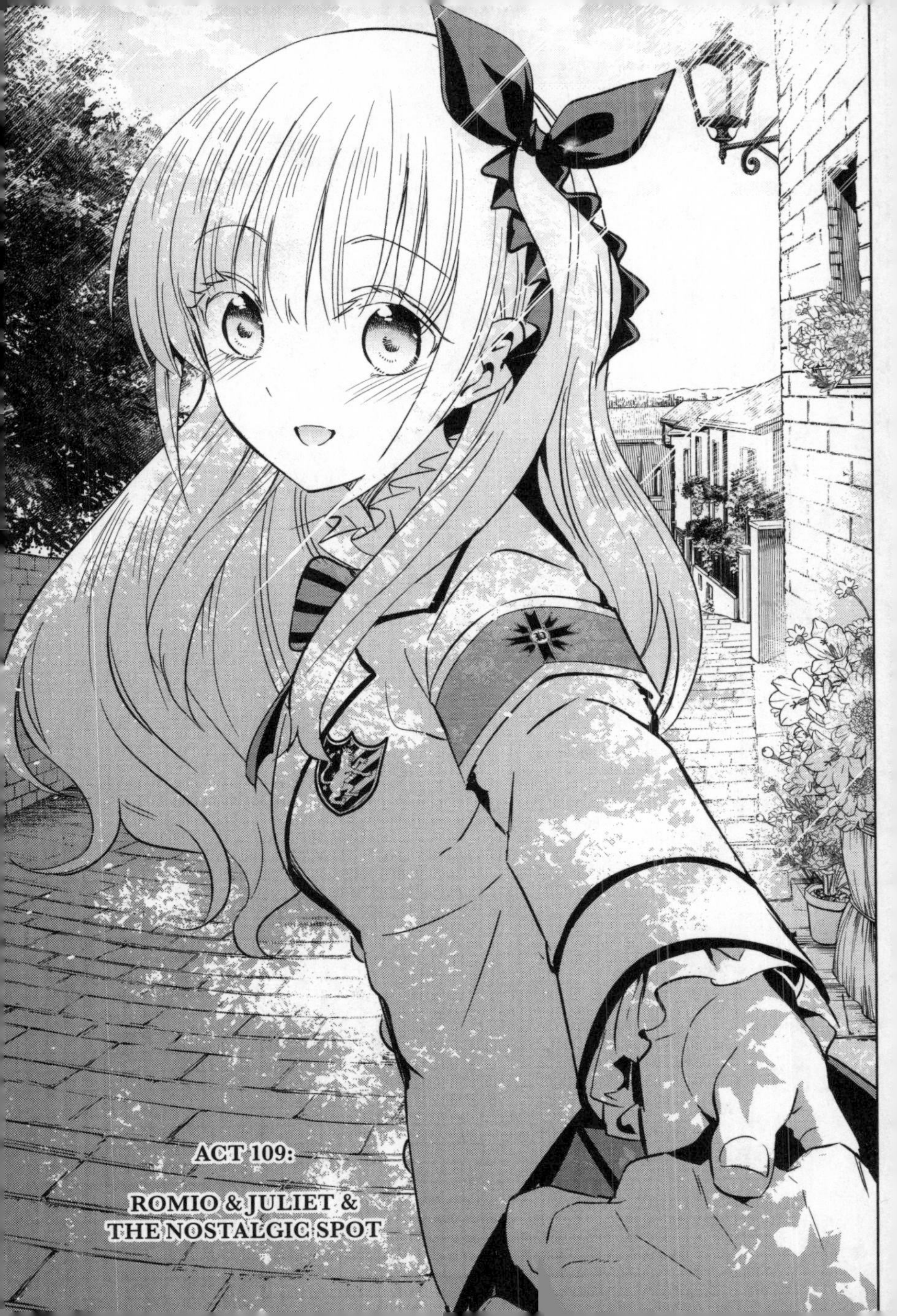
ACT 109:
ROMIO & JULIET &
THE NOSTALGIC SPOT

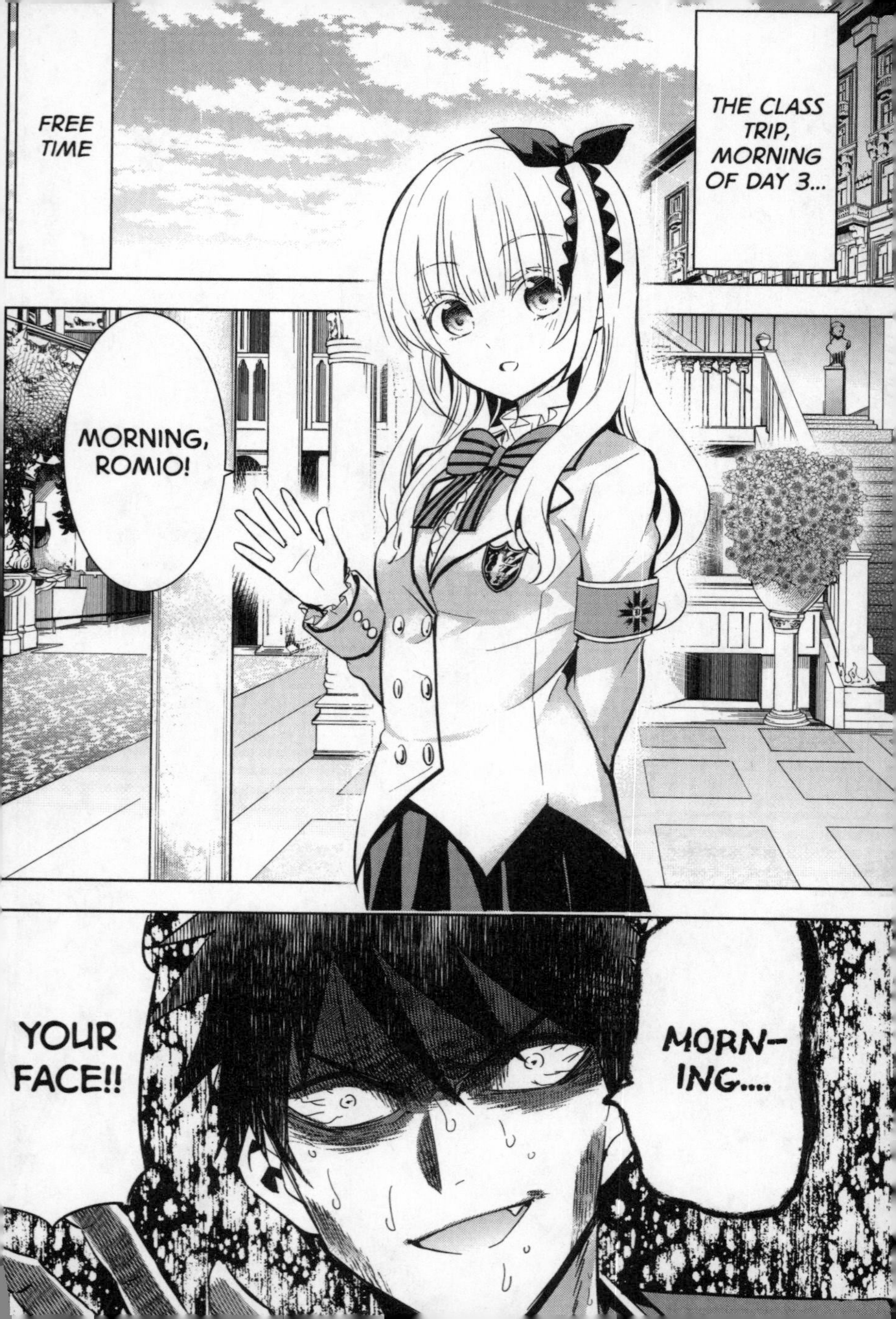
THE CLASS TRIP, MORNING OF DAY 3...
FREE TIME
MORNING, ROMIO!
MORN-ING....
YOUR FACE!!

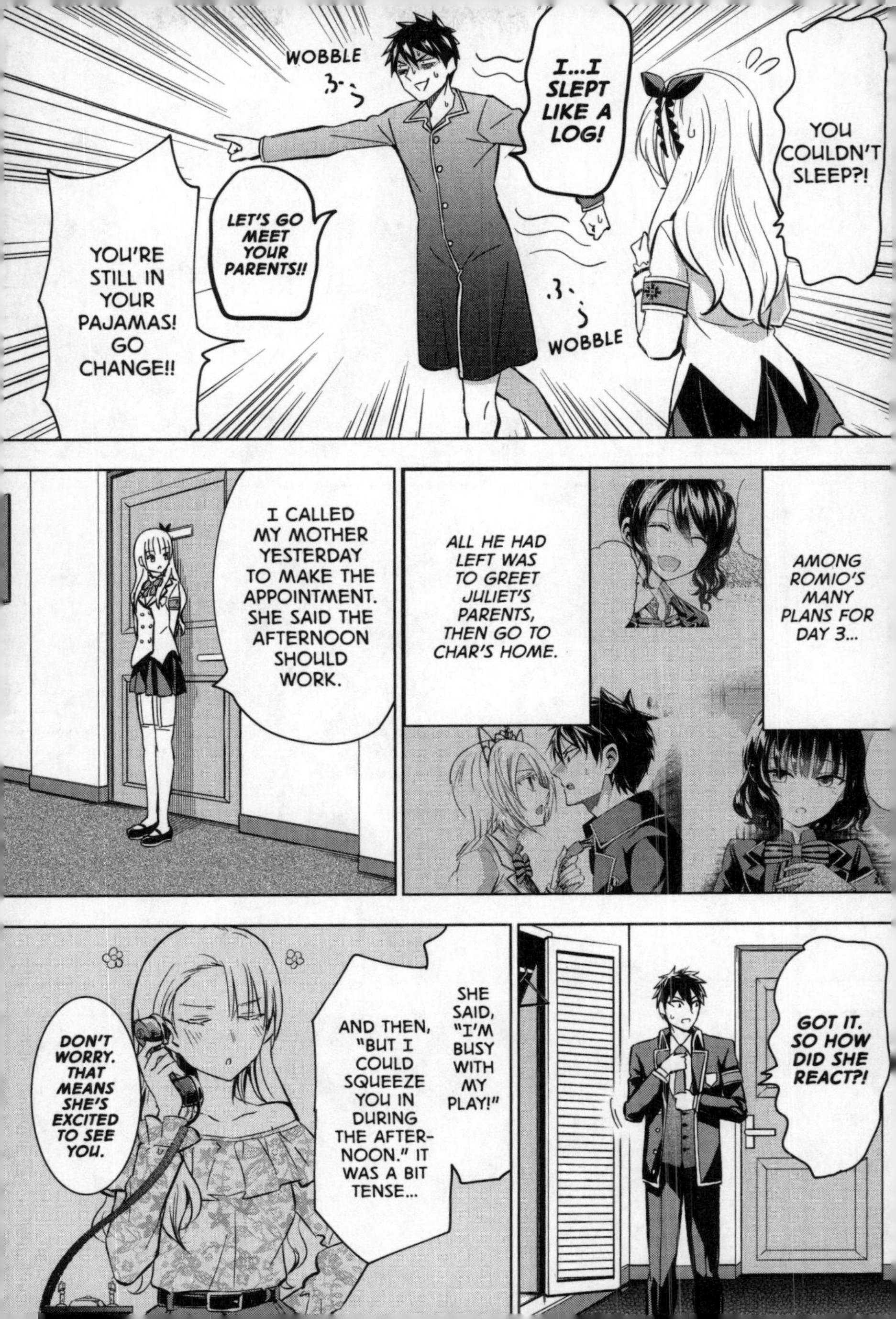
YOU COULDN'T SLEEP?!
I...I SLEPT LIKE A LOG!
WOBBLE
LET'S GO MEET YOUR PARENTS!!
WOBBLE
YOU'RE STILL IN YOUR PAJAMAS! GO CHANGE!!
AMONG ROMIO'S MANY PLANS FOR DAY 3...
ALL HE HAD LEFT WAS TO GREET JULIET'S PARENTS, THEN GO TO CHAR'S HOME.
I CALLED MY MOTHER YESTERDAY TO MAKE THE APPOINTMENT. SHE SAID THE AFTERNOON SHOULD WORK.
GOT IT. SO HOW DID SHE REACT?!
SHE SAID, "I'M BUSY WITH MY PLAY!"
AND THEN, "BUT I COULD SQUEEZE YOU IN DURING THE AFTER-NOON." IT WAS A BIT TENSE...
DON'T WORRY. THAT MEANS SHE'S EXCITED TO SEE YOU.

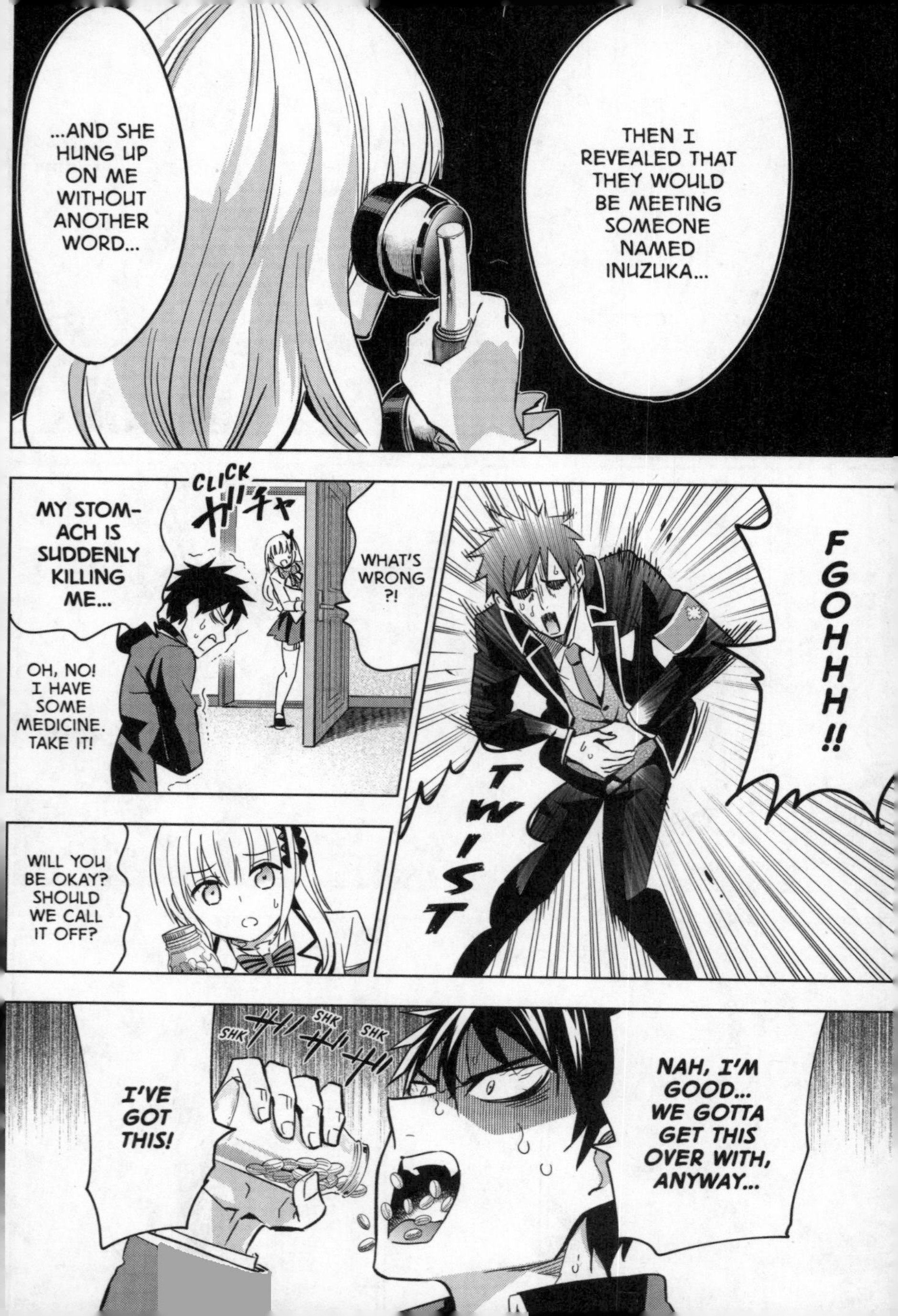
THEN I REVEALED THAT THEY WOULD BE MEETING SOMEONE NAMED INUZUKA...
...AND SHE HUNG UP ON ME WITHOUT ANOTHER WORD...
FGOHHH!!
TWIST
CLICK
ガチャ
WHAT'S WRONG?!
MY STOMACH IS SUDDENLY KILLING ME...
OH, NO! I HAVE SOME MEDICINE. TAKE IT!
WILL YOU BE OKAY? SHOULD WE CALL IT OFF?
NAH, I'M GOOD... WE GOTTA GET THIS OVER WITH, ANYWAY...
SHK
SHK
SHK
I'VE GOT THIS!

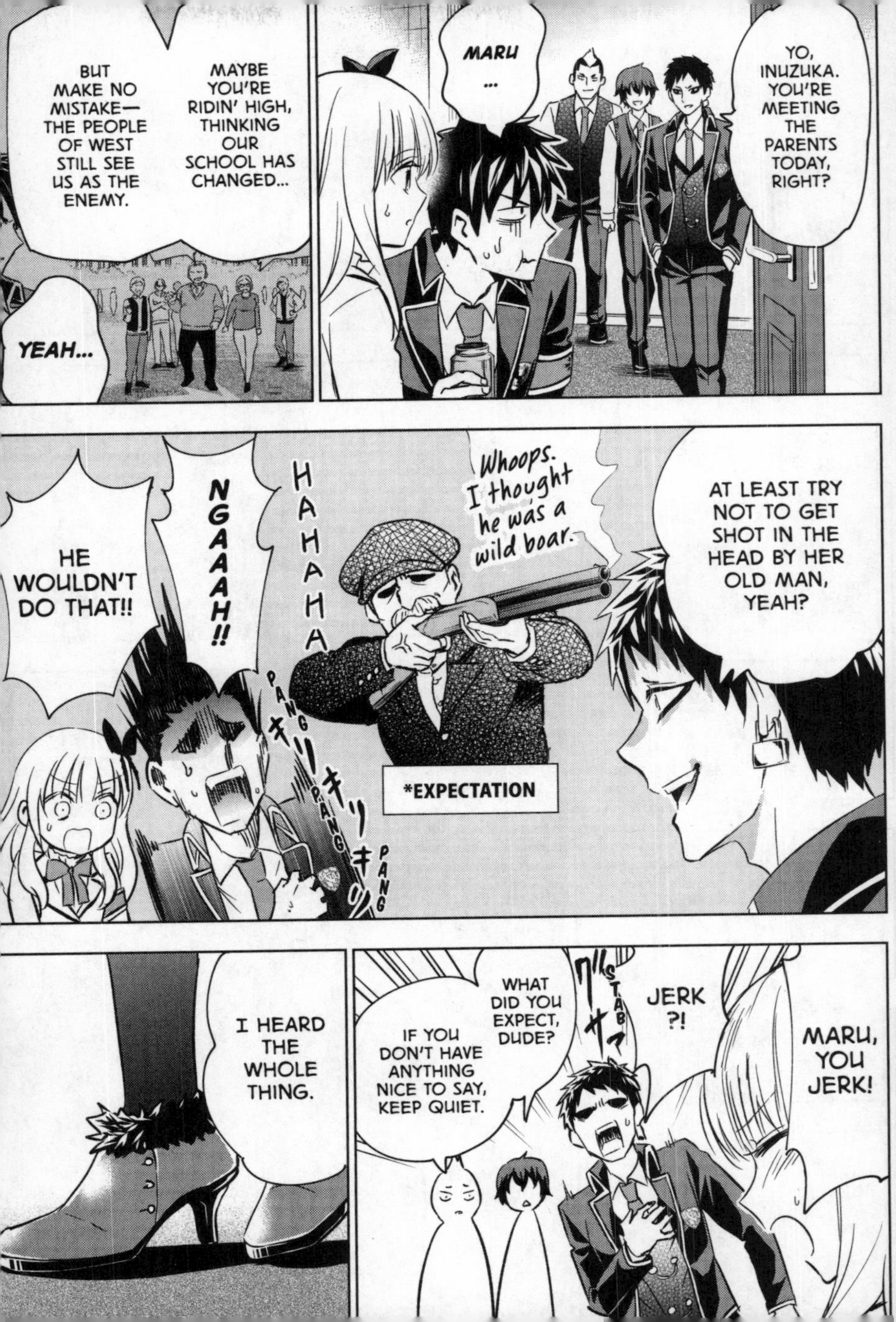
YO, INUZUKA. YOU'RE MEETING THE PARENTS TODAY, RIGHT?
MARU ...
MAYBE YOU'RE RIDIN' HIGH, THINKING OUR SCHOOL HAS CHANGED...
BUT MAKE NO MISTAKE— THE PEOPLE OF WEST STILL SEE US AS THE ENEMY.
YEAH...
AT LEAST TRY NOT TO GET SHOT IN THE HEAD BY HER OLD MAN, YEAH?
Whoops. I thought he was a wild boar.
*EXPECTATION
HAHAHAHA
NGAAAAH!!
HE WOULDN'T DO THAT!!
PANG
PANG
PANG
PANG
MARU, YOU JERK!
JERK ?!
STAB
WHAT DID YOU EXPECT, DUDE?
IF YOU DON'T HAVE ANYTHING NICE TO SAY, KEEP QUIET.
I HEARD THE WHOLE THING.

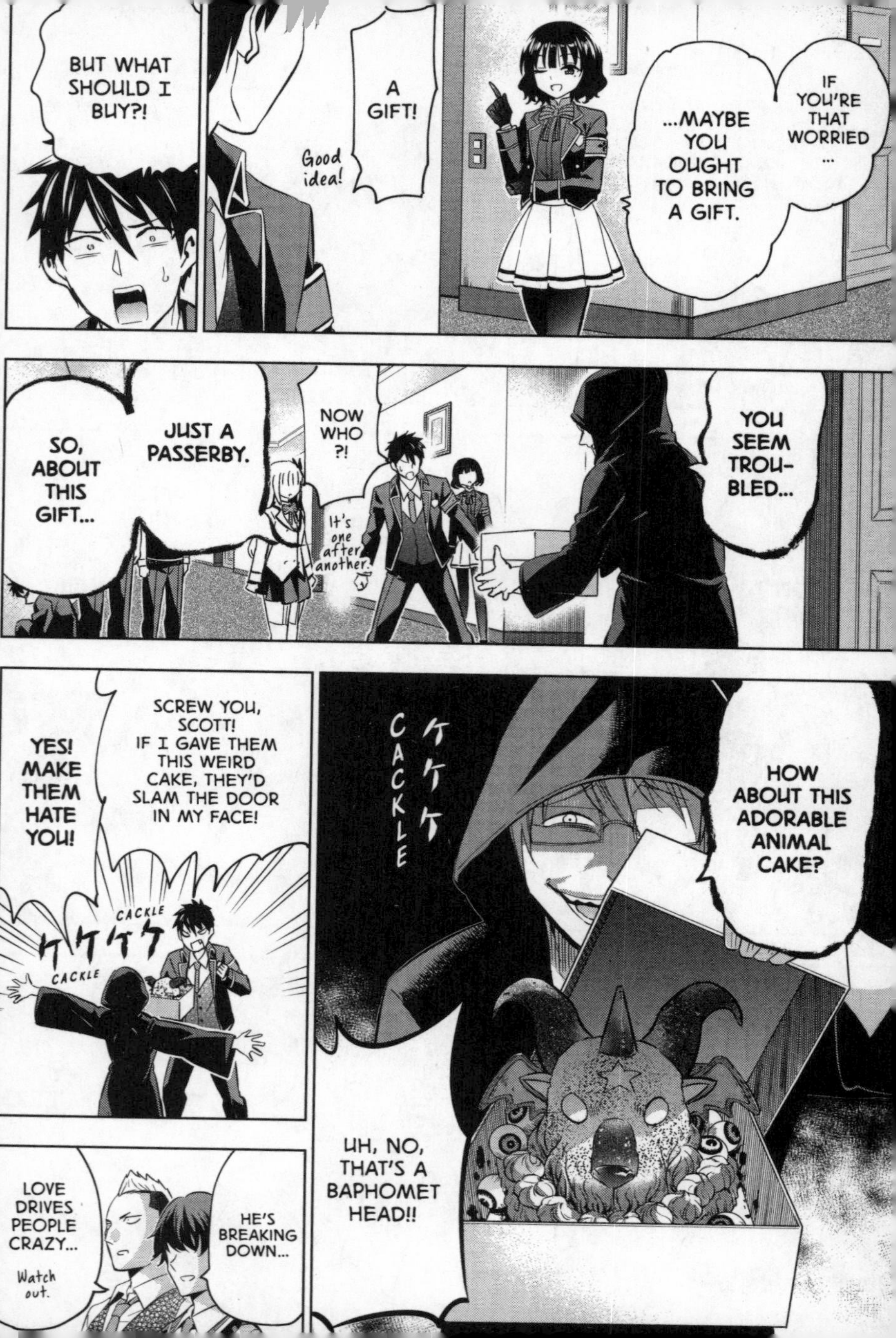
IF YOU'RE THAT WORRIED ...
...MAYBE YOU OUGHT TO BRING A GIFT.
A GIFT!
Good idea!
BUT WHAT SHOULD I BUY?!
YOU SEEM TROU-BLED...
NOW WHO ?!
It's one after another.
JUST A PASSERBY.
SO, ABOUT THIS GIFT...
HOW ABOUT THIS ADORABLE ANIMAL CAKE?
ケケケ
CACKLE
UH, NO, THAT'S A BAPHOMET HEAD!!
SCREW YOU, SCOTT! IF I GAVE THEM THIS WEIRD CAKE, THEY'D SLAM THE DOOR IN MY FACE!
YES! MAKE THEM HATE YOU!
ケケケケ
CACKLE
CACKLE
HE'S BREAKING DOWN...
LOVE DRIVES PEOPLE CRAZY...
Watch out.

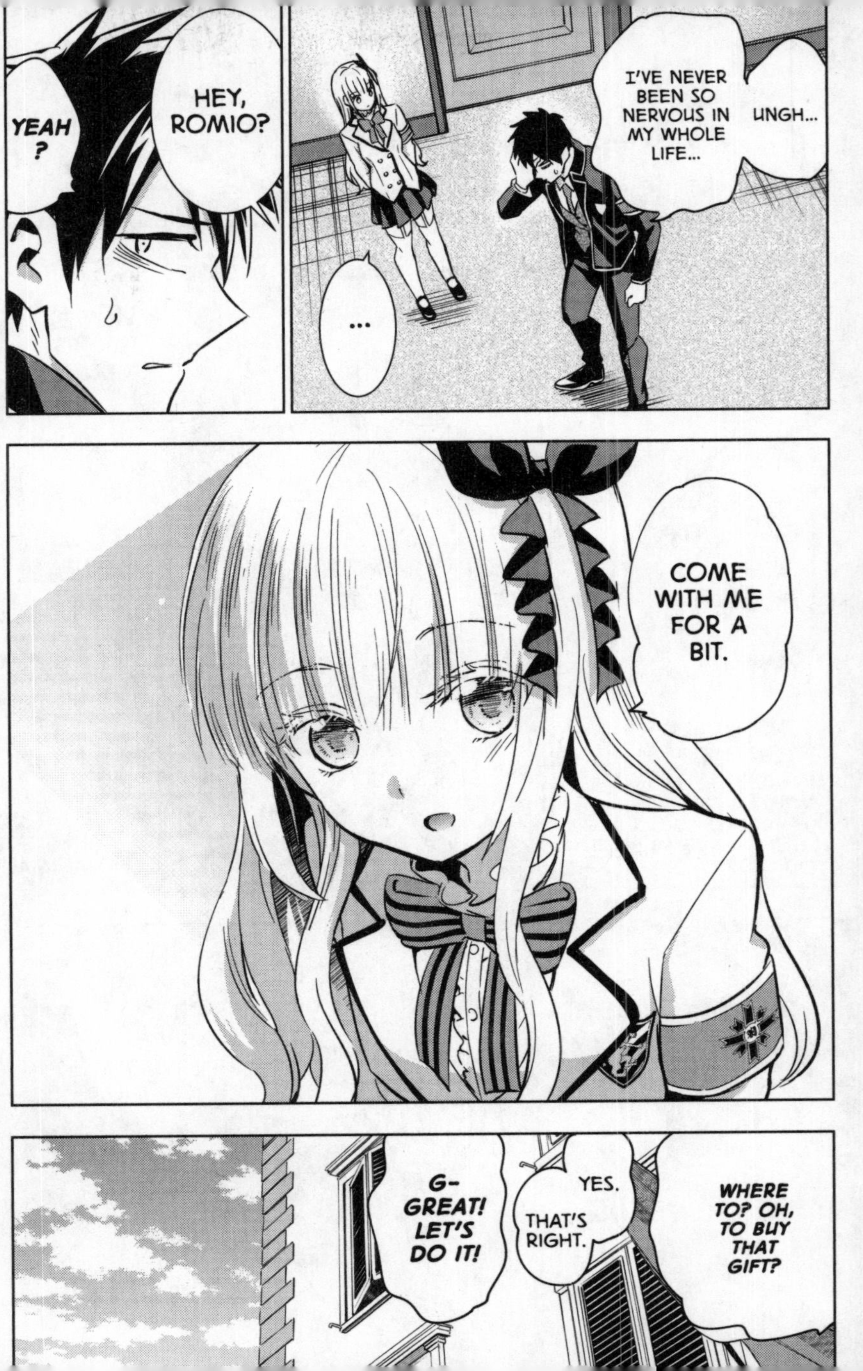
UNGH...
I'VE NEVER BEEN SO NERVOUS IN MY WHOLE LIFE...
...
HEY, ROMIO?
YEAH?
COME WITH ME FOR A BIT.
WHERE TO? OH, TO BUY THAT GIFT?
YES. THAT'S RIGHT.
G-GREAT! LET'S DO IT!

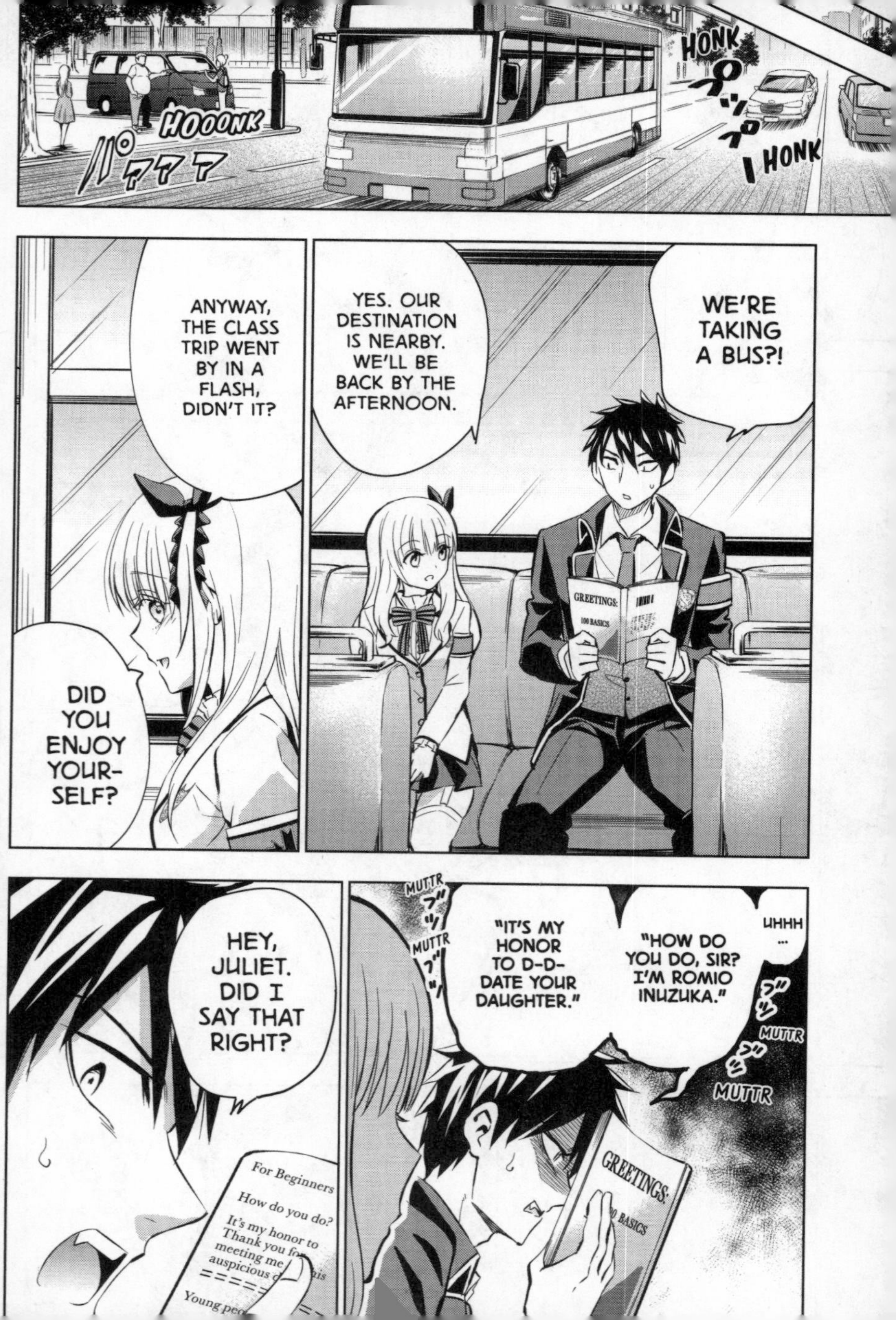
HONK
HONK
HOOONK
WE'RE TAKING A BUS?!
GREETINGS: 100 BASICS
YES. OUR DESTINATION IS NEARBY. WE'LL BE BACK BY THE AFTERNOON.
ANYWAY, THE CLASS TRIP WENT BY IN A FLASH, DIDN'T IT?
DID YOU ENJOY YOURSELF?
UHHH ...
"HOW DO YOU DO, SIR? I'M ROMIO INUZUKA."
"IT'S MY HONOR TO D-D-DATE YOUR DAUGHTER."
MUTTR
MUTTR
MUTTR
MUTTR
GREETINGS:
HEY, JULIET. DID I SAY THAT RIGHT?
For Beginners
How do you do?
It's my honor to

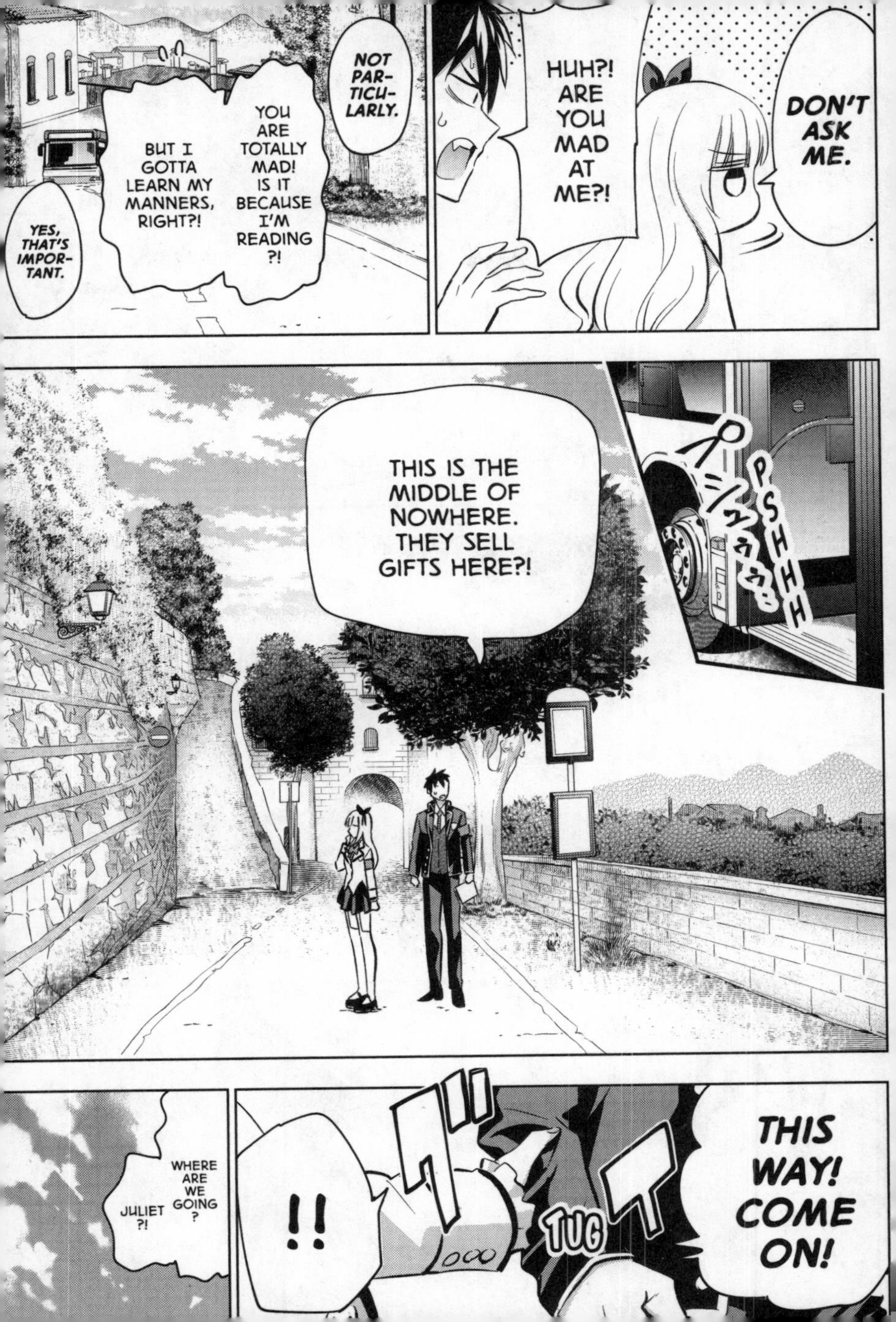

DON'T ASK ME.
HUH?! ARE YOU MAD AT ME?!
NOT PARTICULARLY.
YOU ARE TOTALLY MAD! IS IT BECAUSE I'M READING?!
BUT I GOTTA LEARN MY MANNERS, RIGHT?!
YES, THAT'S IMPORTANT.
PSHHH
THIS IS THE MIDDLE OF NOWHERE. THEY SELL GIFTS HERE?!
THIS WAY! COME ON!
TUG
!!
WHERE ARE WE GOING?
JULIET?!

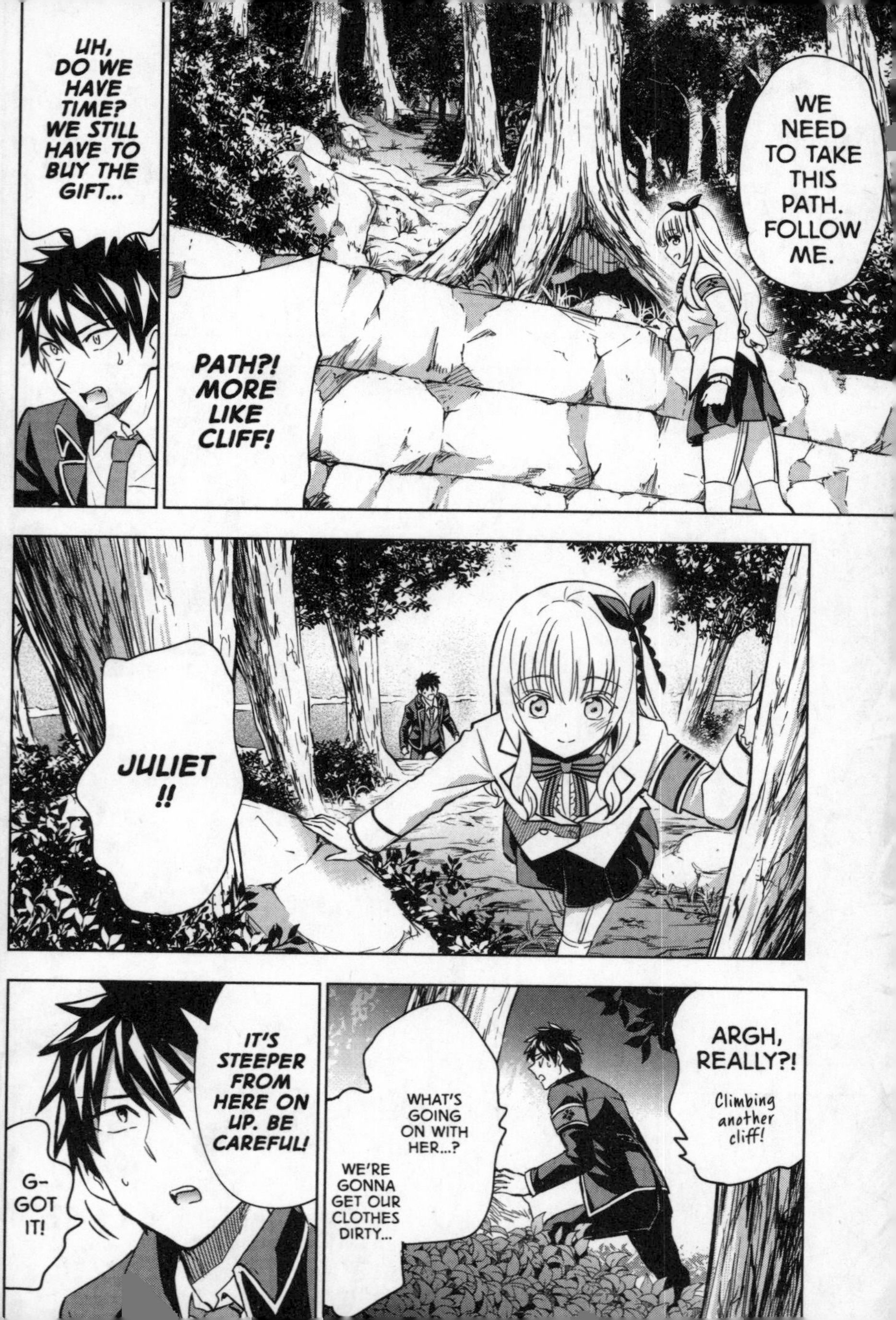
WE NEED TO TAKE THIS PATH. FOLLOW ME.
PATH?! MORE LIKE CLIFF!
UH, DO WE HAVE TIME? WE STILL HAVE TO BUY THE GIFT...
JULIET !!
ARGH, REALLY?!
Climbing another cliff!
WHAT'S GOING ON WITH HER...?
WE'RE GONNA GET OUR CLOTHES DIRTY...
IT'S STEEPER FROM HERE ON UP. BE CAREFUL!
G- GOT IT!

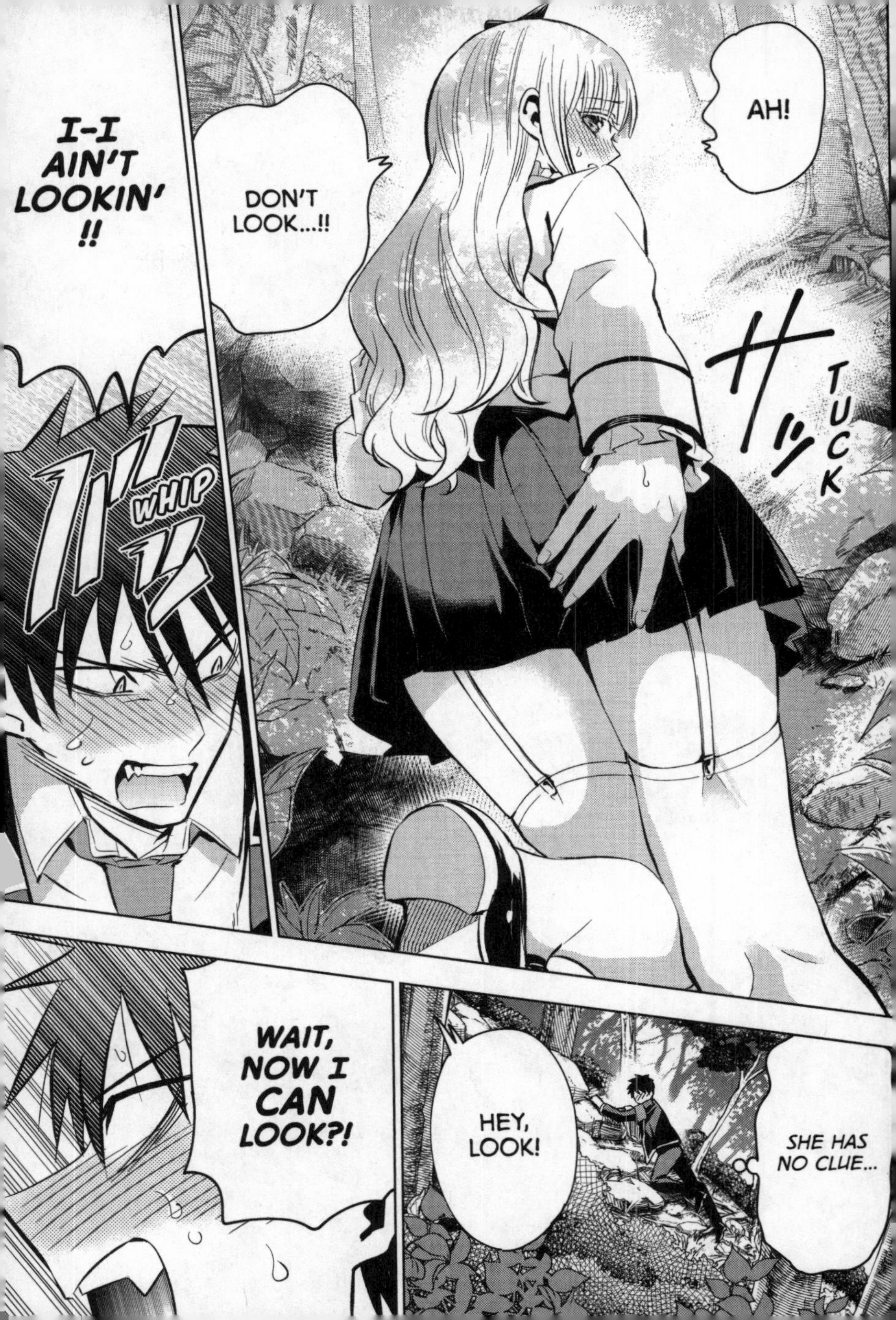
AH!
TUCK
DON'T LOOK...!!
WHIP
I-I AIN'T LOOKIN' !!
SHE HAS NO CLUE...
HEY, LOOK!
WAIT, NOW I CAN LOOK?!

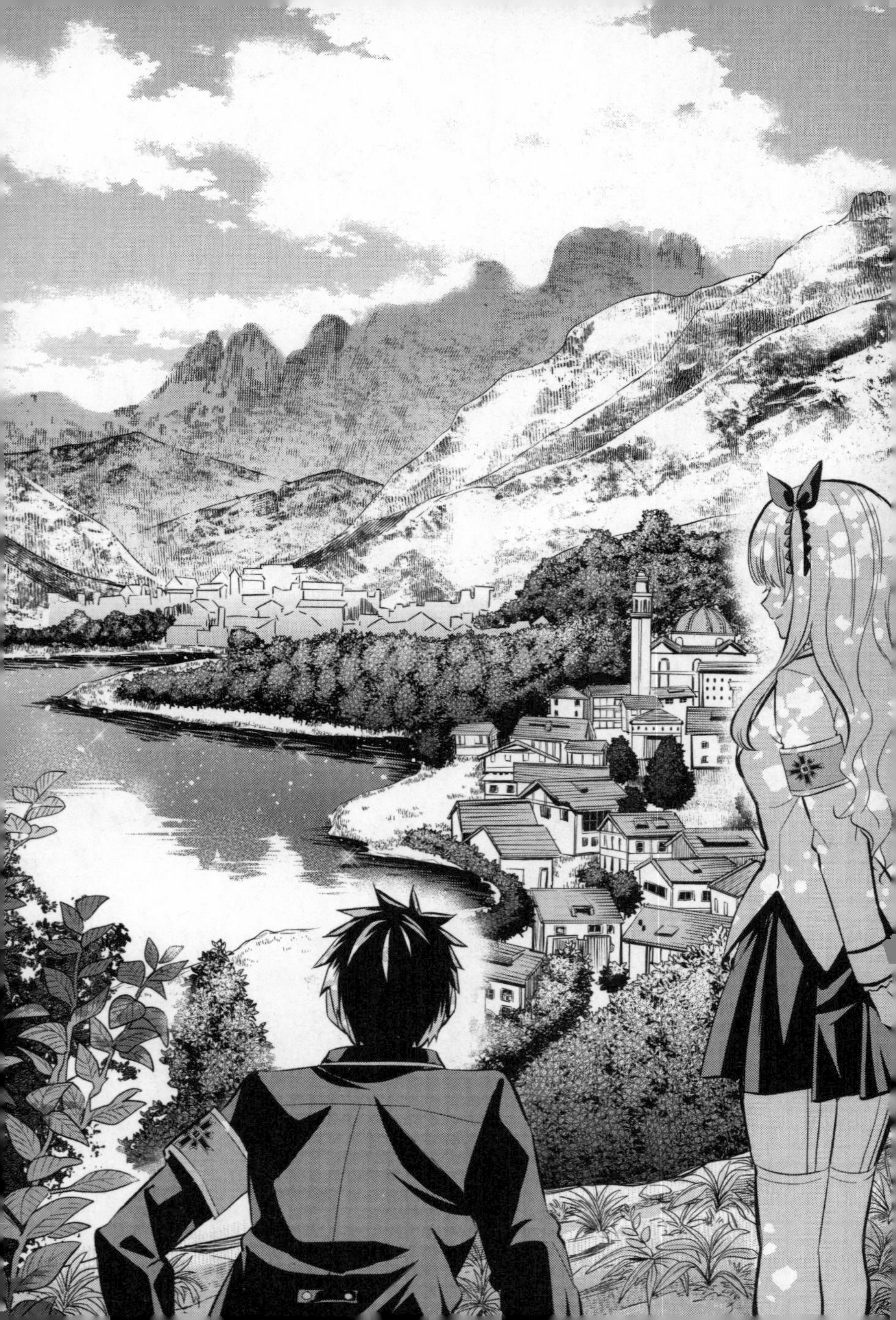

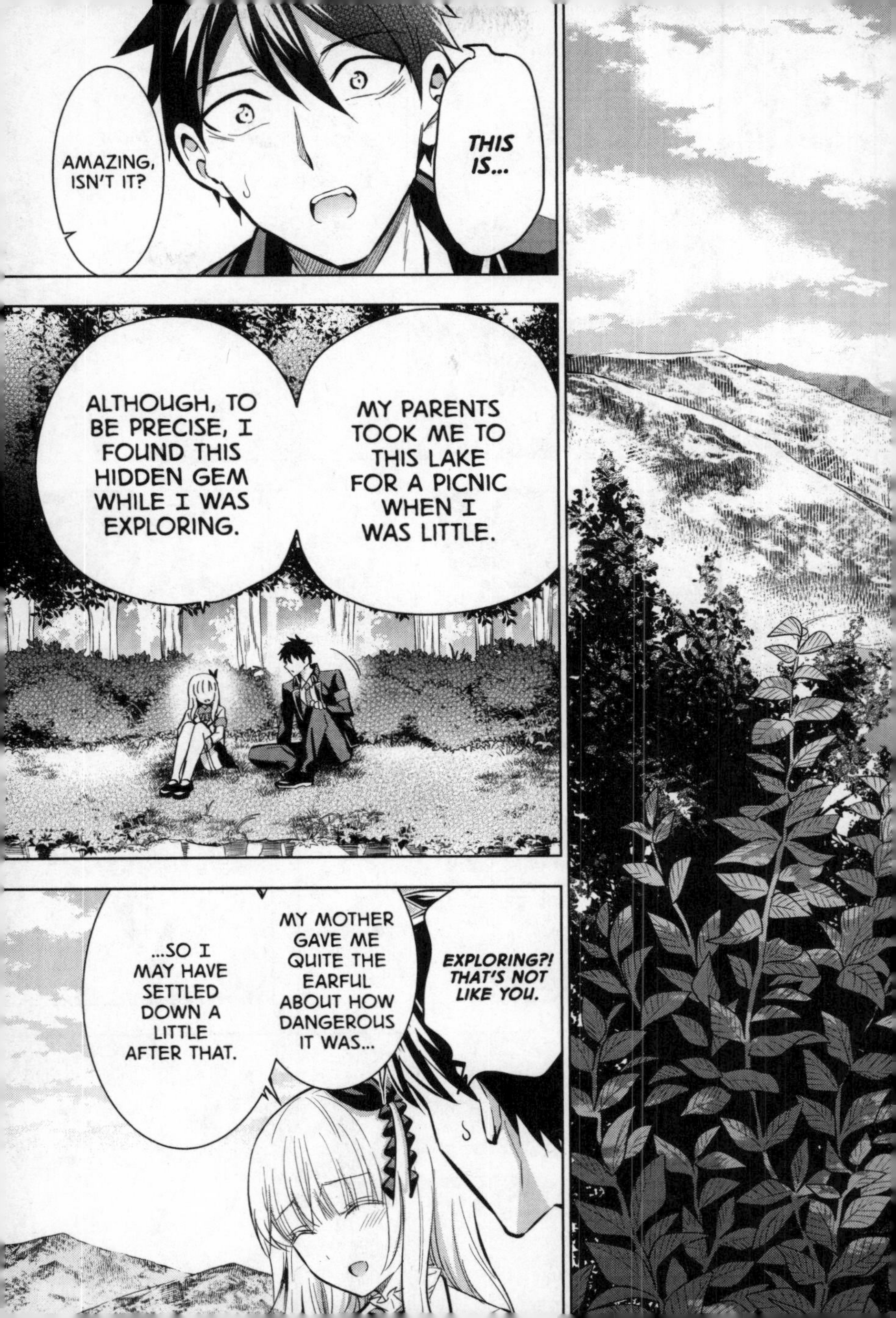
THIS IS...
AMAZING, ISN'T IT?
MY PARENTS TOOK ME TO THIS LAKE FOR A PICNIC WHEN I WAS LITTLE.
ALTHOUGH, TO BE PRECISE, I FOUND THIS HIDDEN GEM WHILE I WAS EXPLORING.
EXPLORING?! THAT'S NOT LIKE YOU.
MY MOTHER GAVE ME QUITE THE EARFUL ABOUT HOW DANGEROUS IT WAS...
...SO I MAY HAVE SETTLED DOWN A LITTLE AFTER THAT.

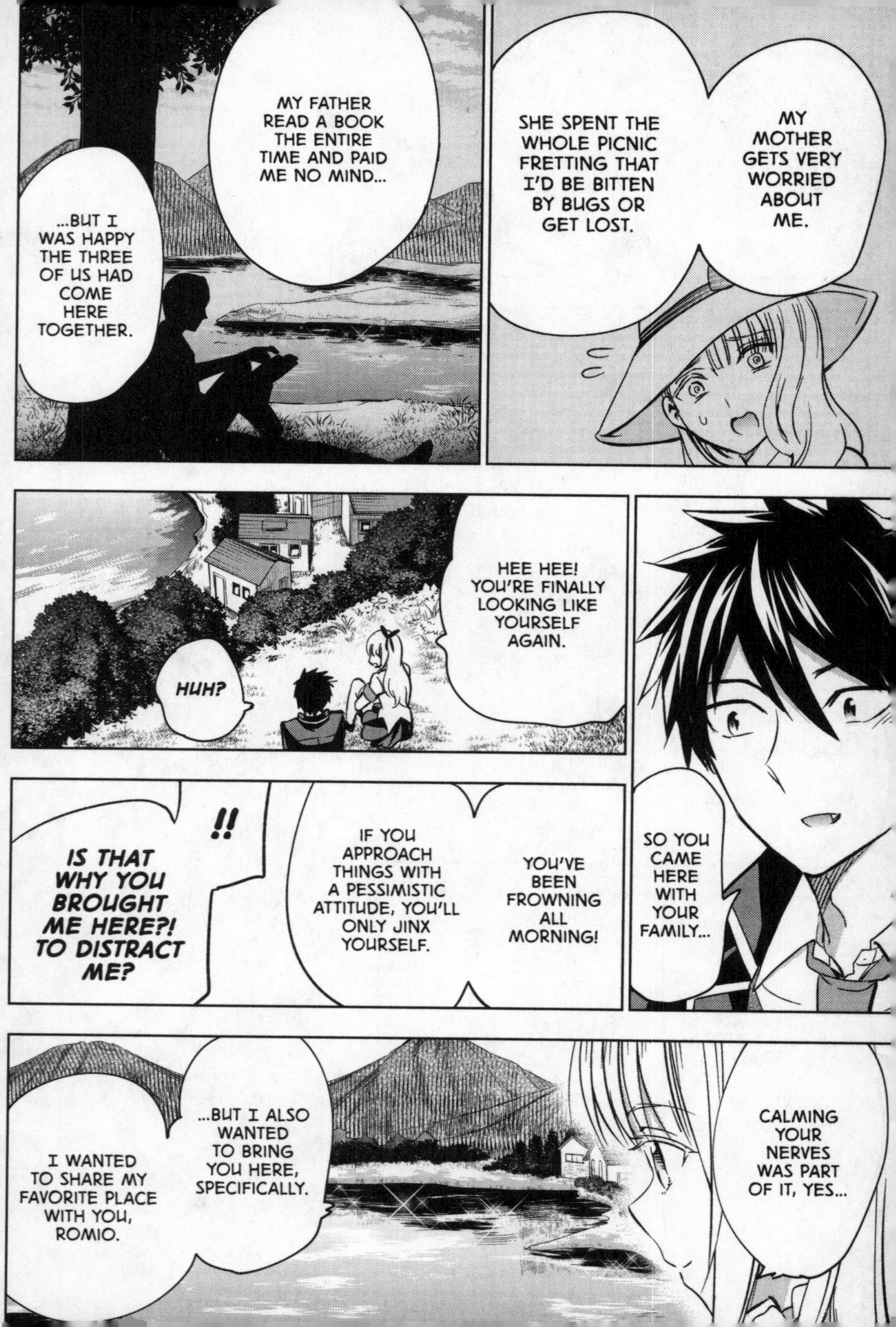
MY MOTHER GETS VERY WORRIED ABOUT ME.
SHE SPENT THE WHOLE PICNIC FRETTING THAT I'D BE BITTEN BY BUGS OR GET LOST.
MY FATHER READ A BOOK THE ENTIRE TIME AND PAID ME NO MIND...
...BUT I WAS HAPPY THE THREE OF US HAD COME HERE TOGETHER.
SO YOU CAME HERE WITH YOUR FAMILY...
HEE HEE! YOU'RE FINALLY LOOKING LIKE YOURSELF AGAIN.
HUH?
YOU'VE BEEN FROWNING ALL MORNING!
IF YOU APPROACH THINGS WITH A PESSIMISTIC ATTITUDE, YOU'LL ONLY JINX YOURSELF.
!!
IS THAT WHY YOU BROUGHT ME HERE?! TO DISTRACT ME?
CALMING YOUR NERVES WAS PART OF IT, YES...
...BUT I ALSO WANTED TO BRING YOU HERE, SPECIFICALLY.
I WANTED TO SHARE MY FAVORITE PLACE WITH YOU, ROMIO.

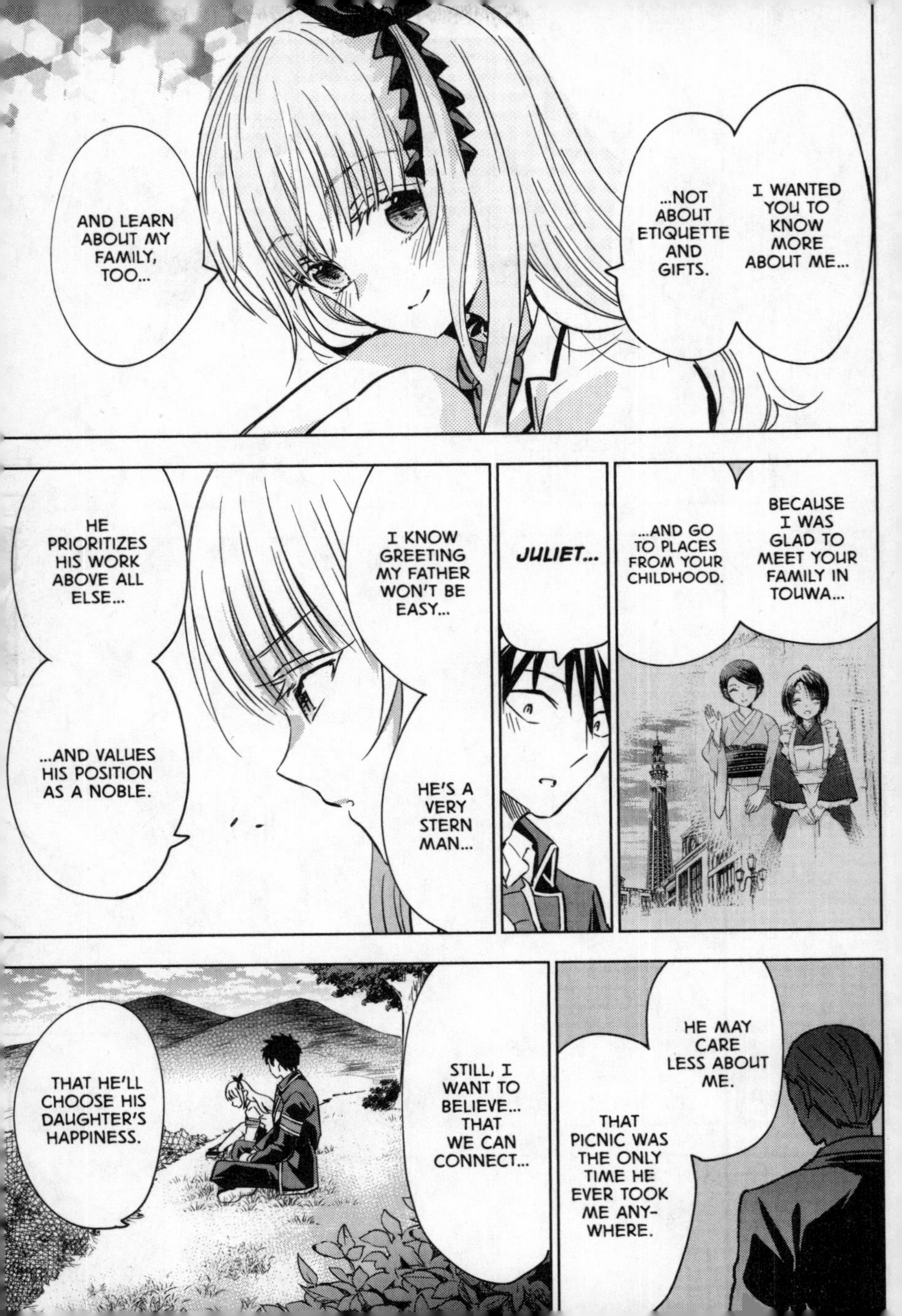

I WANTED YOU TO KNOW MORE ABOUT ME...
...NOT ABOUT ETIQUETTE AND GIFTS.
AND LEARN ABOUT MY FAMILY, TOO...
BECAUSE I WAS GLAD TO MEET YOUR FAMILY IN TOUWA...
...AND GO TO PLACES FROM YOUR CHILDHOOD.
JULIET...
I KNOW GREETING MY FATHER WON'T BE EASY...
HE'S A VERY STERN MAN...
HE PRIORITIZES HIS WORK ABOVE ALL ELSE...
...AND VALUES HIS POSITION AS A NOBLE.
HE MAY CARE LESS ABOUT ME.
THAT PICNIC WAS THE ONLY TIME HE EVER TOOK ME ANYWHERE.
STILL, I WANT TO BELIEVE... THAT WE CAN CONNECT...
THAT HE'LL CHOOSE HIS DAUGHTER'S HAPPINESS.

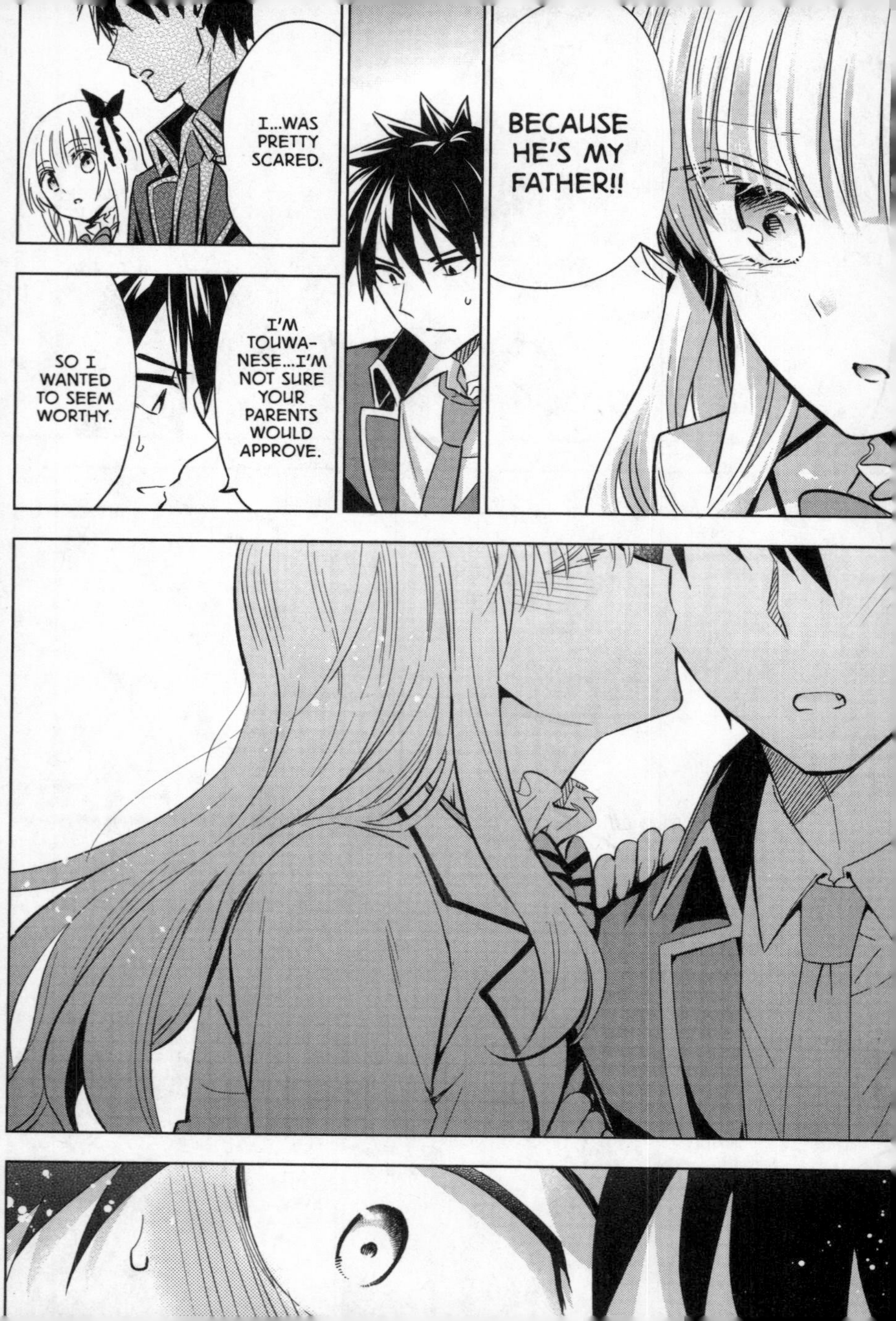
BECAUSE HE'S MY FATHER!!
I...WAS PRETTY SCARED.
I'M TOUWANESE...I'M NOT SURE YOUR PARENTS WOULD APPROVE.
SO I WANTED TO SEEM WORTHY.

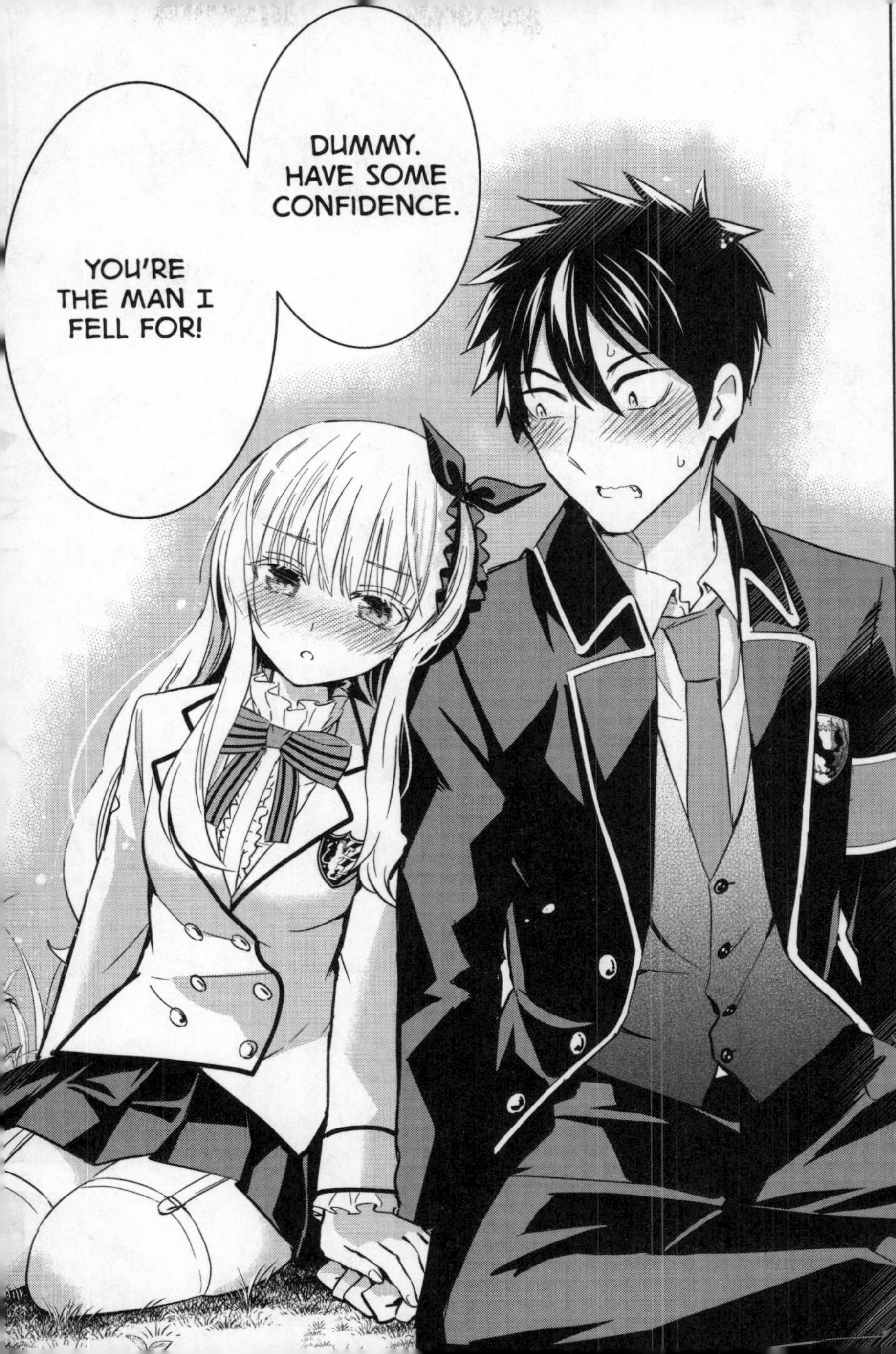
DUMMY. HAVE SOME CONFIDENCE.
YOU'RE THE MAN I FELL FOR!

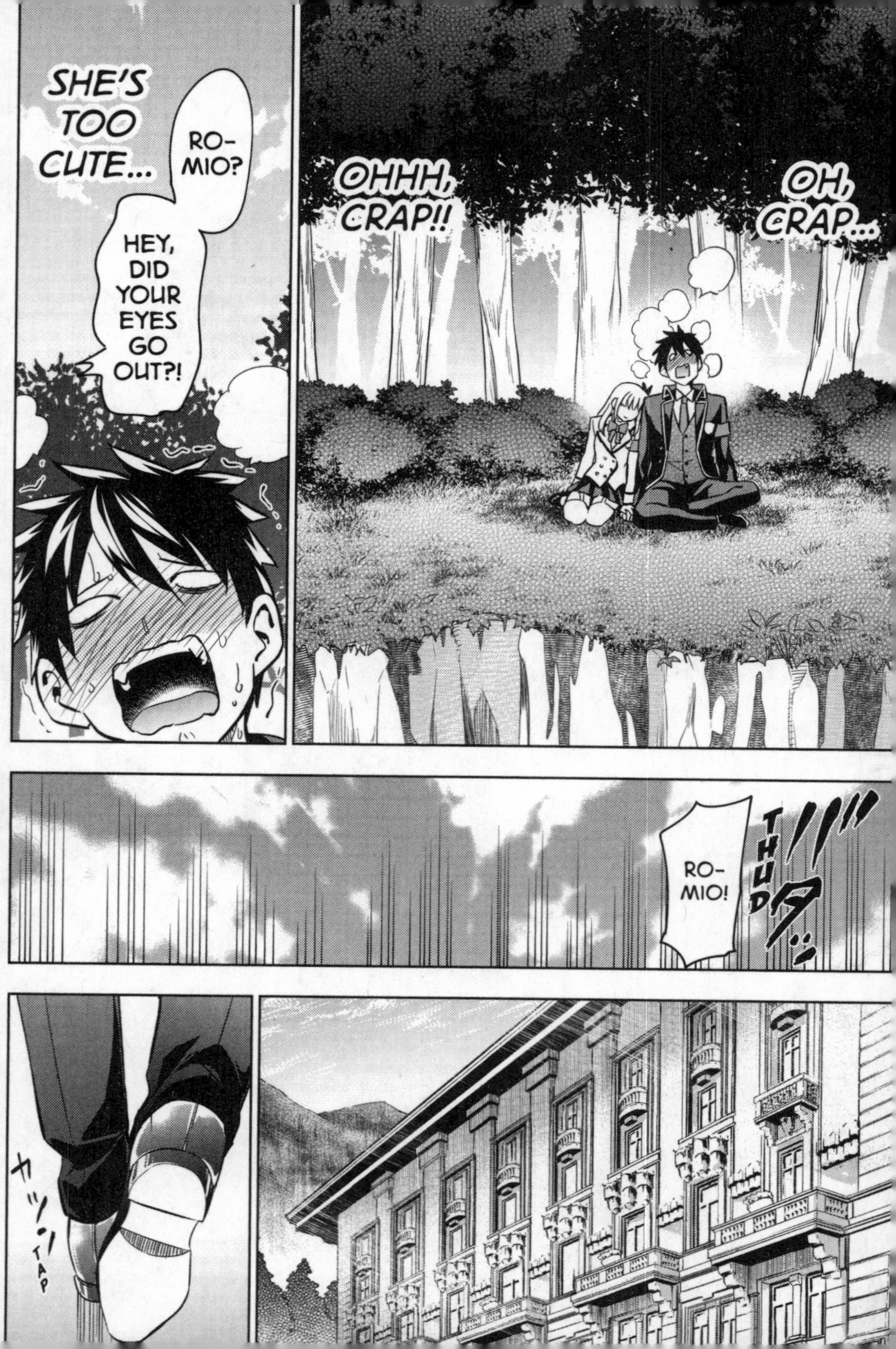
OH, CRAP...
OHHH, CRAP!!
RO-MIO?
HEY, DID YOUR EYES GO OUT?!
SHE'S TOO CUTE...
THUD
RO-MIO!
TAP

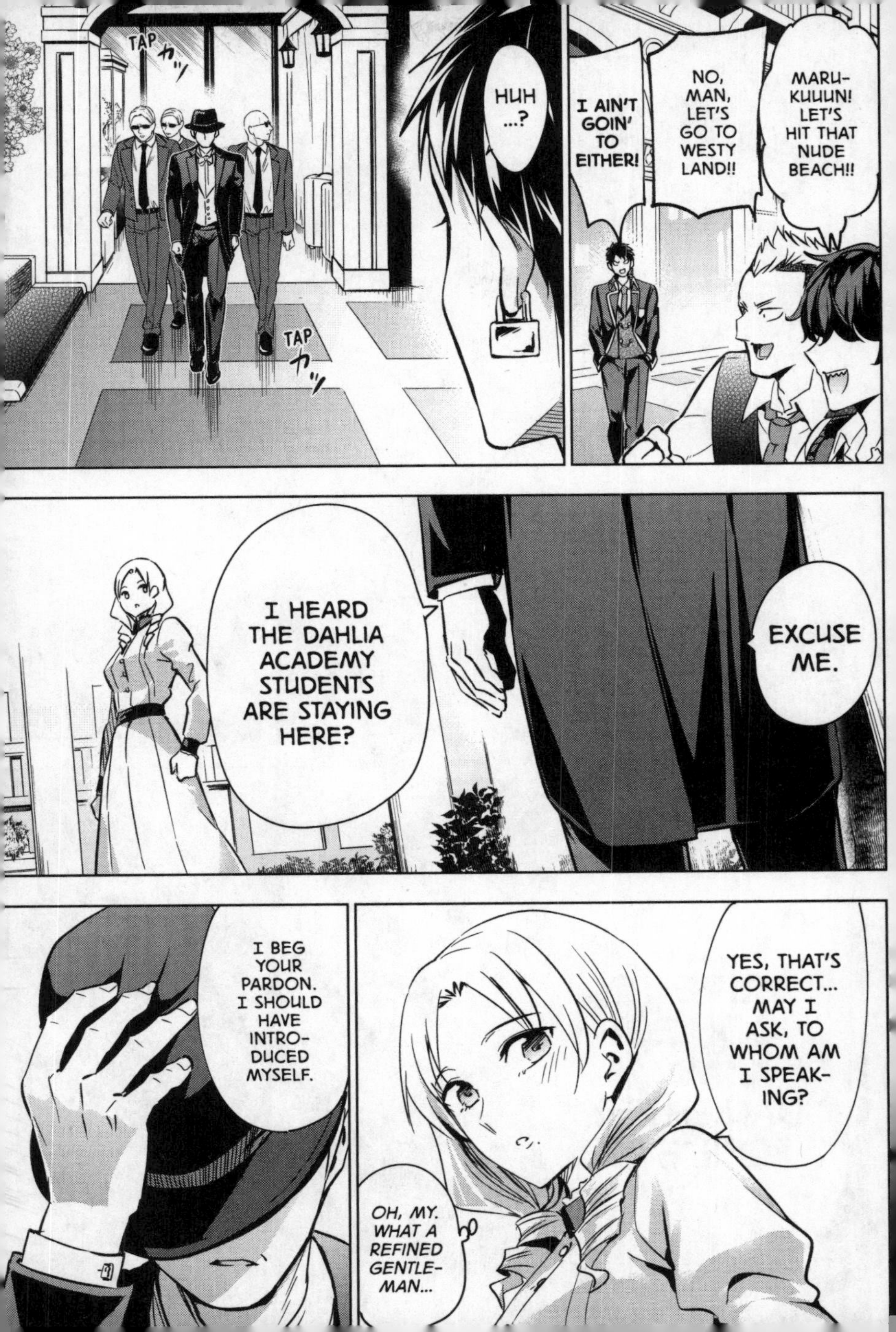
MARU-KUUUN! LET'S HIT THAT NUDE BEACH!!
NO, MAN, LET'S GO TO WESTY LAND!!
I AIN'T GOIN' TO EITHER!
HUH ...?
TAP カッ
TAP カッ
EXCUSE ME.
I HEARD THE DAHLIA ACADEMY STUDENTS ARE STAYING HERE?
YES, THAT'S CORRECT... MAY I ASK, TO WHOM AM I SPEAK-ING?
OH, MY. WHAT A REFINED GENTLE-MAN...
I BEG YOUR PARDON. I SHOULD HAVE INTRO-DUCED MYSELF.

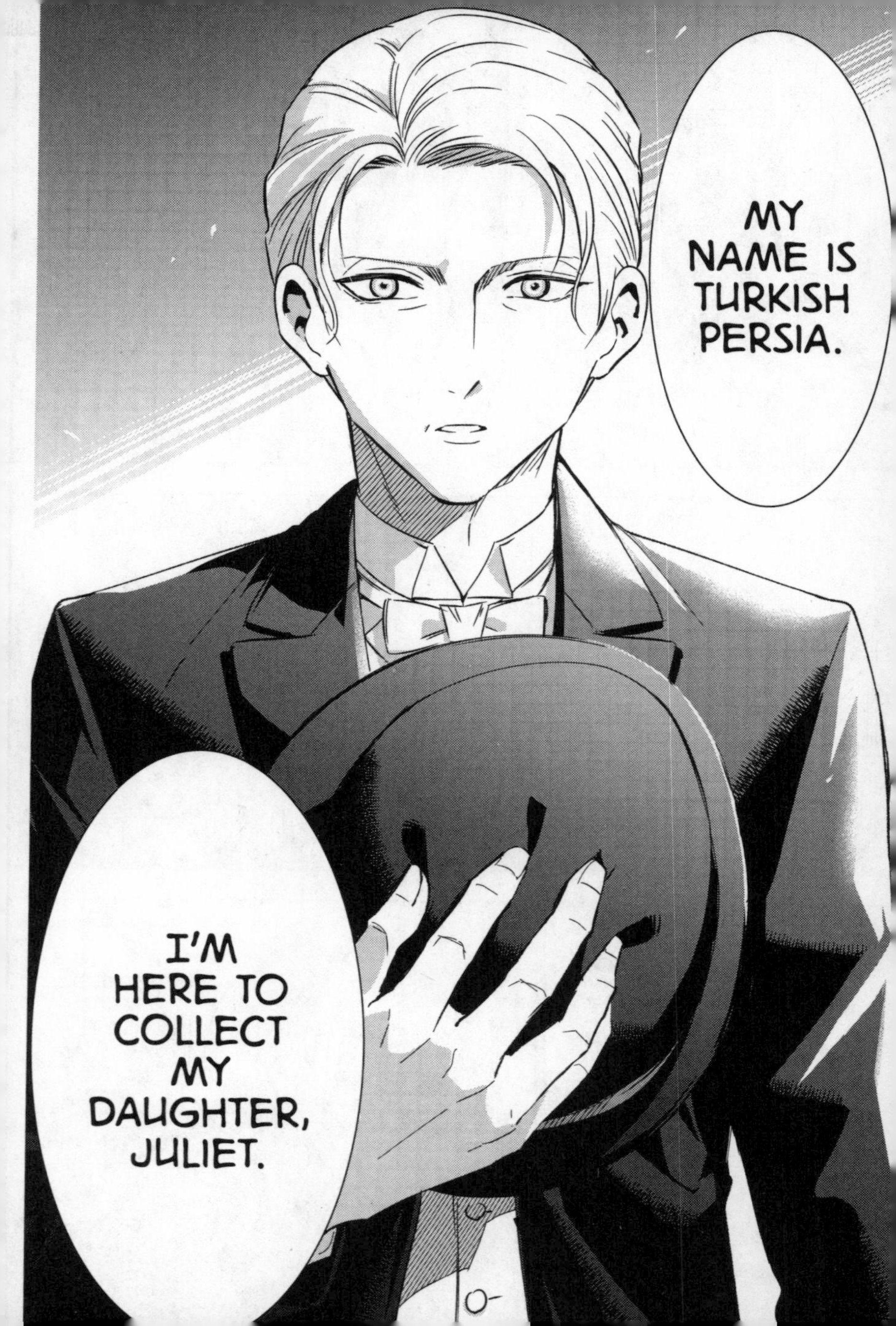
MY NAME IS TURKISH PERSIA.
I'M HERE TO COLLECT MY DAUGHTER, JULIET.

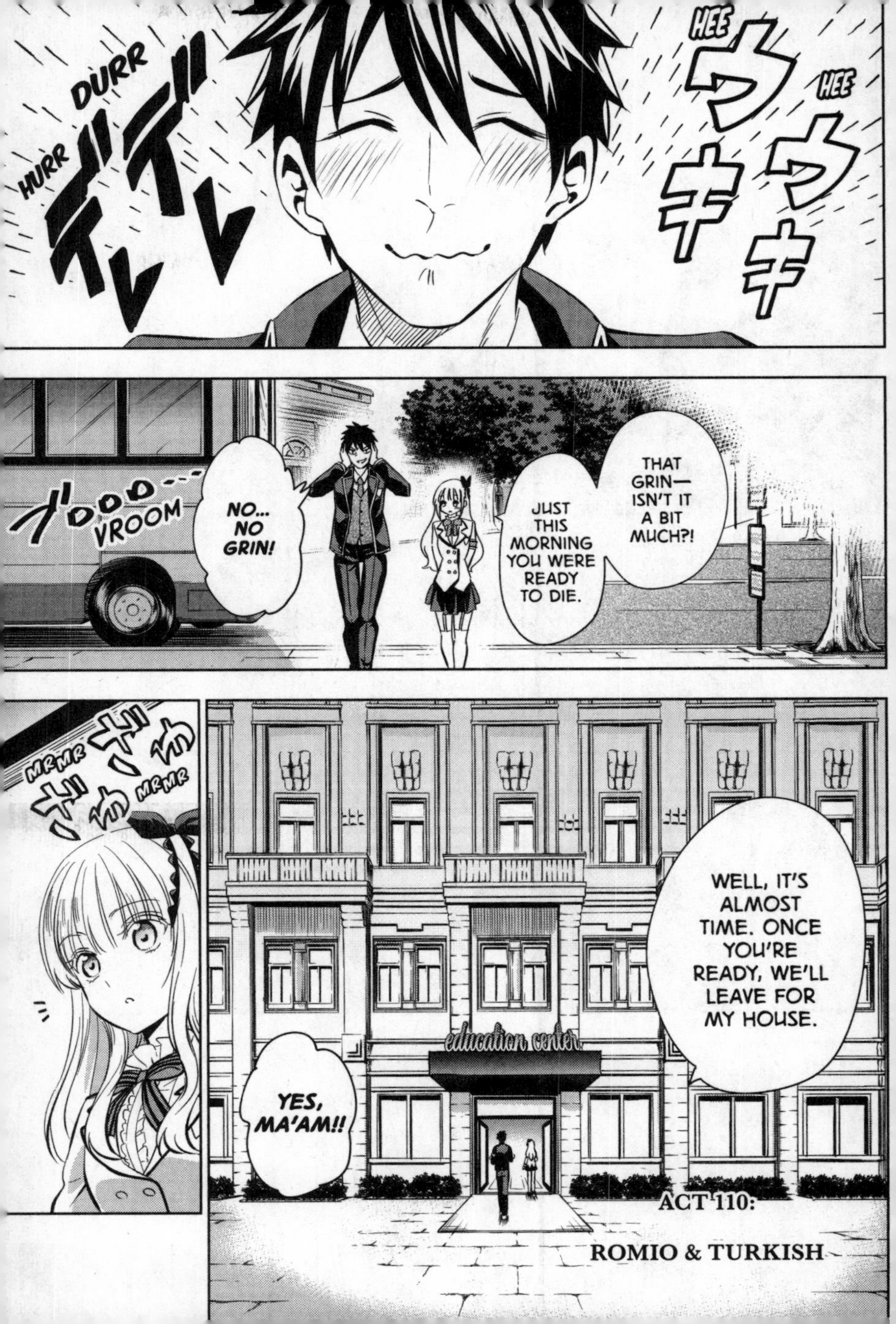
HEE ウキ HEE ウキ
HURR デレ DURR デレ
THAT GRIN—ISN'T IT A BIT MUCH?!
JUST THIS MORNING YOU WERE READY TO DIE.
NO... NO GRIN!
ブロロ... VROOM
WELL, IT'S ALMOST TIME. ONCE YOU'RE READY, WE'LL LEAVE FOR MY HOUSE.
education center
YES, MA'AM!!
ACT 110:
ROMIO & TURKISH
MRMR ざわ ざわ MRMR

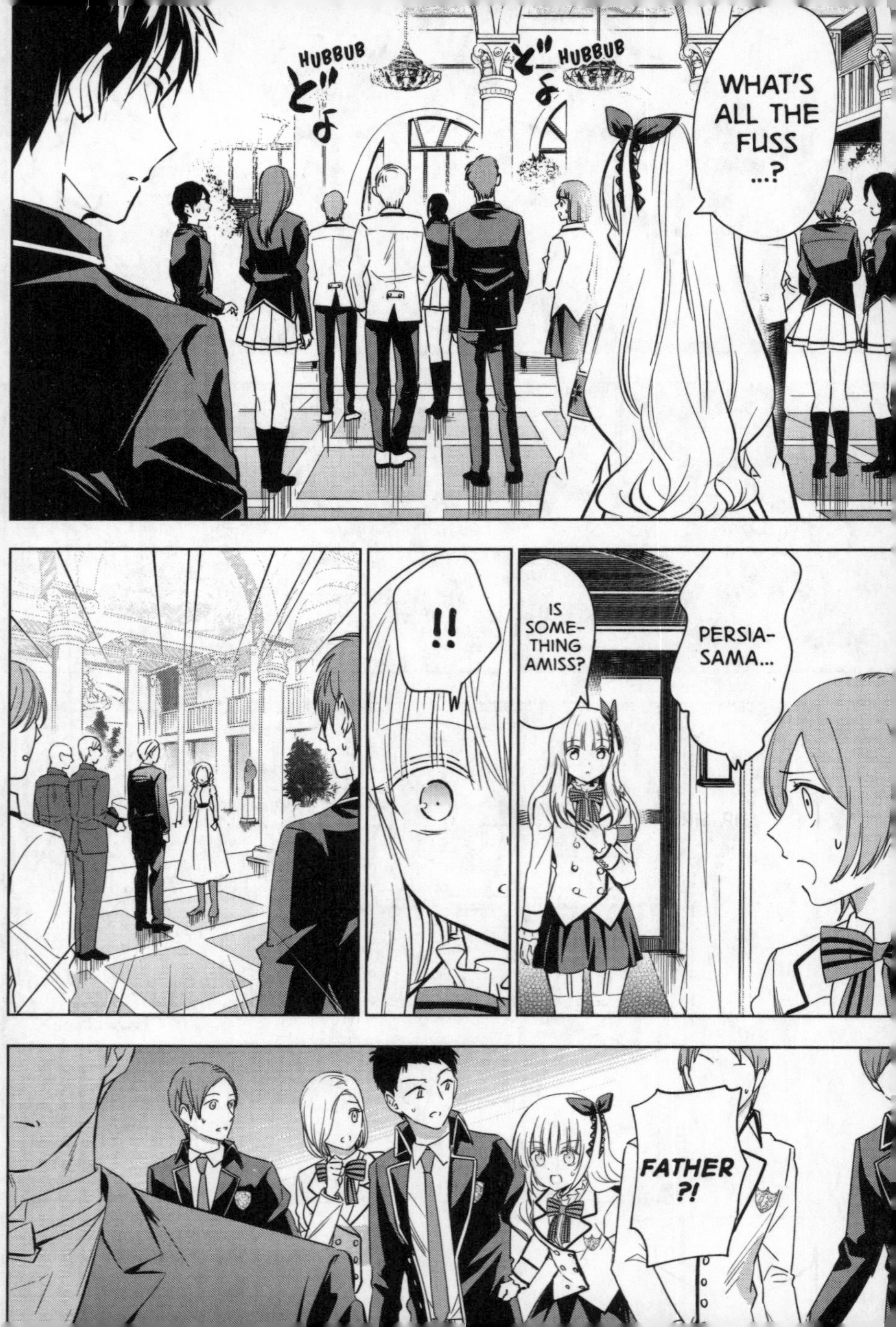
WHAT'S ALL THE FUSS ...?
HUBBUB
どよ
HUBBUB
どよ
PERSIA-SAMA...
IS SOME-THING AMISS?
!!
FATHER ?!

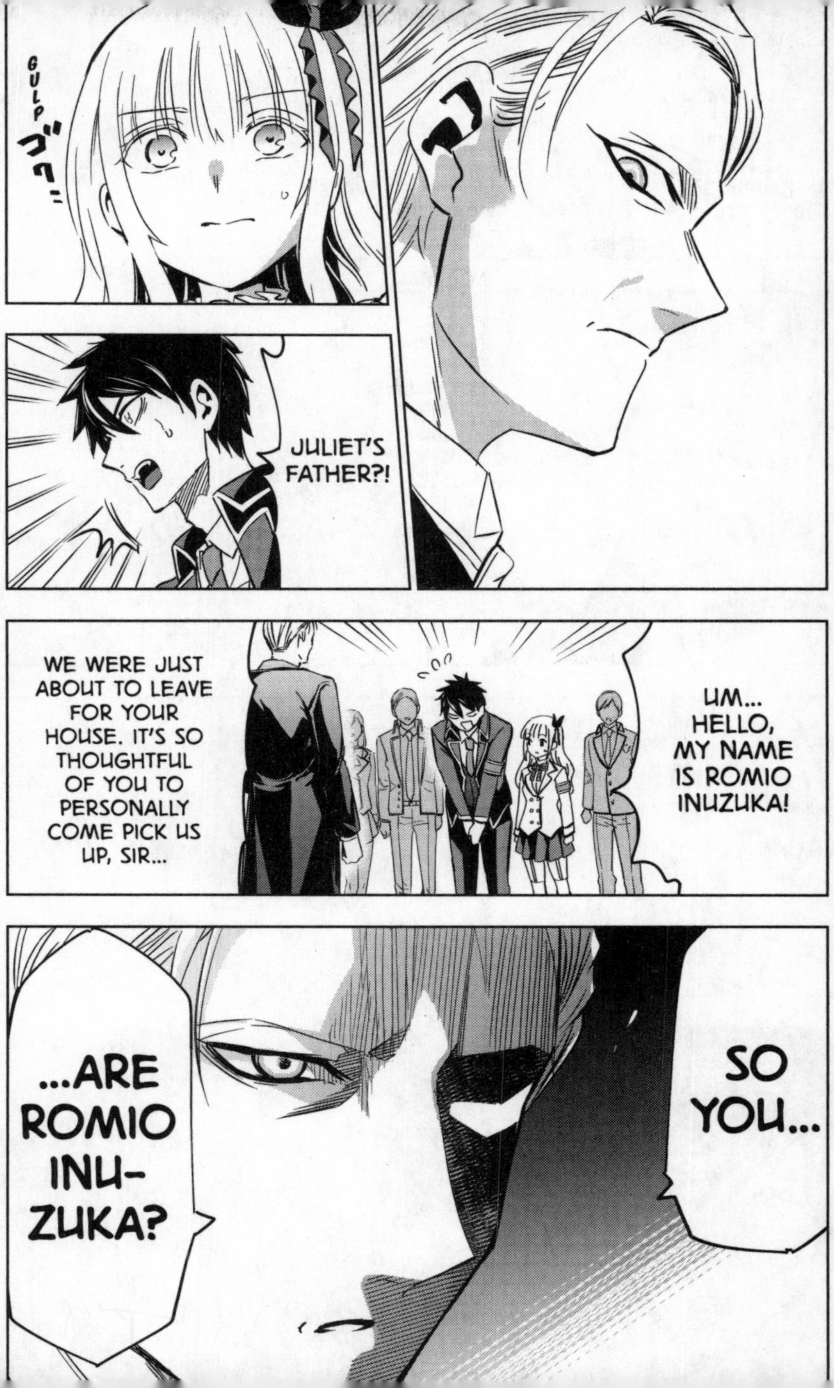
GULP
ゴクッ
JULIET'S FATHER?!
UM... HELLO, MY NAME IS ROMIO INUZUKA!
WE WERE JUST ABOUT TO LEAVE FOR YOUR HOUSE. IT'S SO THOUGHTFUL OF YOU TO PERSONALLY COME PICK US UP, SIR...
SO YOU...
...ARE ROMIO INUZUKA?

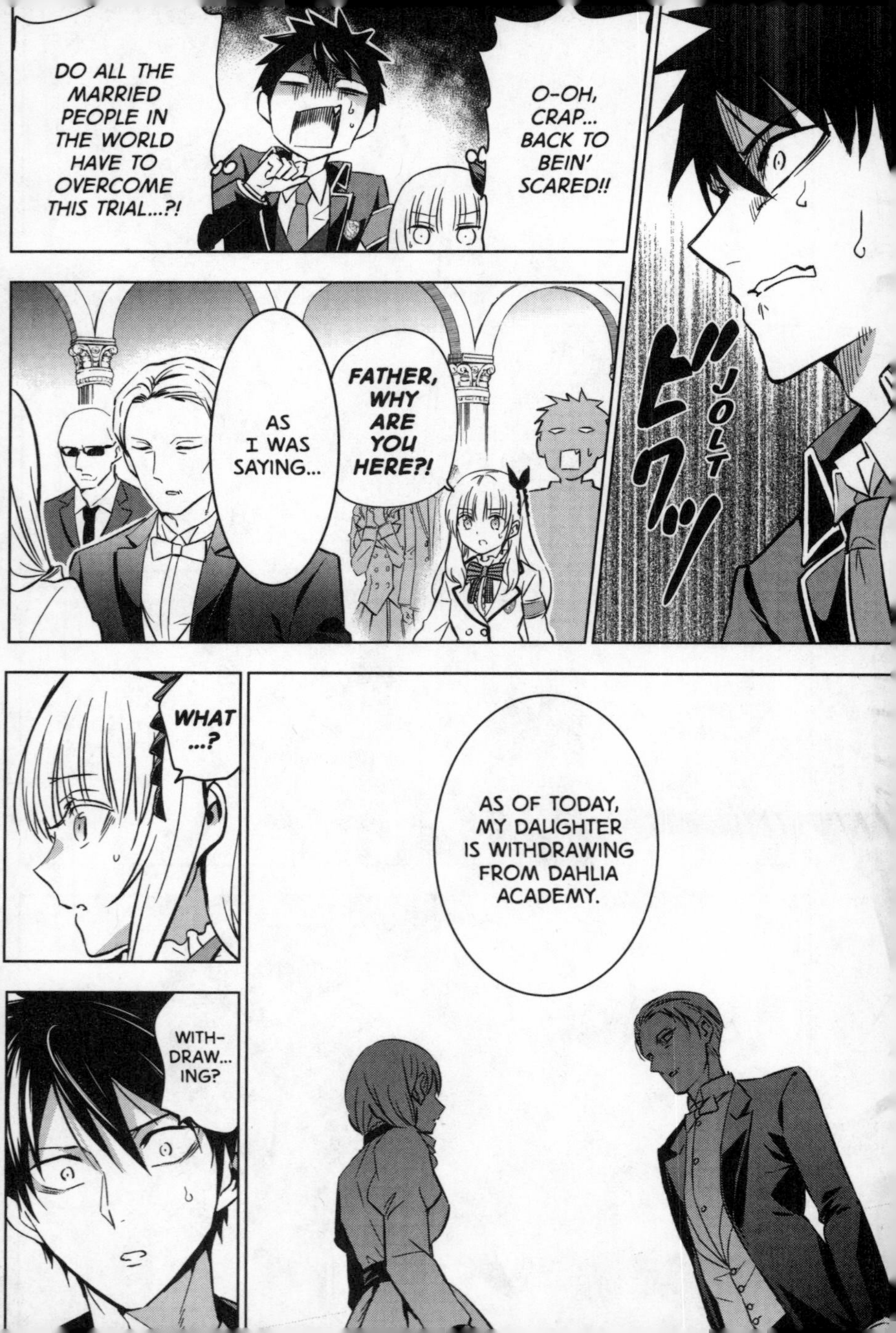
JOLT
O-OH, CRAP... BACK TO BEIN' SCARED!!
DO ALL THE MARRIED PEOPLE IN THE WORLD HAVE TO OVERCOME THIS TRIAL...?!
FATHER, WHY ARE YOU HERE?!
AS I WAS SAYING...
AS OF TODAY, MY DAUGHTER IS WITHDRAWING FROM DAHLIA ACADEMY.
WHAT ...?
WITH-DRAW... ING?

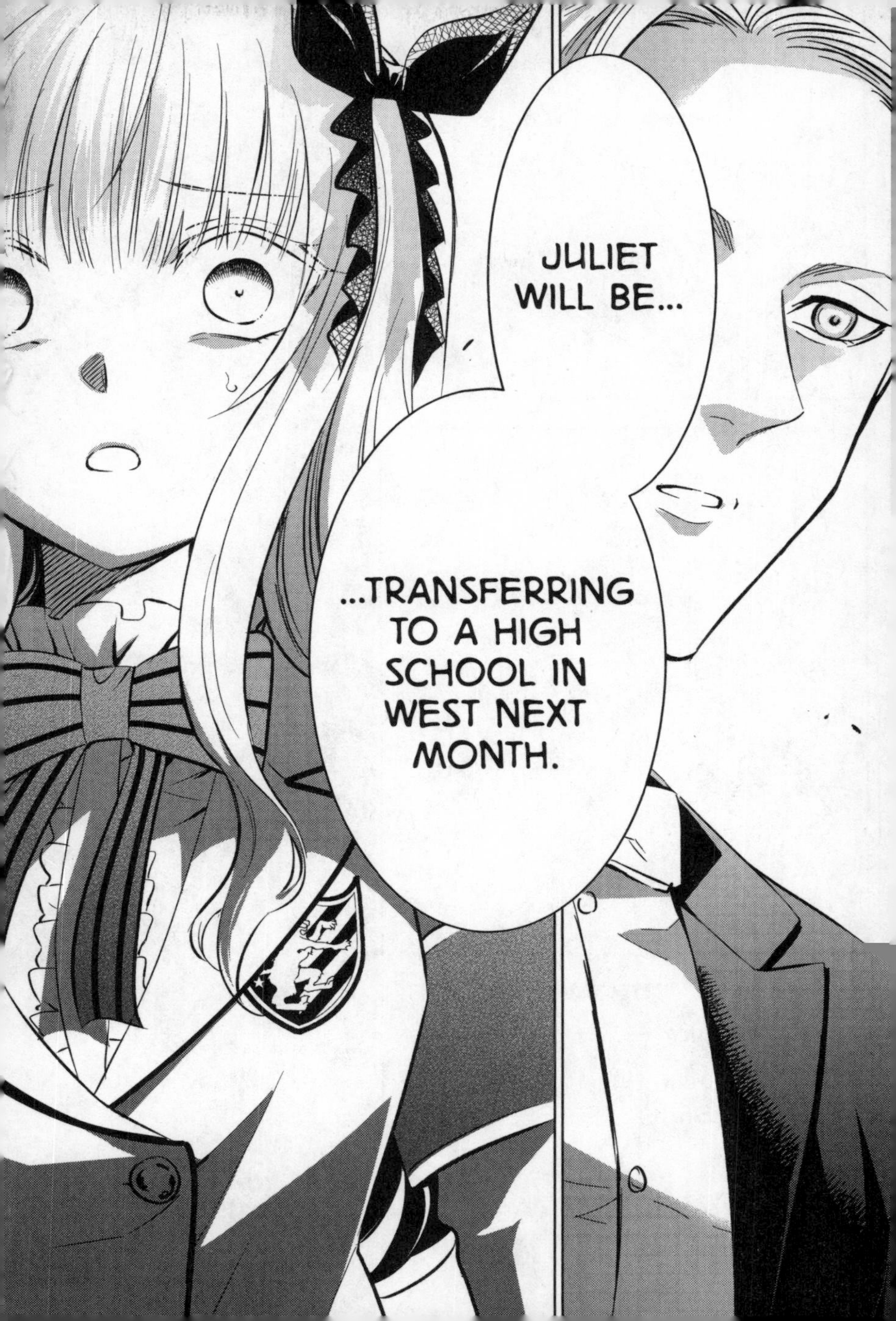
JULIET WILL BE...
...TRANSFERRING TO A HIGH SCHOOL IN WEST NEXT MONTH.

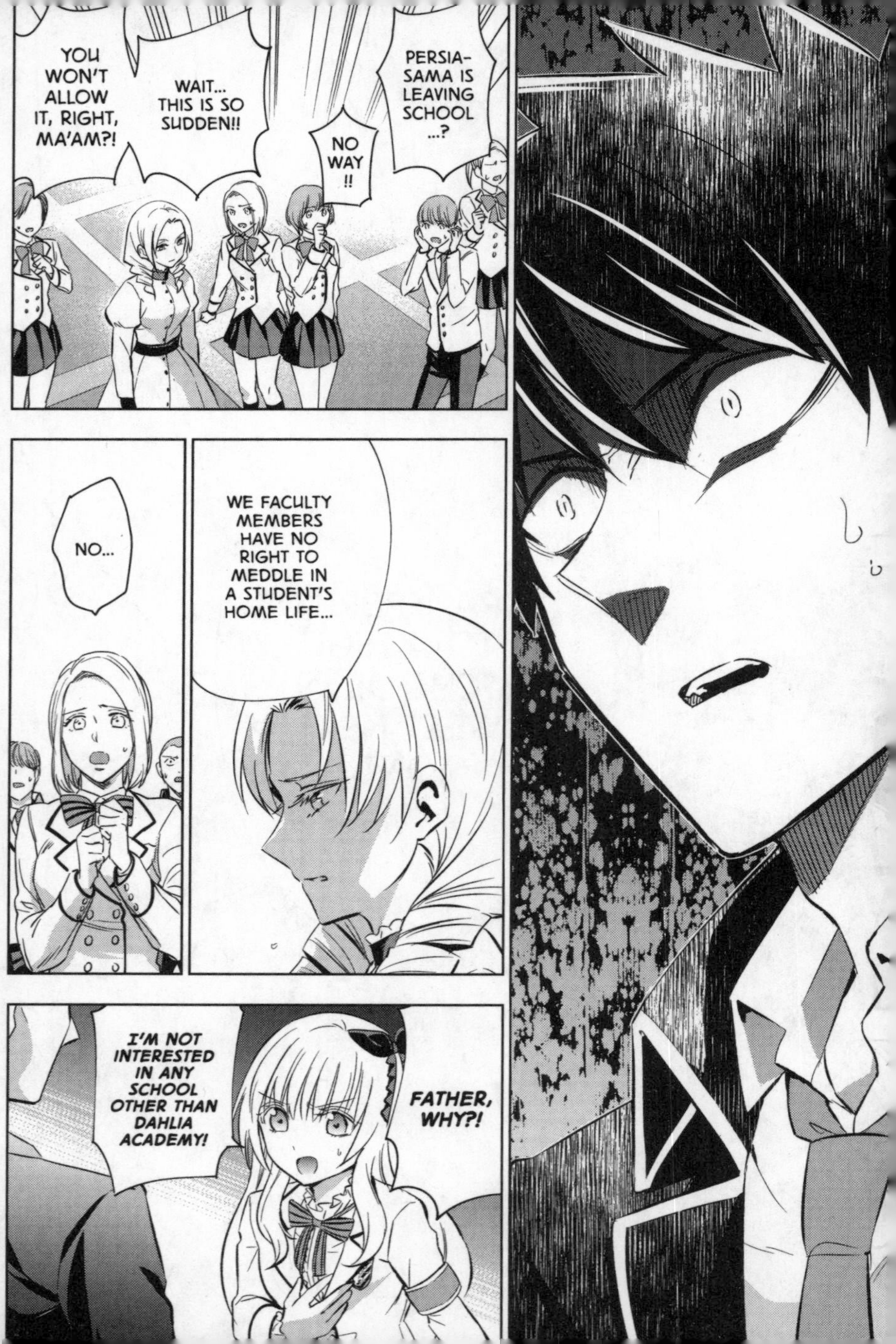
PERSIA-SAMA IS LEAVING SCHOOL ...?
NO WAY !!
WAIT... THIS IS SO SUDDEN!!
YOU WON'T ALLOW IT, RIGHT, MA'AM?!
WE FACULTY MEMBERS HAVE NO RIGHT TO MEDDLE IN A STUDENT'S HOME LIFE...
NO...
FATHER, WHY?!
I'M NOT INTERESTED IN ANY SCHOOL OTHER THAN DAHLIA ACADEMY!

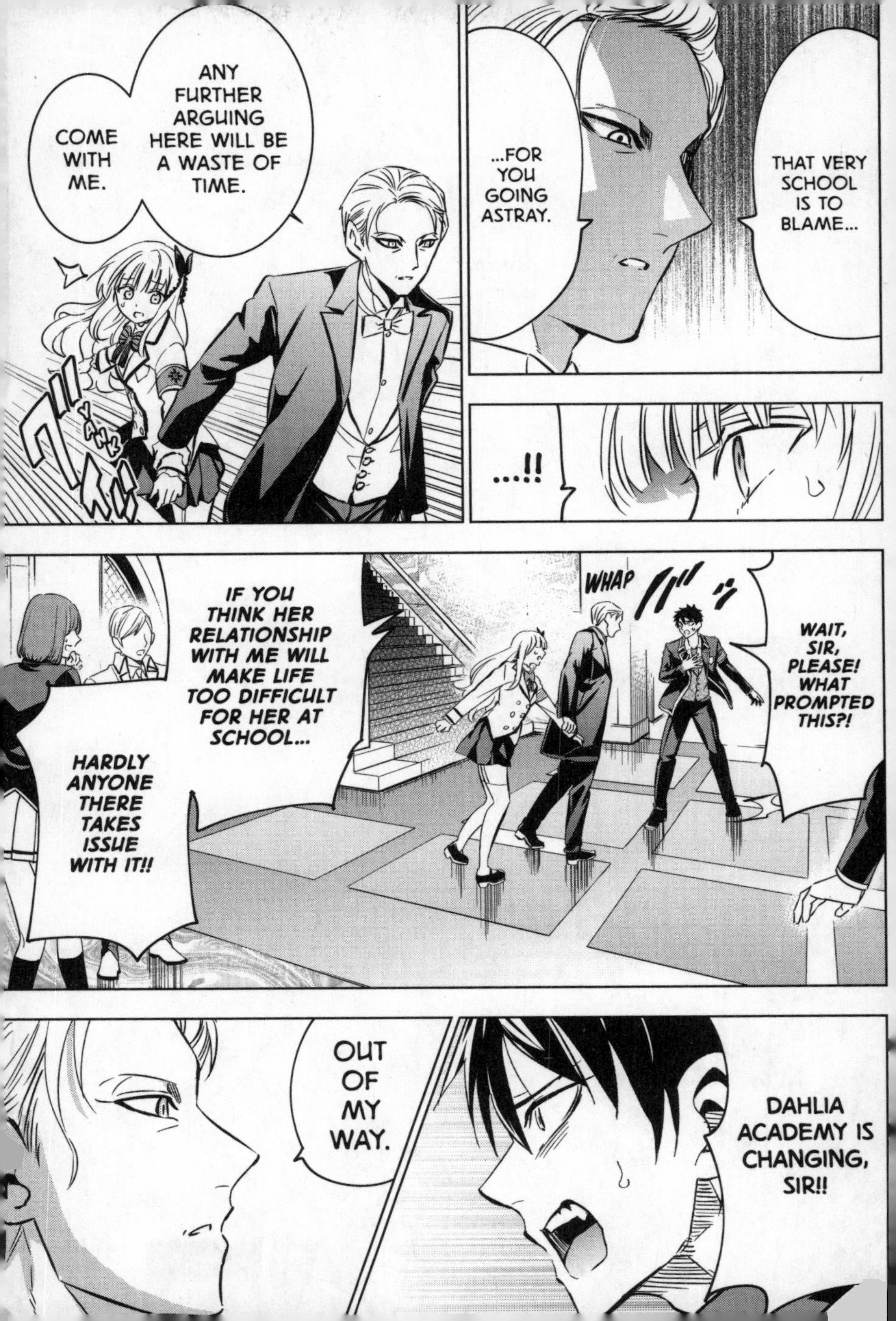
THAT VERY SCHOOL IS TO BLAME...
...FOR YOU GOING ASTRAY.
...!!
ANY FURTHER ARGUING HERE WILL BE A WASTE OF TIME.
COME WITH ME.
YANK
WAIT, SIR, PLEASE! WHAT PROMPTED THIS?!
WHAP
IF YOU THINK HER RELATIONSHIP WITH ME WILL MAKE LIFE TOO DIFFICULT FOR HER AT SCHOOL...
HARDLY ANYONE THERE TAKES ISSUE WITH IT!!
DAHLIA ACADEMY IS CHANGING, SIR!!
OUT OF MY WAY.

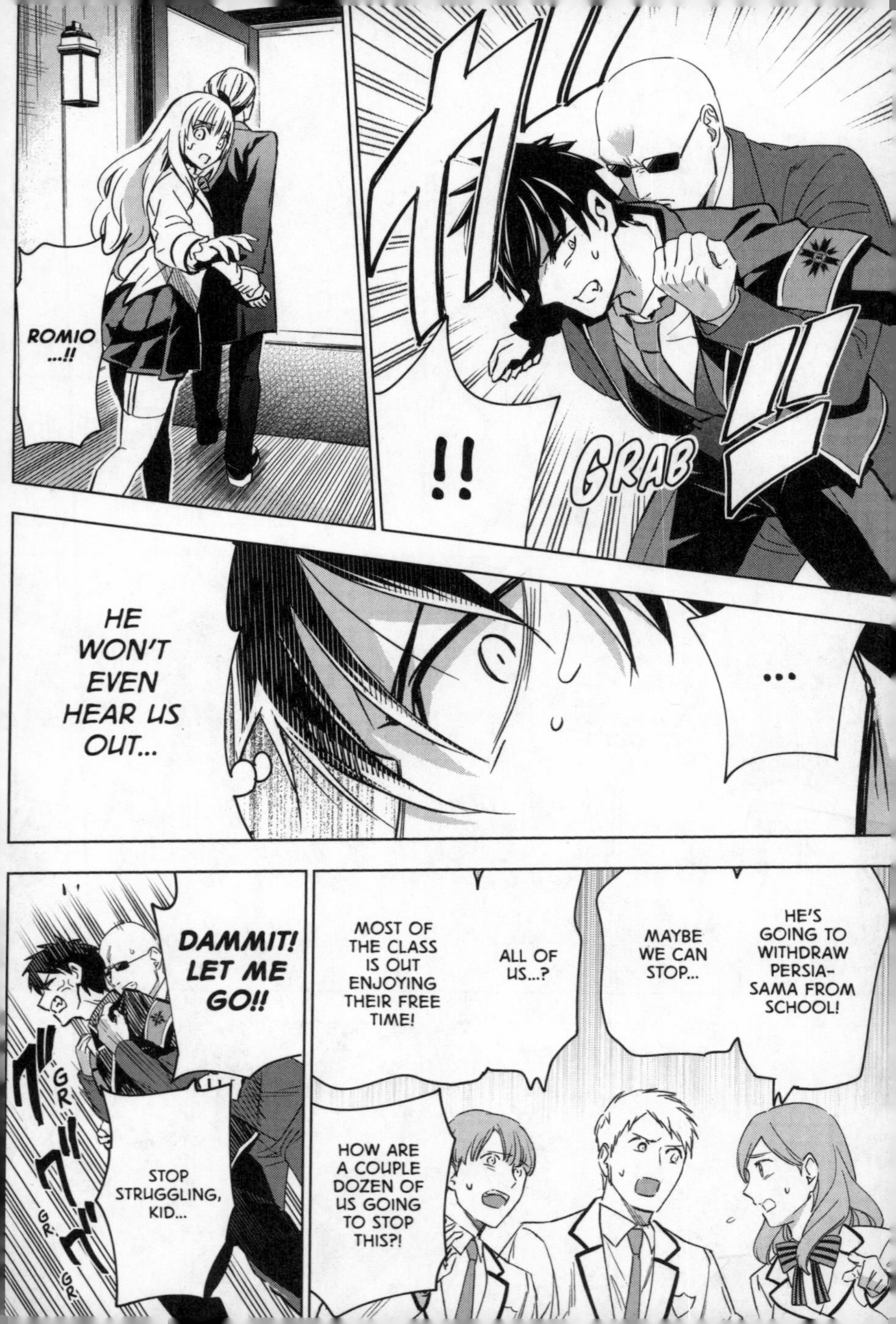
GRAB
!!
ROMIO ...!!
...
HE WON'T EVEN HEAR US OUT...
HE'S GOING TO WITHDRAW PERSIA-SAMA FROM SCHOOL!
MAYBE WE CAN STOP...
ALL OF US...?
MOST OF THE CLASS IS OUT ENJOYING THEIR FREE TIME!
HOW ARE A COUPLE DOZEN OF US GOING TO STOP THIS?!
DAMMIT! LET ME GO!!
STOP STRUGGLING, KID...
GR GR GR

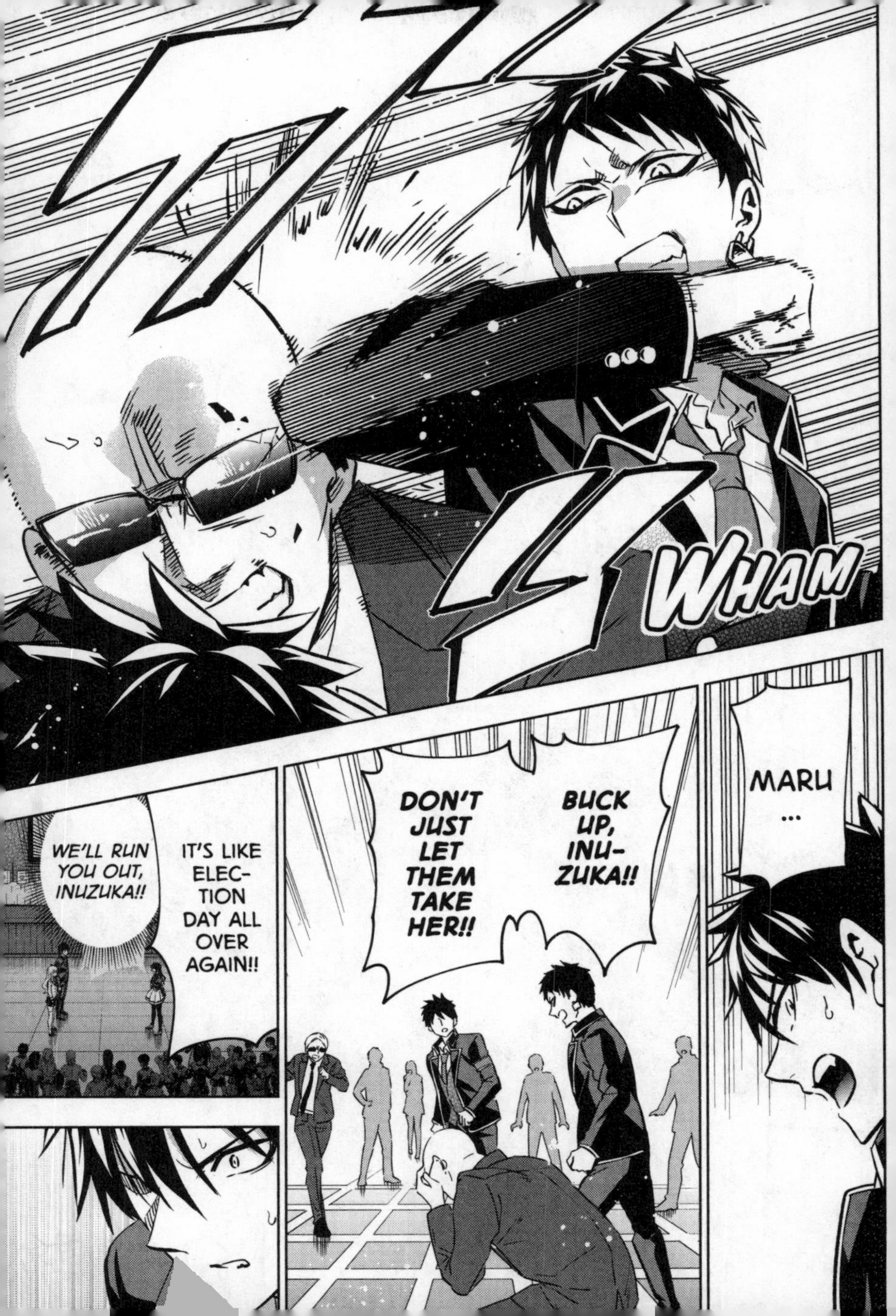
WHAM
MARU ...
BUCK UP, INUZUKA!!
DON'T JUST LET THEM TAKE HER!!
IT'S LIKE ELECTION DAY ALL OVER AGAIN!!
WE'LL RUN YOU OUT, INUZUKA!!

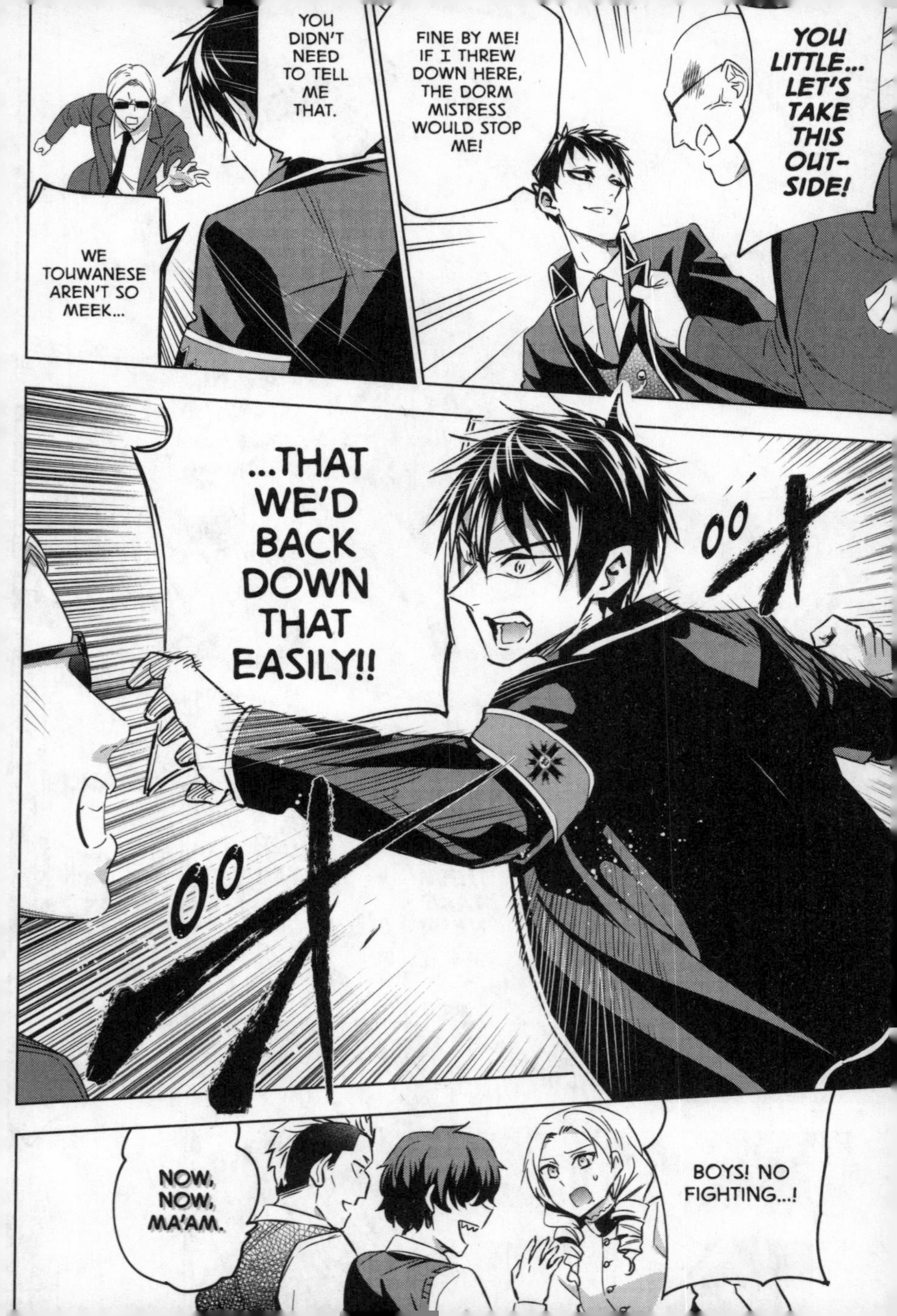
YOU LITTLE... LET'S TAKE THIS OUT-SIDE!
FINE BY ME! IF I THREW DOWN HERE, THE DORM MISTRESS WOULD STOP ME!
YOU DIDN'T NEED TO TELL ME THAT.
WE TOUWANESE AREN'T SO MEEK...
...THAT WE'D BACK DOWN THAT EASILY!!
BOYS! NO FIGHTING...!
NOW, NOW, MA'AM.

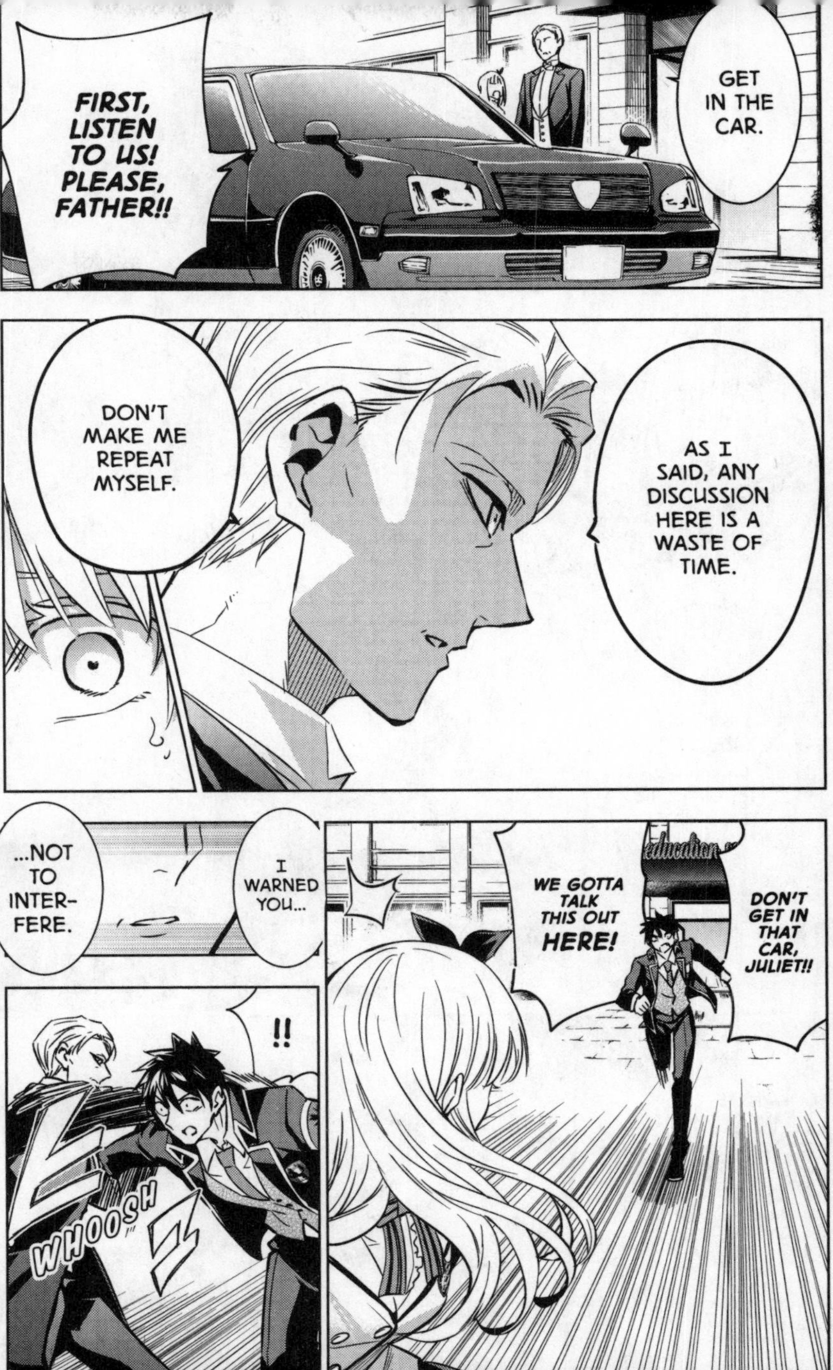
GET IN THE CAR.
FIRST, LISTEN TO US! PLEASE, FATHER!!
AS I SAID, ANY DISCUSSION HERE IS A WASTE OF TIME.
DON'T MAKE ME REPEAT MYSELF.
DON'T GET IN THAT CAR, JULIET!!
WE GOTTA TALK THIS OUT HERE!
I WARNED YOU...
...NOT TO INTER-FERE.
!!
WHOOSH

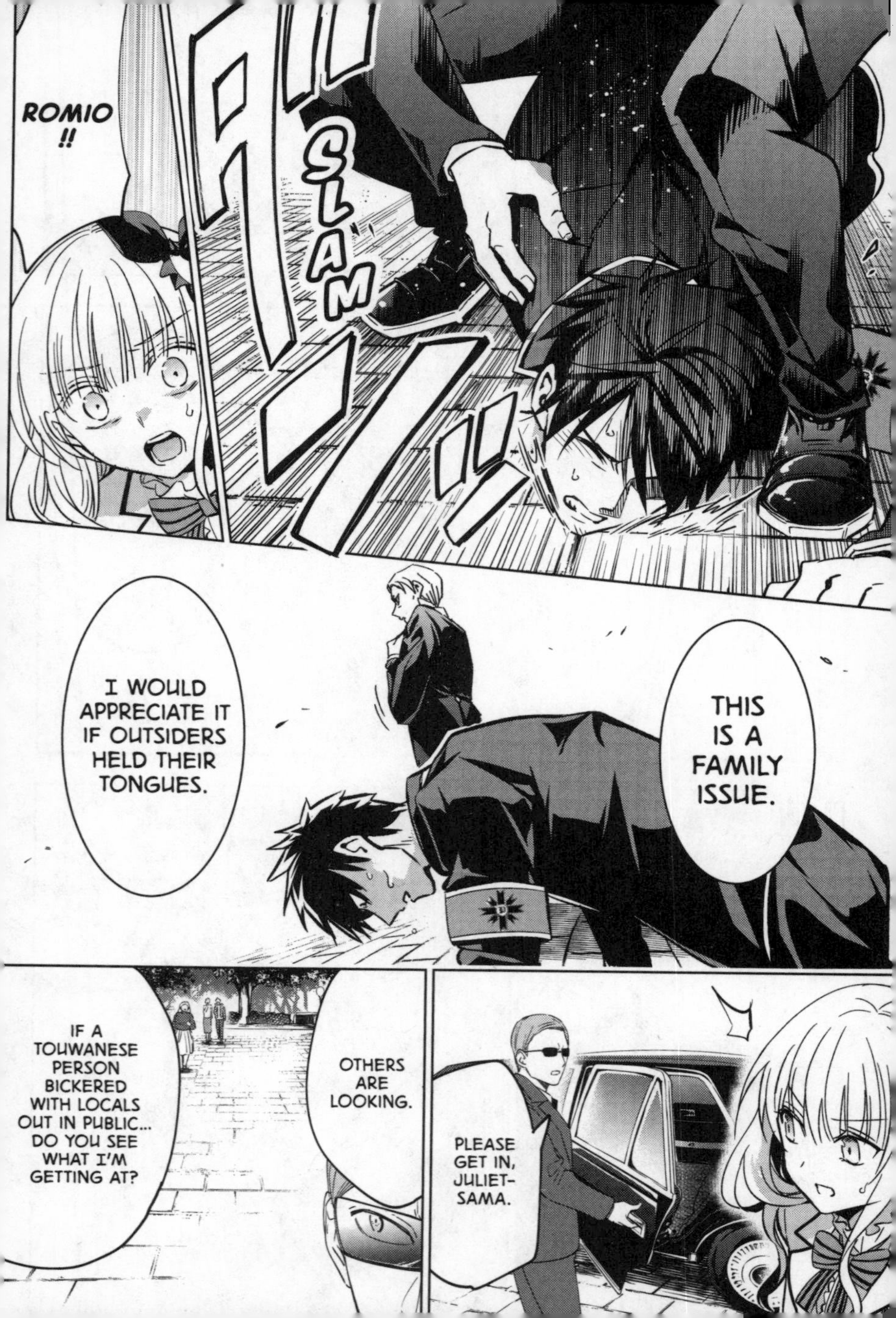
SLAM
ROMIO !!
THIS IS A FAMILY ISSUE.
I WOULD APPRECIATE IT IF OUTSIDERS HELD THEIR TONGUES.
PLEASE GET IN, JULIET-SAMA.
OTHERS ARE LOOKING.
IF A TOUWANESE PERSON BICKERED WITH LOCALS OUT IN PUBLIC... DO YOU SEE WHAT I'M GETTING AT?

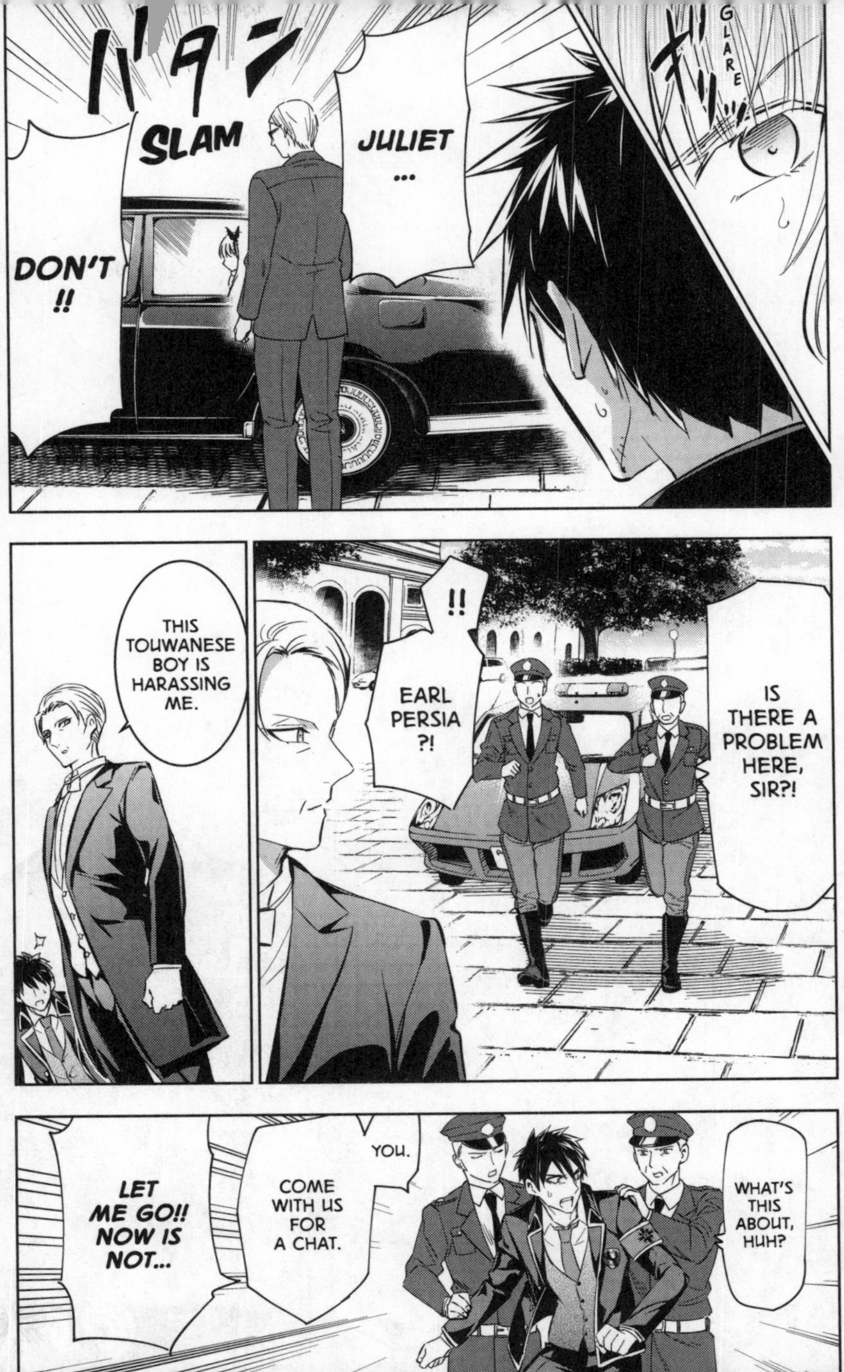
GLARE
JULIET ...
SLAM
DON'T !!
IS THERE A PROBLEM HERE, SIR?!
!!
EARL PERSIA ?!
THIS TOUWANESE BOY IS HARASSING ME.
WHAT'S THIS ABOUT, HUH?
YOU.
COME WITH US FOR A CHAT.
LET ME GO!! NOW IS NOT...

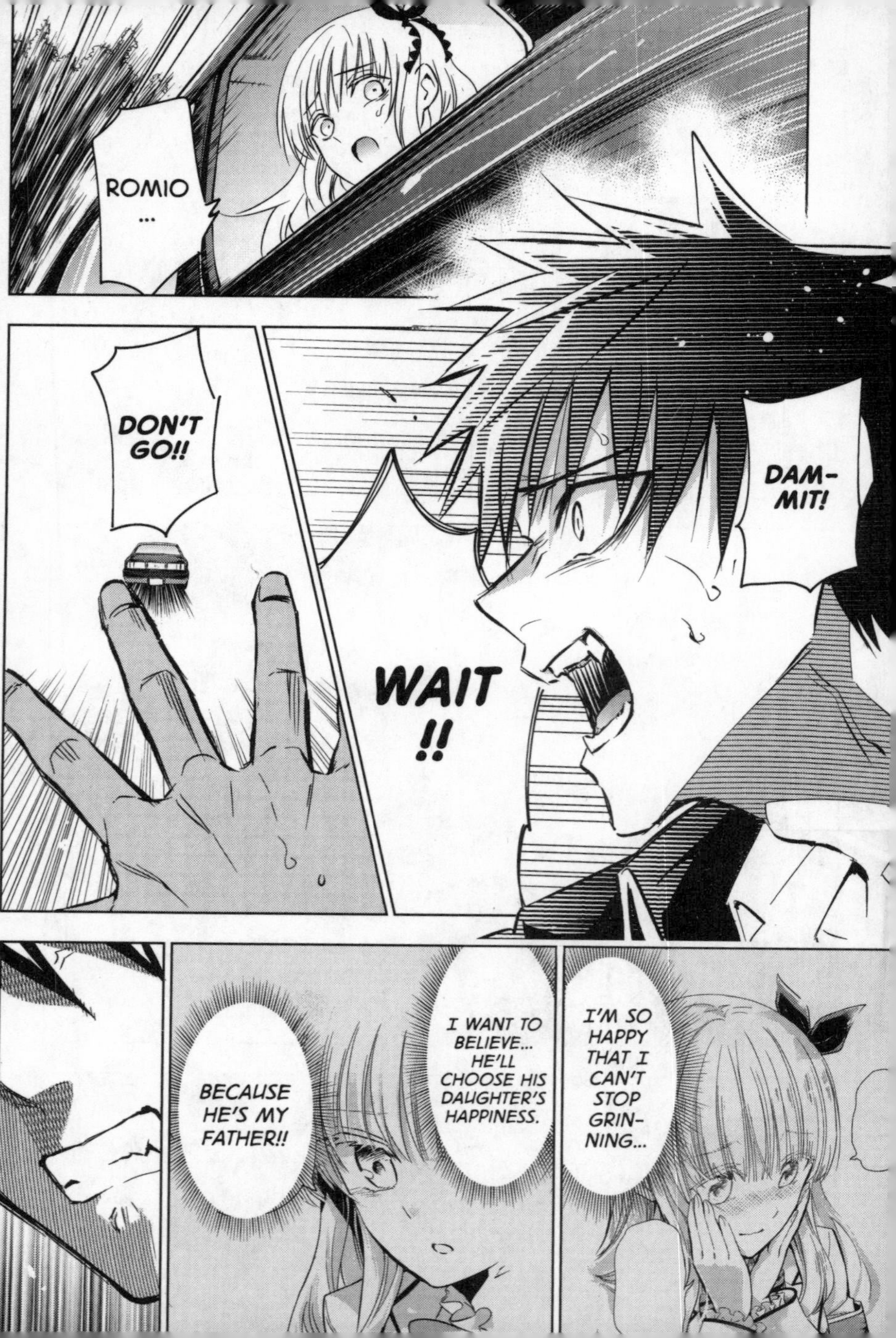
ROMIO ...
DAM-MIT!
WAIT !!
DON'T GO!!
I'M SO HAPPY THAT I CAN'T STOP GRIN-NING...
I WANT TO BELIEVE... HE'LL CHOOSE HIS DAUGHTER'S HAPPINESS.
BECAUSE HE'S MY FATHER!!

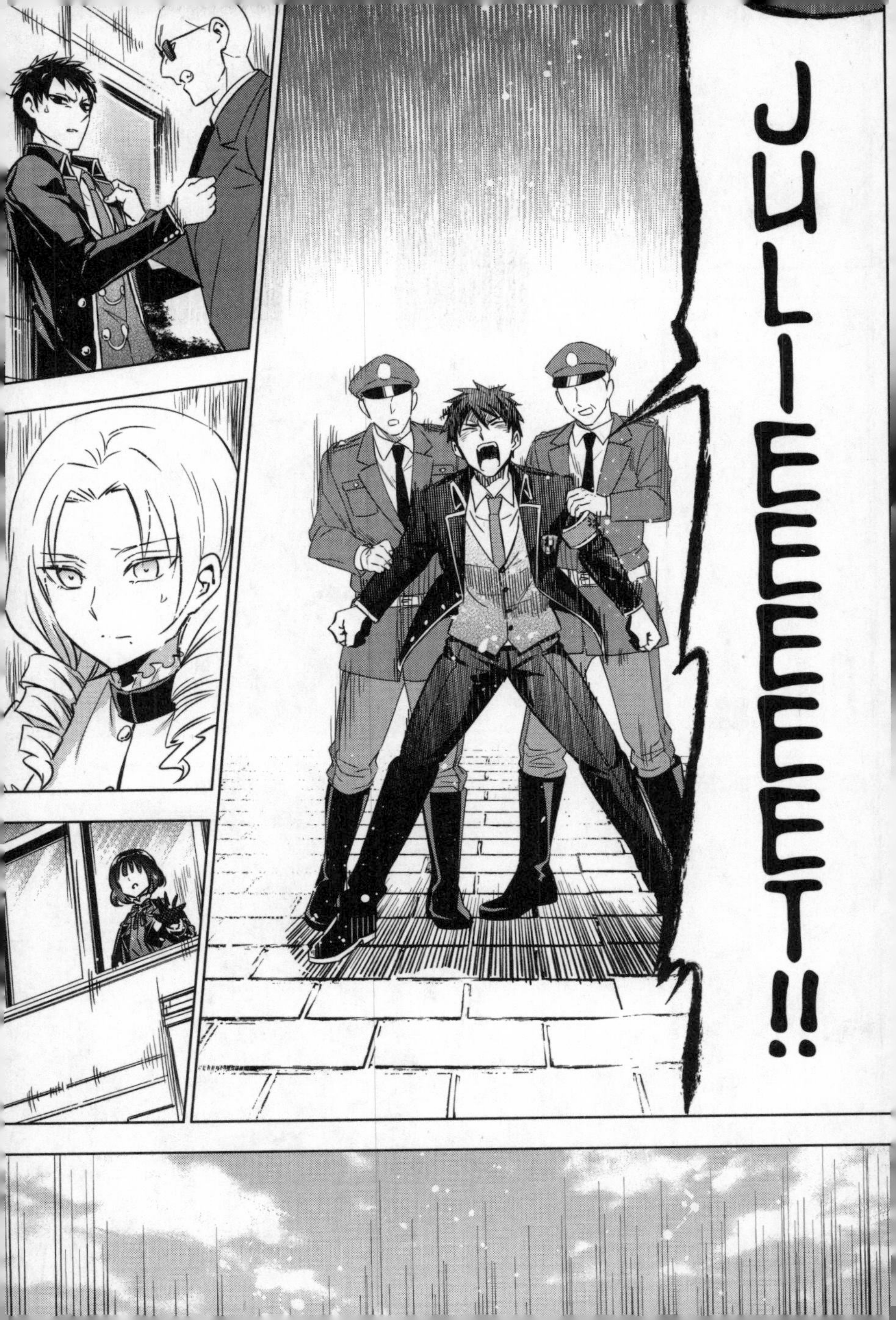
JULIEEEEET!!

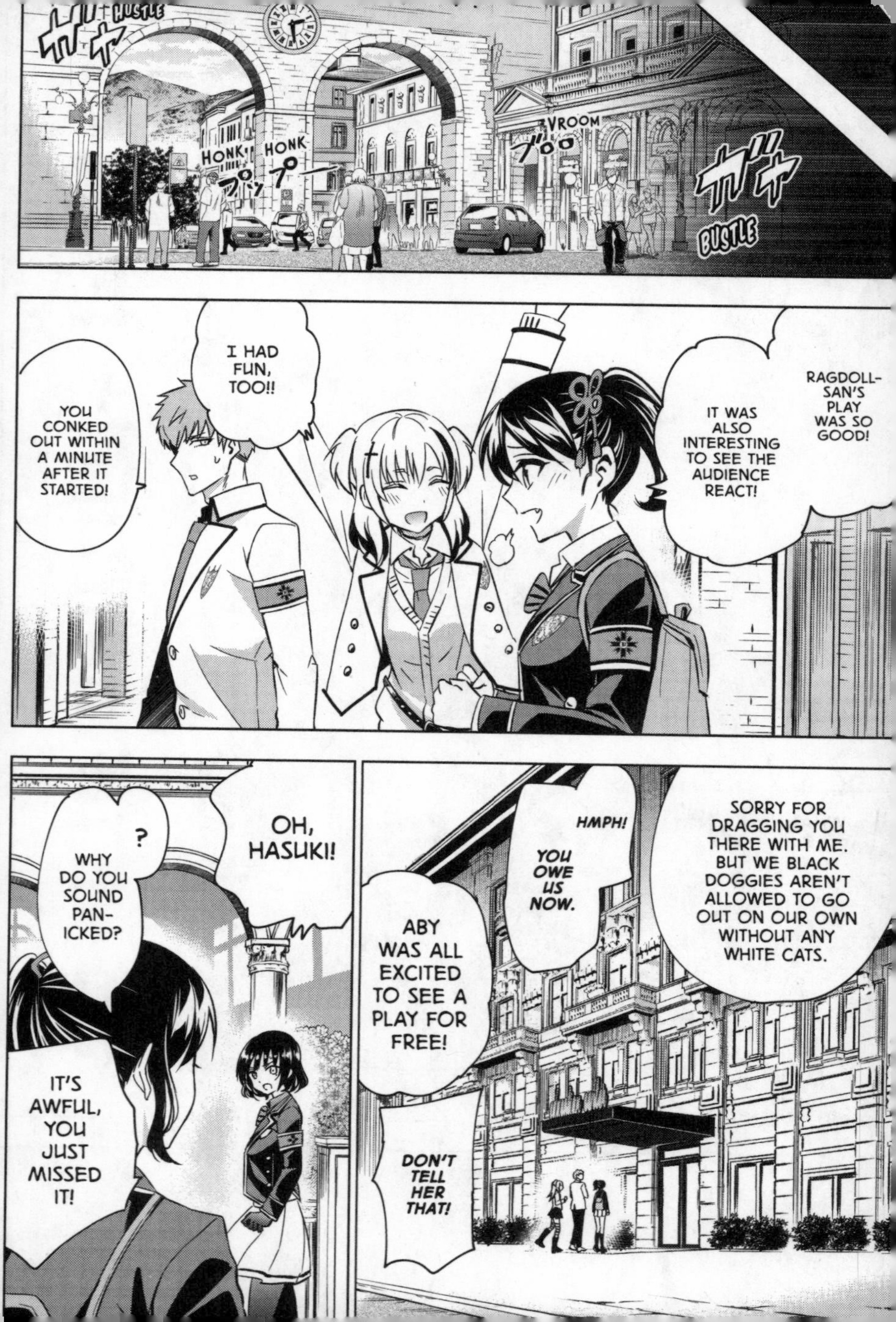
BUSTLE
VROOM
HONK
HONK
HUSTLE
RAGDOLL-SAN'S PLAY WAS SO GOOD!
IT WAS ALSO INTERESTING TO SEE THE AUDIENCE REACT!
I HAD FUN, TOO!!
YOU CONKED OUT WITHIN A MINUTE AFTER IT STARTED!
SORRY FOR DRAGGING YOU THERE WITH ME. BUT WE BLACK DOGGIES AREN'T ALLOWED TO GO OUT ON OUR OWN WITHOUT ANY WHITE CATS.
HMPH! YOU OWE US NOW.
ABY WAS ALL EXCITED TO SEE A PLAY FOR FREE!
DON'T TELL HER THAT!
OH, HASUKI!
? WHY DO YOU SOUND PAN-ICKED?
IT'S AWFUL, YOU JUST MISSED IT!

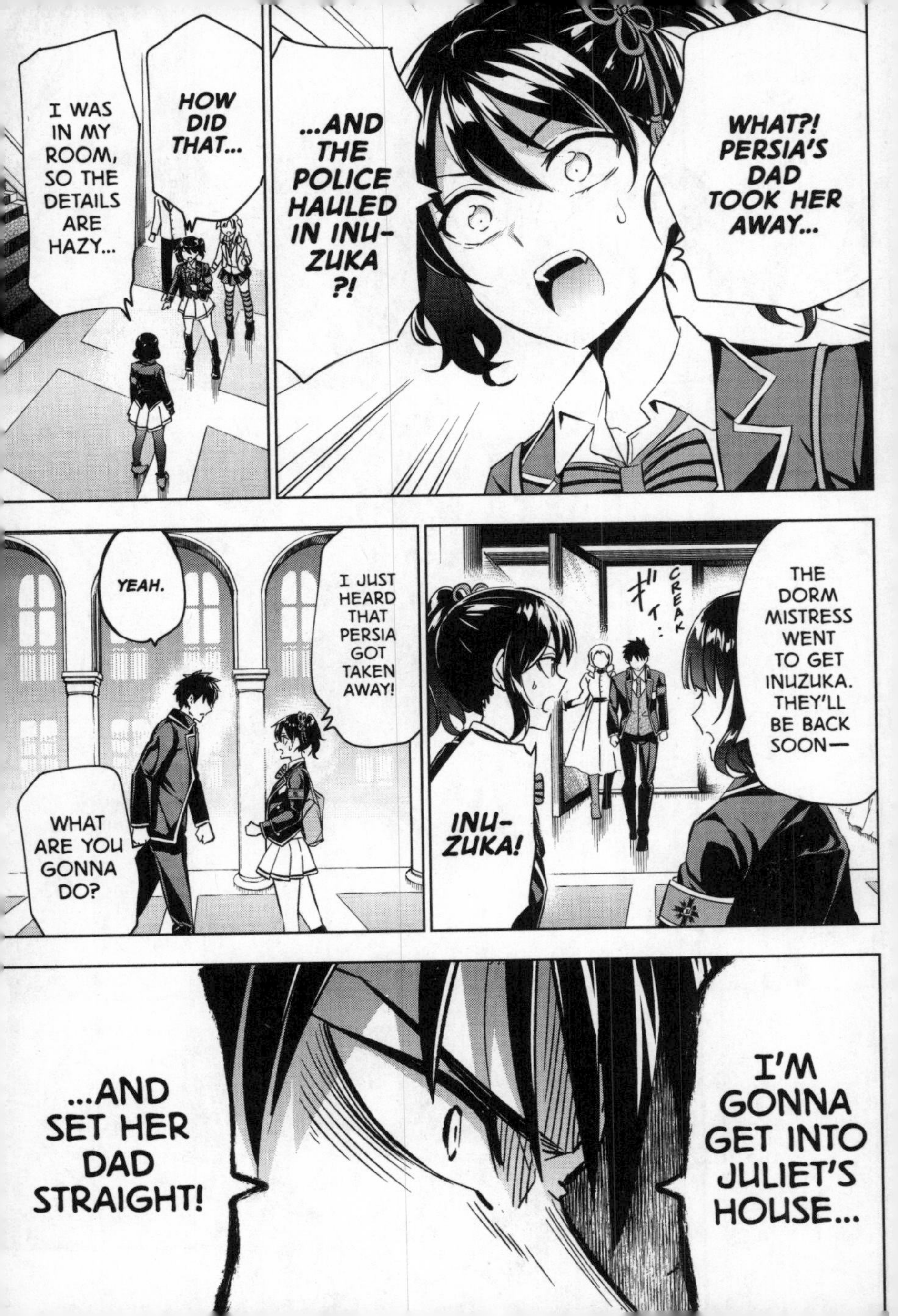
WHAT?! PERSIA'S DAD TOOK HER AWAY...
...AND THE POLICE HAULED IN INUZUKA?!
HOW DID THAT...
I WAS IN MY ROOM, SO THE DETAILS ARE HAZY...
THE DORM MISTRESS WENT TO GET INUZUKA. THEY'LL BE BACK SOON—
CREAK
INUZUKA!
I JUST HEARD THAT PERSIA GOT TAKEN AWAY!
YEAH.
WHAT ARE YOU GONNA DO?
I'M GONNA GET INTO JULIET'S HOUSE...
...AND SET HER DAD STRAIGHT!

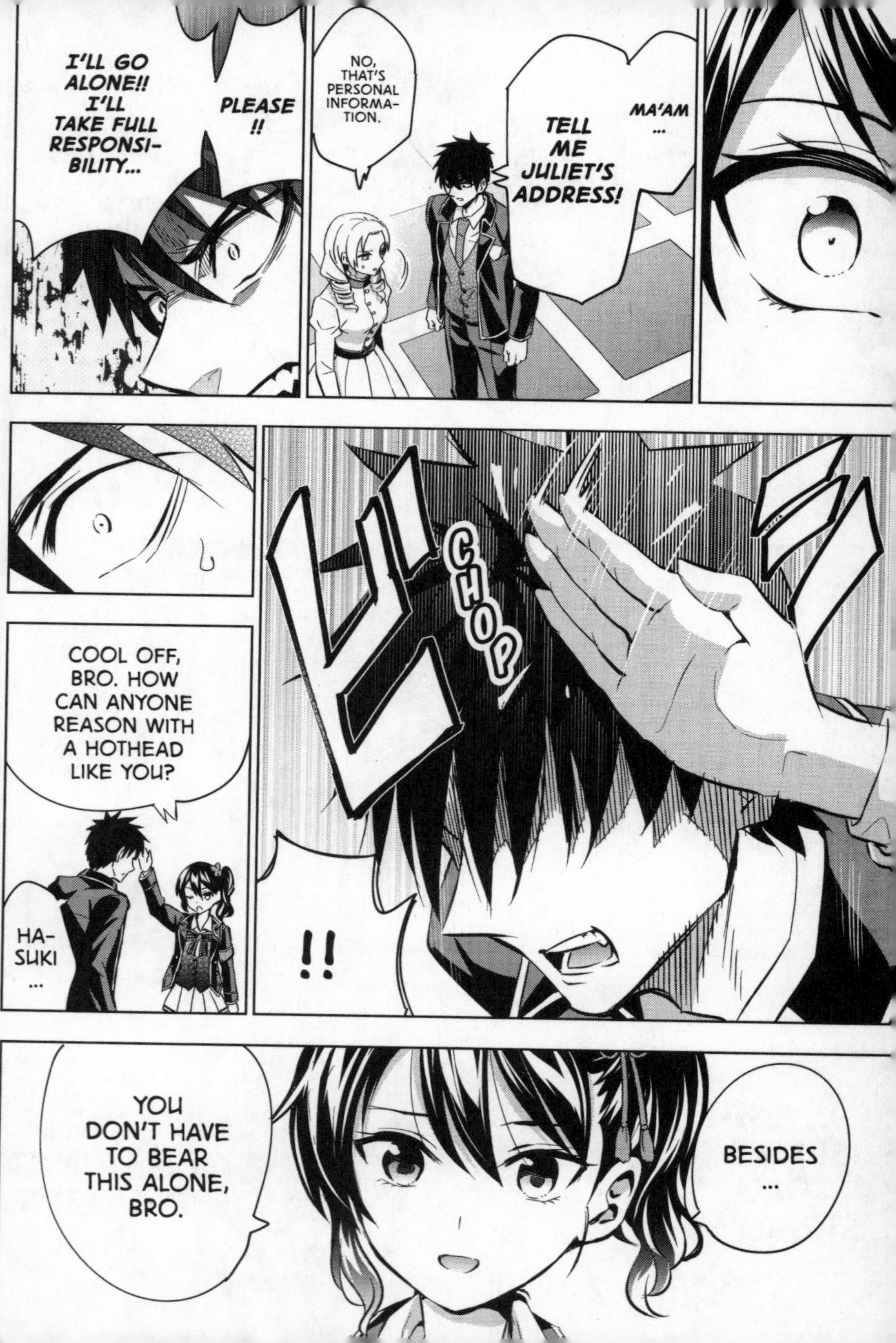
MA'AM ...
TELL ME JULIET'S ADDRESS!
NO, THAT'S PERSONAL INFORMATION.
PLEASE !!
I'LL GO ALONE!! I'LL TAKE FULL RESPONSIBILITY...
CHOP
!!
COOL OFF, BRO. HOW CAN ANYONE REASON WITH A HOTHEAD LIKE YOU?
HA-SUKI ...
BESIDES ...
YOU DON'T HAVE TO BEAR THIS ALONE, BRO.

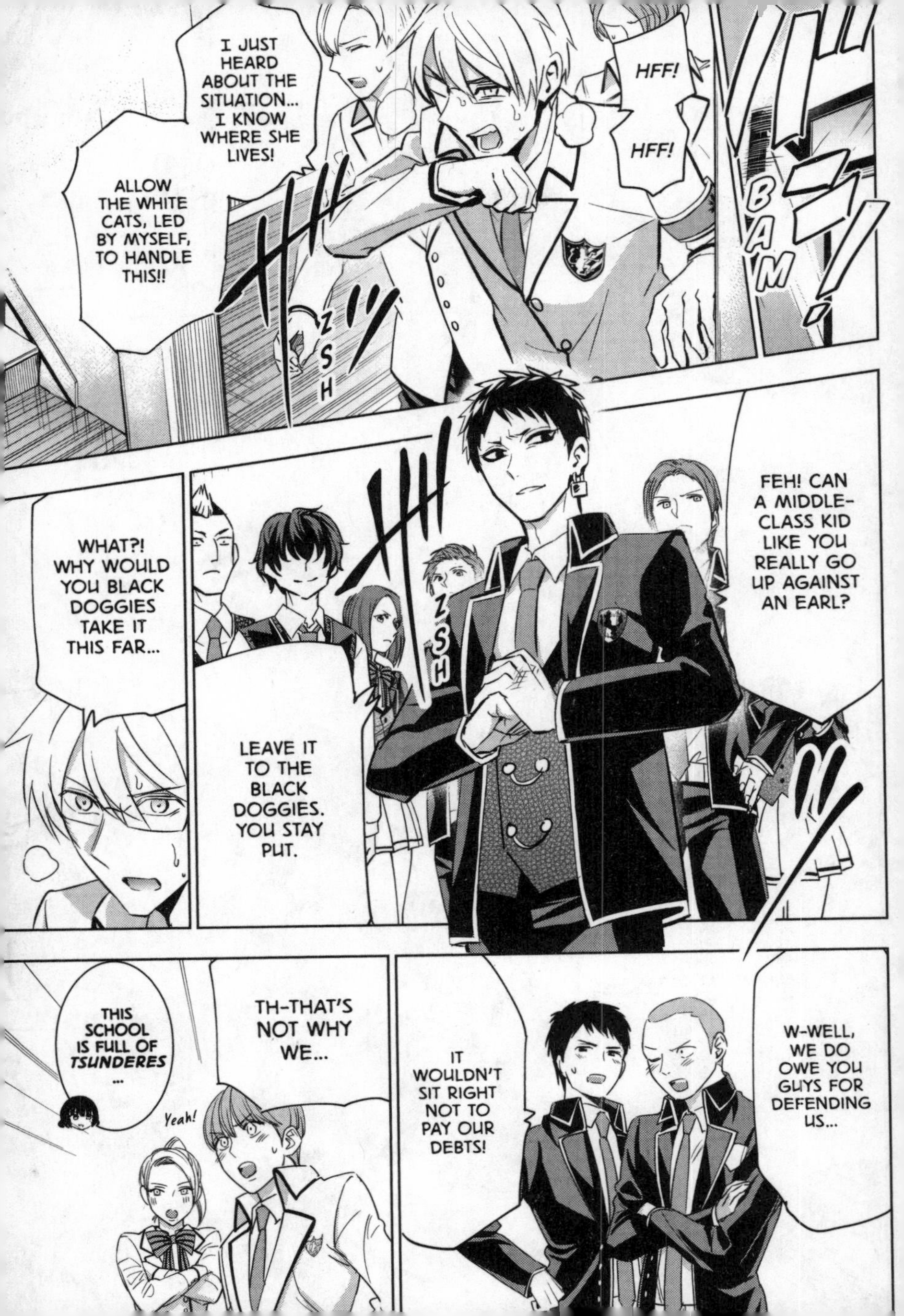
HFF!
HFF!
BAM!
I JUST HEARD ABOUT THE SITUATION... I KNOW WHERE SHE LIVES!
ALLOW THE WHITE CATS, LED BY MYSELF, TO HANDLE THIS!!
ZSH
FEH! CAN A MIDDLE-CLASS KID LIKE YOU REALLY GO UP AGAINST AN EARL?
ZSH
LEAVE IT TO THE BLACK DOGGIES. YOU STAY PUT.
WHAT?! WHY WOULD YOU BLACK DOGGIES TAKE IT THIS FAR...
W-WELL, WE DO OWE YOU GUYS FOR DEFENDING US...
IT WOULDN'T SIT RIGHT NOT TO PAY OUR DEBTS!
TH-THAT'S NOT WHY WE...
Yeah!
THIS SCHOOL IS FULL OF *TSUNDERES*...

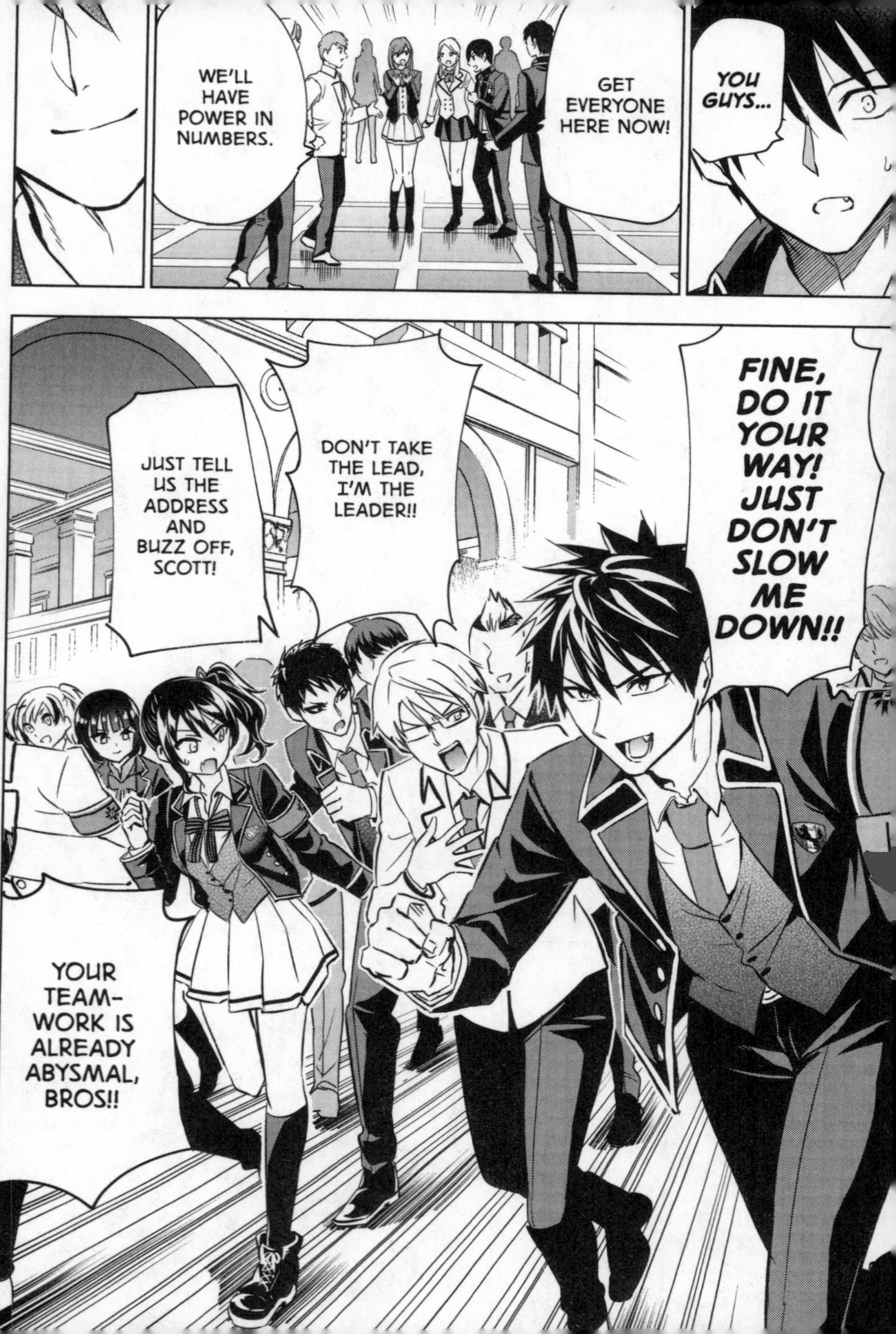
YOU GUYS...
GET EVERYONE HERE NOW!
WE'LL HAVE POWER IN NUMBERS.
FINE, DO IT YOUR WAY! JUST DON'T SLOW ME DOWN!!
DON'T TAKE THE LEAD, I'M THE LEADER!!
JUST TELL US THE ADDRESS AND BUZZ OFF, SCOTT!
YOUR TEAM-WORK IS ALREADY ABYSMAL, BROS!!

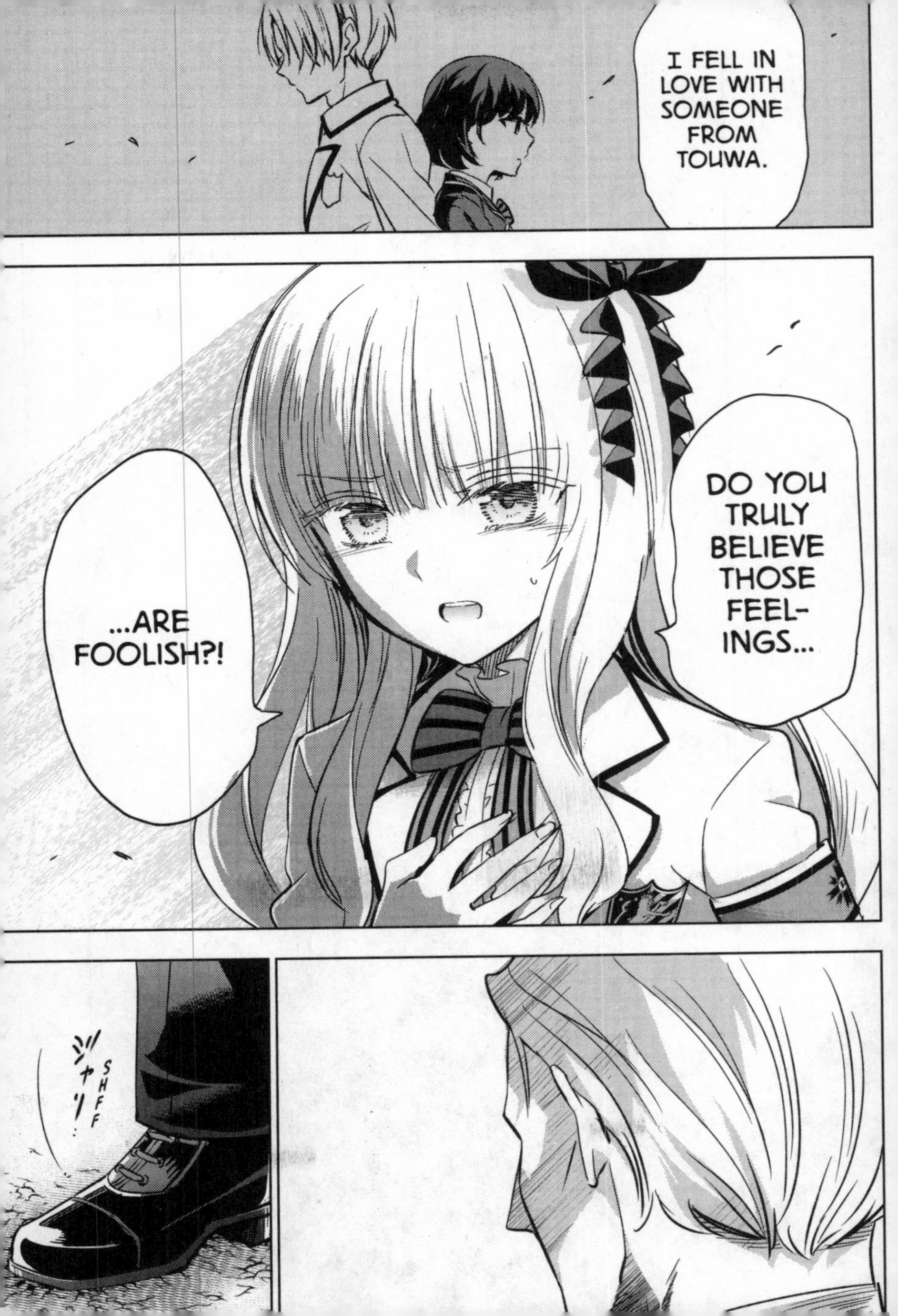
I FELL IN LOVE WITH SOMEONE FROM TOUWA.
DO YOU TRULY BELIEVE THOSE FEEL-INGS...
...ARE FOOLISH?!
ジャリ…
SHFF

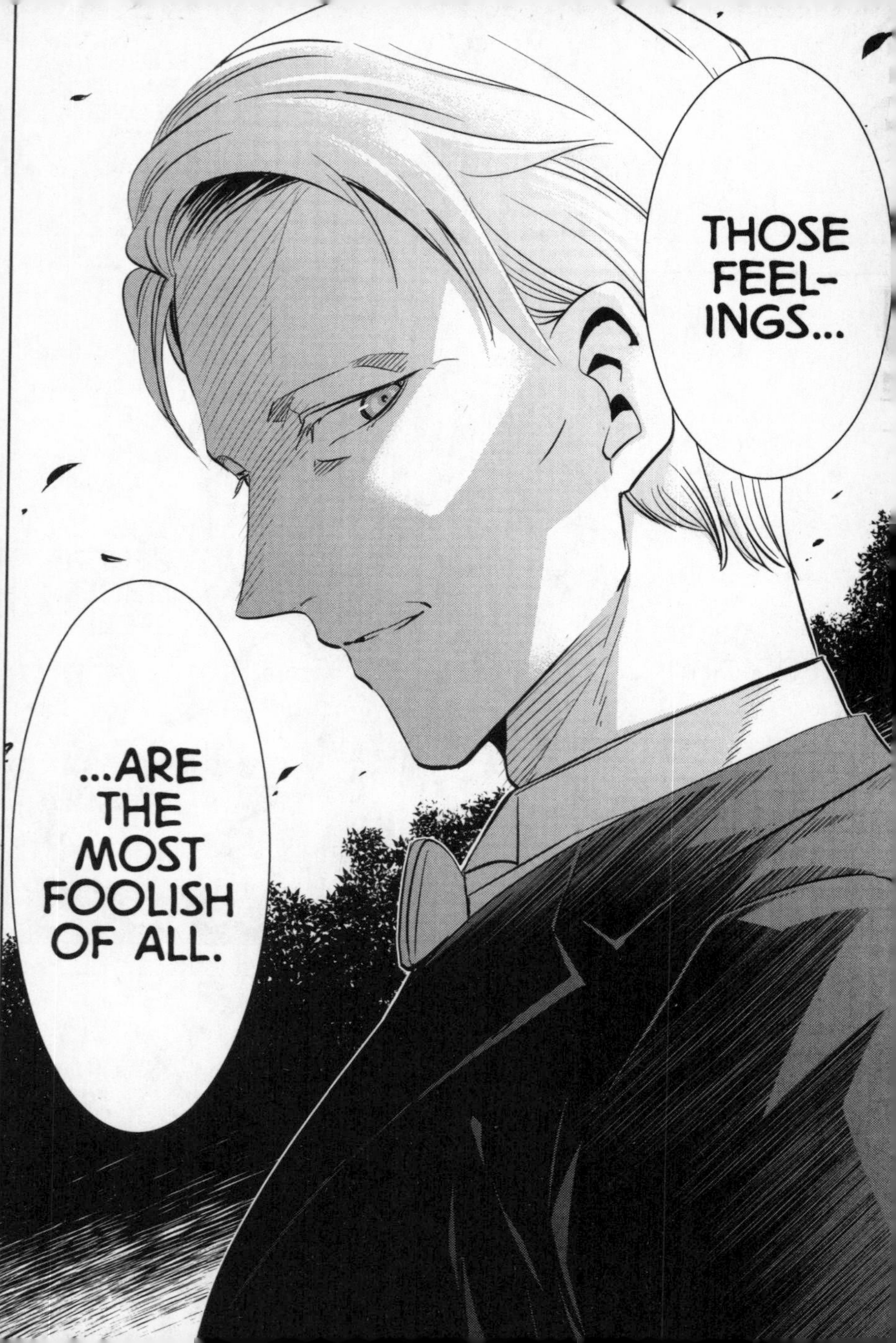
THOSE FEEL-INGS...
...ARE THE MOST FOOLISH OF ALL.

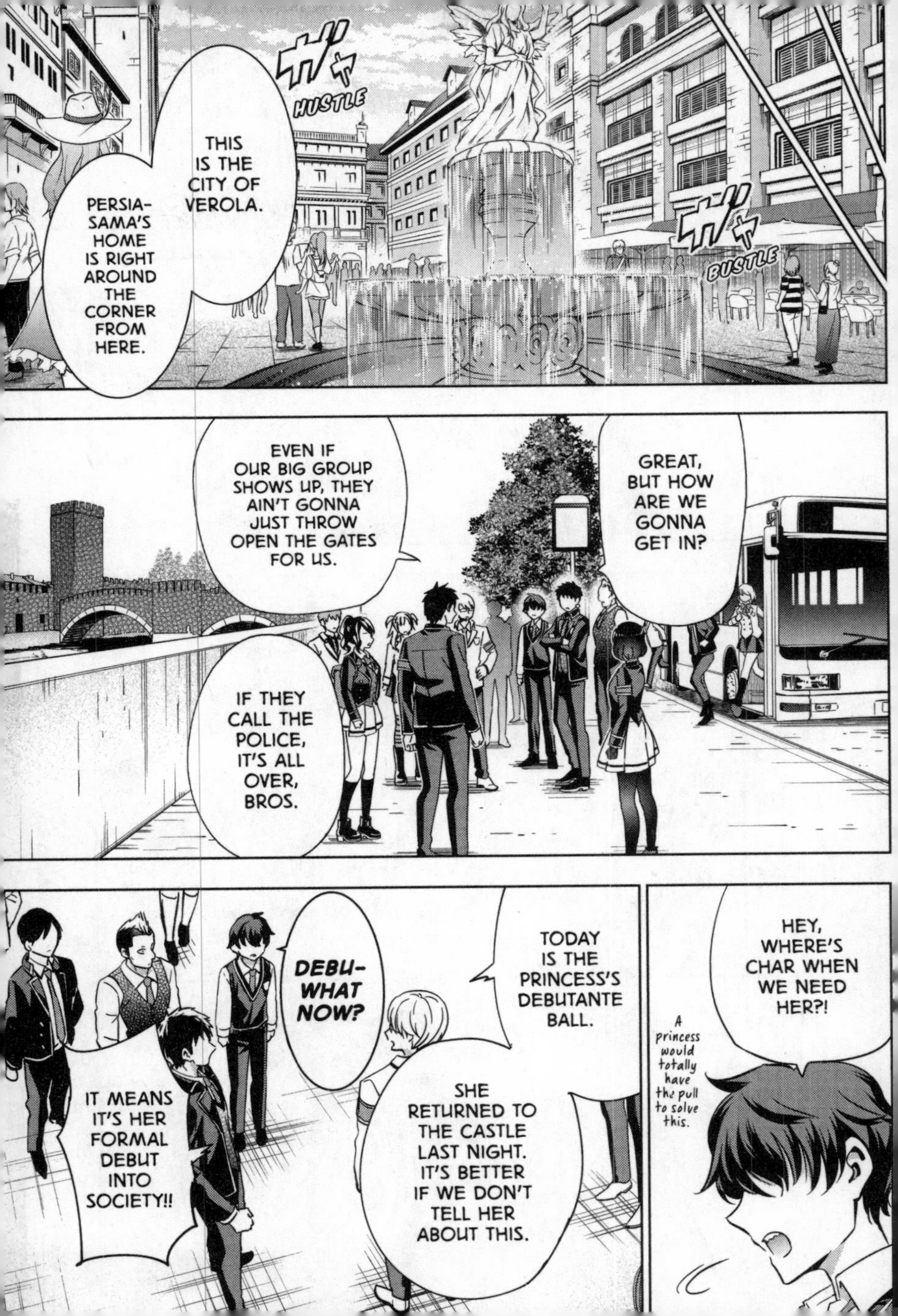
BUSTLE
HUSTLE
THIS IS THE CITY OF VEROLA.
PERSIA-SAMA'S HOME IS RIGHT AROUND THE CORNER FROM HERE.
GREAT, BUT HOW ARE WE GONNA GET IN?
EVEN IF OUR BIG GROUP SHOWS UP, THEY AIN'T GONNA JUST THROW OPEN THE GATES FOR US.
IF THEY CALL THE POLICE, IT'S ALL OVER, BROS.
HEY, WHERE'S CHAR WHEN WE NEED HER?!
A princess would totally have the pull to solve this.
TODAY IS THE PRINCESS'S DEBUTANTE BALL.
DEBU-WHAT NOW?
IT MEANS IT'S HER FORMAL DEBUT INTO SOCIETY!!
SHE RETURNED TO THE CASTLE LAST NIGHT. IT'S BETTER IF WE DON'T TELL HER ABOUT THIS.

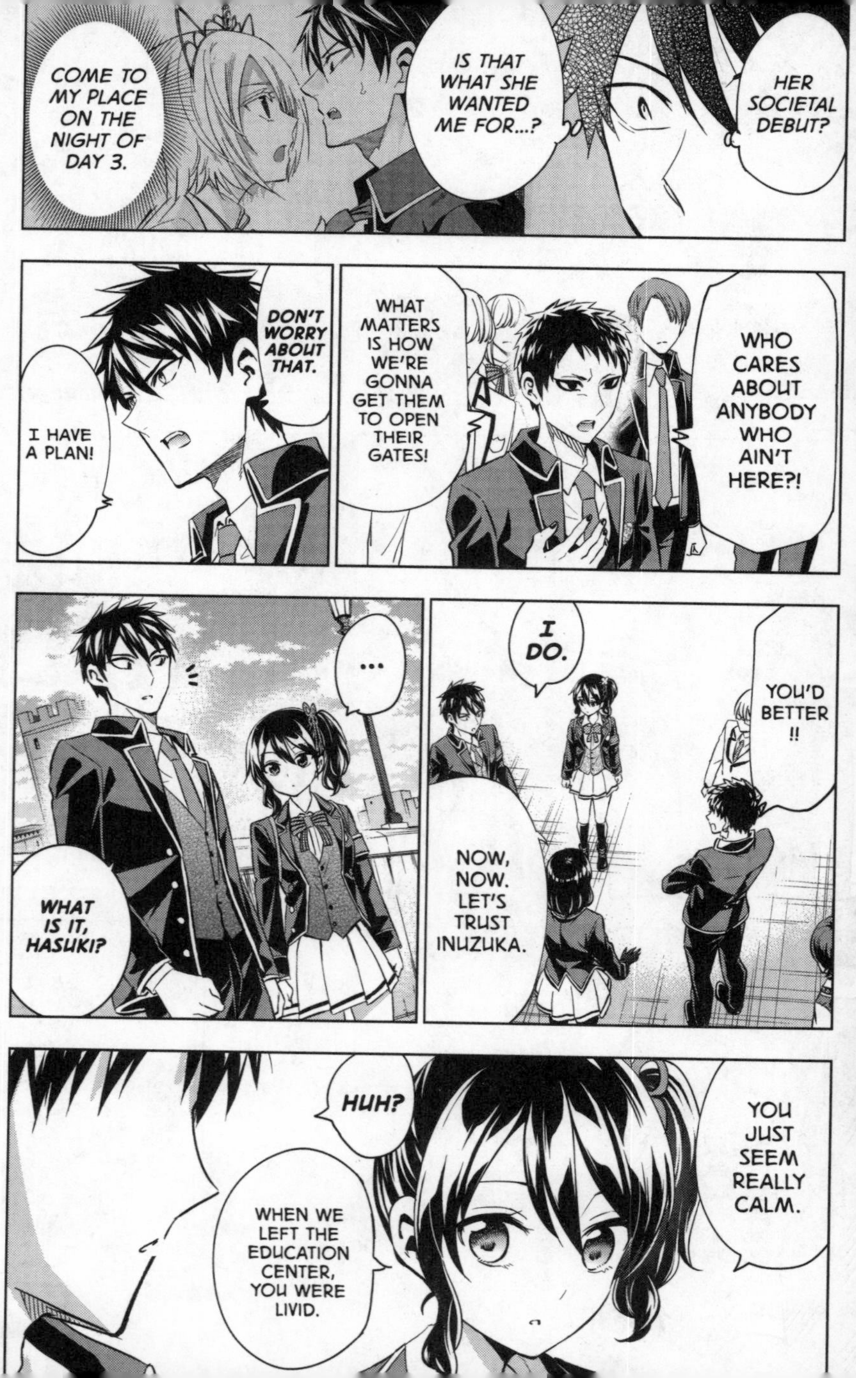
HER SOCIETAL DEBUT?
IS THAT WHAT SHE WANTED ME FOR...?
COME TO MY PLACE ON THE NIGHT OF DAY 3.
WHO CARES ABOUT ANYBODY WHO AIN'T HERE?!
WHAT MATTERS IS HOW WE'RE GONNA GET THEM TO OPEN THEIR GATES!
DON'T WORRY ABOUT THAT.
I HAVE A PLAN!
YOU'D BETTER !!
I DO.
NOW, NOW. LET'S TRUST INUZUKA.
...
WHAT IS IT, HASUKI?
YOU JUST SEEM REALLY CALM.
HUH?
WHEN WE LEFT THE EDUCATION CENTER, YOU WERE LIVID.

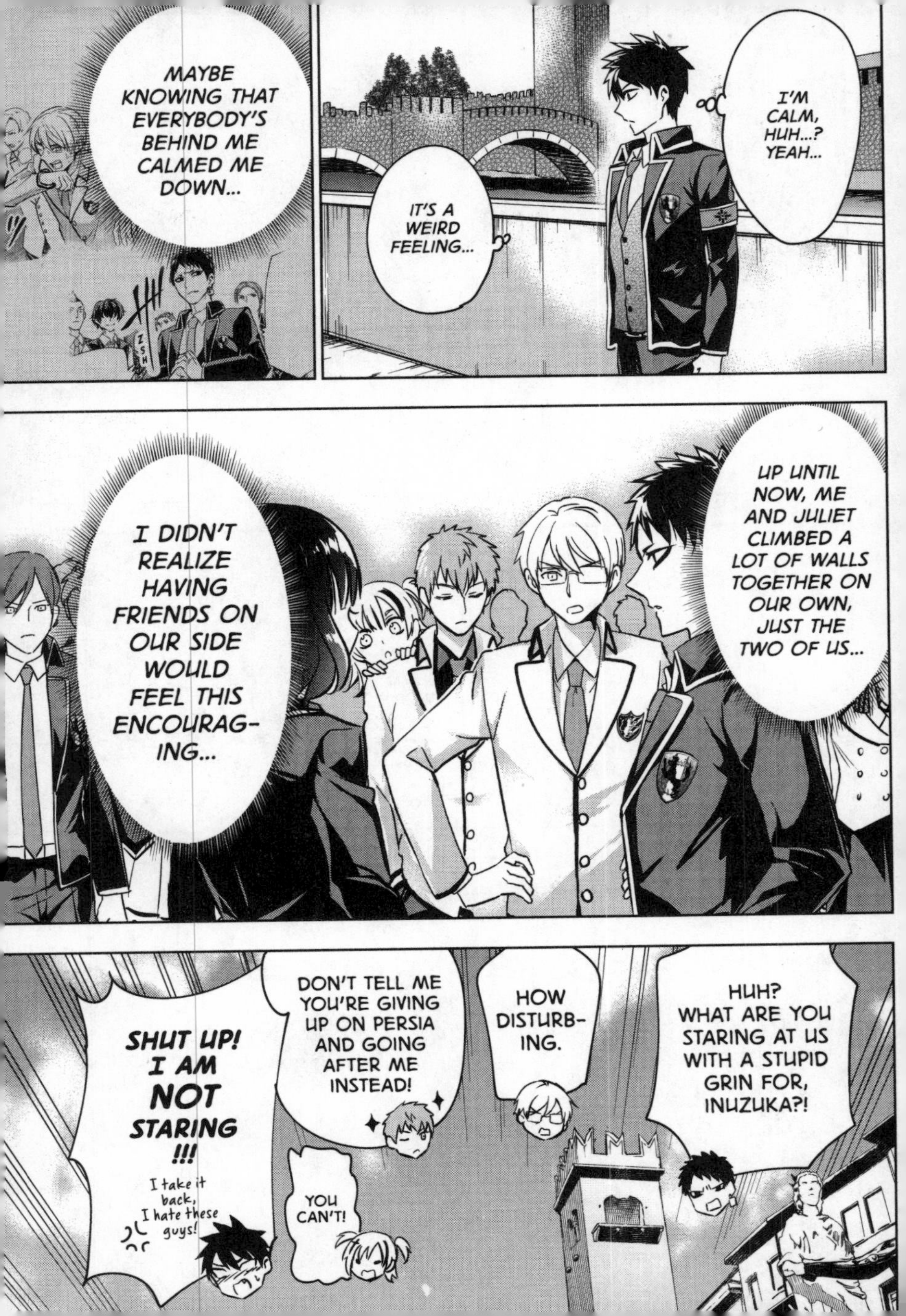
I'M CALM, HUH...? YEAH...
IT'S A WEIRD FEELING...
MAYBE KNOWING THAT EVERYBODY'S BEHIND ME CALMED ME DOWN...
ZSH
UP UNTIL NOW, ME AND JULIET CLIMBED A LOT OF WALLS TOGETHER ON OUR OWN, JUST THE TWO OF US...
I DIDN'T REALIZE HAVING FRIENDS ON OUR SIDE WOULD FEEL THIS ENCOURAG-ING...
HUH? WHAT ARE YOU STARING AT US WITH A STUPID GRIN FOR, INUZUKA?!
HOW DISTURB-ING.
DON'T TELL ME YOU'RE GIVING UP ON PERSIA AND GOING AFTER ME INSTEAD!
YOU CAN'T!
SHUT UP! I AM NOT STARING!!!
I take it back, I hate these guys!

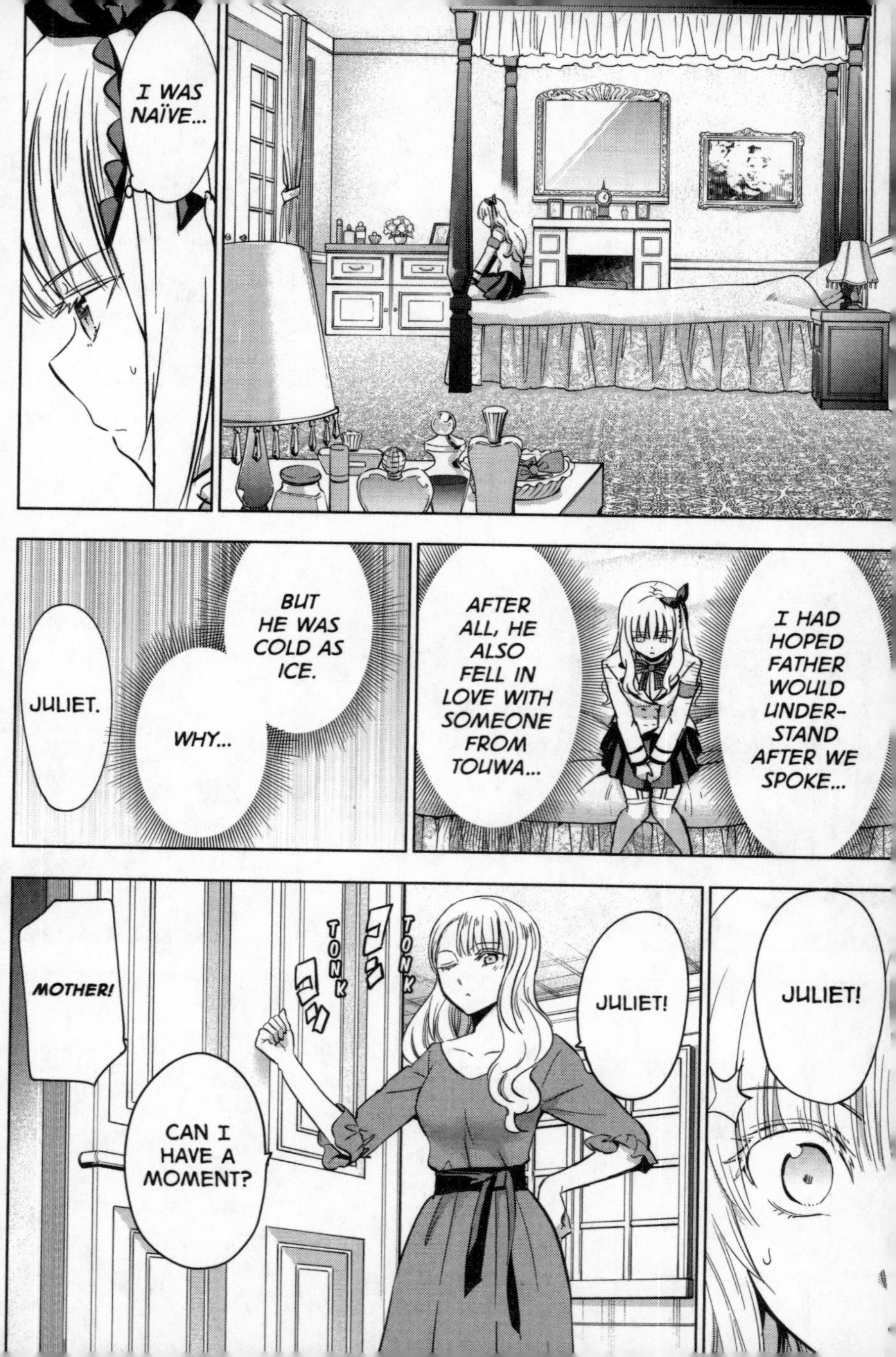
I WAS NAÏVE...
I HAD HOPED FATHER WOULD UNDERSTAND AFTER WE SPOKE...
AFTER ALL, HE ALSO FELL IN LOVE WITH SOMEONE FROM TOUWA...
BUT HE WAS COLD AS ICE.
WHY...
JULIET.
JULIET!
JULIET!
TONK
TONK
CAN I HAVE A MOMENT?
MOTHER!

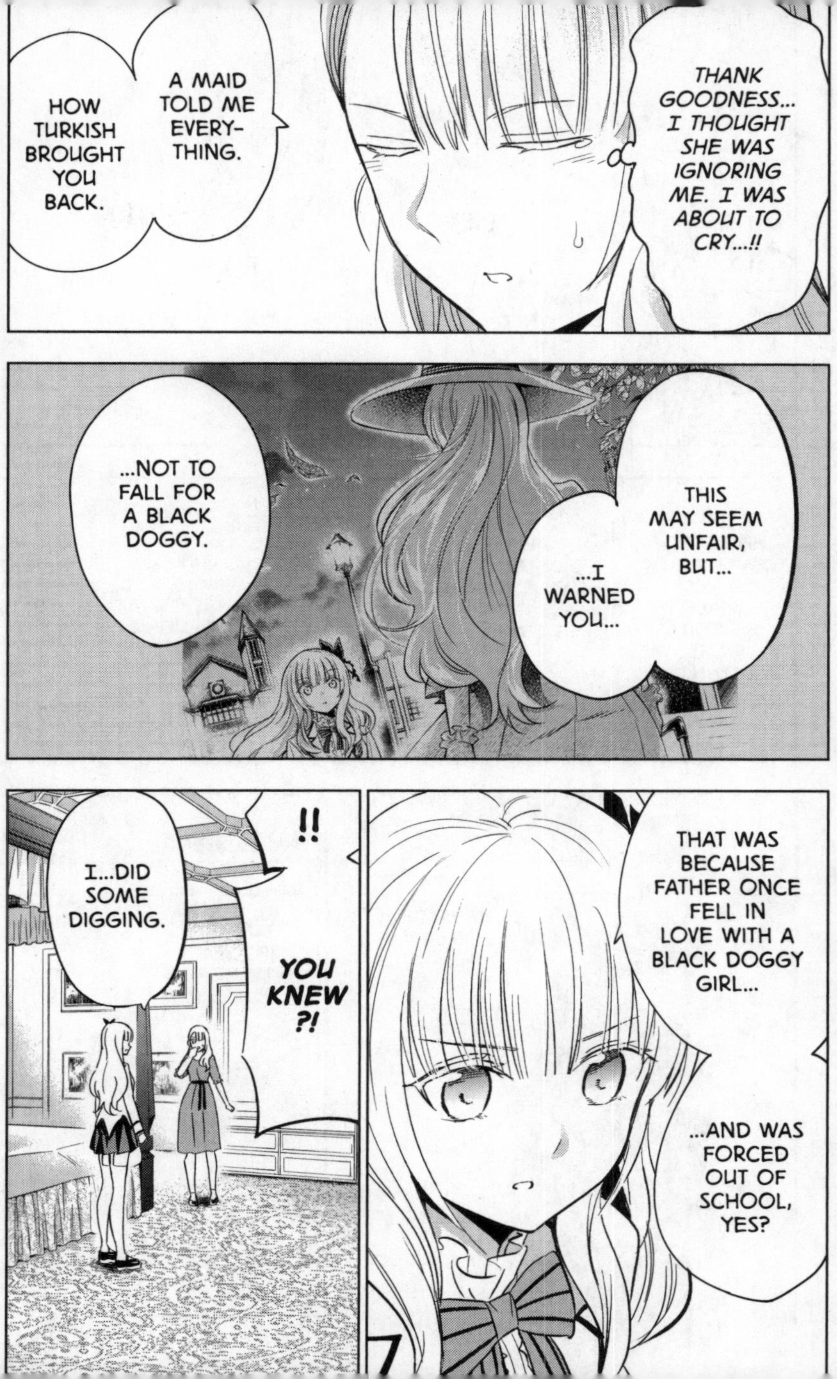
THANK GOODNESS... I THOUGHT SHE WAS IGNORING ME. I WAS ABOUT TO CRY...!!
A MAID TOLD ME EVERY-THING.
HOW TURKISH BROUGHT YOU BACK.
THIS MAY SEEM UNFAIR, BUT...
...I WARNED YOU...
...NOT TO FALL FOR A BLACK DOGGY.
THAT WAS BECAUSE FATHER ONCE FELL IN LOVE WITH A BLACK DOGGY GIRL...
...AND WAS FORCED OUT OF SCHOOL, YES?
!!
YOU KNEW?!
I...DID SOME DIGGING.

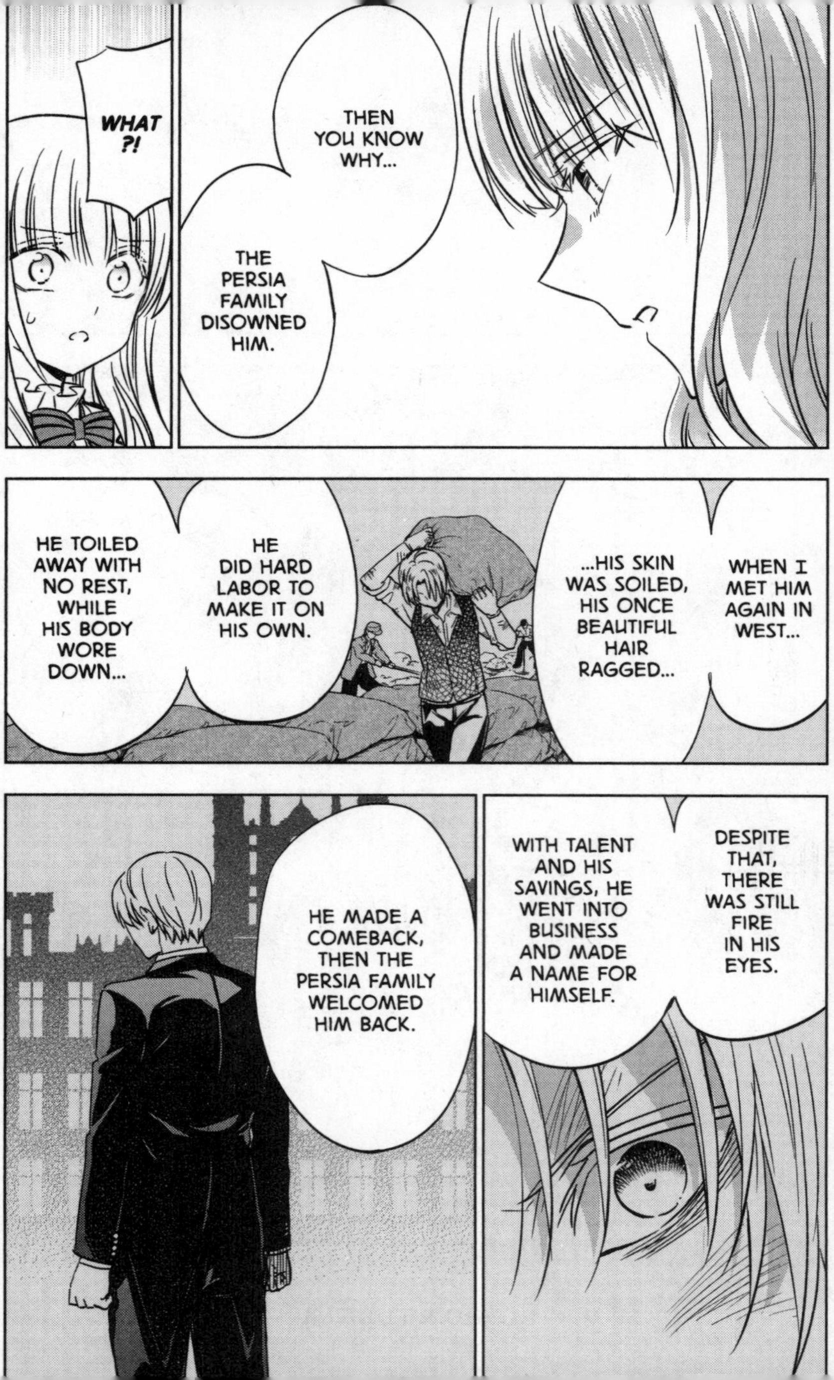
THEN YOU KNOW WHY...
THE PERSIA FAMILY DISOWNED HIM.
WHAT?!
WHEN I MET HIM AGAIN IN WEST...
...HIS SKIN WAS SOILED, HIS ONCE BEAUTIFUL HAIR RAGGED...
HE DID HARD LABOR TO MAKE IT ON HIS OWN.
HE TOILED AWAY WITH NO REST, WHILE HIS BODY WORE DOWN...
DESPITE THAT, THERE WAS STILL FIRE IN HIS EYES.
WITH TALENT AND HIS SAVINGS, HE WENT INTO BUSINESS AND MADE A NAME FOR HIMSELF.
HE MADE A COMEBACK, THEN THE PERSIA FAMILY WELCOMED HIM BACK.

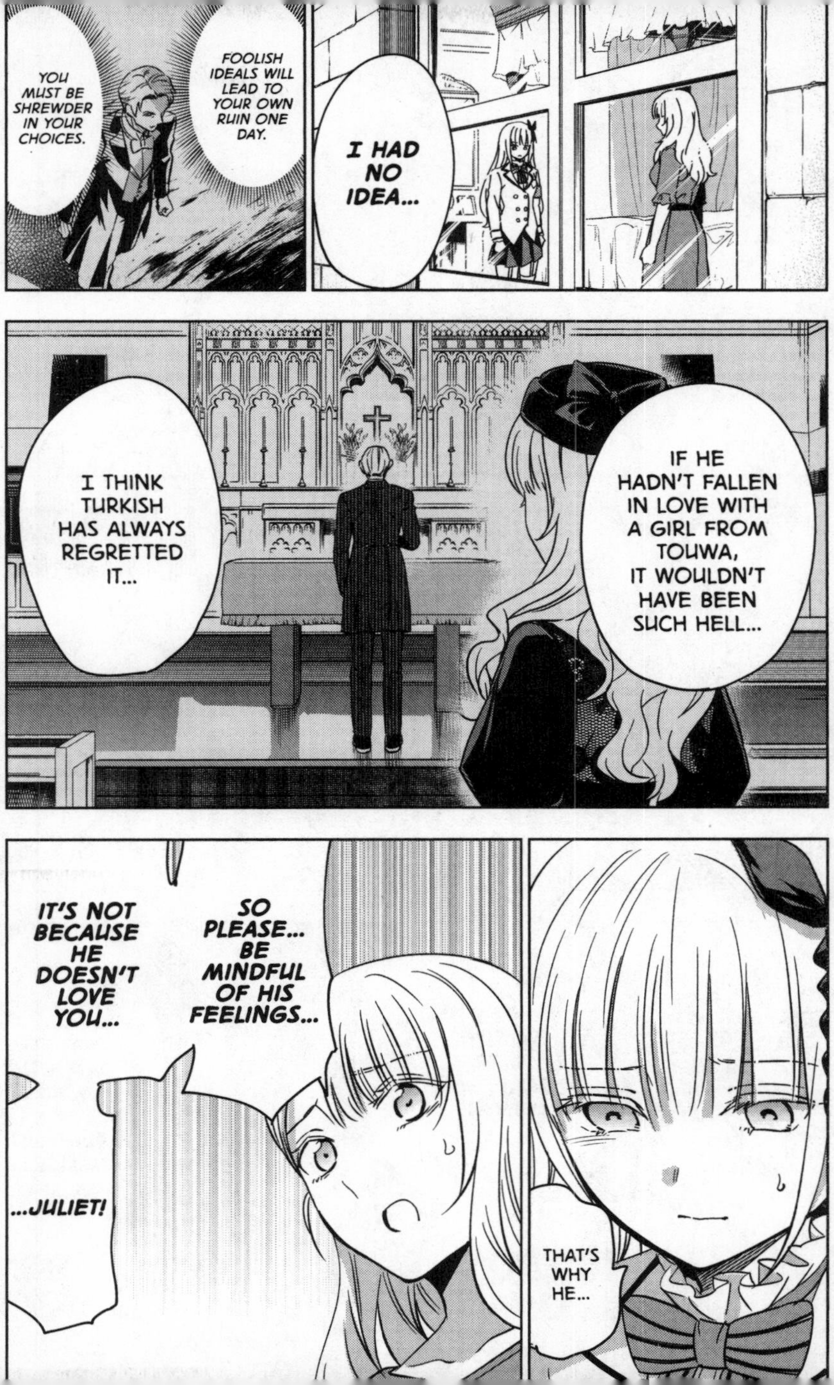
I HAD NO IDEA...
FOOLISH IDEALS WILL LEAD TO YOUR OWN RUIN ONE DAY.
YOU MUST BE SHREWDER IN YOUR CHOICES.
IF HE HADN'T FALLEN IN LOVE WITH A GIRL FROM TOUWA, IT WOULDN'T HAVE BEEN SUCH HELL...
I THINK TURKISH HAS ALWAYS REGRETTED IT...
THAT'S WHY HE...
SO PLEASE... BE MINDFUL OF HIS FEELINGS...
IT'S NOT BECAUSE HE DOESN'T LOVE YOU...
...JULIET!

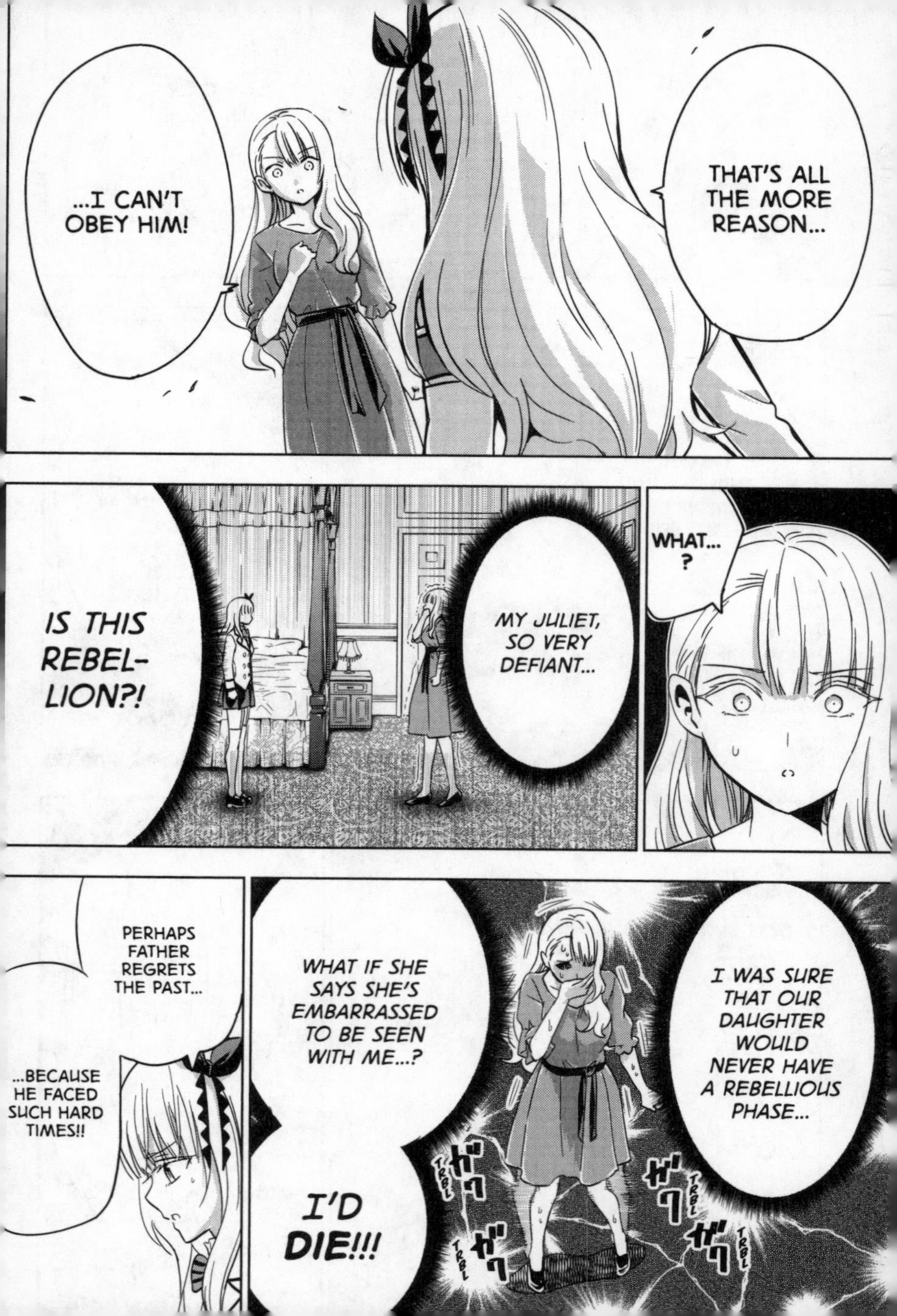
THAT'S ALL THE MORE REASON...
...I CAN'T OBEY HIM!
WHAT... ?
MY JULIET, SO VERY DEFIANT...
IS THIS REBEL-LION?!
I WAS SURE THAT OUR DAUGHTER WOULD NEVER HAVE A REBELLIOUS PHASE...
WHAT IF SHE SAYS SHE'S EMBARRASSED TO BE SEEN WITH ME...?
I'D DIE!!!
TRBL
TRBL
TRBL
TRBL
PERHAPS FATHER REGRETS THE PAST...
...BECAUSE HE FACED SUCH HARD TIMES!!

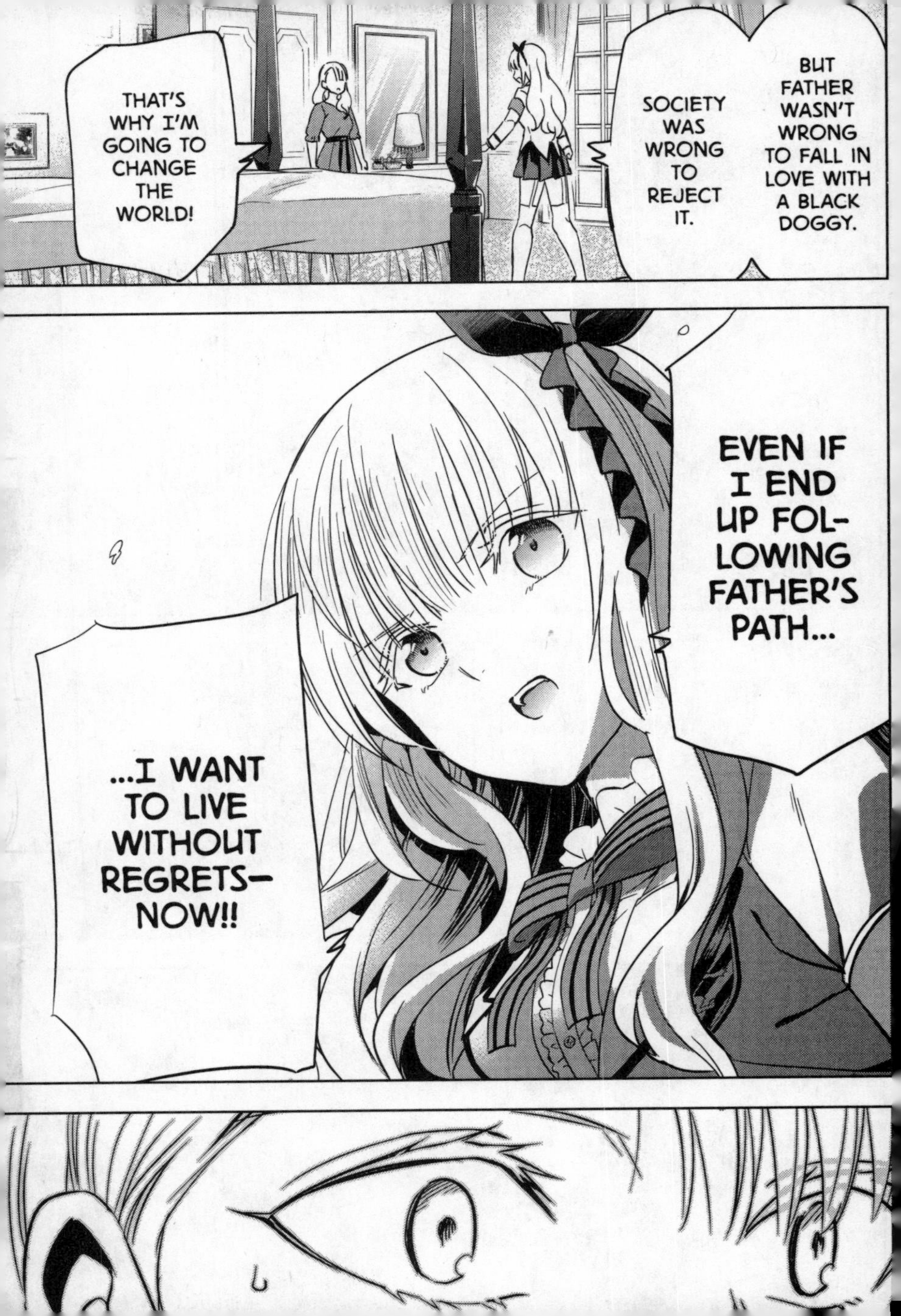
BUT FATHER WASN'T WRONG TO FALL IN LOVE WITH A BLACK DOGGY.
SOCIETY WAS WRONG TO REJECT IT.
THAT'S WHY I'M GOING TO CHANGE THE WORLD!
EVEN IF I END UP FOL-LOWING FATHER'S PATH...
...I WANT TO LIVE WITHOUT REGRETS—NOW!!

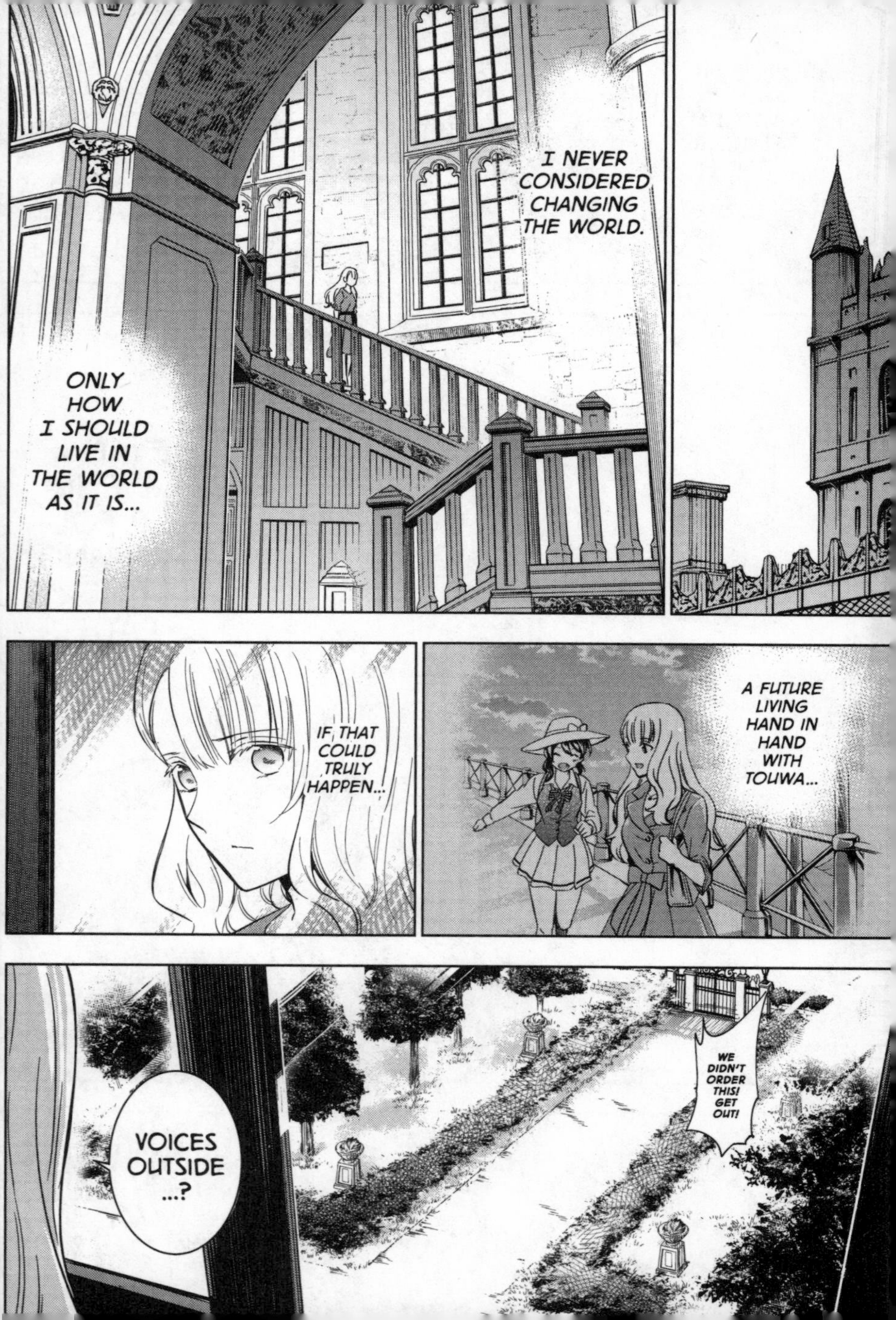
I NEVER CONSIDERED CHANGING THE WORLD.
ONLY HOW I SHOULD LIVE IN THE WORLD AS IT IS...
A FUTURE LIVING HAND IN HAND WITH TOUWA...
IF THAT COULD TRULY HAPPEN...
WE DIDN'T ORDER THIS! GET OUT!
VOICES OUTSIDE ...?

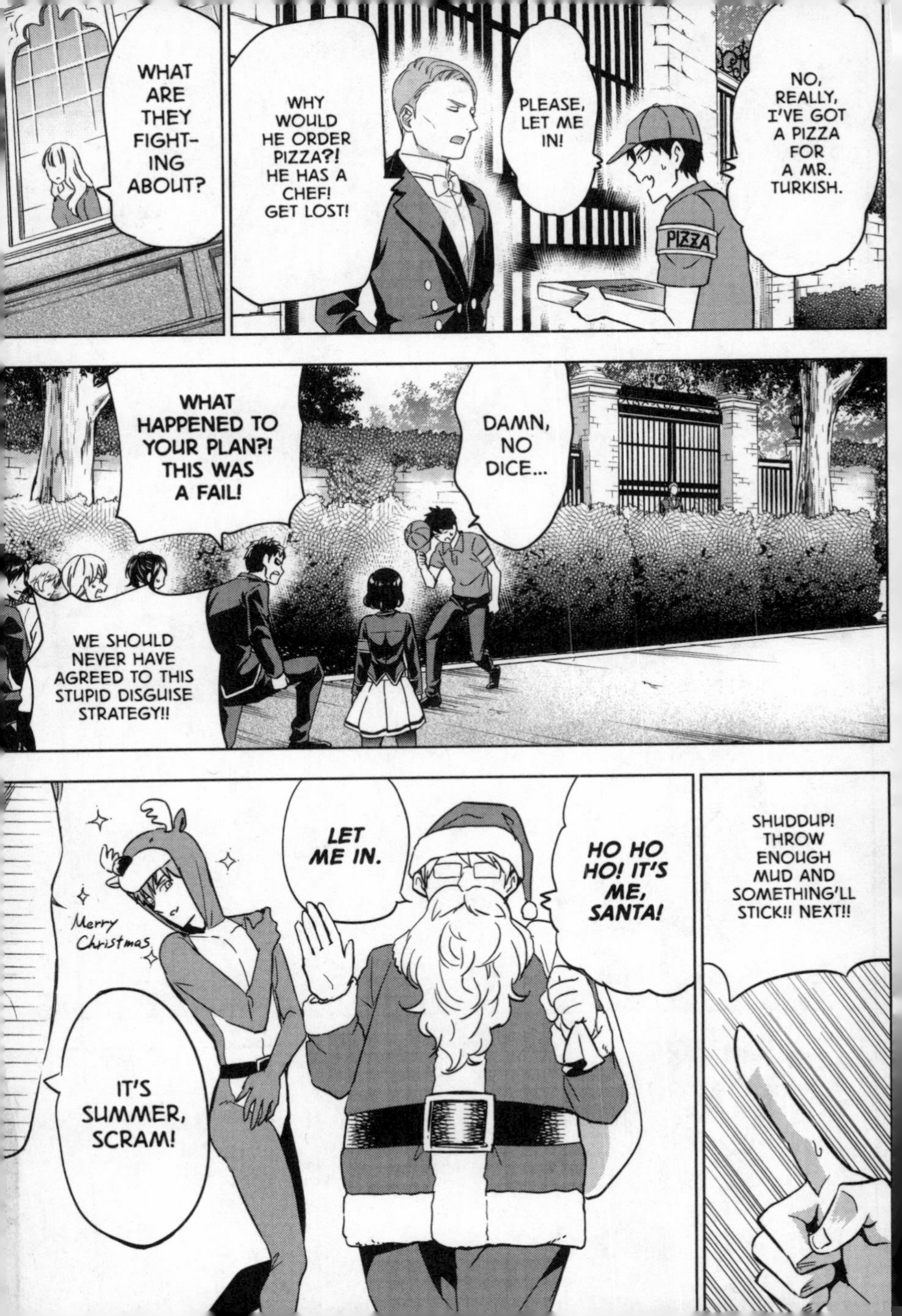
NO, REALLY, I'VE GOT A PIZZA FOR A MR. TURKISH.
PIZZA
PLEASE, LET ME IN!
WHY WOULD HE ORDER PIZZA?! HE HAS A CHEF! GET LOST!
WHAT ARE THEY FIGHT-ING ABOUT?
DAMN, NO DICE...
WHAT HAPPENED TO YOUR PLAN?! THIS WAS A FAIL!
WE SHOULD NEVER HAVE AGREED TO THIS STUPID DISGUISE STRATEGY!!
SHUDDUP! THROW ENOUGH MUD AND SOMETHING'LL STICK!! NEXT!!
HO HO HO! IT'S ME, SANTA!
LET ME IN.
Merry Christmas
IT'S SUMMER, SCRAM!

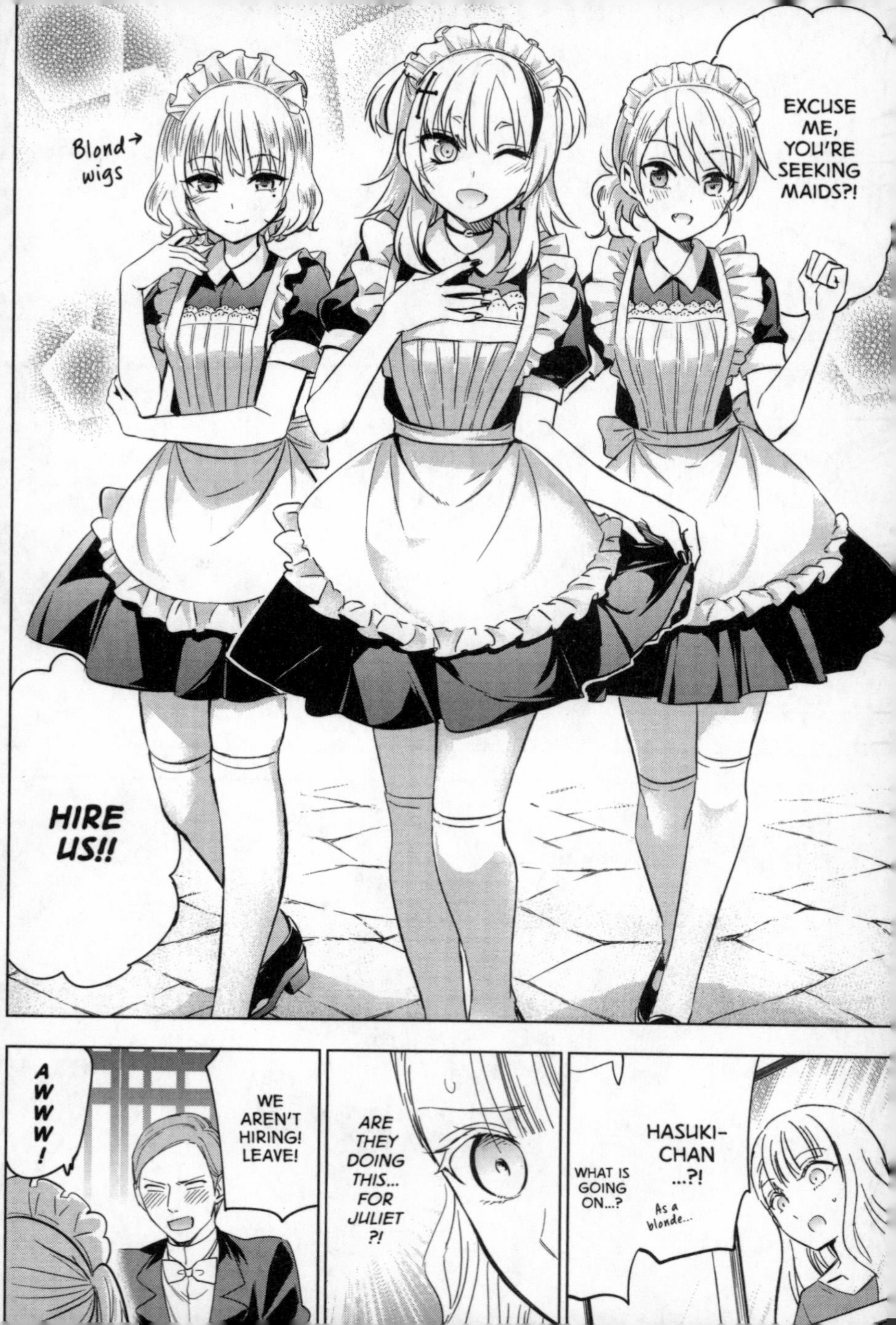
EXCUSE ME, YOU'RE SEEKING MAIDS?!
Blond→ wigs
HIRE US!!
HASUKI-CHAN ...?!
WHAT IS GOING ON...?
As a blonde...
ARE THEY DOING THIS... FOR JULIET ?!
WE AREN'T HIRING! LEAVE!
AWWW!

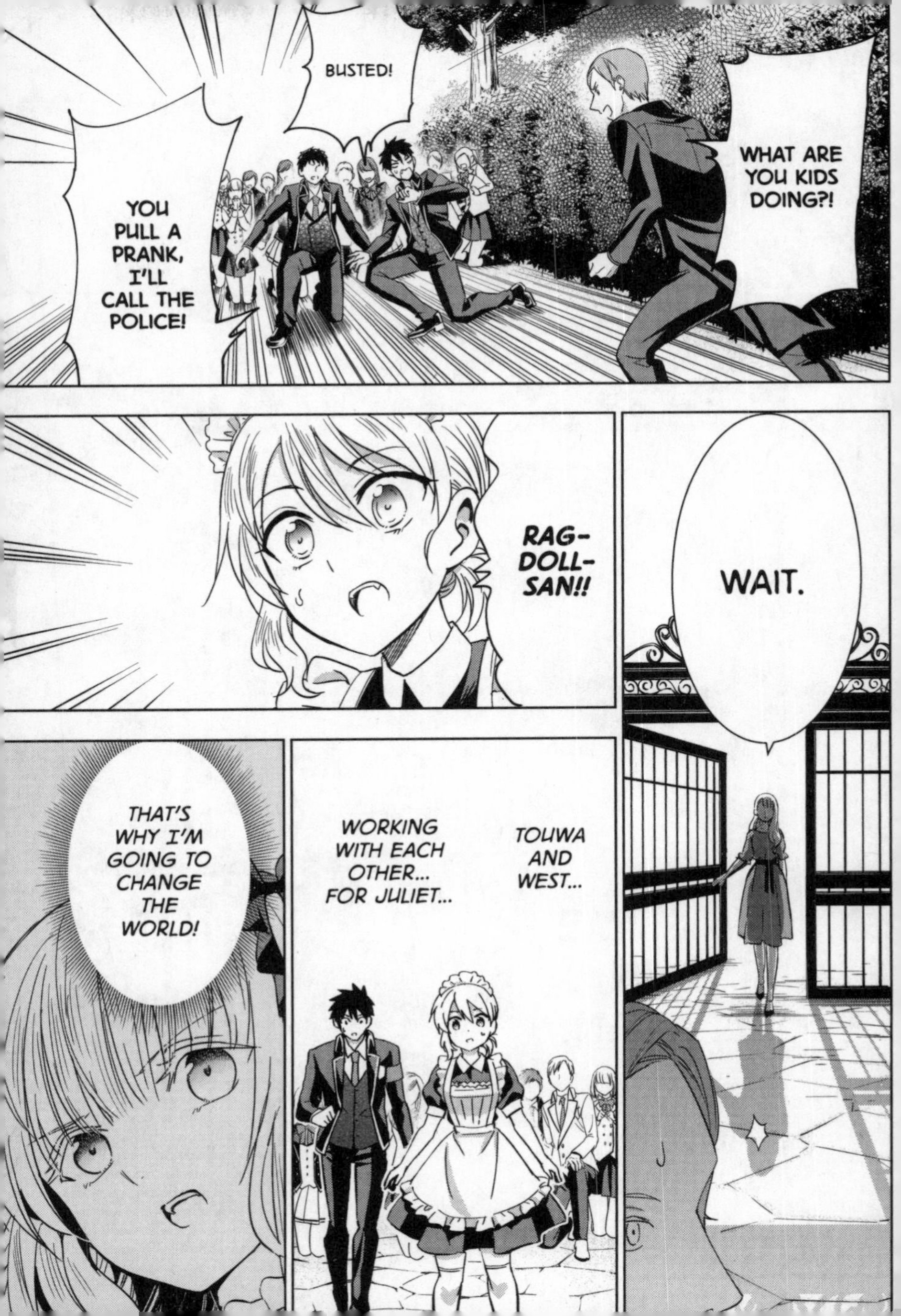
WHAT ARE YOU KIDS DOING?!
BUSTED!
YOU PULL A PRANK, I'LL CALL THE POLICE!
WAIT.
RAG-DOLL-SAN!!
TOUWA AND WEST...
WORKING WITH EACH OTHER... FOR JULIET...
THAT'S WHY I'M GOING TO CHANGE THE WORLD!

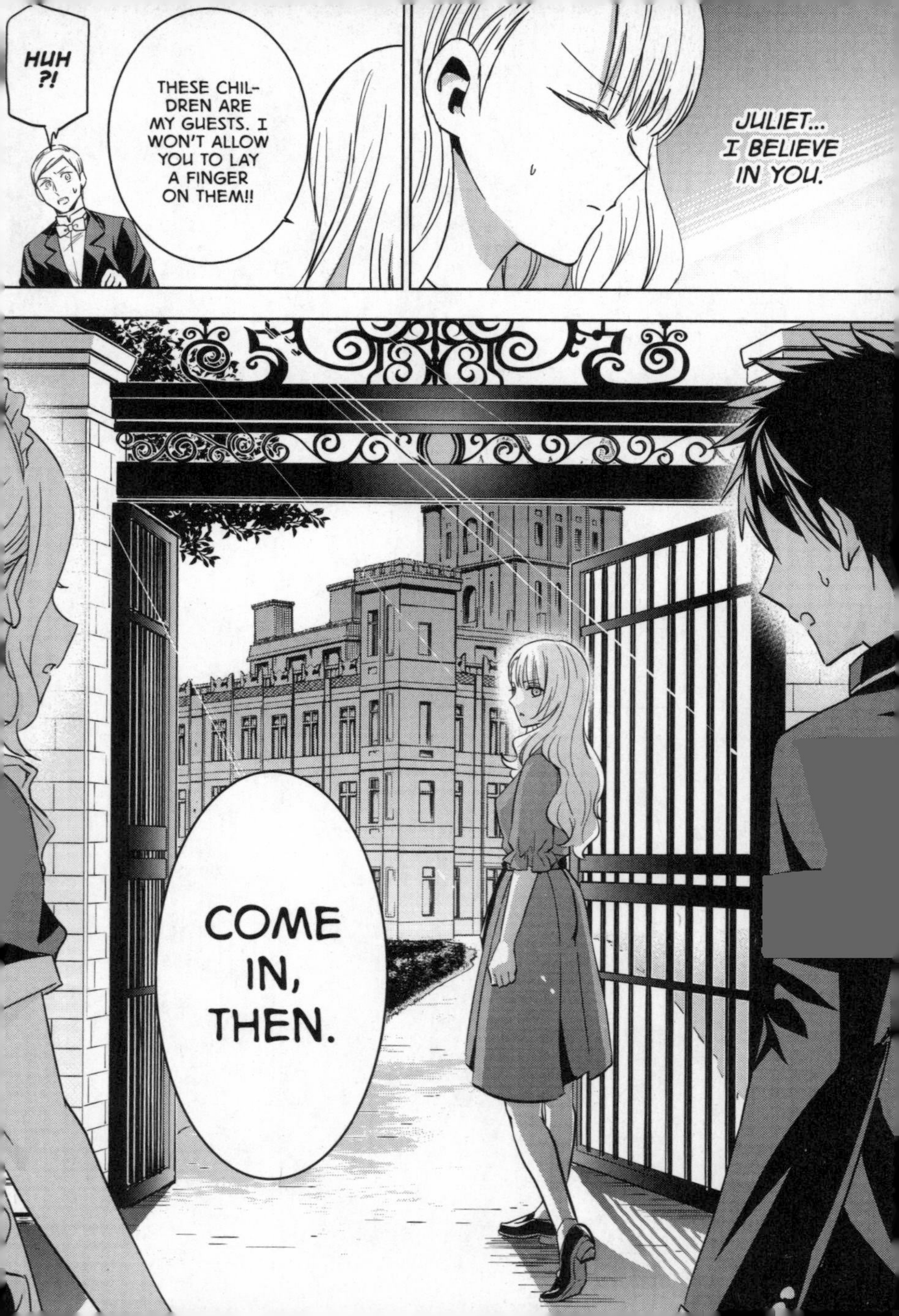
JULIET... I BELIEVE IN YOU.
THESE CHIL-DREN ARE MY GUESTS. I WON'T ALLOW YOU TO LAY A FINGER ON THEM!!
HUH ?!
COME IN, THEN.

CONTINUED IN VOLUME 16

BONUS STORY

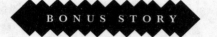

## Boarding School Juliet:

# Romio & Juliet & Halloween

For a change of pace, we present a *Boarding School Juliet* Halloween special on the next page! This standalone bonus chapter ran in *Weekly Shonen Magazine* 2016's issue 48. Chronologically, the story takes place around the time between Acts 47 and 48, back when Romio and Juliet's relationship was still a secret. Please enjoy this trip down memory lane!

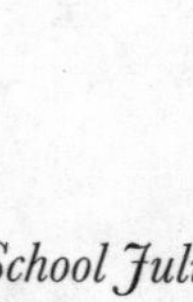

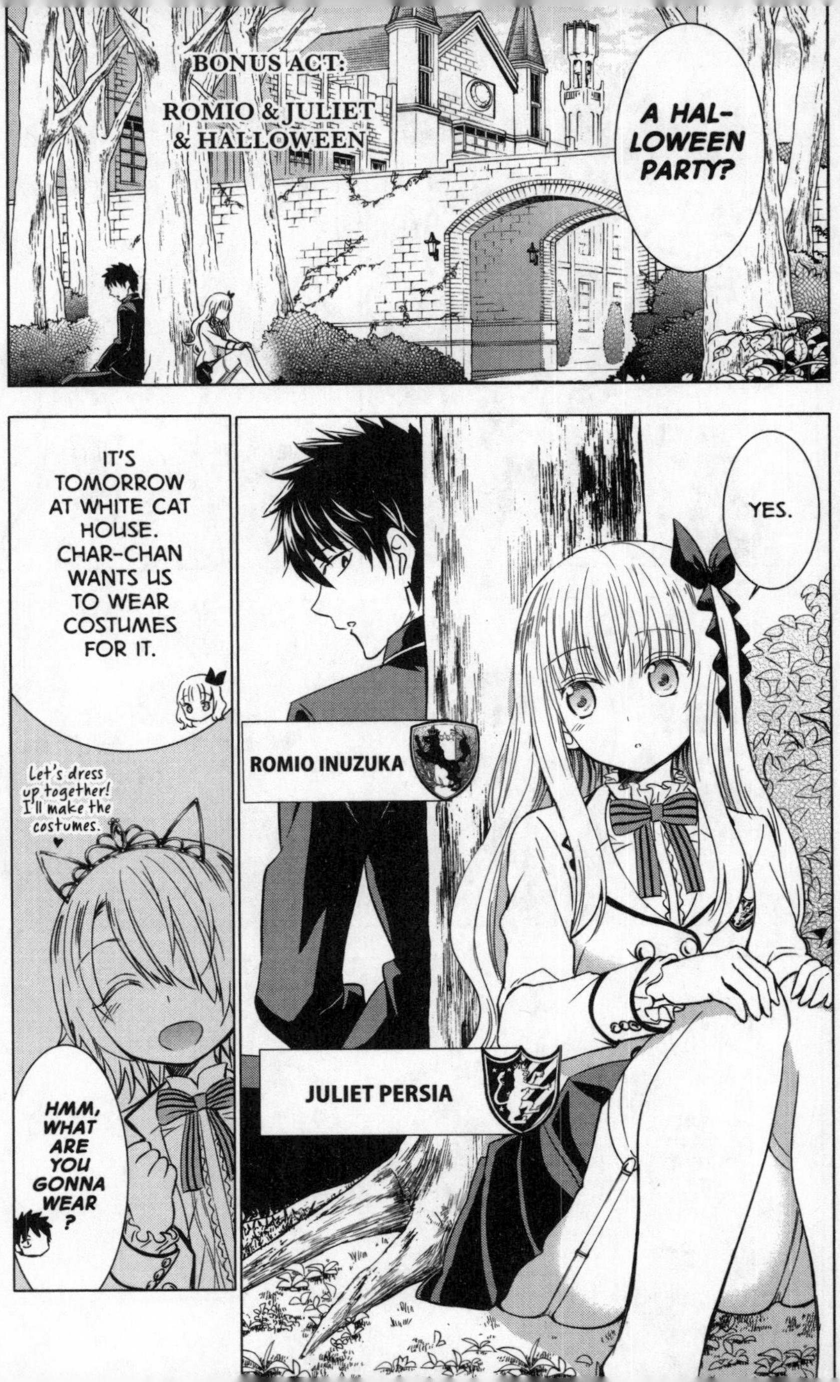
BONUS ACT: ROMIO & JULIET & HALLOWEEN
A HAL-LOWEEN PARTY?
YES.
ROMIO INUZUKA
JULIET PERSIA
IT'S TOMORROW AT WHITE CAT HOUSE. CHAR-CHAN WANTS US TO WEAR COSTUMES FOR IT.
Let's dress up together! I'll make the costumes. ♥
HMM, WHAT ARE YOU GONNA WEAR?

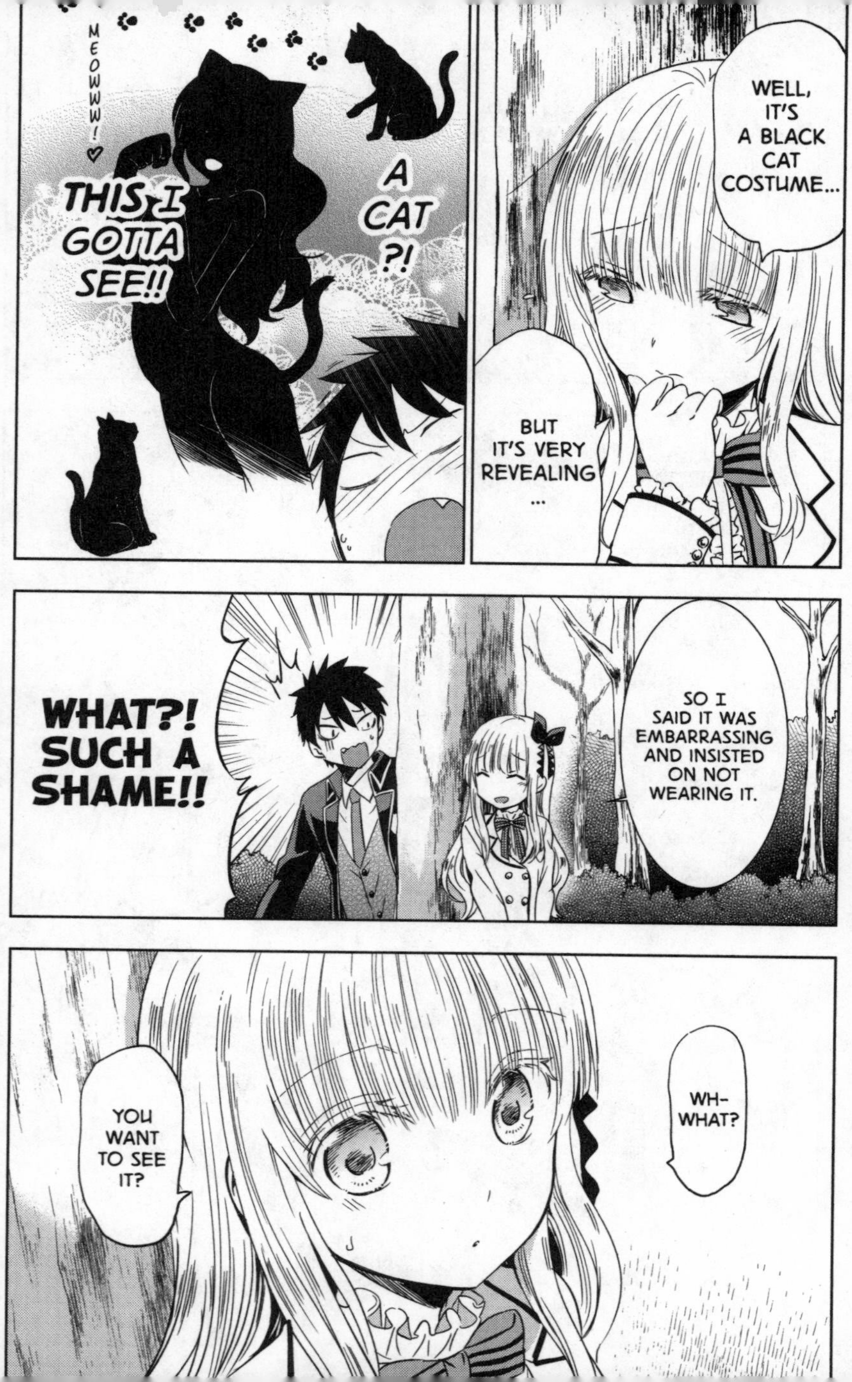
WELL, IT'S A BLACK CAT COSTUME...
BUT IT'S VERY REVEALING...
A CAT?!
MEOWWW!♡
THIS I GOTTA SEE!!
SO I SAID IT WAS EMBARRASSING AND INSISTED ON NOT WEARING IT.
WHAT?! SUCH A SHAME!!
WH-WHAT?
YOU WANT TO SEE IT?

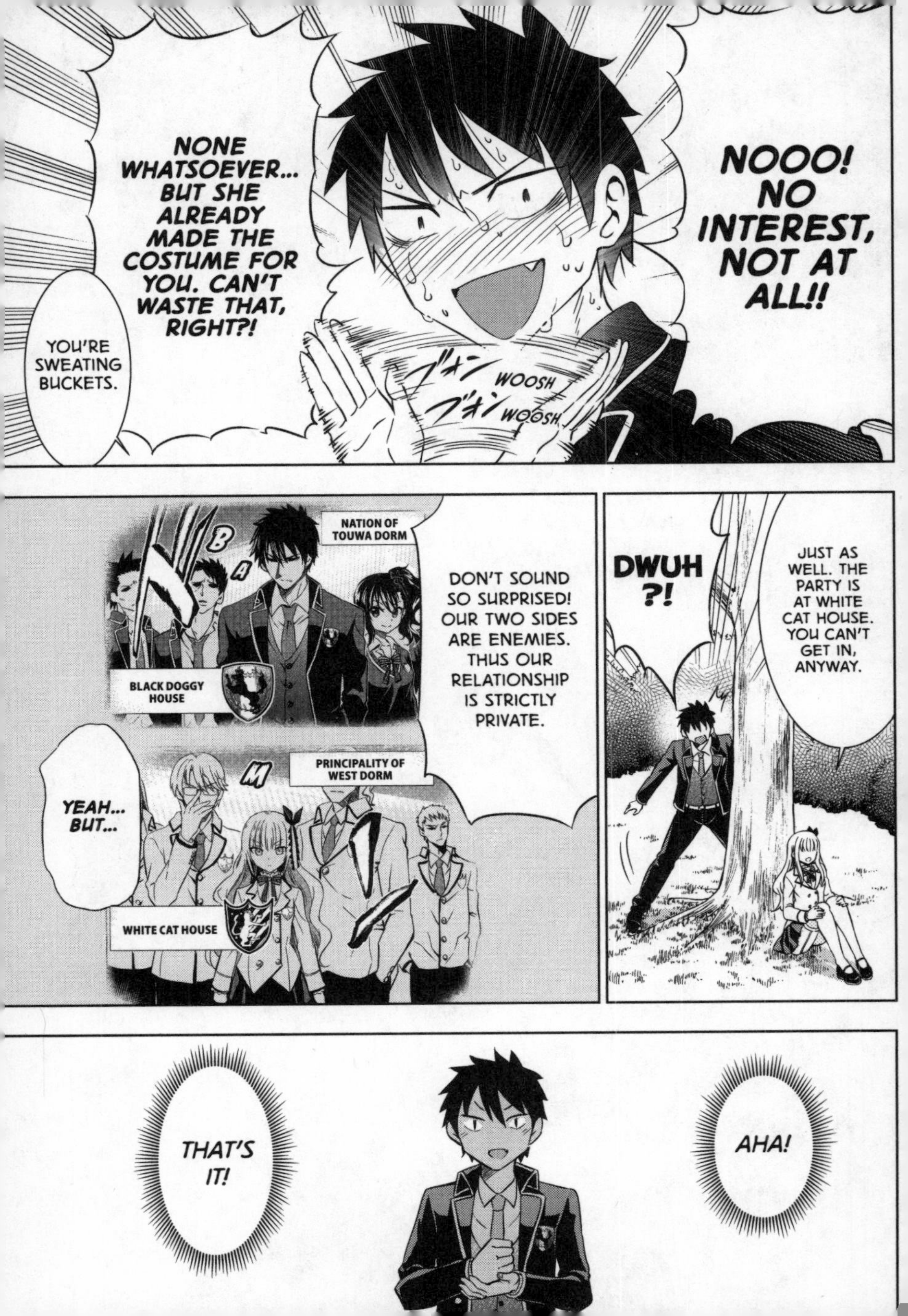
NOOO! NO INTEREST, NOT AT ALL!!
ブォン WOOSH
ブォン WOOSH
NONE WHATSOEVER... BUT SHE ALREADY MADE THE COSTUME FOR YOU. CAN'T WASTE THAT, RIGHT?!
YOU'RE SWEATING BUCKETS.
JUST AS WELL. THE PARTY IS AT WHITE CAT HOUSE. YOU CAN'T GET IN, ANYWAY.
DWUH ?!
DON'T SOUND SO SURPRISED! OUR TWO SIDES ARE ENEMIES. THUS OUR RELATIONSHIP IS STRICTLY PRIVATE.
NATION OF TOUWA DORM
BLACK DOGGY HOUSE
PRINCIPALITY OF WEST DORM
WHITE CAT HOUSE
YEAH... BUT...
AHA!
THAT'S IT!

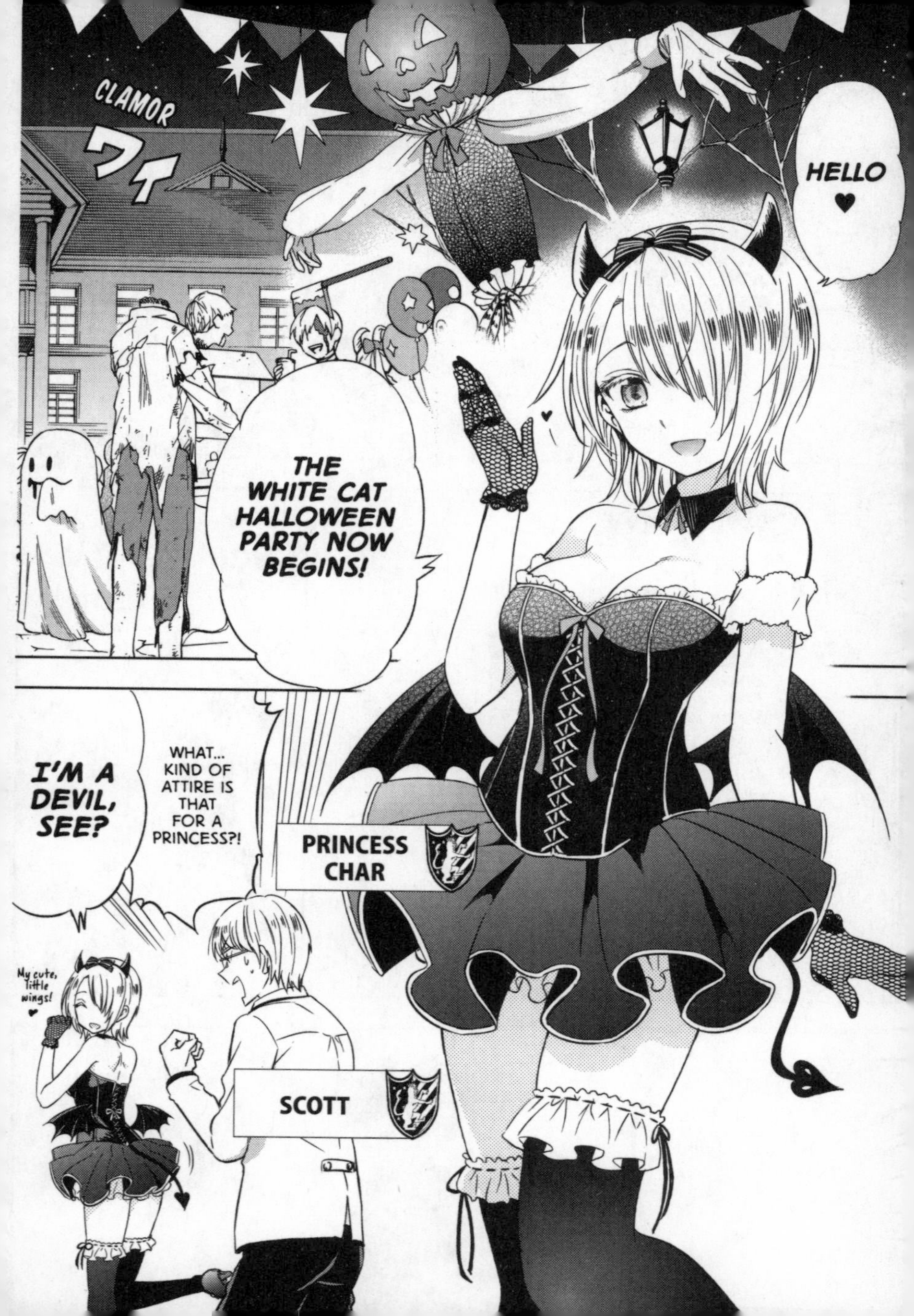
CLAMOR
ワイ
HELLO ♥
THE WHITE CAT HALLOWEEN PARTY NOW BEGINS!
PRINCESS CHAR
WHAT... KIND OF ATTIRE IS THAT FOR A PRINCESS?!
I'M A DEVIL, SEE?
SCOTT
My cute, little wings! ♥

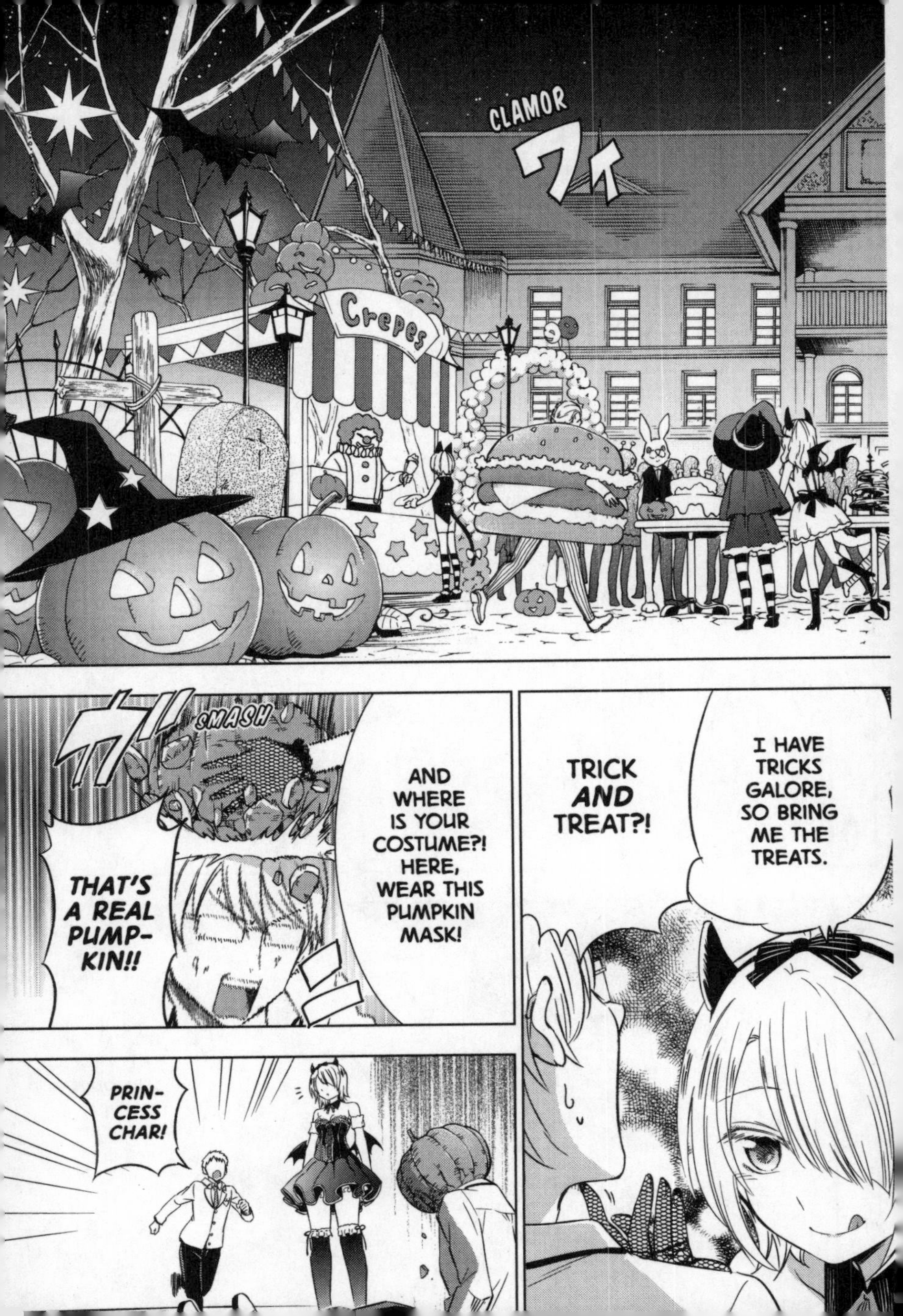

CLAMOR
Crepes
I HAVE TRICKS GALORE, SO BRING ME THE TREATS.
TRICK AND TREAT?!
SMASH
AND WHERE IS YOUR COSTUME?! HERE, WEAR THIS PUMPKIN MASK!
THAT'S A REAL PUMP-KIN!!
PRIN-CESS CHAR!

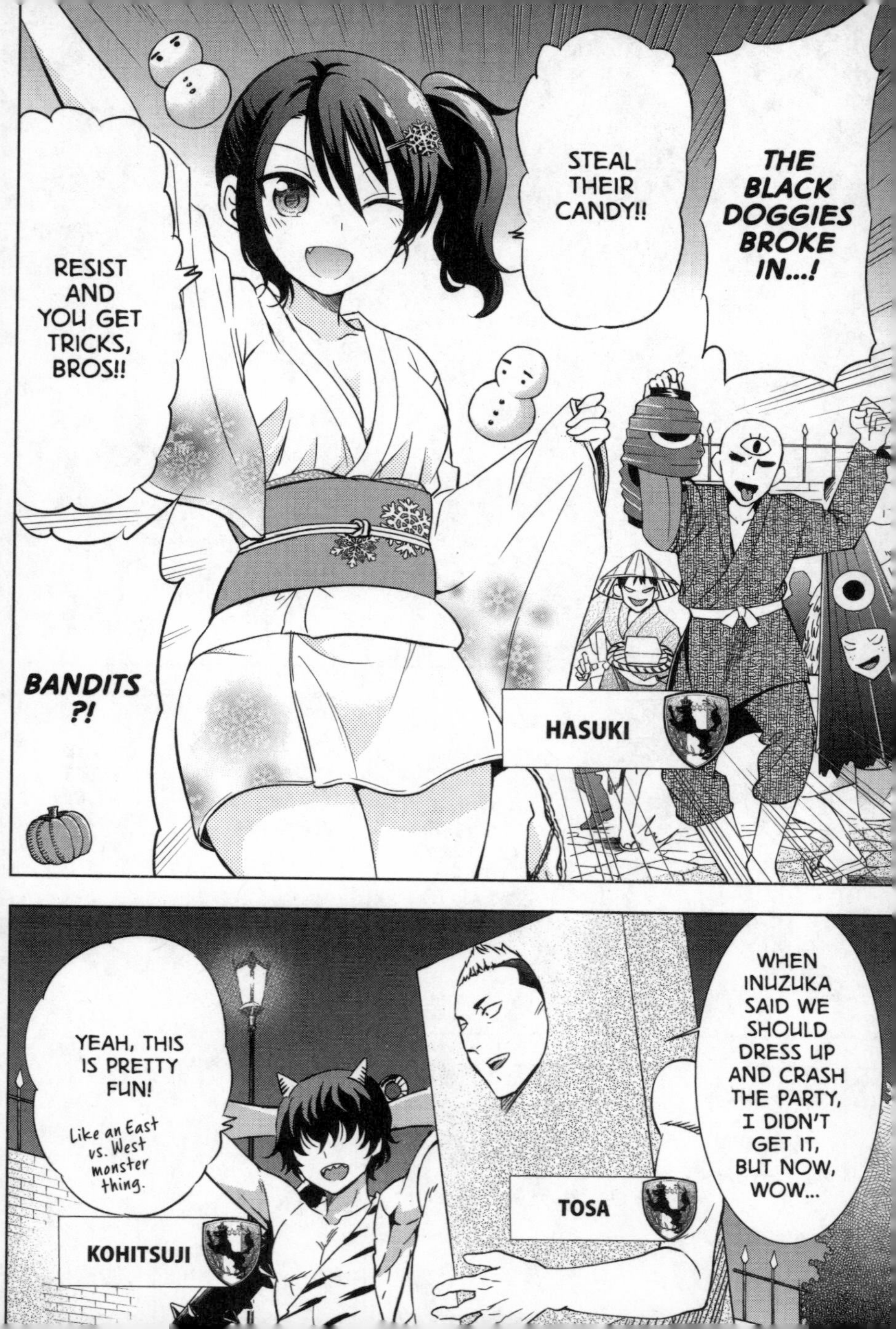
THE BLACK DOGGIES BROKE IN...!
STEAL THEIR CANDY!!
RESIST AND YOU GET TRICKS, BROS!!
BANDITS ?!
HASUKI
WHEN INUZUKA SAID WE SHOULD DRESS UP AND CRASH THE PARTY, I DIDN'T GET IT, BUT NOW, WOW...
YEAH, THIS IS PRETTY FUN!
Like an East vs. West monster thing.
TOSA
KOHITSUJI

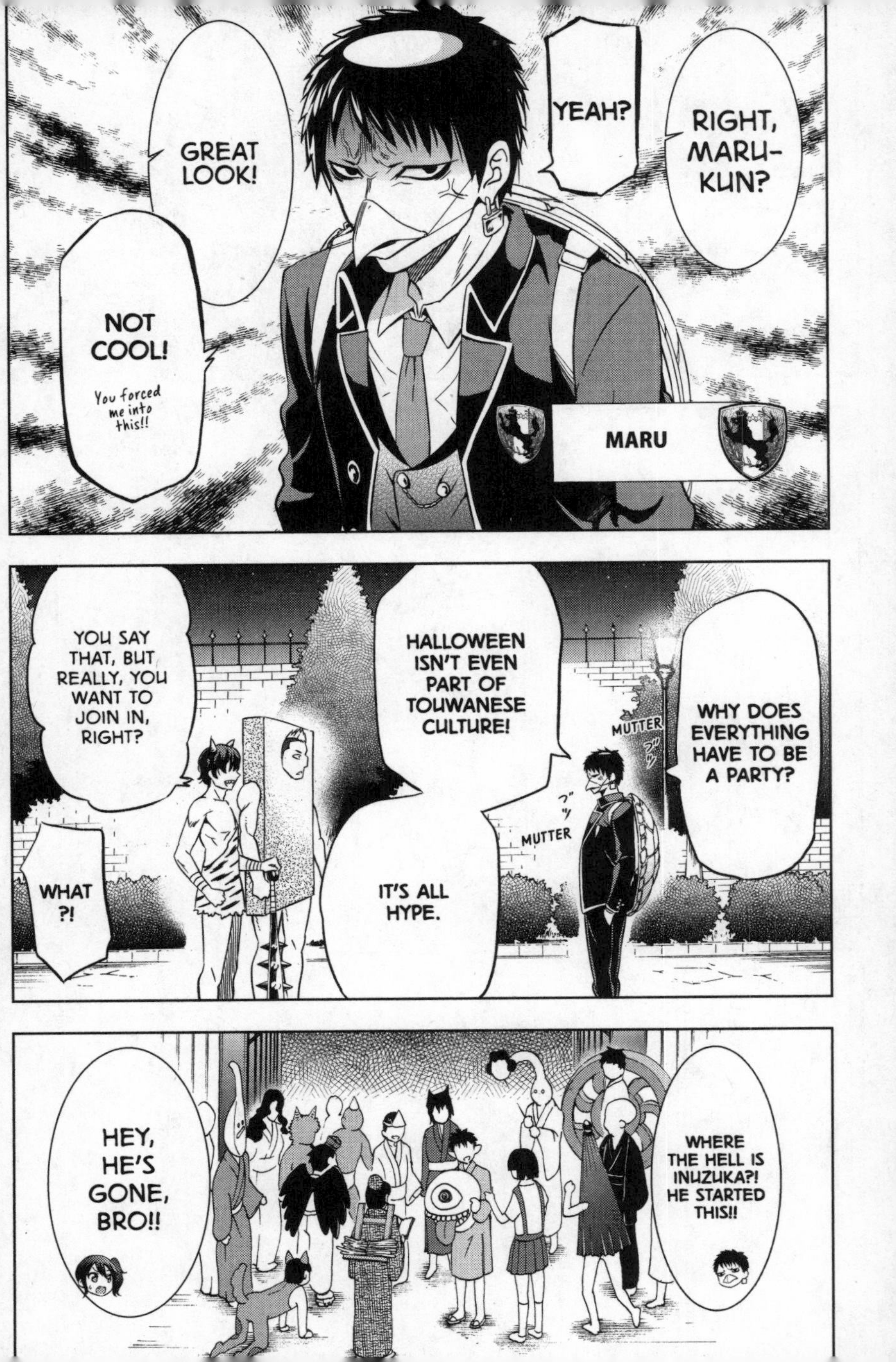
RIGHT, MARU-KUN?
YEAH?
GREAT LOOK!
NOT COOL!
You forced me into this!!
MARU
WHY DOES EVERYTHING HAVE TO BE A PARTY?
MUTTER
MUTTER
HALLOWEEN ISN'T EVEN PART OF TOUWANESE CULTURE!
IT'S ALL HYPE.
YOU SAY THAT, BUT REALLY, YOU WANT TO JOIN IN, RIGHT?
WHAT ?!
WHERE THE HELL IS INUZUKA?! HE STARTED THIS!!
HEY, HE'S GONE, BRO!!

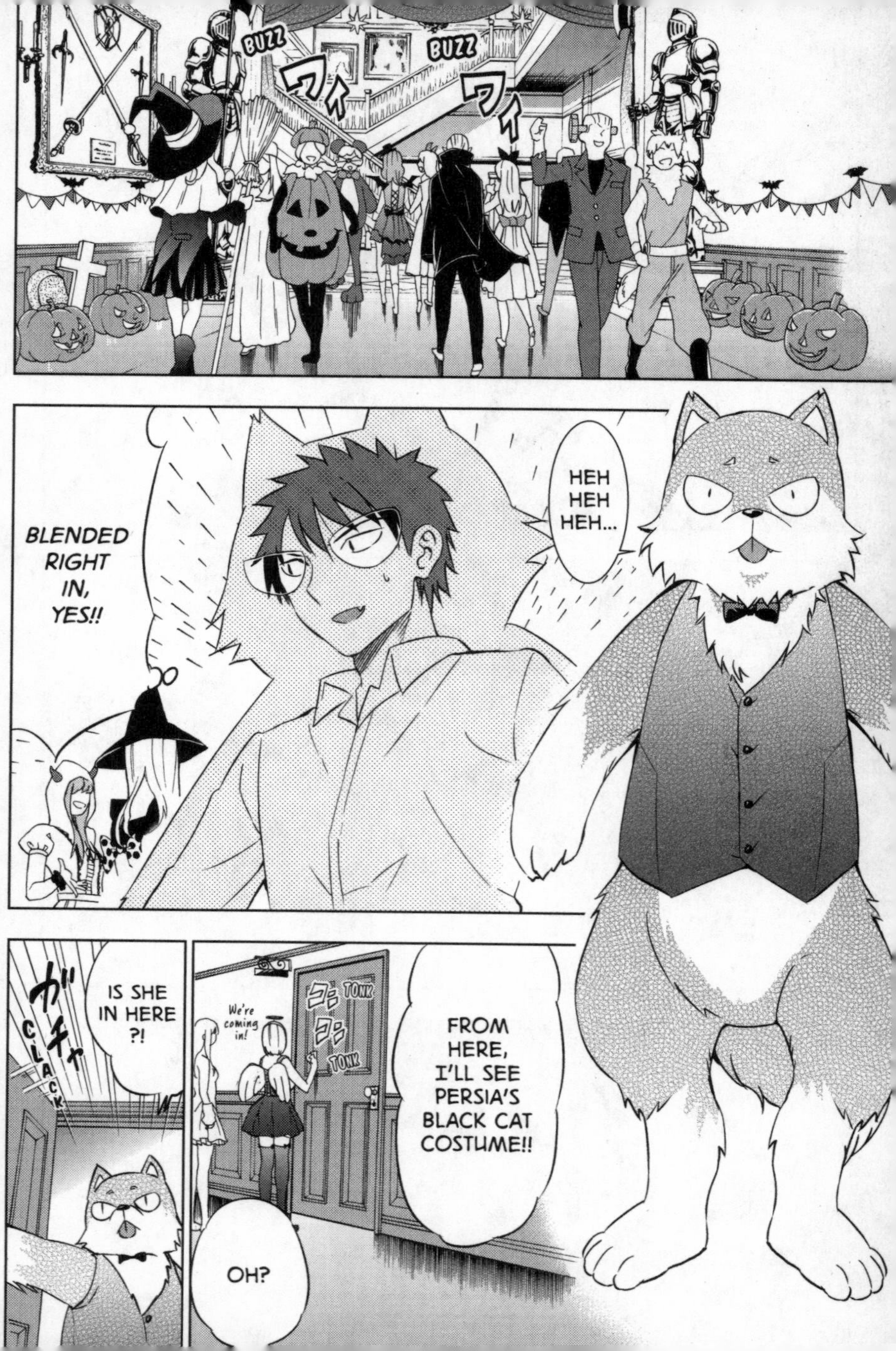
BUZZ
ワイ
BUZZ
ワイ
HEH HEH HEH...
BLENDED RIGHT IN, YES!!
FROM HERE, I'LL SEE PERSIA'S BLACK CAT COSTUME!!
コン TONK
コン TONK
We're coming in!
IS SHE IN HERE ?!
ガチャ
CLACK
OH?

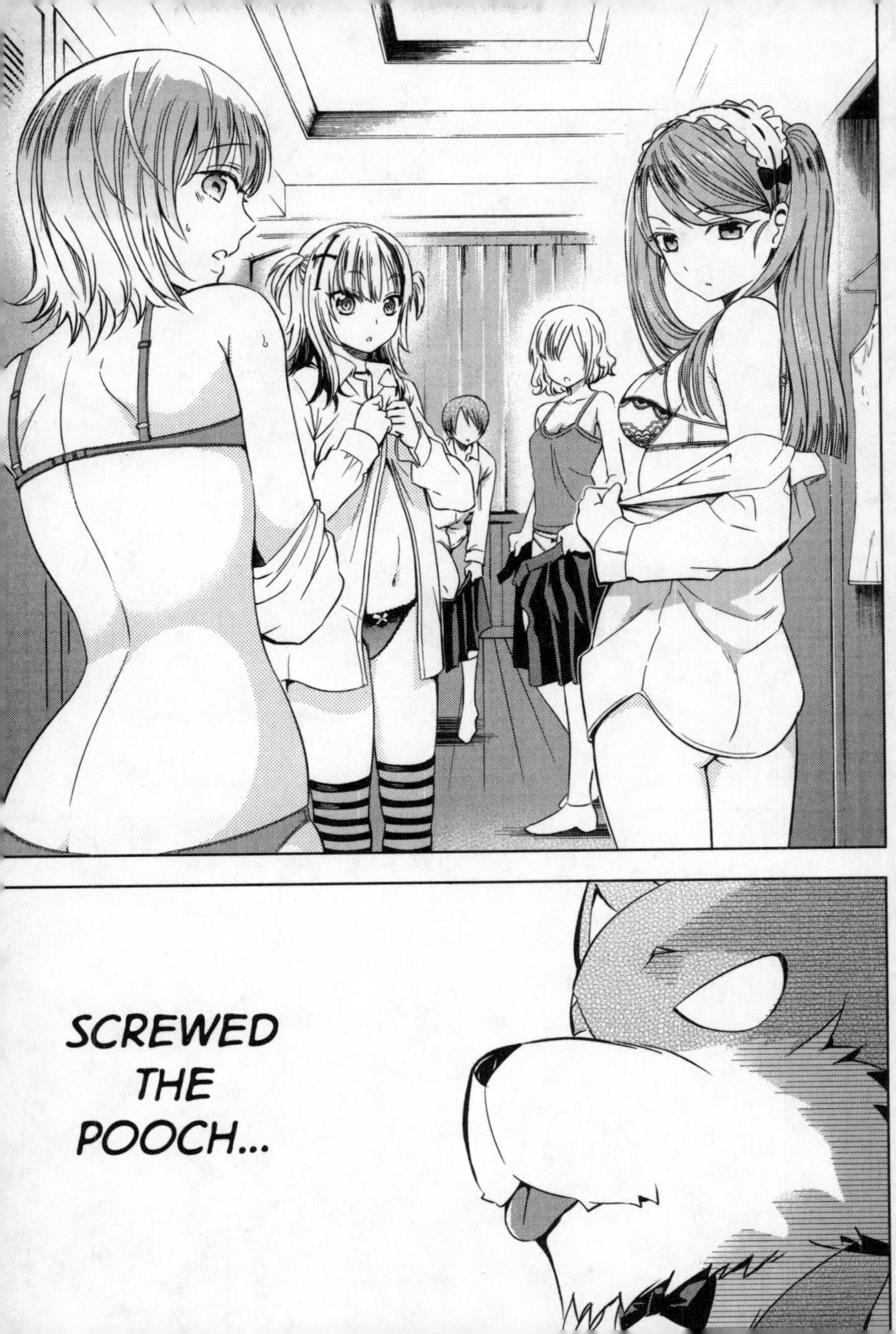
SCREWED THE POOCH...

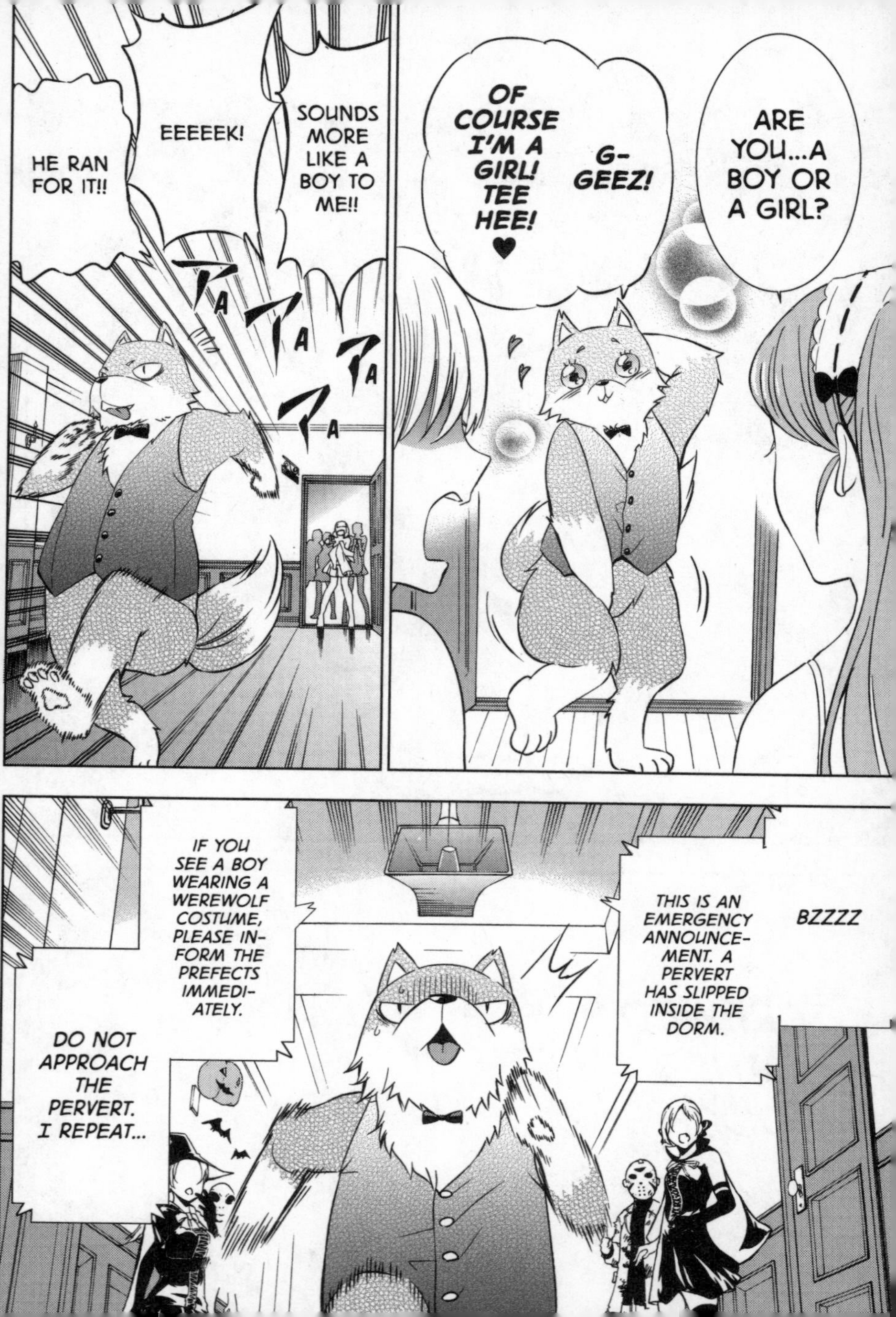

ARE YOU...A BOY OR A GIRL?
G-GEEZ!
OF COURSE I'M A GIRL! TEE HEE! ♥
SOUNDS MORE LIKE A BOY TO ME!!
EEEEEK!
HE RAN FOR IT!!
PA PA PA PA PA
BZZZZ
THIS IS AN EMERGENCY ANNOUNCE-MENT. A PERVERT HAS SLIPPED INSIDE THE DORM.
IF YOU SEE A BOY WEARING A WEREWOLF COSTUME, PLEASE IN-FORM THE PREFECTS IMMEDI-ATELY.
DO NOT APPROACH THE PERVERT. I REPEAT...

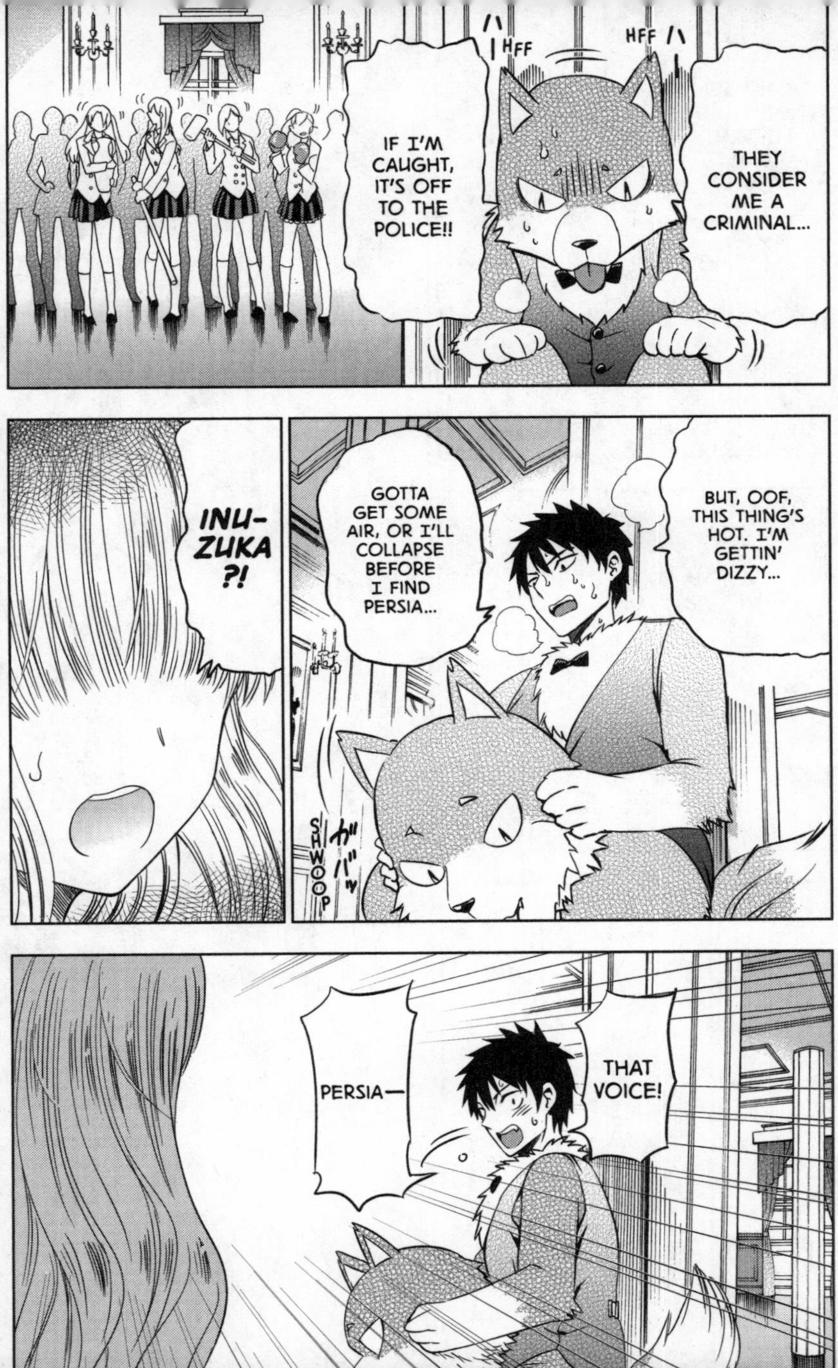

HFF
HFF
THEY CONSIDER ME A CRIMINAL...
IF I'M CAUGHT, IT'S OFF TO THE POLICE!!
BUT, OOF, THIS THING'S HOT. I'M GETTIN' DIZZY...
GOTTA GET SOME AIR, OR I'LL COLLAPSE BEFORE I FIND PERSIA...
SHWOOP
INU-ZUKA ?!
THAT VOICE!
PERSIA—

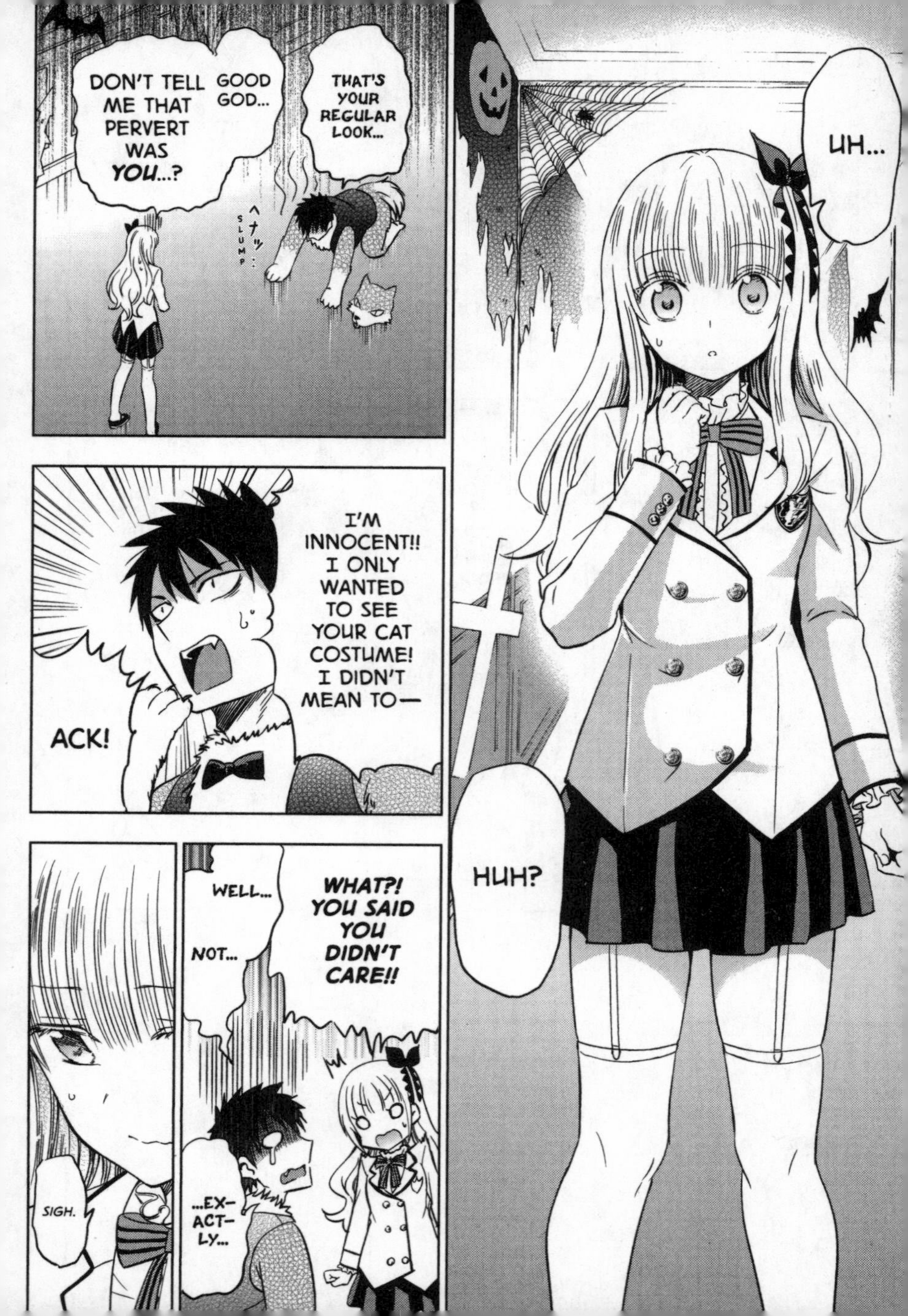
UH...
HUH?
THAT'S YOUR REGULAR LOOK...
GOOD GOD...
DON'T TELL ME THAT PERVERT WAS YOU...?
SLUMP
I'M INNOCENT!! I ONLY WANTED TO SEE YOUR CAT COSTUME! I DIDN'T MEAN TO—
ACK!
WHAT?! YOU SAID YOU DIDN'T CARE!!
WELL...
NOT...
...EX-ACT-LY...
SIGH.

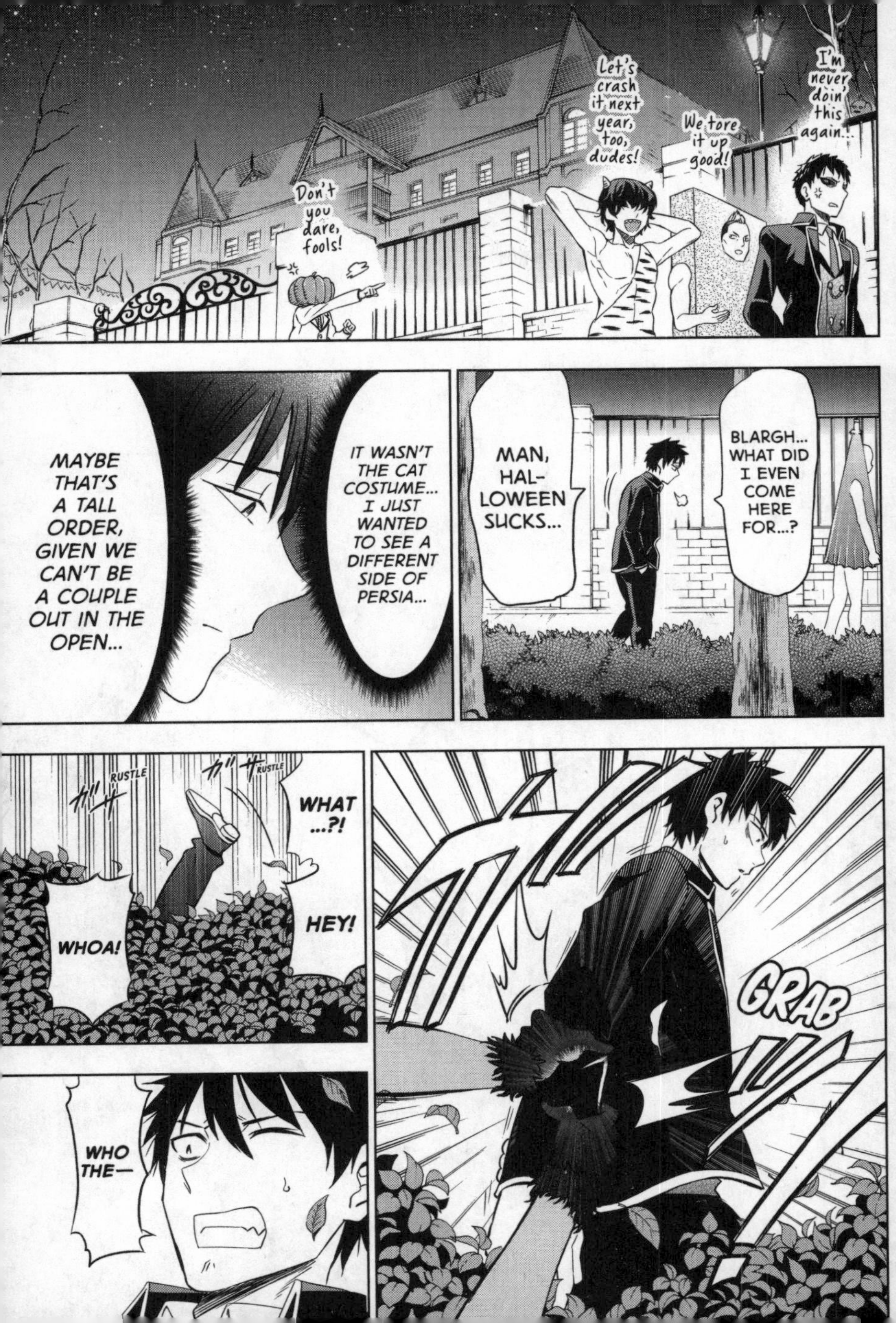
I'm never doin' this again...
We tore it up good!
Let's crash it next year, too, dudes!
Don't you dare, fools!
BLARGH... WHAT DID I EVEN COME HERE FOR...?
MAN, HAL-LOWEEN SUCKS...
IT WASN'T THE CAT COSTUME... I JUST WANTED TO SEE A DIFFERENT SIDE OF PERSIA...
MAYBE THAT'S A TALL ORDER, GIVEN WE CAN'T BE A COUPLE OUT IN THE OPEN...
GRAB
RUSTLE
RUSTLE
WHAT ...?!
HEY!
WHOA!
WHO THE—

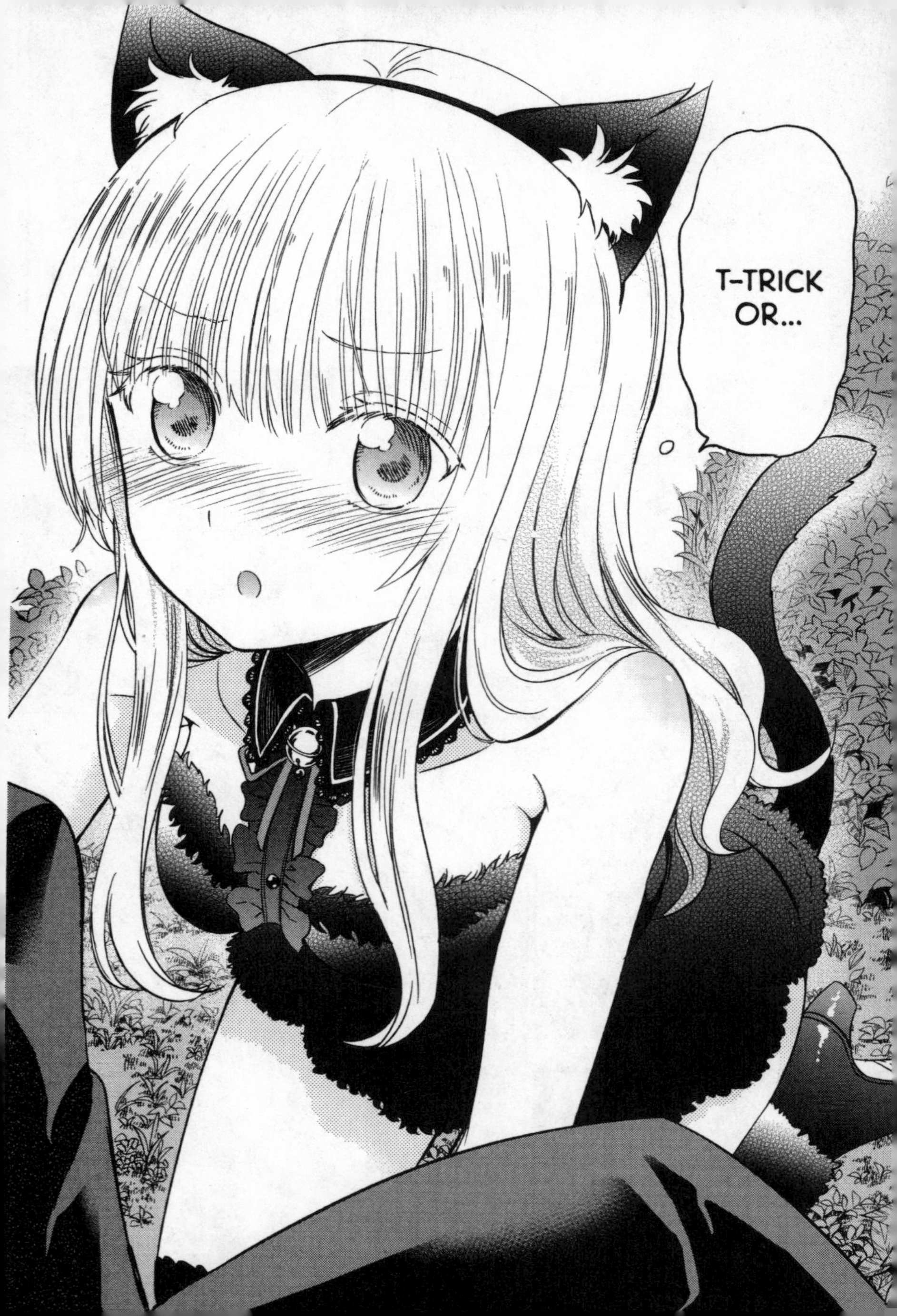
T-TRICK OR...

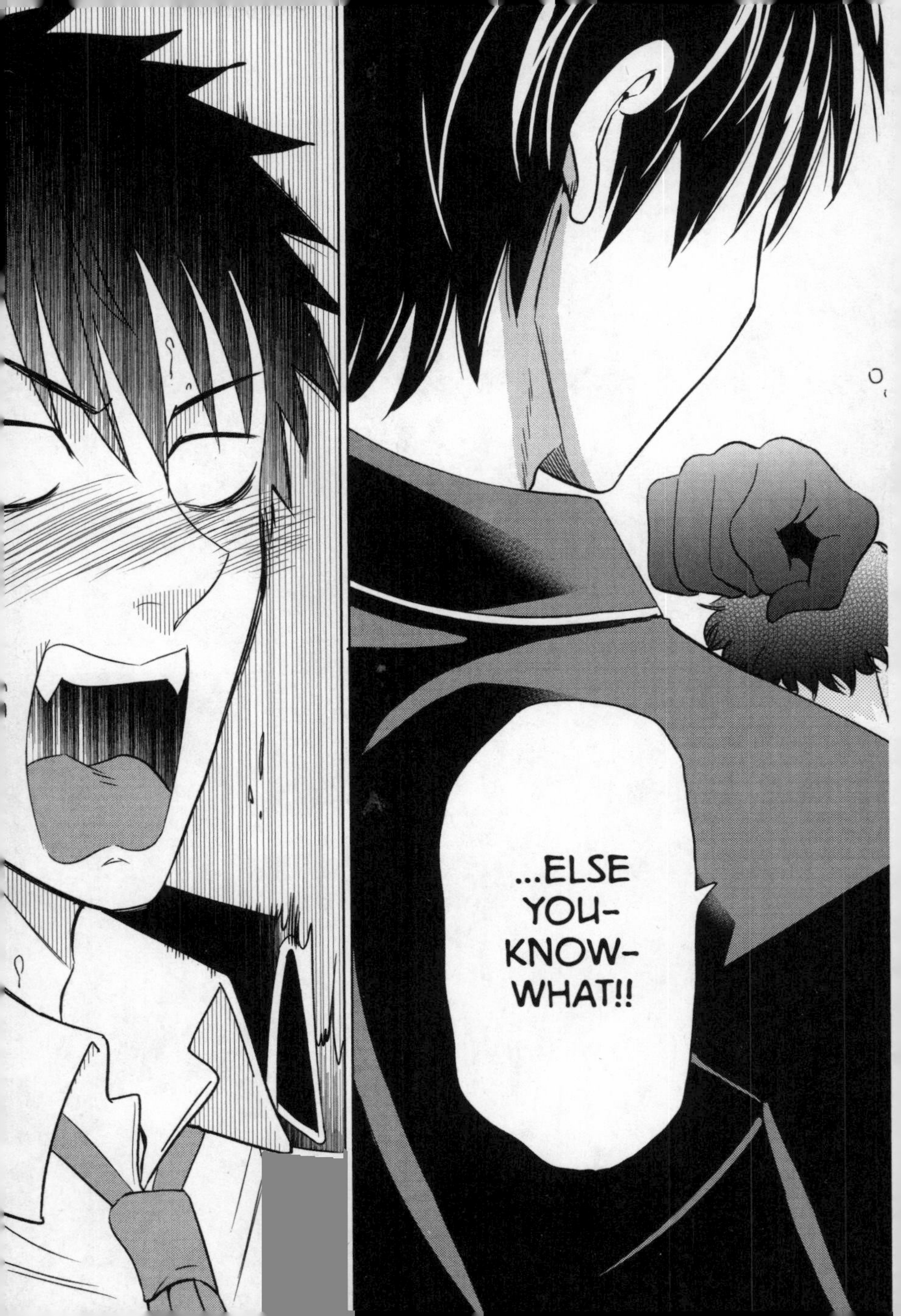
...ELSE YOU-KNOW-WHAT!!

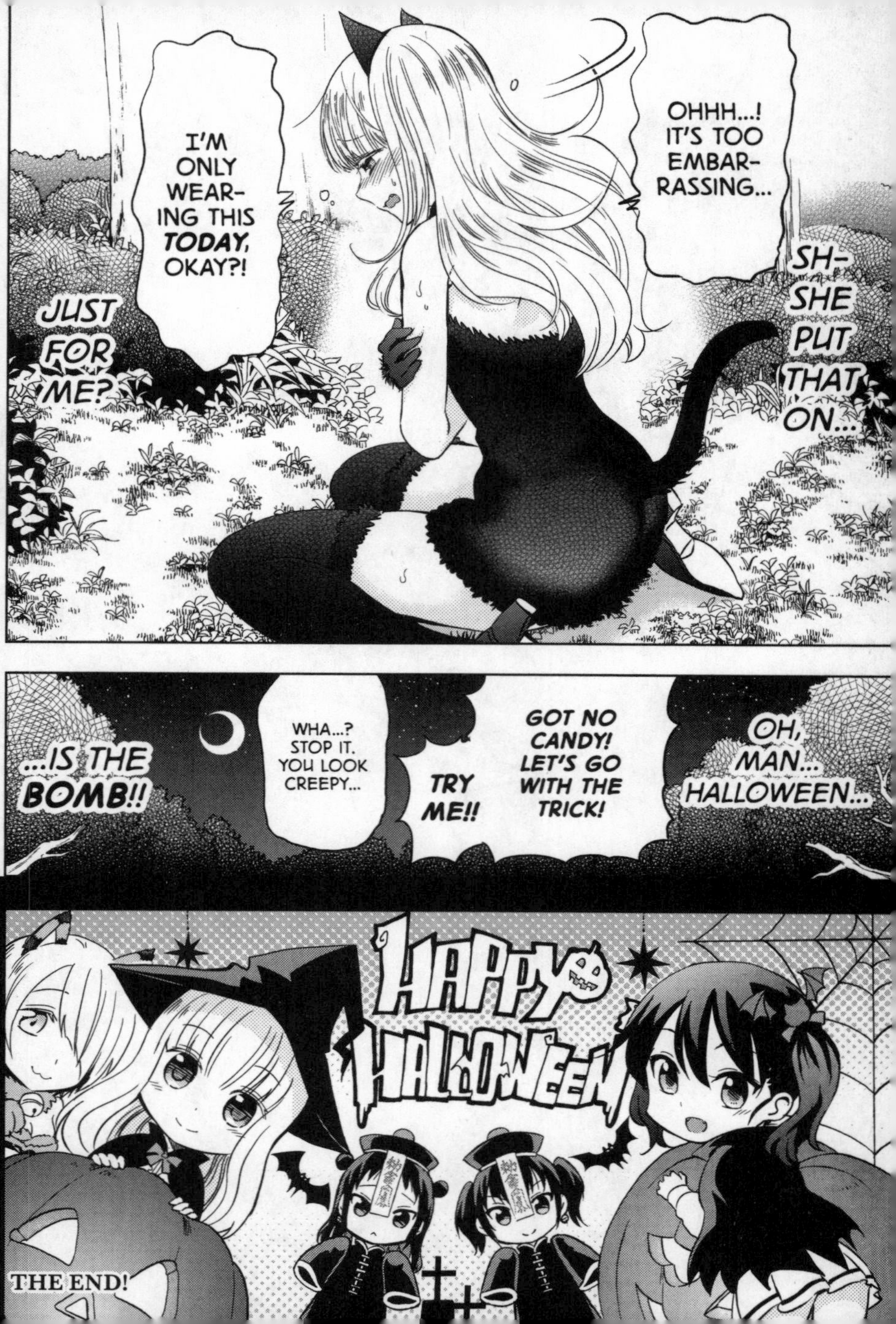
OHHH...! IT'S TOO EMBARRASSING...
SH-SHE PUT THAT ON...
I'M ONLY WEARING THIS *TODAY*, OKAY?!
JUST FOR ME?
OH, MAN... HALLOWEEN...
GOT NO CANDY! LET'S GO WITH THE TRICK!
TRY ME!!
WHA...? STOP IT. YOU LOOK CREEPY...
...IS THE BOMB!!
HAPPY HALLOWEEN
THE END!

4/28

Birthday:
4/27

Can it!

It's "Maru-san" to you.

**BSJ: THE INSIDE STORY**
**EVERY YEAR ON APRIL 27, MARU PLAYS UP HOW HE'S OLDER THAN INUZUKA, JUST FOR THAT DAY.**

# AFTERWORD

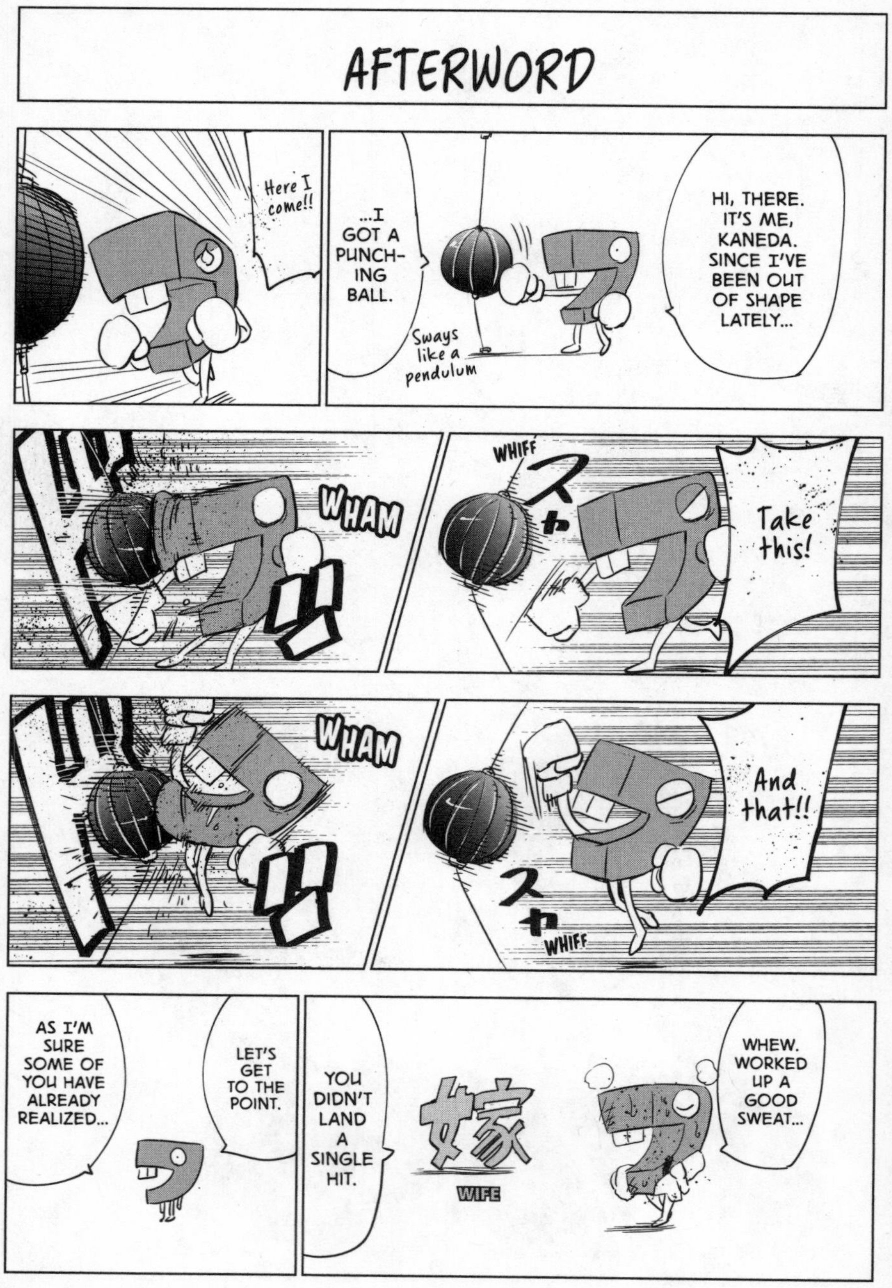
HI, THERE. IT'S ME, KANEDA. SINCE I'VE BEEN OUT OF SHAPE LATELY...
...I GOT A PUNCHING-BALL.
Sways like a pendulum
Here I come!!
WHIFF
Take this!
WHAM
And that!!
WHIFF
WHAM
WHEW. WORKED UP A GOOD SWEAT...
嫁
WIFE
YOU DIDN'T LAND A SINGLE HIT.
LET'S GET TO THE POINT.
AS I'M SURE SOME OF YOU HAVE ALREADY REALIZED...